How to Start and Run a
PROFITABLE
SELF-PUBLISHING
BUSINESS

The Complete Blueprint
With Proven Strategies and Step-By-Step Instructions to Launch and Market Your Book to Become a Bestselling Author

PUBLISHING SERVICES

Copyright © 2025 Publishing Services. All rights reserved.

The content within this book may not be reproduced, duplicated, or transmitted without direct written permission from the author or the publisher.

Under no circumstances will any blame or legal responsibility be held against the publisher or author for any damages, reparation, or monetary loss due to the information contained within this book, either directly or indirectly.

Legal Notice:

This book is copyright-protected. It is only for personal use. You cannot amend, distribute, sell, use, quote, or paraphrase any part of the content within this book without the consent of the author or publisher.

Disclaimer Notice:

Please note the information contained within this document is for educational and entertainment purposes only. All effort has been expended to present accurate, up-to-date, reliable, and complete information. No warranties of any kind are declared or implied. Readers acknowledge that the author is not engaged in the rendering of legal, financial, medical, or professional advice. The content within this book has been derived from various sources. Please consult a licensed professional before attempting any techniques outlined in this book.

By reading this document, the reader agrees that under no circumstances is the author responsible for any losses, direct or indirect, that are incurred as a result of the use of the information contained within this document, including, but not limited to, errors, omissions, or inaccuracies.

ISBN Paperback: 978-0-6486411-4-8

ISBN Hardback: 978-0-6486411-5-5

For inquiries, permissions, or further information, please contact:

Email: support@publishingservices.com

Website: www.publishingservices.com

Table of Contents

Introduction   11

A Quick Start Guide to This Book   13
A Note on AI   15

Chapter 1: Overview of the Self-Publishing Process   17

What Budget Will You Need to Publish a Book?   17
The Self-Publishing Process Graph   19
A Word on Self-Publishing Tools and Distributors   21

Chapter 2: Keyword Research   23

DS Amazon Quick View   23
How and Where to Search for Keywords   26
Keyword Profitability Check (KPC)   26
Key Questions to Consider   30
Target Audience Research Strategies   31
Competitor Analysis Methods   33
Chapter 2 Checklist   35

Chapter 3: Choosing Titles That Sell   37

Words to Avoid   38
How to Find Effective Keywords for Your Title and Subtitle   38
Chapter 3 Checklist   41

Chapter 4: Choosing an Author Name   43

Writing Under a Pen Name   43
Publishing Under Your Real Name   45
Using a Brand Name or Publishing Company Name   45
How to Create a Pen Name   46

Additional Tips ... 46

Chapter 5: Determining the Ideal Book Length — 49

How to Ensure Your Book Meets the 30K Word Count Mark ... 50

Chapter 6: How to Write a Perfect Book Outline — 51

Key Elements of a Book Outline ... 51
Researching for a Strong Outline ... 52
DIY vs. Professional Outlining ... 52
Publishing Services' Book Outline Package ... 56
Publishing Services' Outline Quality Review Package ... 57

Chapter 7: How to Write a Compelling Book Description — 59

Key Elements of a Book Description ... 59
KDP Description Example ... 60
HTML Formatting for KDP Description Example ... 62
Back Cover Description Example ... 63
DIY vs. Professional Descriptions: Which One to Choose ... 64

Chapter 8: From Manuscript to Publication: Ghostwriting Essentials — 67

Where to Find the Perfect Ghostwriter ... 67
How to Collaborate with a Ghostwriter: Best Practices ... 68
Building a Strong Relationship with Your Ghostwriter ... 71
How to Check Your Manuscript for Plagiarism ... 71
Publishing Services' Premium Ghostwriting Package ... 72
AI-Generated Manuscripts: What You Need to Know ... 74
Publishing Services' AIDE Package ... 75

Chapter 9: Understanding ISBNs — 77

ISBN: What It Reveals About a Book and Its Author ... 78
How to Locate a Book's ISBN ... 78
Ebooks & ISBN ... 79
Paperback Books & ISBN ... 79
Where to Buy an ISBN: Trusted Sources and Options ... 80

Purchasing an ISBN from Bowker and Other Providers … 80
FAQs: Common Questions Answered … 81
How to Get a Free ISBN from Amazon … 83

Chapter 10: Designing a Book Cover That Sells … 85

What Makes a Book Cover Stand Out … 85
Effective vs. Ineffective Book Cover Design … 87
How to Write a Brief for Your Designer … 98
Sample Book Cover Brief … 99
Cover Designers Options and Recommendations … 100
Essential Cover Files: What You'll Need for Print and Digital … 105
Designing for Diversity, Equality, and Inclusion: Why It Matters … 107
The Importance of Social Media … 107
Publishing Services' Book Cover Design Packages … 108

Chapter 11: Building Your Facebook Author Page … 111

Step-by-Step Guide: How to Set Up Your Facebook Author Page … 111
Using Audience Polls to Choose Your Book Cover … 113

Chapter 12: Using Images and Graphics to Draw in Readers … 117

What Types of Images to Include in Your Book … 117
Why Image Quality Matters … 118
Choosing Between Black-and-White or Color Images for Your Book … 118

Chapter 13: Refining Your Manuscript: Editing and Proofreading Basics … 119

Who Should Proofread and Edit Your Manuscript? … 119
Understanding the Different Levels of Editing … 120
Publishing Services' Editing & Proofreading Packages … 122

Chapter 14: How to Create Powerful Review Pages … 125

What Should Your Review Pages Include? … 126
How to Secure a Review Link Before Publishing … 127
Mid-Book Review Page Sample … 129
End-Book Review Page Sample … 130

Publishing Services' Review Page Package ... 131

Chapter 15: Book Layout and Formatting — 133

Standard Book Formats ... 133
Differences Between Ebook and Print Formatting ... 134
All About Trim Sizes and Choosing the Right Size for Your Book ... 134
Full-Page Images and Bleed: What to Consider ... 136
How Page Count Affects Formatting ... 136
Understanding Interior Margins ... 137
Making Changes to a Formatted Manuscript ... 138
Designing Your Book Layout ... 138
Preformatting Your Book ... 139
Best Software and Online Tools for Formatting ... 141
Publishing Services' Formatting Package ... 146

Chapter 16: Maximizing Sales with A+ Content — 149

Why A+ Content Makes a Difference ... 149
Goals for Effective A+ Content ... 150
Common Mistakes to Avoid When Designing A+ Content ... 151
Key Features of Effective A+ Content: Examples of What Works and What Doesn't ... 152
How to Design A+ Content ... 156
Publishing Services' A+ Content Package ... 171

Chapter 17: How to Connect with Beta Readers and Get Valuable Feedback — 173

What Makes a Good Beta Reader? ... 174
Where Can You Find Beta Readers? ... 175

Chapter 18: Step-by-Step Guide to Setting Up Your Publishing Accounts — 177

How to Set Up a KDP Account ... 177
Important Tax Numbers and Royalties Information for Authors ... 179
How to Set Up an IngramSpark Account ... 181
How to Set Up an ACX Account ... 183
How to Set Up an Author's Republic Account ... 184
How to Set Up a Findaway Voices by Spotify Account ... 184

Chapter 19: Breezing Through Your Book Pre-Launch Strategy — 185

How Many Copies Should You Send to Potential Reviewers? — 185
Timing Your Book Launch — 186
Working with Your Advanced Reader Copy (ARC) Team — 186
How to Get ARC Readers for Free — 186
Paid Method to Obtain ARC Readers (Via Facebook Ads) — 191
Sample Message to First-Time Reviewers — 195
Sample Message to Past Reviewers — 195
Sample of a Pre-Book Launch Message — 200
Outsourcing the ARC Process: A Hassle-Free Option — 207
How to Get Verified Reviews: A Simple Hack — 208
How to Enroll in KDP Select — 209
Scheduling Your Free Book Promotion — 210

Chapter 20: Uploading Your Book to KDP: Everything You Need to Know — 213

Before You Begin: Key Steps to Take — 213
How to Upload Your Book to KDP — 223
How to Re-upload Your Book to KDP After Making Changes — 242

Chapter 21: Preventing KDP Account Issues — 245

How to Avoid Account Termination — 245
How to Avoid Account Banning on KDP — 250

Chapter 22: The Complete IngramSpark Publishing Process — 253

How to Upload Your Book to IngramSpark — 254

Chapter 23: Exploring Alternative Book Distribution Channels — 271

Print (Paperback & Hardback) Distribution Channels — 271
Ebook Distribution Channels — 272
An Updated List of Book Distribution Channels — 274

Chapter 24: Publishing Your Audiobook: From Script to Sound — **277**

Finding the Perfect Narrator for Your Book — *277*
How to Prepare Your Manuscript for Narration — *281*
Choosing the Right Distribution Services for Your Audiobook — *282*
How to Obtain Reviews for Your Audiobooks — *286*

Chapter 25: Streamlining Your Book Launch Strategy — **289**

Free Book Promotion on Amazon: How to Get Started — *290*
Additional Book Promotion Services to Boost Your Launch — *290*
When Should You Schedule Your Book Promotions? — *291*
Promotion Sites Vetted by Publishing Services — *293*
How to Make the Most of Promotion Websites — *294*
How to Market Your Book on Facebook — *294*

Chapter 26: How to Copyright Your Book — **297**

The Copyrighting Process: Everything You Need to Know — *297*

Chapter 27: How to Write Your Author Bio — **315**

Fulfilling the Wants and Needs of Your Target Audience — *315*
What to Include in Your Author Biography — *316*
Author Bio Samples — *317*
Publishing Services' Author Bio Package — *319*

Chapter 28: How to Set Up and Optimize Your Amazon Author Central and Author Page — **321**

Key Features of Amazon Author Central — *321*
Setting Up Your Amazon Author Central Account — *322*
Setting Up Your Author Page — *322*

Chapter 29: How to Obtain Amazon Editorial Reviews — **325**

Benefits of Editorial Reviews — *326*
Where Can You Get Editorial Reviews? — *327*
How to Obtain Written Permission for Editorial Reviews — *333*

How to Format Editorial Reviews — 333
Uploading Your Editorial Reviews on Amazon Author Central — 335

Chapter 30: Obtaining Verified Book Reviews — 339

Who Can Review Your Book? — 339
Tips for Using Book Review Services Wisely — 345

Chapter 31: Create Winning Amazon Ad Campaigns — 347

Amazon Ads: The Basics — 347
Which Marketplaces Should You Target? — 350
Why Quality Matters in Amazon Ads — 350
The 4 Phases of Your Amazon Ads Strategy — 350
Outsourcing Your Ad Campaign — 367

Chapter 32: Publisher Champ—A Vital and Multifaceted Marketing Tool — 369

How to Set Up Publisher Champ — 370

Chapter 33: Growing Your Publishing Business — 371

Writing Your Next Book — 371
How to Publish Book Collections for More Revenue — 373
Translating Your Book for Global Reach — 374

Chapter 34: How to Transition and Sell Your Publishing Business — 377

Why Would You Sell? — 377
Where Can You Sell Your Publishing Business? — 378
How Much Is Your Publishing Business Worth? — 378
How Empire Flippers Can Help You Sell Your Business — 379
Launching Another KDP Business — 381

A Personal Note to Our Readers from Publishing Services' CEO — 383
Tools & Software — 385
Glossary — 391
References — 393

Introduction

In many ways, this book is Publishing Services' defining work—a book that represents years of hard work, passion, and commitment to self-publishing—one with a mission to show you how to become a best-selling author of self-published books.

Publishing Services (PS) is widely recognized as a top-selling outline, description, and ghostwriting service, known for its exceptional quality and client satisfaction. It was founded in 2019 and has been going strong ever since. As we write these words, we are up to approximately 20,000 completed orders.

Based on more than a thousand reviews, we currently have a 4.9-star rating on Trustpilot. We encourage you to check out the video client testimonials on our website; our customers are your best source of information about our quality and services. In addition to offering outline and description packages, we provide a range of services, including ghostwriting, editing, formatting, design, and more. Over the years, our CEO has assembled a team of seasoned professionals—including multiple bestselling authors, editors, designers, and marketers.

This book is the project of our lifetime because it celebrates what all our team members—managers, writers, editors, formatters, and designers—have been dedicating our hearts and souls to for many years.

We are experts at what we do, and for the very first time in our history, we are giving you a "golden ticket" to see exactly what happens behind the scenes of self-publishing. We are tossing all secrecy out the window, demystifying the publishing process, and openly sharing the specific steps you need to go from an aspiring or new author to a successful authority in your niche. We will help you sell books and show you how to create a thriving, loyal community of readers who fervently look forward to your next publication. Whether you wish to supplement your existing income or live off your book sales, the process begins right here.

Wherever you currently are in your self-publishing pursuit, you may have doubts about the state of the industry. However, the following statistics will confirm that now is the best time to invest time and money into self-publishing (Alliance of Independent Authors 2024):

- Self-published authors earned more in 2023 than those who traditionally published.
- Around 93% of self-published authors are somewhat or extremely positive about self-publishing.
- Self-published authors make up over 50% of Kindle's Top 400 Books for 2023.
- Amazon pays $520 million in royalties to self-published authors each year.
- The global publishing market is expected to grow at 1% CAGR per year, whereas the self-publishing market is expected to grow at 17%.
- The global audiobook market is expected to grow at a CAGR of 26.3% from 2023 to 2030, reaching $35.05 billion by 2030.
- The global ebook market size, valued at $18.13 billion in 2020, is projected to grow at a CAGR of 4.4% from 2021 to 2031.
- $1.25 billion worth of self-published books are sold each year.
- The self-publishing market is expected to grow by 9.2% annually between 2021 and 2028.
- The global ebook market is projected to reach $20.8 billion by 2026.
- In 2023, for the first time in history, 50% of book sales were made online (Bidilică 2023).
- As you can see, we've barely tapped the well; the self-publishing boom is just beginning!

If you are looking for a passive income stream, please understand that very little in self-publishing is "passive." Success in self-publishing is a 100% active pursuit. There are many steps you will need to take to be a self-publisher. Rest assured, we will walk you through every single one of them. Some will take just a few minutes, such as adding your bio to your Amazon author profile. Others will require daily or consistent action, like asking for reviews or checking out the performance of your ads on different social media channels.

Don't worry, though. You won't have to guess a single thing. You will find every actionable step within these pages, but achieving success will involve ticking each item on the many checklists we will provide. Consistency, commitment, and a belief in the book you are publishing are all key.

A Quick Start Guide to This Book

This book is written for new publishers as well as established publishers and those with existing books that have not quite hit the sales mark.

New Publishers

If you are new to publishing, here is what you can expect from this guide:

- Step-by-step guidance on the entire publishing process, from outline drafting to marketing
- Clear explanations of the terms you need to know and key industry practices
- Practical tips and advice for overcoming common challenges and avoiding beginner mistakes
- Inspiration and motivation to pursue your publishing dreams with confidence

Publishers Looking to Improve

If you already have books on the market but are displeased with reviews or sales, you are likely looking for insights on what went "wrong" to improve your process. These aspects of this book may resonate with you:

- An analysis of common mistakes and pitfalls that occur in self-publishing
- Practical solutions and actionable advice for improving your book quality, marketing efforts, and reading engagement
- Case studies or success stories of authors who have turned their publishing careers around after initial setbacks
- Strategies for evaluating market demand, identifying target audiences, and positioning your book for better sales and visibility

Established Publishers

If you are an established, moderately successful publisher, this book is also for you. Chances are, your primary concern lies in optimizing your process and increasing your sales or diversifying your income streams. This book will offer you:

- Advanced tips and strategies for maximizing book sales, royalties, and overall profitability
- Insights into emerging trends and opportunities in self-publishing, including audiobooks, translations, and international markets
- Resources for ongoing education and professional development, including recommended books and courses

We will leave no stone unturned, and that includes budgets and sales figures. At the beginning of this book, we will present a definitive list of budgets for the entire publishing process—from start to finish. As we progress, we will reveal exactly how many sales you must make to earn hundreds or thousands of dollars from your books.

We will present this information through numerous means, catering to different learning styles and ensuring we remain in tune with the digital age. In a time of ever-present connectivity, consumers are as excited about social media, video tutorials, and interactive content as they are about books. This book will connect you to a wide array of sources—including video tutorials, checklists, websites, and audiovisual tools. Because prices, processes, and tools are constantly changing or being updated, we will provide QR codes, links, and resources that will keep you up-to-date and informed of changes in a timely manner.

Important Note: This book is designed as a hands-on guide, not a traditional read-through. Rather than reading it cover to cover, we recommend following each step in the sequence to fully engage with the process. If you try to read it front to back, some of the information may feel abstract or disconnected. But by actively working through the steps, you'll see how each piece fits together.

This book contains affiliate links. This means that if you click on a link and make a purchase, we may earn a small commission at no additional cost to you. In some cases, clicking our affiliate links may also grant you exclusive discounts. These opportunities will be clearly outlined (see the next section).

Throughout this book, you'll find sections marked by three unique icons, each offering specific insights or opportunities.

Look for this symbol to find **exclusive deals** and discounts from companies we trust and recommend. These partners have been selected based on our positive experiences with their services, and they offer special terms for Publishing Services customers.

This icon highlights additional **insights, tips, and tricks** related to the topic at hand. These expert suggestions are designed to help you get even more out of the publishing process.

When Publishing Services offers a **specialized service** for a step in the publishing process—such as outline creation or formatting—you'll see our logo. These sections provide details on the service and instructions on how to place an order.

Let's get right to the steps involved in creating, publishing, and marketing a successful book. In the first chapter, we will provide you with a select list of budgets and a brief overview of the entire publishing process so you can highlight or tick each step as you move along.

Feel free to email support@publishingservices.com if you have any questions or thoughts about our services or this book! You can also check out our website: www.publishingservices.com.

PS also has an active social media presence. We regularly update information, publish newsletters, and share posts on Facebook. We encourage you to join our Facebook group, *The Self-Publishing Network—Powered by Publishing Services*, to stay informed on the latest developments!

A Note on AI

No discussion of publishing would be complete without giving due importance to artificial intelligence (AI)—arguably the most disruptive force in self-publishing in recent years. This book will show you how to use AI for research purposes and brainstorming while maintaining the unique value of human writers, editors, and designers. Ethical, legal, and copyright issues are hot topics regarding AI-produced material, and we will keep you informed of important legal developments as they arise.

Chapter 1

Overview of the Self-Publishing Process

In this chapter, we will present two handy pieces of information you may wish to return to as you progress throughout the book. The first is a selection of budgets, and the second is a visual map of the entire publishing process.

What Budget Will You Need to Publish a Book?

The answer to this question is that no single budget suits all needs. We have crafted a list of five budgets for book creation, ranging from $0 to $3,700+. Consider the "no budget" option as an indication that it is theoretically possible to create a book without paying a cent. However, this option is for those with no budget at all who can do all the necessary work themselves (such as writers with editing experience). Each range is self-explanatory, but we always recommend going for the best package you can. We consider the ultra-premium option a "Publishing Services-level" book. This level of book is informative, engaging, visually appealing, and professionally proofed and edited, maximizing your chances of publishing a bestseller.

No Budget ($0)

- DIY everything

Minimal ($1,590–$2,100)

- Book outline & book description ($397)
- Entry-level writer ($990)
- Cover design ($35–$350)
- Formatting ($97–$300)
- KDSpy ($67)
- DIY the rest

Entry-Level ($2,200–$2,820)

- Book outline & book description ($397)
- Top-level writer ($1,300)
- Proofreading ($270–$400)
- Cover design ($35–$350)
- Formatting ($97–$300)
- KDSpy ($67)
- DIY the rest

Mid-Range ($2,300–$3,150)

- Book outline & book description ($397)
- Premium-level writer ($1,350–$1,500)
- Proofreading ($270–$400)
- Cover design ($35–$350)
- Formatting ($97–$300)
- A+ content ($70–$130)
- KDSpy ($67)
- DIY the rest

High-End ($2,850–$4,200)

- Book outline & book description ($397)
- Premium-level writer ($1,800–$2,300)
- Proofreading ($270–$400)
- Cover design ($35–$350)
- Formatting ($97–$300)
- A+ content ($70–$130)
- Review pages ($130)

- KDSpy + other software ($67–$300)
- DIY the rest

Ultra-Premium ($3,800+ per book)

- Book outline & book description ($397)
- Premium-level writer ($2,300)
- Proofreading ($270–$400)
- Cover design ($350)
- Formatting ($97–$300)
- A+ content ($127)
- Review pages ($130)
- KDSpy ($67)
- Software ($97+)
- No DIY!

The Self-Publishing Process Graph

The following graph indicates a step-by-step description of self-publishing, from creating your book to marketing it, nurturing it, and building a loyal community of readers. You may find that you turn to this graph many times during your reading journey. Doing so is a great way of working out where you're at. Take a quick look and join us on the first step of becoming a successful self-published author: conducting your audience research!

YOUR PATH TO SUCCESSFUL SELF-PUBLISHING

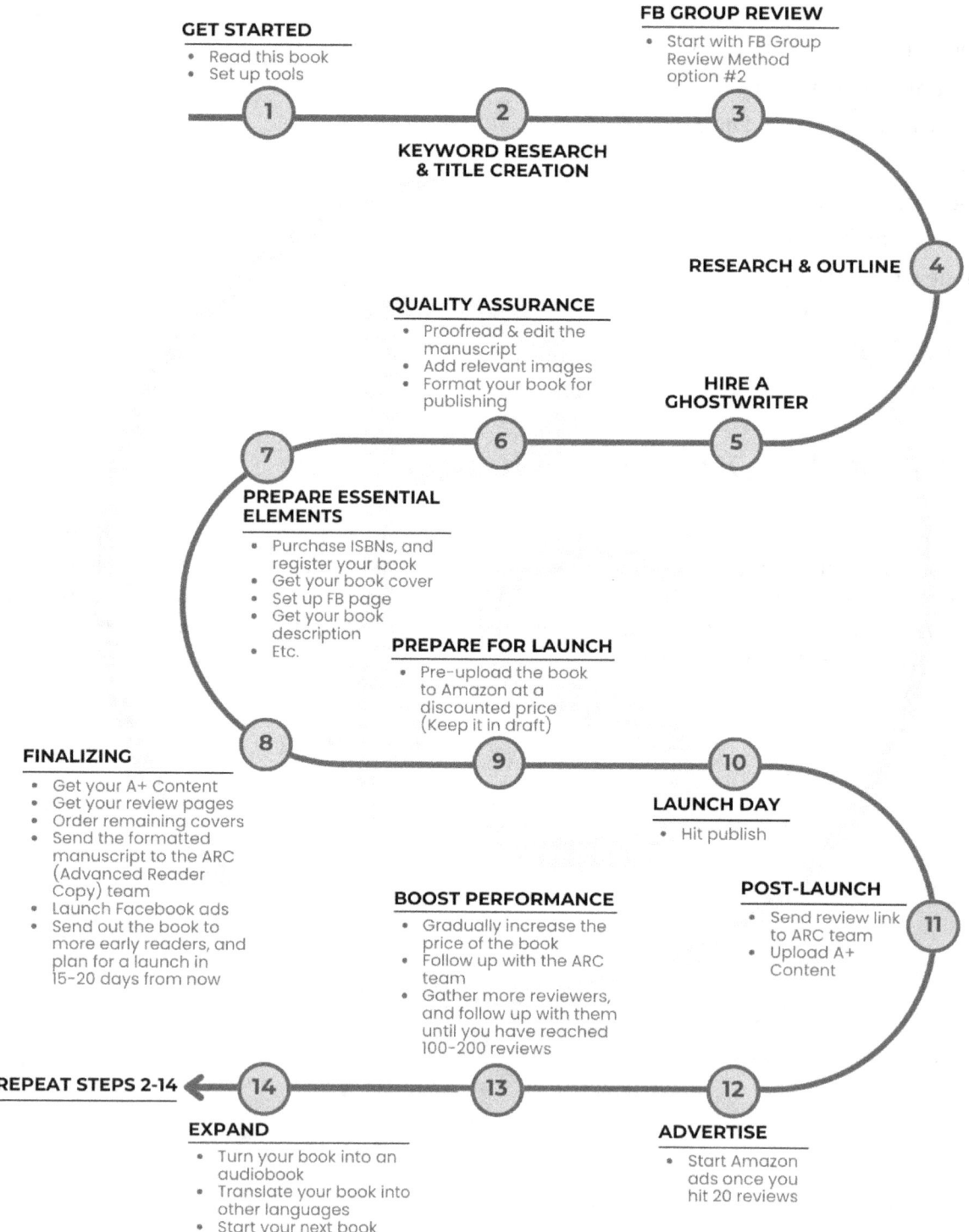

A Word on Self-Publishing Tools and Distributors

Before we get to Chapter 2, it would be helpful to provide you with a list of the leading self-publishing platforms and distributors, as various steps will involve opening accounts and following regulations stipulated by these organizations. In Chapter 18, we will explain how to open an account for all these platforms.

Amazon Kindle Direct Publishing (KDP)

Amazon Kindle Direct Publishing (KDP) is a self-publishing platform that allows you to publish and sell books directly to Amazon's sizeable consumer base. Amazon dominates over 50% of the market share for print and ebooks, making it an optimal choice for self-published authors (Nafees 2022).

IngramSpark

IngramSpark is a print-on-demand and ebook publishing service for authors wishing to distribute their work globally. It is owned by Ingram Book Group, one of the world's largest book distributors. The company distributes books to over 39,000 retailers, libraries, and online stores, including Amazon, Walmart, Target, and Barnes & Noble (IngramSpark 2019).

ACX

Audiobook Creation Exchange (ACX), which is a part of Audible (an Amazon.com, Inc. subsidiary), allows self-publishers residing in the US, Canada, Ireland, and the UK to produce and distribute digital audiobooks. It helps you audition voice talent, review recorded work, and distribute your audiobook through popular audio bookstores. The audiobook market is currently worth around $6.4 billion (Research and Markets 2024), so turning your book into an audiobook should definitely be a priority. If you do not reside in the US, you cannot use ACX. Instead, you have to use Author's Republic or Findaway Voices by Spotify, which are below.

Author's Republic

This platform allows you to produce quality audiobooks and sell them to 50+ distribution channels, including Amazon, Apple, Spotify, and Google.

Findaway Voices by Spotify

Findaway Voices by Spotify is the platform for independent authors who want to unlock the world's major audiobook platforms, including Spotify, Audible, and Apple Books. To use Findaway Voices, simply open an account, upload your audiobook, and distribute it.

With a solid overview of the publishing process and budget examples in mind, you're ready to start planning your next step. Remember that your budget and publishing strategy should match your goals. Whether you're working with a limited budget or have more flexibility, knowing where to focus your resources will make a big difference. In the next chapter, we'll take a closer look at keyword research—the crucial first step toward a bestseller.

Let's get started!

Chapter 2

Keyword Research

You may write a fascinating book with a gorgeous cover and useful information inside, but if there is no demand for it, it is unlikely to become a bestseller. This is where research comes into play. To make money as a self-publisher, you need to write a book with a high demand but a relatively low supply, meaning the topic and niche are not saturated with high-quality books. Your book must also match your audience's keywords—a list of words or phrases your audience uses to find a book on a topic they are interested in. When it comes to self-publishing, the sequence of steps involved in research and the tools you need to discover a profitable topic is well-defined and easy to access. Continue reading to learn each step of the process.

01 >> DS Amazon Quick View

DS Amazon Quick View is a Google Chrome extension for Amazon shoppers who wish to save time and view product details quickly without clicking on each product. You need this tool for research because it will provide you with vital information about profitable niches and sub-niches. This tool can only be installed on Chrome, and the free, basic version is sufficient for your research needs.

To install DS Amazon Quick View, search for it in the Chrome Webstore or go to www.publishingservicesbook.com/ds-amazon-quick-view and add it to Chrome.

Search Using Incognito Mode

In addition to installing DS Amazon Quick View, you must open your browser in incognito mode when searching for keywords. Doing so will put you in a similar position to target readers searching for a book on your topic. If you search Amazon using your own profile, the results will be based on *your personal* browsing interests and history. Unless you want to sell the book to yourself, this isn't your best bet!

Enable DS Amazon QuickView

To enable DS Amazon Quick View for incognito mode, go to Chrome and click the three dots in the top right corner of your browser. Select Extensions, and click Manage Extensions. Next, click Details in DS Amazon Quick View and select Allow in Incognito.

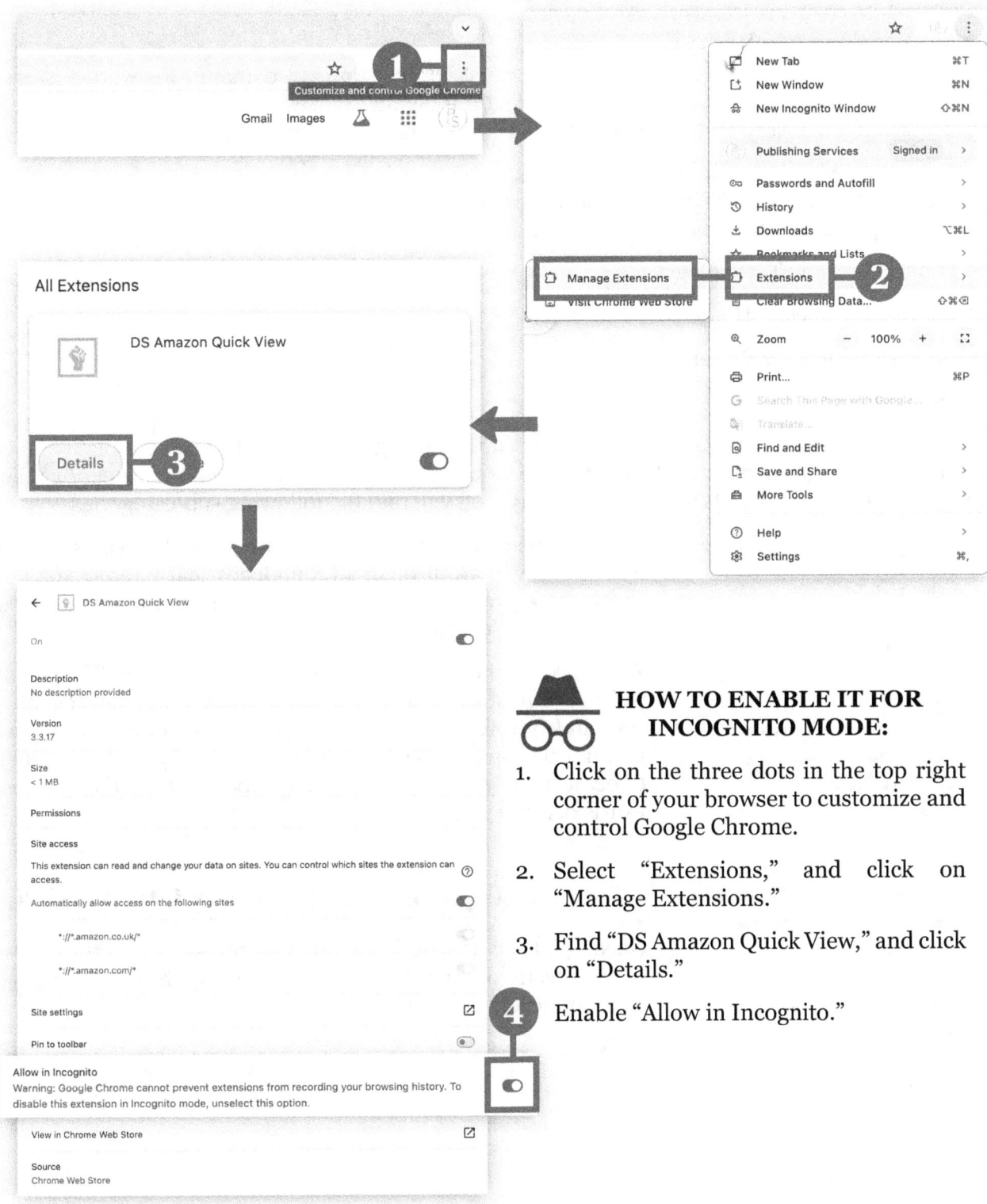

HOW TO ENABLE IT FOR INCOGNITO MODE:

1. Click on the three dots in the top right corner of your browser to customize and control Google Chrome.

2. Select "Extensions," and click on "Manage Extensions."

3. Find "DS Amazon Quick View," and click on "Details."

4. Enable "Allow in Incognito."

02 ▶▶ How and Where to Search for Keywords

If you want a book to sell, its title and content must cover a topic in demand. Keyword research used to be a laborious process. Fortunately, there are tools that make the process easy, and we are introducing you to the very best of them. Let's go through the search process from start to finish.

Open your browser in incognito mode. (Click the three dots in the top right corner of your browser and select **New Incognito Window.**) Go to Amazon's Best Seller tab and click **Books** to review different categories. You will find numerous options, such as:

- Computers and Technology
- Crafts, Hobbies, & Home
- Health, Fitness, & Dieting
- Self-Help

These are broad categories. During a keyword search, your goal is to narrow your topic as much as possible so you can find an in-demand niche to target. To find niches, click the categories. For instance, if you click **Computers & Technology**, you will find the following sub-categories.

‹ Books
Computers & Technology
Business Technology
Certification
Computer Science
Databases & Big Data
Digital Audio, Video & Photography
Games & Strategy Guides
Graphics & Design
Hardware & DIY
History & Culture
Internet & Social Media
Mobile Phones, Tablets & E-Readers
Networking & Cloud Computing
Operating Systems
Programming
Programming Languages
Security & Encryption
Software
Web Development & Design

Now, you need to do some digging, otherwise known as *niching down*. You will go through all the niches that interest you and check the keywords. For example, let's say you want to write a book on cybersecurity.

You click on the **Security & Encryption** niche. There, you will find a host of books. Look at the titles and subtitles—they contain keywords you can investigate. For instance, our search found titles and subtitles like *Cybersecurity for Dummies*, *Cybersecurity for Beginners*, and *Cybersecurity Bible*. Those words become your keywords and phrases.

03 ▶▶ Keyword Profitability Check (KPC)

Once you have 50-100 keywords and phrases like these, enter them directly on our Keyword Profitability Check (KPC) page. You can access the page at www.publishingservicesbook.com/kpc.

Niching down is important because the more specific your niche is, the greater your chance of publishing a bestseller, provided your keywords also fulfill some additional requirements. Your keyword profitability check (KPC) will tell you which keywords can potentially be transformed into a profitable book.

For your keywords to pass the profitability check, they must be present in at least three relevant books with fewer than 150 customer reviews and a Best Seller Rank (BSR) of under 150K. BSR is a metric that shows how a product is selling in the Amazon store compared to other products listed in the same category. The closer a BSR is to 1, the better the book is selling.

This step can be even easier thanks to a tool called KDSpy. In one click, KDSpy shows you all the key information you need; you no longer have to search book by book to make sure specific keywords have potential. KDSpy has a one-off purchase cost of $69 and is worth the investment—even if you go the full DIY route. To purchase this software, go to www.publishingservicesbook.com/kdspy.

KDSpy lists all the books ranked on the first page for your keywords or niche. These are the books you want to compete with. You want your book to pop up on the first page of your target audience's search results because buyers rarely look beyond the first page when searching for books and other products on Amazon.

To use KDSpy, make sure you are in incognito mode. (Open Chrome, click the three dots on the top right, and select **New Incognito Window**.)

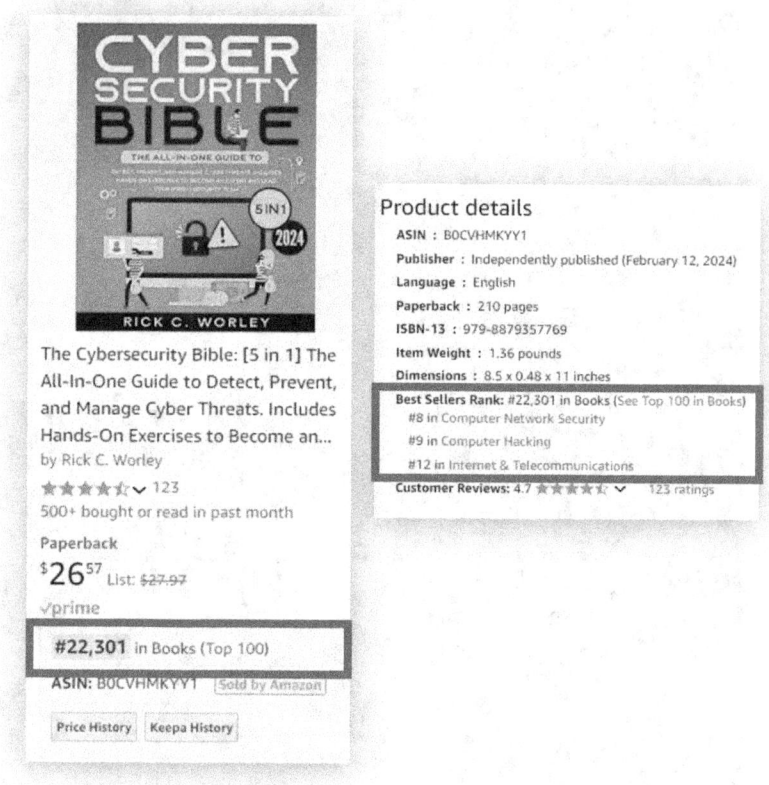

1. Take the keywords you wrote in your KPC file and go to Amazon Best Sellers at www.publishingservicesbook.com/amazon-best-sellers.
2. Type the keywords from your list in the search bar and click the search symbol.
3. Next, open KDSpy and click on **Reviews** so your list will be sorted from low to high.
4. See if these keywords are found in at least three books with fewer than 150 customer reviews and a BSR of under 150K. If so, those are your winning keywords!

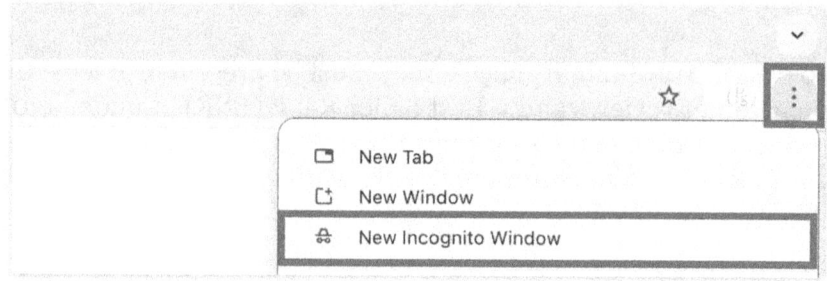

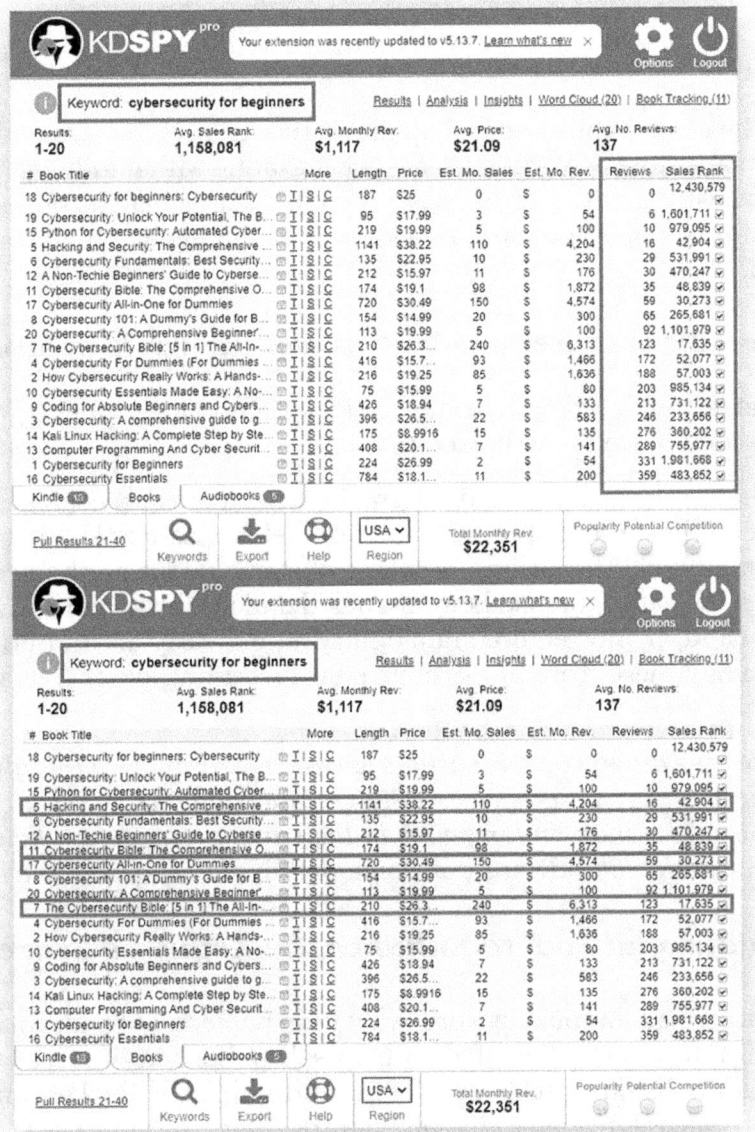

 **Pro Tip:** You can also use trend-centered websites like Meetglimpse.com to find new trends. This website is linked to Google Trends, which means that its data is accurate.

04 >> Key Questions to Consider

1. Does the topic have lasting relevance?

You wouldn't want to invest in publishing a book that is too "trendy" or seasonally tied. For instance, if you searched in December for keywords such as "getting along with family," you might find a host of books on "getting along with family at Christmas." A book like this may be selling like hotcakes when you look it up, but chances are, by January, nobody will be buying it. Try to select topics that are of interest all year round.

2. Are there any specific obstacles making this niche tough to publish?

You need to ensure that no major financial, time-related, or other impediments will make your chosen keywords or niche too complicated to write about.

For instance, a complicated topic like quantum gravity or statistical mechanics may not be a great idea unless you and your ghostwriter specialize in these fields. Readers looking for this type of book will likely specialize in the field themselves. Another obstacle might be the need for illustrations—especially colored ones. If your book needs numerous detailed illustrations, this will increase your budget. On the other hand, if you require simple illustrations—say around 60 illustrations of wall pilates poses—you can buy these from professionals on Fiverr and other freelance sites for around $250.

Disclaimer: Any books we discuss or screenshots we use as examples in this guide are simply ways to demonstrate specific points. Aspects such as BSRs change, and by the time this guide is published, the books we use as examples may no longer be in the same positions as they were at the date of writing. As such, it is essential to find your own keywords rather than relying on our examples.

BookBeam: An Additional Tool to Enhance the Keyword Search Process

KDSpy is the tool you need to follow our keyword evaluation process, but additional tools are available. One of these is BookBeam, a toolset created to help self-publishers increase their Amazon sales. BookBeam is known in publishing circles as "KDSpy and Publisher Rocket (another popular piece of software that we will discuss in a later chapter) put together." It helps users find their niche (and alternative keywords) and sort self-published books from those published by traditional publishing houses.

One of the best Bookbeam features is their service to track and optimize your book listing on Amazon. They offer a variety of handy tools, such as competitor tracking, ad efficiency improvement, sales and profit data analysis, etc. They also give suggestions on how you can rank higher than your competitors (for instance, by adding A+ Content—more on this in the following chapters).

BookBeam also has a trademark checker. Trademarks are essentially the rights to a word or group of words that other companies or writers own. That means you cannot use them in your title or subtitle. For instance, if you search the phrase "cybersecurity for dummies," you will see that the phrase "for dummies" is trademarked. So are terms like "Pokémon" and "Lego." It's a good idea to ensure your search terms, book title, and content do not contain trademarked terms. Failing to do so can result in potential trademark infringement issues. The search process is straightforward. You simply type your proposed title or keywords into the search bar and immediately receive information on whether they are trademarked. If you choose not to use Bookbeam, you can check trademarks for free at www.uspto.gov/trademarks/search.

 **Exclusive Deal:** BookBeam is an affiliate partner of Publishing Services. Go to www.publishingservicesbook.com/bookbeam and type **PS10** to get **10% off** for the yearly plans or **PS50** to get **50% off** on the first month. (BookBeam is a monthly subscription service.)

05 ▸▸ Target Audience Research Strategies

Knowing your target audience—what moves and pains them, how they think, how old they are, and how their culture might impact their demand for your book—is vital. Target research is imperative at two stages of self-publishing: during this initial stage and again when crafting your book's outline.

When searching for your target audience, you are looking for the segment of the market that you can serve best: those who have a need that you can fulfill and who are willing and able to pay for the value of what you are offering them. Knowing this segment well will keep you focused while you conduct your marketing efforts. It will also be needed when writing your book outline or manuscript—since, in order to resonate with your target audience, you need to speak to them in the right voice. Below are a few key questions that will help you "step into the shoes" of your target audience.

1. **What are your audience demographics?** You can identify this by targeting the following criteria:
   - Gender
   - Age
   - Cultural background (if relevant)
   - Family situation (Are they likely to be married, single, or have kids?)
   - Work or financial situation
   - Any biases they might have
   - Tendency to trust (or mistrust) science
   - Tendency to trust (or mistrust) authorities
   - Any relevant religious or political leanings

2. **What wants or needs will your book fulfill?** To discover this, ask and answer the following questions:
   - Who does your target reader want to please?

- What problem/s do they have that your book can help them solve?
- Is there anything they do not want to be told or any overused advice that should not be in your book?

3. **What will make your book stand out from its competition?** This is your book's unique selling point (or USP).

4. **What is your aim when publishing this book?**

We will go deeper into these questions when discussing how to write a great outline. For now, answering the four questions above is a great start. There is no "one-size-fits-all" solution for conducting audience research. Let's look at some of the tools that successful published authors use.

Google Searches and AI

If you wish to write a book on osteoporosis, searching for "osteoporosis statistics" will instantly show you that this health problem affects one in three women and one in five men over the age of fifty. This suggests that most of your readers may be women but that you can benefit from targeting men as well. In that case, it's best to set a gender-neutral tone in your book to appeal to all sides.

When using AI tools like Perplexity, always check the sources they provide. AI sometimes offers incorrect sources or makes a claim and then provides a source that says something different. If you are basing your conclusions on studies, make it a point to at least read the abstract and the study discussion so you can ensure the statistics you have found are accurate.

In our experience, AI is particularly helpful for identifying pain points (the reasons why your readers want to buy a book like yours). For instance, if you are writing a book about anxiety in teens, you may immediately think of main pain points such as "the desire to have a normal social life," "a wish to be in control of their anxiety rather than vice versa," or "the hope to lessen anxiety so that school and work are easier/more enjoyable." However, AI may point out additional pain points you may not otherwise have thought of—including the role that social media plays in teen anxiety.

Popular Forums like Reddit and Quora

These forums are invaluable sources of real-life stories. For instance, we conducted a search for "parenting a child with ADHD." We found a thread from a parent who was worried about the effect that increasingly higher doses of Ritalin were having on their child, and they spoke to other parents on the forum about an alternative, non-stimulant medication. As such, one of the pain points for a book on this topic might be "finding alternative solutions to traditionally prescribed medications." This is just one example of many pain points you will find as you delve into the issues people are sharing and seeking advice for online.

Competitor Reviews

It is amazing to see the extent to which many reviewers share a bit about their own story when reviewing a book. Spend a generous amount of time reading what readers liked and disliked about the book, and read up about the pain points they share. This will come in handy for identifying who your target audience is and addressing key points to be addressed in your book. Reviews will also tell you a lot about the kind of advice readers want (and do not want) to hear, the type of content they are looking for (they may mention checklists, journaling exercises, or tests), and similar.

06 >> Competitor Analysis Methods

You have one clear advantage over all other books listed under your category: yours is yet to be written. That means you can look at your competitors' books and identify what went wrong, what went right, and how you can make your book even better than the current top-selling book. To conduct a competitor analysis, click the listings of your strongest competitors' books and identify the positive and negative aspects of each of the following:

- Title and subtitle
- Description
- Amazon A+ Content (a tool within Amazon's Seller Central that allows brand owners to create beautifully designed Amazon product descriptions for their product listings)
- Reviews
- Table of contents

The book title and subtitle help show you which keywords are being targeted. The description provides vital information on the following aspects of the book:

- Pain points it seeks to solve
- Solution(s) offered by the book
- The most interesting, useful content within the book
- Possible objections the target reader may have to buying the book and how to counter these objections

As mentioned above, Amazon A+ Content is beautifully designed promotional content. Check out what your competitors have created so you can make your Amazon A+ Content more visually appealing and write more engaging marketing text.

Reviews are, without a doubt, one of the most important ways to leave your competition in the dust. They are a great indicator of what you should include in or leave out of your book. When you enter a book listing and click **Ratings**, you will see 5-, 4-, 3-, 2-, and 1-star ratings. By all means, browse the 5-star ratings to see what readers found most valuable about the book, but also pay close attention to the 4-star and 3-star ratings, as they will identify flaws you can ensure are absent from your book.

For instance, we clicked on one book on cybersecurity for beginners and found the following useful comments:

- **4-Star Rating:** "The book was easy to read and focused on Windows and MacOS. However, it ignored Linux, Servers, and Tablets. Most importantly, it does not deal with cellular devices. I wish this book included ransomware."

- **4-Star Rating:** "The work seems a bit short on browsers, clone sites, 'useful' downloads that contain more than expected, certificates, HTTPS lock, and certs. Also, it would be good to have information regarding RDP security risks."

- **3-Star Rating:** "Great book if you don't know anything about cybersecurity, but it lacks examples and in-depth analysis. Not very hands-on."

- **2-Star Rating:** "There is nothing in this book that you can't find with a basic online search."

Finally, we suggest reviewing the table of contents of your competitors. Most books on Amazon allow browsers to read a free sample. Usually, the table of contents can be found in this sample. This part of your competitors' books will be even more pertinent when you or your copywriter writes the outline for your manuscript. However, even at this stage, it is useful to review because it shows you the basic structure of the book and the main points it covers.

Congratulations on making it through our guide on how to conduct your keyword, audience, and competitor research. In Chapter 3, we will focus on how to create a best-selling book title that will capture your target audience's attention and make them click the **Add to Cart** button without delay!

 **Chapter 2 Checklist**

Research Steps	Check When Completed

Step 1:
Install DS Amazon Quick View on Google Chrome and enable it for incognito mode. Open your browser in incognito mode. ☐

Step 2:
Search for Keywords by niching down and writing down around 50-100 keywords used by books in your niche. ☐

Step 3:
Conduct your Keyword Profitability Check (KPC) on your keywords. ☐

- Purchase KDSpy. ☐
- Purchase Bookbeam (if within your budget). ☐
- Look for keywords present in at least three relevant books with fewer than 150 customer reviews and a BSR of under 150K. ☐

Step 4:
Ask yourself if the book is evergreen and if there are major impediments to choosing a specific niche/set of keywords. ☐

Step 5:
Conduct your trademark search. ☐

Step 6:
Conduct your competitive analysis. ☐

Chapter 3

Choosing Titles That Sell

All your work in Chapter 2 will be important for Chapter 3 because when choosing a book title and subtitle, keeping keywords in mind is vital. Let's take a look at two titles in the same niche. One hits the spot, and the other is way off the mark. Can you spot what's wrong with the second one?

Book One: *How Cybersecurity Really Works: A Hands-On Guide for Total Beginners* (This title exists on Amazon.)

Book Two: *The Cybersecurity Starter Kit: Everything You Need to Know About Online Security, Identity Protection, Threat Detection, Data Encryption, and Safe Browsing for First-Timers and Tech Novices with Practical Tips for Enhancing Online Privacy for New Users* (We have created this title to show you what not to do.)

If you identified wordiness as one problem in Book Two, you're right. Your title and subtitles should be pertinent and sound appealing when you read them aloud. Book Two's title sounds like someone stuffed every keyword they could think of into their title so they could rank well when customers were searching for a book on their topic. It is confusing and cluttered, and very few customers will likely be attracted to it. Keep clarity and simplicity at the forefront when writing anything, selecting keywords with a purpose instead of resorting to keyword stuffing or bunching.

A professional book title has the following qualities:

- It clearly states what the book is about.
- It contains the phrases your target audience will be using.

- The title contains your main keywords.
- The subtitle addresses the pain points and desired outcomes from reading your book.
- The title and subtitle have a combined character count of no more than 200.

Words to Avoid

A strong title does not contain profanity, acronyms, or asterisks hiding swears (STFU, F**K, SHTF). Sure, you can theoretically use these words in your title and upload your book to Kindle Direct Publishing (KDP), but when you want to run ads for your book on Amazon, you won't be allowed to. To avoid having to redo a significant portion of your work, simply avoid swear words.

Other words to avoid include:

- Unauthorized use of trademarked terms (If you use these, you risk having your KDP account terminated.)
- Words with health promises such as "cure," "heal," and other words that make unsubstantiated claims
- Repeated generic keywords like "notebook," "journal," "gifts," "books," and similar
- Unauthorized reference to other titles or authors
- Reference to sales rank (for example, "best-selling")
- Reference to ads or promotions (such as "free")
- Excessive punctuation (for instance, "?????" or "!!!!")
- Using "none," "not applicable," "null," and similar
- HTML tags

How to Find Effective Keywords for Your Title and Subtitle

From this point onward, we will use a sample niche and title to show you the different steps you must undertake to publish a profitable book. We have chosen the sample niche of "raising chickens." Please note that this is NOT a profitable niche; we do not advise you to write about it. We will simply use this niche to show you how to find keywords, design an eye-catching cover, obtain reviews, and more. Our intention is for you to use the advice we give you and apply it to *your* chosen niche and title. Let's get straight to finding and selecting winning keywords for your title and subtitle. To make sure you reach your target audience, follow these steps.

01 ▶▶ *Research the Keywords Used in Top-Ranking Competitors' Titles and Subtitles*

Don't limit yourself to the most obvious ones, like "raising chickens." Make sure to also look for long-tail keywords, which are longer, more specific keyword phrases your audience is most likely to use when making a purchase or using voice search. Let's check out our example niche. Go to Amazon Books and type in "raising chickens." On the day we typed this in, we found the following suggested keywords and long-tail keywords in the titles and subtitles of top-ranked books:

1. Raising chickens for beginners
2. Raising chickens for eggs
3. Raising backyard chickens
4. Raising backyard chickens for beginners
5. Beginner's guide to raising chickens
6. Raise a happy backyard flock
7. Raising happy, healthy chickens
8. Guide to raising chickens
9. Breed selection, facilities, feeding, health care, managing layers and meat birds
10. Egg production
11. Urban chickens
12. How to raise chickens in your backyard

Prioritize those that appear in the list of autosuggested books, working from top to bottom (in order of how many people look them up).

 *Use Your List to Create at Least Two Titles*

Read them out loud and ask others' opinions about which title rolls off the tongue better. Include the main keyword/s in the title, and address the pain points and outcome in the subtitle.

For instance, a relevant title and subtitle for your book might be *Become a Backyard Chicken Farmer—Master Breed Selection and Feeding—Uncover the Importance of Facilities and Health Care to Effortlessly Increase Egg Production*. The keywords should describe what your audience will find in your book. The title lets you know what the book is about, while the subtitle shows what tasks your book can help readers with.

Another great example can be found in the book you are reading right now: *How to Start and Run a Profitable Self-Publishing Business: The Complete Blueprint With Proven Strategies and Step-By-Step Instructions to Launch and Market Your Book to Become a Bestselling Author*. The main title shows this will help you become a self-published author, and the subtitle indicates that it will take the confusion out of the process ("step-by-step instructions") and that the strategies will give you the outcome you desire ("to become a bestselling author").

Remember to check your title and subtitle for those prohibited words before you finalize your choice.

 **Pro Tip:** Remember that relevant keywords change continuously. As you move closer to the book-writing stage, you may decide to use in-demand keywords that may not have existed during your first search.

As you can see, selecting the best book title is closely tied to keyword research. But your title isn't the only first impression you'll make. In the next chapter, we'll focus on another important decision: choosing your author name. It's a brief but important discussion that can impact how readers perceive and connect with you.

 **Chapter 3 Checklist**

Research Steps   Check When Completed

Step 1:
Look into the keywords and long-tail keywords utilized by competitors ranked on the first page of your search on Amazon. Type your keywords into the Amazon and Audible search bars and see what they auto-suggest. Create a long list of keywords, ensuring you include main and long-tail keywords.

☐

Step 2:
Create two or more book titles (with subtitles), ensuring that the combined total of the title and subtitle is no more than 200 characters without keyword stuffing/bunching, and choose the one that sounds better to yourself and others.

☐

Step 3:
Check that nothing in your chosen title or subtitle is trademarked.

☐

Step 4:
Check that nothing in your chosen title and subtitle contains prohibited words.

☐

Chapter 4

Choosing an Author Name

You have three choices when it comes to choosing a name. You can use your real name, a pen name, or a brand name. A pen name is used by writers who wish to hide their real name or who wish to create a writer persona that they feel would resonate more strongly with their readers. A brand name is used to imply authority in a chosen niche.

The name you select will show up on your public profile page. It is important to weigh the pros and cons of using your name vs. a pseudonym or brand name because once your book is published, you won't be able to change your book's primary author field on Amazon. You can create a new edition with a new author name, but this will involve additional time and expense.

Writing Under a Pen Name

Below are a few pros and cons of using a pen name (Sreepoorna 2021).

Pros

- You can avoid people prying into your personal life and stay out of controversy.
- Your name may be hard to remember, making it more difficult for them to recommend your book to other readers.

- In some cases, your name may be too similar to another author's or, in your view, not the best fit for your niche.
- You may not want others (for instance, people in your current job) to know you are involved in self-publishing. For example, you may write a book that clashes with the values of your current employer, and you don't want your job security to be threatened.
- You can see how your book is received first, without receiving hate or excessively negative backlash. Reviews can be scathing—even if your book is good. Sometimes, these reviews are left by competitors who meticulously point out the tiniest flaws and inflate their importance. Publishing under a pseudonym gives you time to get used to this (and to jot down any complaints they make) so that if you later publish a new book with your own name, you'll know more of what to expect.
- Your book may be private, and using a pseudonym enables you to share your story but not your identity.
- You can write books in different genres or niches and use different author personas as desired. That way, if one book is selling well, you can push that persona and write more books in the same niche.

Cons

- Many authors enjoy creating a personal connection with their readers. Using a pseudonym prevents you from doing so.
- Your marketing efforts can be curtailed, as you may not be able to attend meetups or use social media to speak about your book in the first person. That is unless you share your real identity further down the line. Many authors choose to do this.
- You may have to pay a copywriter to create an author persona for you. Anything related to this persona—including your logo design, website, and marketing materials—should align with the fictional persona.
- If you write books in more than one genre, you will need to create a new persona for each one and invest in building trust and recognition for each name.

Famous Pen Names

Fun Fact: Some of the most famous pen names (and their real-life equivalents) include:
- Mark Twain: Samuel Langhorne Clemens
- George Orwell: Eric Arthur Blair
- Lewis Carroll: Charles Lutwidge Dodgson
- Dr. Seuss: Theodor Seuss Geisel

- George Eliot: Mary Ann Evans
- J.K. Rowling: Joanne Rowling (she wrote using the pseudonym Robert Galbraith)
- Stan Lee: Stanley Martin Lieber
- Lemony Snicket: Daniel Handler
- Richard Bachman: Stephen King
- Anne Rice: Howard Allen Frances O'Brien

And here's another cool fact: Daniel Handler came up with the memorable name "Lemony Snicket" while researching his novel, *The Basic Eight*. He needed information from political organizations but didn't want to be on their mailing lists. When asked his name, he blurted out, "Lemony Snicket." It became a longstanding joke among his friends, and eventually, when he started a series of children's books, he knew it would make the perfect pen name.

Publishing Under Your Real Name

Below are a few pros and cons of using your real name:

Pros

- You can create a personal brand that can be useful if you wish to establish yourself as an expert in your chosen niche.
- You can attend in-person events, interviews, and meet-ups.
- Using your name gives you the power of authenticity and the ability to connect with your readers without creating a persona.
- Over time, readers may develop a strong loyalty to you as an author and purchase all the books you publish.

Cons

- Your privacy can be affected, and you may not be ready to let superiors at work or other people know that you are a self-published author.
- Your name might become strongly associated with one niche or genre, and readers may not be as open if you decide to publish a book in a completely unrelated genre.

Using a Brand Name or Publishing Company Name

A third option that resonates with some self-publishers is a brand name. For instance, if you are in the coloring book niche, you might use "Artful Designs" or "Color Whimsy" as your brand name.

Below are a few pros and cons of using a brand name:

Pros

- It looks professional and lends an air of authority to your book.
- It helps create a business entity encompassing various authors and genres without confusion.

Cons

- As with pen names, it may lack a personal connection.
- Building brand loyalty can be more challenging when not using a person's name.
- It requires a high degree of marketing consistency.
- It suits some genres more than others. For instance, it works well in education, wellness, and art genres but not so well in self-help books centered on personal experiences and anecdotes.
- If you write books in more than one genre, you will have to invest in building trust and recognition for each of these brand names.

How to Create a Pen Name

You can choose any name that aligns with your niche and target audience. You can also use a site like Reedsy, which creates various pen names you can select. To access the generator, go to www.publishingservicesbook.com/pen-name-generator. All you need to do is indicate the first letter of your pseudonym, pick a genre, and choose a language of origin. Then, click **Generate Name** and repeat the process as many times as you like.

Additional Tips

- **Ensure your chosen name resonates with your target audience.** Conduct polls among people you know and trust. Don't offer your name on public forums, as you don't want to risk someone else taking a name you spent time dreaming up.
- **Remember that sounds, consonants, and syllables convey specific qualities.** For instance, "plosive sounds" (the kinds of sounds usually associated with the letters *p, t, k, b, d, g*, in which airflow from the lungs is interrupted by a complete closure being made in the mouth) can sound harder than *m, n, s, and sh* sounds (Maddieson, n.d.).

- **Names can have a meaning that lends them a specific quality.** For instance, names like Axel, Hunter, or Maverick can impart a sense of power and strength, while names like Noah, Milo, Emily, or Lily can have a softer feel. Of course, the sensations evoked by specific names can vary among cultures, so it's a good idea to research, inquire, and rely on opinions without exposing your shortlist to a wider public.
- Check that the name you choose is not already in use on Amazon.
- **Run a Google search to ensure your chosen name is not associated with anything controversial.** Try to ensure your name does not mean something you don't want it to in another language. Use Google Translate or ChatGPT to check this.
- **If you choose a brand name, you must also do a trademark search.** You can do so on this site: www.uspto.gov/trademarks/search

This chapter does not have a checklist, as choosing a name is simply a matter of weighing your options. In the next chapter, we will cover a short but important topic: the ideal length for your book!

Chapter 5

Determining the Ideal Book Length

There is no hard and fast rule when choosing the ideal length for your book. However, after many years in the industry, the standard Publishing Services recommendation is 30,000 (30K) words. This is an ideal minimum number to aim for because:

- A 30K-length book contains plenty of information but isn't so long that a reader may tire of reading it.
- Keeping your book to around 30k allows you to stick to a manageable budget with regards to ghostwriting, editing, formatting, translation, and printing.
- If your book is much longer, it will also take longer to go through each of these stages.
- 30K is a typical word count for non-fiction books in the self-publishing world. One reason for this is that audiobook sales and royalties rise significantly when works exceed the three-hour mark, and a 30K book produces around three hours of narration.
- A 30K-word book can easily be transformed into a host of formats, including ebook, print, and audiobook.

 **Pro Tip:** You do not have to stick with an exact length of 30K words. Customers have asked, "Is a 35K-45K word count still okay?" The answer is yes! 30K is considered an "ideal minimum," as it enables your audiobook to fall into a higher royalty tier.

How to Ensure Your Book Meets the 30K Word Count Mark

To ensure you or your ghostwriter can meet the 30K mark, consider creating or investing in a quality outline. Your outline should contain enough detail and sources that the ghostwriter has a clear map to follow. The outline (more on this later) will contain a breakdown of the word count the writer should aim for in each chapter. A little variation may be necessary when you or your ghostwriter starts writing. If a chapter is a little longer or shorter than expected, the writer can make up for it by adjusting other chapters as you go along. It isn't difficult to do, especially if you count on an experienced ghostwriter who is accustomed to writing books of this length or more.

Speaking of outlines, the next chapter is all about how to create an excellent outline. At Publishing Services, we've written thousands of these, so we are in the perfect position to share a few secrets with you!

Chapter 6

How to Write a Perfect Book Outline

For very different reasons, your book outline and description are two of the most important requirements for publishing a best-selling book. Your outline is research-based; it outlines the precise structure of your book and its complete list of contents. The idea is for your ghostwriter to base what they write on the instructions in your outline, utilizing the sources it contains. The ghostwriter is not meant to conduct significant additional research.

The description is a piece of commercial copywriting intended to convince your target audience that buying and reading your book will be worth their time and money because it will help them solve or deal with their problems. When the reader clicks on your book listing on Amazon, they will review your description to see whether it contains the information they are seeking. You will learn more about the art of writing book descriptions in Chapter 7.

In this chapter, we will present what needs to be included in your outline, as well as weigh the pros and cons of a DIY vs. professional approach.

Key Elements of a Book Outline

A book outline should have various components so the ghostwriter knows exactly what contents to include and what style and tone to use. Your outline should contain the following information:

- Title and subtitle of your book
- Author name

- A general overview of the book, including:
  - A summary of its contents
  - Information on your target audience (including audience demographics, pain points, and outcomes from reading your book)
  - Information on the tone or style of your book
  - A list of pertinent terminology or jargon
  - Specific instructions the ghostwriter should take into account
  - Information on the author or author's persona
- An overview of the chapters (chapter titles and word count per chapter)
- A chapter-by-chapter outline with information on the content of the chapter and its goal, engaging chapter hooks, supporting content, and optional stories
- An introduction and a conclusion

It is also helpful for the ghostwriter if each chapter has additional sources they may find pertinent, plus any suggested interactive elements or exercises and, finally, a segue to the next chapter.

Researching for a Strong Outline

There are various parts of the outline that require extensive research, including the target audience and chapter-by-chapter sections. This is a laborious process that requires you or your outline writer to find relevant, recent, and interesting information from the following sources:

- Studies and reports
- Reviews and opinions of other books
- Specialized websites and blogs
- Competitors' books (to see the content they include)
- Worksheets, activities, and journaling ideas
- YouTube and other video sites containing useful information

If you want to create your own outline, you can use our student template, which can be found here: www.publishingservicesbook.com/outline-template.

DIY vs. Professional Outlining

In Chapter 1, we mentioned several budgets. However, all budgets include a professionally written outline by a dedicated team of researchers. While, theoretically, you can write an outline yourself, it pays to consider that outline writing is a specialized field, and many writers spend years simply learning how to write a professional outline in college.

A good outline doesn't just indicate the topics and subtopics that need to be covered; it contains a clear hierarchy, with sources placed beneath the corresponding points and sub-points. It instructs the ghostwriter on specific things to watch out for, interactive elements the writer should add, etc. It also provides precise, authoritative, and updated sources that permit the writer to craft an informative, engaging book.

The outline should provide a complete, thorough, and well-researched work that the ghostwriter can immediately work with without having to find their own sources or invent activities as they go along. When you read your completed outline, you should see every relevant topic and subtopic, source, story idea, and activity listed so you can make any changes before your ghostwriter commences working on your manuscript. Failing to use a top-quality outline can lead to rewrites, wasted time, and more significant costs in the long run.

 **Pro Tip**: Go to www.publishingservicesbook.com/outline-sample to review a Publishing Services outline sample!

Comparison: DIY Outline and a Publishing Services Outline

DIY Outline	Publishing Services Outline
It is free.	Our Book Outline and Description Package costs $397.
A separate description must be written.	Ours comes with a description (with a back cover version and HTML coding for KDP) written by a highly experienced, professional copywriter.
It is time-consuming.	Your professionally written outline is delivered within 10 business days.
You may not include enough details or sources for your ghostwriter to write the book you want.	Your outline contains detailed information written in the correct hierarchy, with a full set of instructions for your ghostwriter, detailed sources for each point made, and links to ideas for stories and interactive elements.
You risk being too similar to your competitors.	Your outline will be completely original and include a signature framework if you desire one.

 **Pro Tip:** You may wonder what an acronym-based signature framework is. Signature frameworks take quite a bit of thinking and creativity; here's an example. Say you are writing a book titled *Become a Backyard Chicken Farmer: Master Breed Selection and Feeding*. Without a framework, your chapters might look like a mere collection of useful strategies. For example:

- **Chapter 1**: Getting Started: Why Raise Chickens in Your Backyard?
- **Chapter 2**: Choosing Your Flock
- **Chapter 3**: Coop Basics: Building a Safe and Comfortable Home for Your Chickens
- **Chapter 4**: Feeding Your Flock
- **Chapter 5**: Caring for Chicks: From Hatchlings to Hens
- **Chapter 6**: Daily Care and Maintenance
- **Chapter 7**: Keeping Chickens Safe: Predator-Proofing and Coop Security
- **Chapter 8**: From Backyard to Table: Recipes and Ideas for Using Fresh Eggs

The book might be straightforward and informative, but the chapter headings are not the most eye-catching or interesting. Let's add a signature framework into the equation to make it stand out and help the reader recall its contents. For instance, we could call our signature framework **C.H.I.C.K.E.N.S.** Each chapter would comprise one of the letters in our acronym. As such, in the introduction to your book, you would mention that the reader will achieve their desired outcome (to raise heathy chickens) by following your signature **C.H.I.C.K.E.N.S** method. The new chapter layout would look something like this:

- Chapter 1: **C**hoosing the Right Breeds
- Chapter 2: **H**ealthy Habitats for Happy Hens
- Chapter 3: **I**nspecting for Illness
- Chapter 4: **C**ultivating a Nutritious Diet
- Chapter 5: **K**eeping Chickens Safe from Predators
- Chapter 6: **E**gg Laying Essentials
- Chapter 7: **N**urturing Young Chicks
- Chapter 8: **S**ustaining Your Flock for the Long Term

Remember to check that your signature term is not trademarked!

What About AI?

It has become a trend to rely on AI to create an entire outline. However, problems with AI-generated outlines and manuscripts have led to a demand for reviewing, rewriting, and humanizing these materials. We offer this service at Publishing Services. See our Outline Quality Review Package for further information.

"Why would I need someone to revise an AI-generated outline?" you may ask. The answer is that although AI is a useful research tool and can point out interesting pain points and topics for your outline, it simply cannot produce a top-quality outline. That's still an exclusively human skill. Below are just a few problems our clients with AI-generated outlines have asked us to fix:

- Repeated content appearing in different chapters
- A lack of instruction to the ghostwriter (Content is simply laid out bare with no specific instructions to the ghostwriter.)
- A lack of resources (Many AI outlines provide two or three resources for every chapter, giving a total of around 25 sources for the whole book, compared to 75+ in professionally written outlines.)
- Lack of originality in the content (We have seen the same structure repeatedly in some niches. What's more, AI outlines do not have an original framework, which you can ask a professional outline writer from Publishing Services to provide.)
- No real-life stories and anecdotes, only artificial-sounding ones that have little value for the reader
- Source links that seem legitimate but lead to paid-for content or error notices
- Sources that are too academic or specific; others that are completely irrelevant

In our experience writing original outlines and reviewing AI outlines, we have concluded that AI is a useful research tool but cannot replace human-written outlines. The risk of publishing unoriginal (and potentially copyrighted) content, the scarcity of sources, and the lack of instructions to the ghostwriter are flaws that result in low-quality books. AI has another big problem that its developers are still trying to solve—bias. AI is dependent on what human beings have uploaded. That means that if a source is biased, AI cannot determine it as such, and it may suggest biased sources for your outline (IBM 2023).

With your book outline ready, you now have the blueprint for your content. But creating a great book doesn't stop there. Once your manuscript is complete, you'll need to grab readers' attention with an interesting book description. In the next chapter, we'll explore how to write a captivating description that hooks readers and ensures they hit that **Add to Cart** button.

 **Publishing Services' Book Outline Package**

At Publishing Services, our copywriters dedicate time to research your topic thoroughly so that your outline contains more than superficial blog entries. They conduct extensive audience research, consult tables of contents, read hundreds of reviews of competitor books, read other works from your niche if they require more information, and consult the latest studies and reports. This puts them in the perfect position to write the outline for a top-selling book.

To place an order, visit the Publishing Services website at www.publishingservices.com. Scroll down and select **Book Outline and Description Package**. Fill in the required fields, including your book's title, subtitle, word count, author name, niche, summary, any specific requests you may have, and whether you desire a unique framework. You can also upload an additional file with your notes if you wish. Some of our clients provide just a brief description of their chosen book. Those who want to can provide detailed notes containing topics, authors, and specific works they would like included.

When you're done filling out the order form, click **Add to Cart.**

You will see that you can select **Add-ons** if you desire, such as an ACX description, formatting, or fast delivery (5 business days).

Once you receive your outline, if you have any questions or requests for changes, you can contact us via email at support@publishingservices.com. To request changes, use the comment feature on Google Docs and state your requests within the outline document. You can also provide an additional document with detailed instructions.

 # Publishing Services' Outline Quality Review Package

This package has been exclusively tailored to enhance book outlines created by AI.

While AI can assist with research, it fails to deliver the depth, originality, and precision needed for a high-quality outline.

Our process involves extensive research, often incorporating several dozen credible sources compared to the few that AI typically provides. We also address important issues like repeated content, lack of clear instructions for ghostwriters, and the absence of unique frameworks or real-life anecdotes.

To place an order, visit the Publishing Services website at www.publishingservices.com. Scroll down and select **Outline Quality Review Package**. Fill in the fields, including your book title and subtitle.

Upload your book outline in Word format, and upload your customer research document if it is in a separate document. Click **Add to Cart.**

You will receive your package back in four business days.

Chapter 7

How to Write a Compelling Book Description

Your book description is a summary of the book's content and appeal that is visible on the book's product page in the Amazon marketplace. It's one of the first things a potential buyer reads when deciding whether or not to purchase, so it's critical for capturing attention and driving sales. The description is your first and sometimes your only chance to make an impression on potential readers. It needs to grab attention quickly and communicate what makes the book valuable or intriguing. A clear description sets realistic expectations about the book's content, tone, and style, which leads to higher reader satisfaction.

Key Elements of a Book Description

As stated above, when you click on a book that piques your interest on Amazon, you are presented with a brief summary. The key components of a book description are:

- **The KDP Description:** This is a maximum of 4,000 characters (not including title and subtitle) in HTML format—around 600 words.
- **The Back Cover:** This should be a shortened version of the KDP description—around 350 words maximum.
- **The HTML Version of the KDP Description:** This is your description, minus the title and subtitle, and it should ideally be formatted in HTML. HTML enables you to insert formatting elements such as line breaks, bolding, italics, and bullet points. A handy tool for formatting

your description is the Kindlepreneur Book Description Generator, which you can find at www.publishingservicesbook.com/html-generator. This tool allows you to create headings, choose your font style (bold, italic, underline), and include bulleted lists. You should also check out KDP's description formatting rules, as you can't use all the heading types available on Kindlepreneur for this. If you wish to create your own HTML, review KDP's formatting rules, available at www.publishingservicesbook.com/kdp-formatting-rules. After formatting your description, check that everything looks good by cutting and pasting it onto the ABlurb preview tool, which you can find at www.publishingservicesbook.com/ablurb.

- **The ACX Description:** If you publish an audiobook on the Audiobook Creation Exchange (ACX) platform, you will need a shorter description with a maximum of 2000 characters in HTML format. This description will also have to be converted to the ACX-accepted HTML format. The coding is the same as for KDP, with the one exception that you cannot use regular H4 headings—only normal size and bold font.

Pro Tip: Below you'll find an example of a bestselling book description we created for our example book, along with a back cover and an HTML code for KDP.

KDP Description Example

Fresh eggs and happy chickens… all in your own backyard! Are you ready to make your dream of becoming a backyard chicken farmer come true?

What could be better than walking into your backyard and collecting eggs, knowing your breakfast is as fresh as it gets?

There's nothing like the taste of home-raised eggs!

Growing your own flock of chickens has many benefits. They're going to be living their best life in your backyard, pecking away at bugs and grass and absorbing far more nutrients than any chicken in a poultry house will ever get, and that means amazing eggs!

Your eggs will have **more vitamin E, more healthy Omega-3 fatty acids, and more beta carotene** than a store-bought egg… and better yet, they'll have less saturated fat and cholesterol, too!

Now, that's all well and good, but you're not a farmer. Do you really have what it takes to raise healthy, happy chickens and keep yourself in a steady supply of fresh eggs?

You absolutely do!

Raising chickens is easy and rewarding. All you need to do is choose the right breed and understand how to nurture them so that they're healthy and well taken care of, and this essential guide to becoming a backyard chicken farmer will show you everything you need to know.

Inside, you'll discover:

- Why it's so important to **choose the right breed from the outset**—and all the guidance you need to make sure you do
- **The secret to raising happy chickens** (It's all in their habits—and that's something you have control over!)
- Everything you need to know to inspect your chickens for illness and make sure you deal with any concern before it becomes a problem
- Exactly how to feed a chicken well... and how their nutrition impacts your eggs
- **How to make sure your chickens are always safe from predators** (no matter what other animals like to creep around in your backyard)
- Your complete guide to egg laying—with some surprising secrets to increasing production
- How to be a mother hen, **nurturing your chicks** as they grow into happy, healthy hens
- Essential advice for keeping your flock healthy, happy, and productive in the long term
- Expert advice from experienced chicken farmers and all the tips and tricks you need to fall in love with raising chickens

And much more.

If you've been overwhelmed by the amount of information there is about rearing chickens, you might doubt how realistic your chicken-raising dream really is.

But with the right guidance, you'll see how fun and easy this is and have all the confidence you need to get started.

Raising chickens is the most rewarding endeavor you'll ever take on. You'll soon be giggling at all their little quirks and marveling at how each character stands out from the flock, and you'll be eating the best eggs ever!

This comprehensive and accessible guide is exactly the solution you've been looking for, and all your chicken-rearing dreams are about to come true!

Are you ready to become a backyard chicken farmer? Scroll up and click "Add to Cart" right now!

HTML Formatting for KDP Description Example

```
<h4>Fresh eggs and happy chickens... All in your own backyard! Are you ready to make your dream of becoming a backyard chicken farmer come true?<br></h4><p>What could be better than walking into your backyard and collecting eggs, knowing your breakfast is as fresh as it gets?<br></p><p>There's nothing like the taste of home-raised eggs! <br></p><p>Growing your own flock of chickens has many benefits. They're going to be living their best life in your backyard, pecking away at bugs and grass and absorbing far more nutrients than any chicken in a poultry house will ever get... and that means amazing eggs!<br></p><p>Your eggs are going to have<b> more Vitamin E, more healthy Omega-3 fatty acids, and more beta carotene</b> than a store-bought egg... and better yet, they'll have less saturated fat and cholesterol too!<br></p><p>Now, that's all well and good, but you're not a farmer. Do you really have what it takes to raise healthy, happy chickens and keep yourself in a steady supply of fresh eggs?<br></p><p>You absolutely do!<br></p><p><b>Raising chickens is easy and rewarding</b>—all you need to do is choose the right breed and understand how to nurture them so that they're healthy and well taken care of... and this essential guide to becoming a backyard chicken farmer will show you everything you need to know.<br></p><p>Inside, you'll discover:<br></p><ul><li>Why it's so important to <b>choose the right breed from the outset</b>—and all the guidance you need to make sure you do</li><li><b>The secret to raising happy chickens </b>(it's all in their habits—and that's something you have control over!)</li><li>Everything you need to know to inspect your chickens for illness and make sure you deal with any concern before it becomes a problem</li><li>Exactly how to feed a chicken well... and why their nutrition is so important to your eggs</li><li><b>How to make sure your chickens are always safe from predators</b> (no matter what other animals like to creep around in your backyard)</li><li>Your complete guide to egg laying—with some surprising secrets to increase your egg production!</li><li>How to be a mother hen—<b>nurture your chicks</b> as they grow into happy, healthy hens</li><li>Essential advice for keeping your flock healthy, happy, and productive in the long term</li><li>Expert advice from experienced chicken farmers... and all the tips and tricks you need to fall in love with raising chickens</li></ul><p><em>And much more.</em><br></p><p>If you've been overwhelmed by the amount of information there is about rearing chickens, you might have started to doubt how realistic your chicken-raising dream really is. <br></p><p>But with the right guidance, you'll see how fun and easy this is, and you'll have all the confidence you need to get started.<br></p><p><b>Raising chickens is the most rewarding endeavor you'll ever take on.</b> You're soon going to be giggling at all their little quirks and marveling at how each character stands out from the flock... and you're going to be eating the best eggs ever!<br></p><p>This comprehensive and accessible guide is exactly the solution you've been looking for... and all your chicken-rearing dreams are about to come true! <br></p><h4>Are you ready to become a backyard chicken farmer? Then scroll up and click "Add to Cart" right now!</h4>
```

Back Cover Description Example

Fresh eggs and happy chickens... all in your own backyard!

What could be better than walking into your backyard and collecting eggs, knowing your breakfast is as fresh as it gets?

There's nothing like the taste of home-raised eggs!

They have **more vitamin E, more healthy Omega-3 fatty acids, and more beta carotene** than a store-bought egg... and better yet, they'll have less saturated fat and cholesterol, too!

Now, that's all well and good, but you're not a farmer. Do you really have what it takes to raise healthy, happy chickens and keep yourself in a steady supply of fresh eggs?

You absolutely do!

This essential guide to becoming a backyard chicken farmer will show you everything you need to know.

Inside, you'll discover:

- Why it's so important to **choose the right breed from the outset**
- **The secret to raising happy chickens**
- Everything you need to know to inspect your chickens for illness
- Exactly how to feed a chicken well... and how their nutrition impacts your eggs
- **How to make sure your chickens are always safe from predators**
- Your complete guide to egg laying—with some surprising secrets to increase production
- How to be a mother hen, **nurturing your chicks** as they grow into happy, healthy hens
- Essential advice for keeping your flock healthy, happy, and productive in the long term
- Expert advice from experienced chicken farmers

And much more.

Raising chickens is the most rewarding endeavor you'll ever take on. You'll soon be giggling at all their little quirks and marveling at how each character stands out from the flock, and you'll be eating the best eggs ever!

This comprehensive and accessible guide is exactly the solution you've been looking for... and all your chicken-rearing dreams are about to come true!

DIY vs. Professional Descriptions: Which One to Choose

Because book descriptions can be the thing that makes or breaks your book, hiring a professional copywriter for this task is the ideal way to go. A large-scale study by The Nielsen Company (US), LLC found that book descriptions are a massive contributor to ebook sales in volume terms. They influence around 17.7% of all sales. The study concluded that in the UK alone, book descriptions influenced over 60M UK consumer book purchases, worth a whopping £400m, which is approximately $500m USD (Nielsen Book 2021).

Your description should let the reader know what they can expect to find inside, but it can't reveal too much. A talented description writer knows how to pinpoint that sweet spot by revealing just enough content to interest the reader and entice them to buy the book.

The description also has to show that you understand the reader's pain points and that they will achieve their desired outcome by the time they turn the last page of your book. Professional copywriters study your target market thoroughly and know how to get "into your audience's heads." There is too much at stake to just "wing it" if you are not a professional writer.

Comparison: DIY Description and a Publishing Services Description

DIY Description	**Publishing Services Description**
As a DIY option, this is free.	You will pay $67 for our Book Description Package (plus $10 if you need ACX formatting). If you purchase the Outline and Description Package, you will not need to purchase a separate description; it will already be included in the price.
It can be time-consuming.	We have a turnaround time of 5 business days.
It may lack SEO optimization.	Our descriptions are SEO-friendly and optimized for keywords.
Quality can vary based on personal writing skills.	The quality is consistent, high, and polished.
It may be potentially less compelling.	It is tailored to capture the reader's interest.
Revisions can be annoying.	You have unlimited free revisions.

Writing the manuscript is next up in the process of breathing life into your book. Unless you are an expert in your niche and a prolific writer, you may consider hiring a ghostwriter. In Chapter 8, we'll look at all your options so you can ensure your book looks good, has an attractive description, and fulfills every promise you have made to your readers.

 # Publishing Services' Book Description Package

Description writing is copywriting. It requires a high level of skill and experience, and it usually pays to hire a professional for this task. Your description is an advertisement for your book. It has to entice the reader and convince them that among all the top-selling books in your genre, your book is the one they should buy because it contains something your competitors lack. It also needs to follow certain restrictions and guidelines and include phrases and formulas proven to increase sales.

This is where PS comes in!

To place an order, visit the Publishing Services website at www.publishingservices.com. Scroll down and select **Book Description Package**. Fill in the fields required, including your book's title, subtitle, and author name. You will need to upload your manuscript, as the copywriter reads your manuscript beforehand so they can write a thorough description. When you're done, click **Add to Cart**.

The turnaround time is five business days. You can include special requests if you wish, as well as add-ons, such as an ACX description formatting and fast delivery (2 business days).

Chapter 8

From Manuscript to Publication: Ghostwriting Essentials

We have mentioned how important your outline is, but it is only one piece of the puzzle. The second half is your manuscript. This is arguably the cornerstone to entering bestseller territory. Without a book that solves your readers' problems, you won't get the reviews you need to reach a wider segment of your audience. Your book has to be unique and provide readers with genuine value. Anyone can go online and find a host of advice on everything from teen life skills to wall Pilates. There are also a lot of affordable books created by your competition.

In order to establish yourself as an authority in your niche, your book has to be better than what everyone else is publishing. It should have a good flow and the right tone. It must make your audience feel understood and speak to their hearts, making them feel like it's the ultimate guide to make their life better, fuller, or easier. This is why, much like outlines and descriptions, we recommend opting for a professional ghostwriter.

Where to Find the Perfect Ghostwriter

Our extensive experience, passion for great customer service, and high Trustpilot rating are just a few reasons why Publishing Services is your go-to company for ghostwriting services, and you can learn more about our services at the end of this chapter.

However, there are other companies and freelance platforms that offer ghostwriting services, including:

- Upwork.com
- PeoplePerHour.com
- Linkedin.com
- Reedsy.com

In addition to the sites above, you can search Google for quality ghostwriters. Use Google's advanced search options to exclude any terms you wish. For instance, excluding terms like "budget" and "cheap" can help you avoid low-quality writing. Meanwhile, you can include the specialty you are looking for. For instance, you can type in "business book ghostwriter" or "psychology book ghostwriter" to limit your results to those who write entire manuscripts, not just blogs or other shorter content (Fox, n.d.).

How to Collaborate with a Ghostwriter: Best Practices

No matter where you look for that perfect ghostwriter, there are several handy tips you should keep in mind to both protect yourself and ensure you hire a high-quality writer who will do your book justice.

- **Check their previous work and resume**. If you're hiring via a freelance platform, read all the reviews of past jobs the writer has done and ask for several writing samples. Be sure to mention you are looking for AI-free writing and use online AI checkers and plagiarism software to ensure the sample passes both tests (more information on this below). Ask them how many books they have written and in which niches they have experience.

- **Define your project**. Describe the niche, target audience, and key themes of your book. Knowing these details will help you communicate your vision to the ghostwriter and ensure they understand your goals. All this information should be present in your book outline. This is why you can benefit from a human-written, top-tier book outline. It is the very foundation upon which your book is built.

- **Conduct interviews**. Some writers prefer to communicate online, without phone or video communication. If they pass all other checks and their writing samples are great, this is not a problem. However, it's always best to speak to your future writer face-to-face or via video conference. That way, you can ask about their previous projects, the writing process, and how they handle revisions.

- **Be very clear on terms and budget**. Talk to the writer about payment milestones, deadlines, and any additional costs, such as research or revisions. Both sides should have a clear understanding of the project timeline. For instance, paying per word is a good idea because if you need additional content, it is very easy to calculate how much more you owe. Some writers charge by project or per hour rather than by word, so be prepared to come across various payment proposals.

- **Consider paying them for a trial.** After your initial search, you may find that you cannot decide between two or three writers. If you have the budget for it, consider asking them to complete a trial. You might, for instance, ask them to write the introduction and first chapter of a book from your outline. If you are using your own outline, only send them the introduction and first chapter information. Using your outline will ensure the following:
    - Everyone uses the same sources.
    - The writer knows the tone and target audience. (This should be indicated in the customer research part of the outline.)
    - You can get a good feel for what different writers are capable of doing with the same material. It will also help you pick the writer whose style best suits the book you want to publish.
    - You can gather how good they are at telling a story and engaging the audience. Even non-fiction books benefit from stories interjected here and there. Stories are more memorable than facts alone. Studies have shown, for instance, that people recall only 5% to 10% of statistics. However, they remember 65% to 70% of the information in stories (Klongerbo 2023).
- **Be prepared to wait for a great ghostwriter.** Ghostwriters are sometimes working on more than one project at a time. If you have found the perfect writer for your book and have to wait a month or two until they are ready to start on yours, it pays to be patient. Your book's content will be a dealmaker or breaker, so avoid hiring someone whose work you like less simply because you are in a rush.

Stipulating Terms and Conditions Clearly

If you hire a freelance writer, signing a contract with them is very important. It will protect your privacy and ensure you fully own the copyright of the contents.

Your contract should contain the following information:

- **Scope of the Project:** Clearly lay out the length of the book and the type of work it is.
- **Prices and Payment Terms:** Indicate how much the writer will be paid and include a schedule of payments and a payment method. The common practice is to set up milestones, fund them, and then release each milestone after the work for this milestone has been completed. For instance, you might set milestones as follows and pay the writer per milestone completed:
    - **Milestone #1** = 10k words completed
    - **Milestone #2** = 20k words completed

- ◇ **Milestone #3** = 30k words completed

You can, of course, adjust the number of milestones or determine a different payment schedule. This is totally up to you and the writer.

Once you have set up your milestones, you should fund the first milestone. Most freelance platforms, like Upwork, for example, will hold this money until you approve the release of the funds.

Once the ghostwriter has completed a milestone, they will inform you and ask for the funds to be released. After checking that you liked the content and that the writer is on the right track, you release the funds and fund the next milestone. This process is repeated until the book is finished and all funds have been released.

- **Client and Ghostwriter Responsibilities:** Stipulate what outline you will use, who will do the research, and whether you will be contributing some content to the book. Some clients enjoy including their personal anecdotes if they publish the book under their real name.
- **Writing Pace:** Look at the milestones you've set up and create a timeline. Generally, a seasoned ghostwriter should be able to pen a 30K book in one month or less. Of course, the more technical a book is, the longer it will take, so be prepared to give your writer leeway while always having a deadline to work toward.
- **Your Goals:** Let your ghostwriter know what you want to achieve. Will your book be part of a series? Will you be using the same pen name? Do you want the book to have theoretical and practical information, too? Write down all the ideas you want them to bring life to through their words.
- **Termination Rights:** If, for any reason, the ghostwriter does not want to continue with your book or you decide you want someone else to complete it, ensure you have the rights to the content written until the point of termination. The ghostwriter should receive payment for the content they have completed.
- **Non-Disclosure Act (NDA):** The ghostwriter should sign an NDA to establish a duty of non-disclosure.

Pro Tip: We cannot provide you with a sample contract because this should be drafted by a legal professional to ensure it is watertight. However, the list of terms and conditions stated above can serve as a starting point for your discussions with your lawyer.

Building a Strong Relationship with Your Ghostwriter

Early in your dealings with the ghostwriter, talk about how often you would like to discuss the book. A good time to talk is after new chapters are uploaded to your project management app. You can also decide to chat once or twice a week. In practice, you may not need to talk after every chapter. Many ghostwriters and clients leave comments or suggestions on a shared document containing the manuscript, reserving actual conversations for special requests, longer suggestions, or brainstorming sessions.

Once your ghostwriter has started penning your book, aim to establish rapport with them. Tell them a little about yourself and your book's goals, and ask them a little about themselves, too. When you communicate openly, it is much easier to give feedback, ask for what you need (for instance, a story or further explanation in some parts of the book), or request a change in tone.

Your ghostwriter should also feel free to make suggestions as they move through research. They may have ideas for new chapters, sections, or activities. The more your writer cares about your project, the more motivated they will be to produce top-quality work. If you are happy with them, it pays to let them know they are appreciated. For a stellar job, consider gifting them an Amazon gift card or sending them a token of your thanks. Let them know you would love to work with them in the future and, if you're ready, book them for your next work! It will ensure the same tone and style are present in all the works you publish under the same author name.

How to Check Your Manuscript for Plagiarism

At Publishing Services, our professional ghostwriters and editors check each manuscript to ensure that the contents are original. However, if you have written your manuscript or hired a ghostwriter, don't forget to conduct a plagiarism check. You can use Grammarly (www.publishingservicesbook.com/grammarly) or ProWritingAid (www.publishingservicesbook.com/prowritingaid). Unfortunately, the best online checkers come at a price. Many free versions are available, but they either have a word limit or are not super reliable. For instance, Duplichecker is pretty good but has a 1000-word limit. As such, if you want to use this, you have to cut and paste less than 1000 words at a time.

These tools will show you which parts of your text are showing up as "flagged." You can take the time you need to rewrite these sections, then run it through the same checker again to make sure you have the all-clear. Bear in mind that when you run a plagiarism check, a few commonly used phrases may pop up as being plagiarized. Direct quotes may also come up as being plagiarized. When running the check, it will be clear when large chunks have been taken from another source. Use your common sense to make sure that only a small percentage of commonly used phrases are flagged. If there are large sections of text that pop up on the checker, rewrite the relevant sections or ask your ghostwriter to do so.

 # Publishing Services' Premium Ghostwriting Package

At Publishing Services, we have conducted a rigorous testing process to find a select, highly-talented team of ghostwriters. When you use our services, you don't have to worry about finding or reviewing writers; we handle that for you. We only work with experienced writers who are skilled in many different niches, so you can trust your project is in good hands.

All PS ghostwriters have authored numerous 30K+ manuscripts and workbooks. They have diverse experience and backgrounds, including business, education, film and screenwriting, fitness, gardening, health, herbalism, languages, law, nutrition, parenting, psychology, real estate investing, relationships, technology, the outdoors, popular culture, and prepping. Our writers are customer-oriented and highly capable of fulfilling customers' needs. Once a customer is assigned to a ghostwriter, a project is set up on dedicated software, and from that point on, the customer and the writer can communicate directly.

Upon assignment, the ghostwriter completes the first milestone, the book's introduction and first chapter. Once the customer approves this milestone, they continue writing until they reach the second milestone of writing 50% of the book. They then continue until the book is finished. In actual practice, the writer and client discuss each chapter or small group of chapters. The client leaves comments on the shared document, where they can request changes, say what they liked, or ask for something new. Doing so guarantees that the book is progressing according to their wishes.

Publishing Services' **Premium Ghostwriting Package** includes absolutely everything you need to get your book written from scratch, including your:

- Book Outline Package
- Book Description Package with HTML coding for KDP & ACX
- Ghostwriting Package
- Book Review Package
- Proofreading Package
- Book Cover Design Package
- Book Formatting Package with Vellum (formatting) Source Files
- A+ Content Package

This package is priced at $3,350 for a 30K book. If you already have a Publishing Services outline for the book you want us to ghostwrite, we'll deduct the outline package price from the total.

One thing to note is that we do not accept AI-generated outlines or those from other companies. This is because an outline is a crucial component of a good book, and for ghostwriters to write a great book, they need to work from an equally great outline.

This package is easy to order. Just visit the Publishing Services website at www.publishingservices.com. Scroll down and select **Premium Ghostwriting Package – Shortlist**. Tick the box that states that you will be added to our shortlist and contacted as soon as a ghostwriter in our team matches your project. Fill in the required fields, including your book's title, subtitle, word count, author, and information about the author/pen name. Choose your niche, indicate if you want your book to have a unique framework, and let us know if PS has already written an outline for you.

Summarize your vision for your book, and upload any additional information you wish to share. Click **Add to Cart.**

As soon as we receive your information, we'll contact you with information on writer availability.

Once you are assigned a ghostwriter, you can communicate with them as often as you like via our project management software.

AI-Generated Manuscripts: What You Need to Know

AI-generated manuscripts are on the rise in 2025. They have many of the problems mentioned earlier, including repetitive information, artificial-sounding language filled with overused metaphors, and un-cited references. These books also lack a personal touch. They contain "stories" that sound AI-generated and, therefore, do not connect with the reader. The language in these manuscripts is often very generic. They may point out that resources, groups, or websites exist but fail to provide you with the names of these sources. The manuscripts lack the personal touches of unique insights, comments, and anecdotes that are the products of human experiences. They do not do justice to the human reader and cannot solve their pain points.

Check Your Manuscript for AI-Generated Content

It is a good idea to check your manuscript for AI-generated content. When publishing a book on KDP, you are asked to inform Amazon of any AI-generated content—including text, images, or translations. You will also have to do this when you make edits to and republish an existing book through KDP (Kindle Direct Publishing, n.d.-a). You do not need to disclose AI-assisted content. What is the difference between the two? KDP states that AI-generated content is comprised of text, images, or translations created by an AI-based tool. **This is the case even if you applied substantial edits after generating this content.** AI-assisted content, on the other hand, is content you created yourself and then perhaps used AI tools to proof, edit, refine, or otherwise improve it.

As it stands, we still do not know what KDP is doing with this information, but we advise you to avoid using AI-generated content in the event that KDP decides to place restrictions or impose changes on such content.

To ensure your manuscript is not classified as having AI-generated content, we recommend that you run it through one or more of the following tools:

Undetectable AI	Go to www.publishingservicesbook.com/undetectable-ai
Originality.ai	Go to www.publishingservicesbook.com/originality-ai
GPTZero	Go to www.publishingservicesbook.com/gptzero
QuillBot	Go to www.publishingservicesbook.com/quillbot

Pro Tip: AI-generated content checkers are not 100% accurate. Both AI software and AI checkers are continuously changing and advancing, so you might get a different score from various checkers for the same text. The same goes for plagiarism checkers. The best ones usually come at a cost, and even then, there is no guarantee that they will catch everything.

Now that we've explored how ghostwriting can transform your ideas into a manuscript, let's move on to the next critical step in the publishing process: obtaining an ISBN. This unique identifier is a small but important detail that ensures your book can be professionally cataloged and easily accessible to readers.

# Publishing Services' AIDE Package

As a result of low-to-medium quality AI-generated manuscripts, many clients have asked us to rewrite their AI manuscripts. We call this package the AI Manuscript Developmental Editing & Humanization Package.

There are two main features of this package. First, we developmentally edit AI-generated manuscripts by thoroughly researching all information and ensuring all included information is factual. Second, we humanize the content by removing AI language, adding interesting and compelling anecdotes, and reorganizing information into a logical order.

During this process, three of our well-vetted, professional writers and editors go through these manuscripts line by line to make sure nothing is missed and that you are as ready for publication as possible.

To place an order for this package, head over to the Publishing Services website at www.publishingservices.com. Scroll down and select **AI Manuscript Developmental Editing & Humanization Package**. Choose the correct word count of your book in the drop-down menu. Fill in the required fields, including your book's title, subtitle, and author. Choose a style guide (CMOS or APA) and upload the files we will need: your book manuscript, your outline, and customer research (if you have it).

Fill in the other sections, and choose if you'd like to add extra packages to this order, such as a Review Page Package or a Book Description Package. Click **Add To Cart.**

You should receive your manuscript back in eighteen business days. We will thoroughly edit, rewrite, fact-check, and proofread your book. Our expert services ensure that your text meets professional standards and truly connects with your audience, setting the stage for a successful publication once formatted. If you see that the package is sold out, do not fret! We have a short waitlist that you can get on by emailing us!

Chapter 9

Understanding ISBNs

All published books have an International Standard Book Number (ISBN)—a unique numeric commercial book identifier. An ISBN is 10 digits long if it was assigned before 2007 and 13 digits long if assigned from January 1, 2007 onward. Some very old books have an ISBN comprising just nine numbers. In this case, publishers usually add a "0" before the number to bring it up to 10 digits.

If you publish several editions of the same book, an ISBN is assigned to each separate edition and variation of your book. Keep in mind this does not apply to a simple reprint. Each format will also need its own ISBN. Say you have a paperback, ebook, and hardback edition of your book. Each of these needs its own ISBN, but if you were to simply reprint any of these editions, the reprints would carry the same ISBN as the originals, provided there were no significant additions or modifications.

ISBN: What It Reveals About a Book and Its Author

An ISBN gives a wealth of information. Its 13 digits are divided into groups of 3-1-2-6-1 digit(s), as follows (Allan 2023).

In the diagram above, you will see that:

- The first 3 digits indicate that you are looking at an ISBN.
- The 4th digit tells us what language the book is in or what country it is from. When a book is in English, it is usually identified with 0 or 1.
- The 5th and 6th digits identify the publisher.
- Digits 7 to 12 identify the title, edition, and format of the book.
- Digit 13 is called the "check digit." It is just a number that is mathematically calculated as a fixed digit.

How to Locate a Book's ISBN

There are various places where this could be, including the back cover (close to the publisher's barcode), the copyright page (at the front of the book near the title page), or online. It can also be found on the Amazon product page. Visit ISBNsearch.org and type in an ISBN, title, or author to obtain more information about any book.

Ebooks & ISBN

KDP does not require ebooks to have their own ISBN. Once your content is published on KDP, Amazon assigns it a 10-digit Amazon Standard Identification Number (ASIN), which is an identification number for the Kindle ebook on Amazon. Note that the ASIN is not the same as an ISBN!

An ISBN is the universal number that identifies a book. If you already have an ISBN for your ebook, you can enter it during your title setup. Some distributors will require you to have an ISBN to distribute your book to Kindle and other stores.

If you sell a print or ebook directly from your own website, you are not obligated to have an ISBN. But if you want to sell it in a store, the store or the distributor (for example, IngramSpark) may stipulate that your book needs an ISBN (Author Imprints 2024). To avoid complications, we suggest purchasing your own ISBN (more on this below).

Paperback Books & ISBN

When you publish your paperback book on KDP, you have the option to use a free ISBN provided by Amazon. However, as stated above, we recommend that you purchase your own ISBN for the following additional reasons:

- It allows you to create a review link (in which you ask for reviews, which are great for boosting your book's visibility) before your book is published.
- You do not end up with multiple listings for the same book. This is because different stores or distributors (for instance, Amazon, and Draft2Digital) sometimes offer you their own ISBN. However, these individual numbers may not be valid if you want to sell your book in a different store. Having one ISBN you can use across various platforms (including Amazon, Barnes & Noble, IngramSpark, and more) keeps things simple.
- Free ISBNs are nontransferable. You will need your own ISBN to upload your book to other platforms outside of Amazon. Purchasing an ISBN gives your publishing company a stronger brand identity with which you can align your name.
- You retain full ownership and control of your book. When you use the free Amazon ISBN, you must list Amazon as the publisher.
- Owning your ISBN makes you appear more professional to stores, libraries, and other professionals in the field.
- If you plan on publishing a series, you can purchase a block of ISBNs, which brings consistency to your numbering and makes for easier management.
- You will need a paid-for ISBN for your book to be accepted in libraries. This ISBN must be registered by its publisher (which, in this case, would be you).

Overall, buying your own ISBN is more convenient, gives you greater control, and lends your publications a professional image.

Where to Buy an ISBN: Trusted Sources and Options

- If you reside in the United States, you can buy an ISBN from Bowker, the official US ISBN agency for publishers, or through your local ISBN agency. ISBNs purchased from Bowker can be used to publish titles in any language, and KDP authors get a discounted rate from them. www.myidentifiers.com
- If you are a resident of the United Kingdom or Ireland, the official IBSN agency is Nielsen. www.isbn.nielsenbook.co.uk
- If you reside in Canada, you can obtain a free number from ISBN Canada by emailing isbn-canada@bac-lac.gc.ca.
- If you reside in Australia, your official ISBN agency is Thorpe-Bowker. www.myidentifiers.com.au
- If you reside in New Zealand, visit Thorpe-Bowker at www.myidentifiers.com/nz.
- For other countries, consult the International ISBN Agency at www.isbn-international.org/agencies. There, you will find a list of all national ISBN agencies. Simply select your country from the dropdown menu "Select an Agency," and you will find all the information you need.

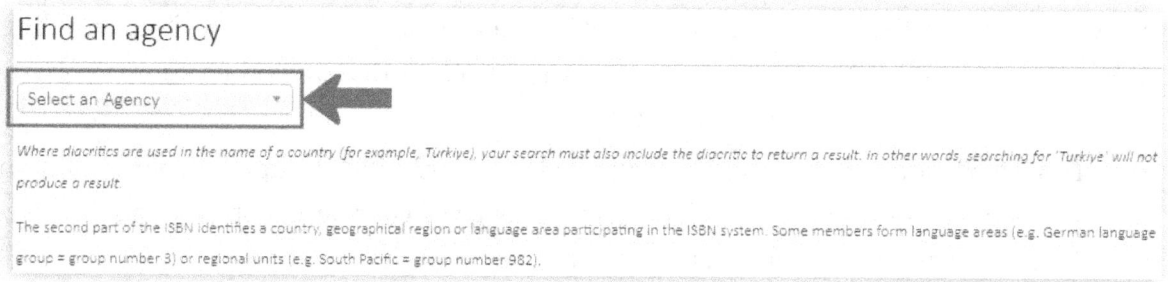

Purchasing an ISBN from Bowker and Other Providers

Generally, each organization will provide clear instructions on what to do on their websites. On Bowker, for instance, you set up an account, choose the package you are interested in, provide information about your book, and pay. The process is simple and can be completed in a matter of minutes.

FAQs: Common Questions Answered

Q: Does your book have to be published before you get an ISBN?

No. You can get one before it is published.

Q: What type of changes would require you to assign an additional ISBN to a book?

The following are a few cases where you would need a different ISBN:

- You published the book in large print.
- You published the book in any language other than English.
- You have added new material to an already published book, or you are publishing a second or subsequent edition.
- You have changed the book's binding.
- You have published the book in different sizes. (More information on this is in Chapter 15, where we will discuss formatting.) Say your book is published in the following sizes: 5 x 8, 5.5 x 8.5, and 6 x 9—each will have to have its own ISBN.

By contrast, you will not need a new ISBN if you simply change the book price, cover design, distributor, or printer. The same goes for minor grammatical and factual corrections.

Q: How much does an ISBN Cost?

This varies, but in general, a single ISBN costs $125 (on Bowker). Generally, the more ISBNs you buy, the lower the unit price is. As we write, prices on Bowker are as follows:

Q: Will I need to register my ISBN once it has been approved?

Yes, you should. You can do so on Bowkerlink (www.bowkerlink.com) or as indicated by an official agency. Note that you will have to register your book in both paperback and hardback versions (meaning you will need two ISBNs).

How to Get a Free ISBN from Amazon

When you obtain a free ASIN from KDP, Amazon automatically registers it with Bowker (the official ISBN agency for the United States). The process is as follows (Kindle Direct Publishing, n.d.-b):

1. When you upload your book to KDP, click **Create**, and select the type of book for which you wish to obtain the ISBN (Kindle ebook, paperback, or hardback).

2. You will then be led to a details page where you will fill in a few boxes, including:
   - Language
   - Book title and subtitle
   - Author name
   - Book description
   - Primary marketplace categories
   - Seven backend keywords (covered in Chapter 20)
   - Edition number (if applicable)
   - Disclosure of any sexually explicit content

   Once you have completed the information, click **Save and Continue**.

3. You will then be led to a second page called "Content." Here, you can either get a free ISBN by clicking **Assign ISBN** or add your own by providing the one you've secured and the publisher.

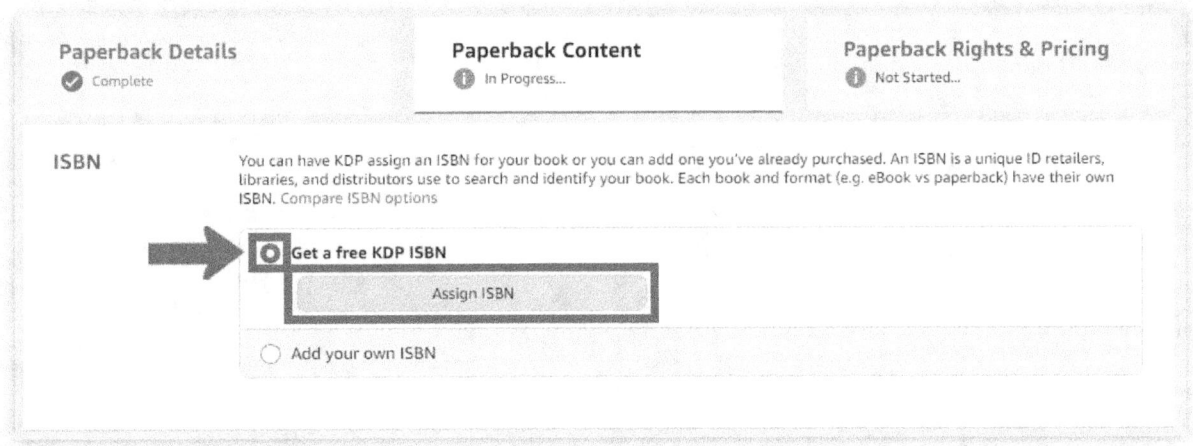

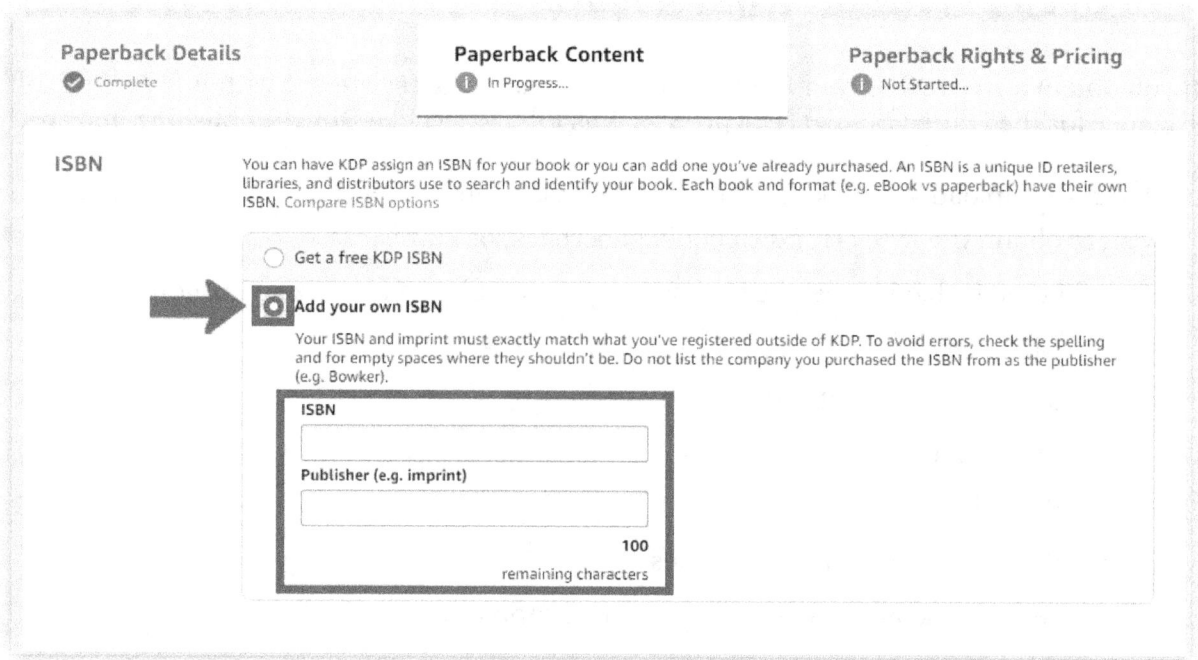

4. Fill in the rest of the information required on the page and upload it.

Important Note: Once you are assigned a free ISBN or you add your own ISBN, it cannot be changed.

In the next chapter, we will discuss one of the most creative aspects of self-publishing: your book cover!

Chapter 10

Designing a Book Cover That Sells

Forget everything the philosophers told you. In self-publishing, you definitely *should* judge a book by its cover—after all, everyone else will be! A study by Reedsy found that professionally redesigned covers increased click-through rates by an average of 35%, with individual improvements ranging from 12.5% to 50% (Reedsy 2022).

The cover is the first thing people see when browsing for books, whether online or in a bookstore. In a market flooded with options, it's often the cover that grabs potential readers' attention first. If the cover doesn't stand out or appeal to the target audience, readers may not even bother reading the description or reviews.

What Makes a Book Cover Stand Out

There are so many factors that make a book cover stand out. A great designer knows how to use color, fonts, and symbolism to capture the essence of what your book is about. A good cover has the following basic characteristics:

- It makes a great first impression.
- It is consistent with your brand identity.
- It creates an emotional connection or captures your reader's attention, standing out from your competitors' covers.

- It provides visual cues as to what your book is about.
- It has a catchy spine containing the book's title, the author's name, and the publisher's logo (if the publisher has one).
- It has a back cover with the same tone, fonts, and colors as the front cover.
- It also contains all the following information: a blurb, the publisher's details, the ISBN or barcode, a testimonial (if you wish), the price of the book, the category of the book (optional), and the name of the cover designer (optional).

Go the Extra Mile

To set your cover apart, look for a cover that goes further than the basics. Some of the more nuanced details of a good cover can be lost in the hustle. Let's look at those and break them down for you.

Your cover should match the expectations for your chosen genre. A cover can be beautifully produced and artistically illustrated or designed, but if it lacks the elements or style associated with your genre, it's not the right cover for you. For instance, mystery books often feature design elements like shadows or silhouettes; historical books typically incorporate vintage imagery or sepia tones; and biographies usually favor subdued colors, clear and bold typography, and symbolic items related to the subject's life rather than just a simple portrait. For this reason, your designer should ideally have experience and an attractive portfolio of covers in your genre (Rapovets 2024).

Also, remember that font choices matter. If you have to pay a little more to purchase a dedicated font or have your designer create one, do so. Avoid using free fonts from Microsoft Word, as they can cheapen the design and compromise your credibility. Also, steer clear of quirky typefaces that are unsuitable for professional work. Use two different fonts at most to ensure the cover is clear and easy to read. Consider combining complementary serif and sans serif fonts. Serif fonts have decorative lines or tapers (commonly called "tails" or "feet"), while sans serif fonts don't. Because they don't have tails, sans-serif fonts comprise simple, clean lines that are the same width throughout (deBara, n.d.).

The following are excellent font choices for book covers (Cover Design Studio, n.d.):

- Sans serif: Helvetica, Microsoft Sans, Arial, Futura, Myriad, Geneva, Verdana, Gill Sans, Franklin Gothic, Tw Century, Calibri, Simplified Arabic
- Serif: Bodoni, Baskerville, Garamond, Palatino, Times, Lucida Bright, Cambria, Minion, Didot, Book Antiqua, Georgia

Your cover art should have the right colors for your genre. For instance, books from the mystery/thriller genre favor black and gray, horror suits red elements, romance usually incorporates pinks and reds, science fiction and fantasy are often associated with deep blue, purple, and green hues, and blue or purple is often chosen for non-fiction books from the self-help genre, since these colors inspire trust and calm and exude intelligence (Harrison, n.d.).

Finally, make sure that your cover has the right hierarchy of information. Designers create hierarchy via size differentiations, weight, font style, and alignment. That is, bolder, thicker, larger fonts capture more attention than finer ones. The correct hierarchy for a book cover is as follows:

- Title
- Author's name
- Subtitle

Effective vs. Ineffective Book Cover Design

Let's get back to our sample book, *Become a Backyard Chicken Farmer—Master Breed Selection and Feeding—Uncover the Importance of Facilities and Health Care to Effortlessly Increase Egg Production*. Check out our examples of ineffective and effective designs below.

Ineffective Book Covers

Let's take a look at the following covers and discuss why they are not very likely to captivate an audience or make them buy the book:

Cover #1

Poor Image Choice

It's easy to see how unappealing this cover is. Let's start with the chickens, which seem to be squished into uncomfortable positions. The main image says everything but "I am a successful chicken farmer with happy, thriving chickens." It is impersonal and oddly cropped, and the farmer seems to care very little about the welfare of the animals.

Poor Typeface/Font Choice

The font selected for the cover seems to be a standard, visually unappealing one obtained for free on Word. The italicized font is a little hard to read and is likely to be totally missed when one is browsing online.

Overall Comment

The cover does not stand out, the image is unpleasant, and it looks unprofessional.

Scan the QR code to view this image in color.

Cover #2

Poor Image Choice

The chickens seem to be aimlessly wandering and uncared for. There is no indication that the book involves managing chickens.

Poor Typeface/Font Choice

The correct hierarchy for book covers is title, author, and subtitle. Here, the title is small and barely visible, while the subtitle is huge. Once again, the fonts chosen are unappealing. Moreover, the spacing between the author's name and subtitle is too insignificant.

Overall Comment

This cover does not align with the book's interior; in fact, it seems not to say anything at all. The fonts clash, and the hierarchy is all off.

Scan the QR code to view this image in color.

Cover #3

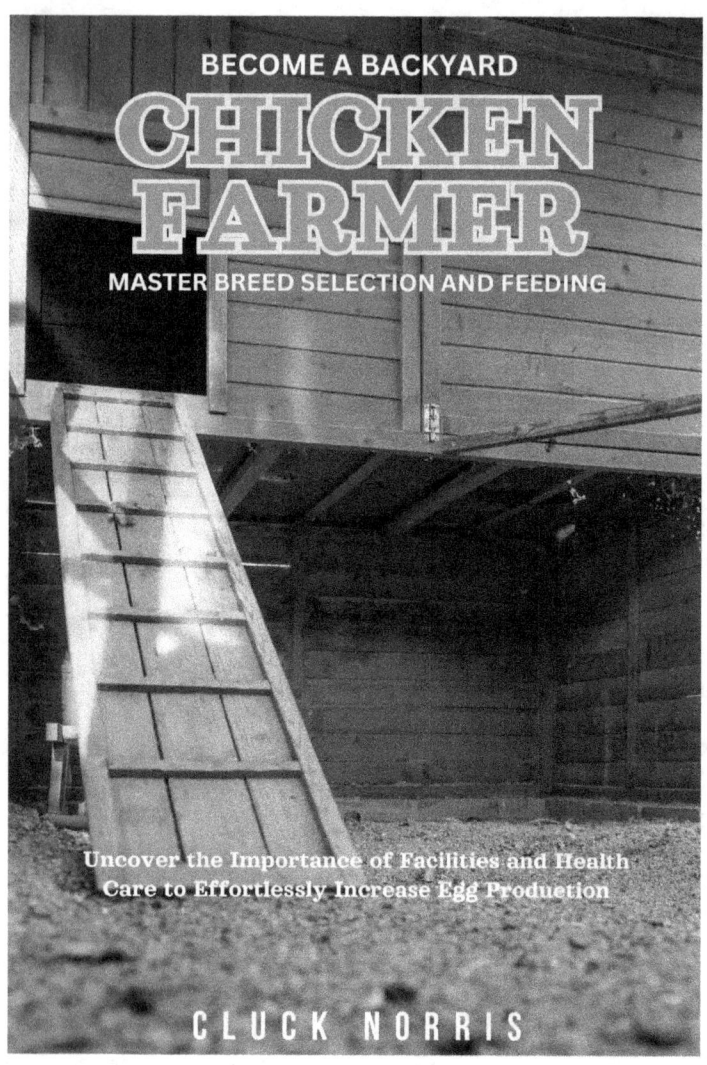

Poor Image Choice

Where are all the chickens? What has the farmer done to them? This cover seems more suited to a horror novel than a book about raising chickens.

Clashing Fonts

It isn't difficult to see how poor the font choices are here. Some text is so tiny it is barely legible, the style of the title is unappealing, and the title is written in two different fonts. The subtitle is also tiny, and the author's name blends into the image.

Overall Comment

It is very hard to work out what this book is about, and the image seems downright menacing.

Scan the QR code to view this image in color.

Cover #4

Stylistic Issues

The strange diagonal line separating the top of the design from the bottom does not make sense. The style is not suited to the contents of the book.

Color Choices

The color choices (bright yellow and purple) are all wrong for a book on chicken farming. A book of this nature begs for simple, nature-inspired colors rather than loud, unnatural ones.

Problematic Fonts

Once again, the font choice is all off. There are four different fonts on the same page, and the title is very difficult to read. The author's name is written in a smaller font than the subtitle.

Overall Comment

This cover seems to be heavily inspired by 1970s pop art, but as a cover, it misses the mark completely because it fails to capture the book's interior.

Scan the QR code to view this image in color.

Cover #5

Image Issues

There are too many images on the cover, making it messy and confusing. The images are also poorly cropped.

Font Issues

Once again, the fonts used are boring and oddly sized. The author's name, for instance, is tiny, and the name is misspelled. The subtitle is also barely noticeable.

Overall Comment

This cover is so busy that it's an eyesore.

Scan the QR code to view this image in color.

Effective Book Covers

Cover #1

Appealing Imagery

The imagery is simply lovely. We can see numerous eggs and seemingly happy chickens roaming in the background.

Correct Hierarchy

As you will see, everything that needs to stand out (particularly the title and author name) does.

Great Font Choices

The font is attractive, and the yellow letters speckled with green are catchy. The typeface isn't boring or cheap-looking.

Appealing Color Choice

The designer has chosen analogous colors (yellow and green), which work well together and lend the cover a warm touch.

Overall Comment

The book lets you know what the interior will be about. It is suitable for the genre and is aesthetically pleasing, with good font and color choices.

Scan the QR code to view this image in color.

Cover #2

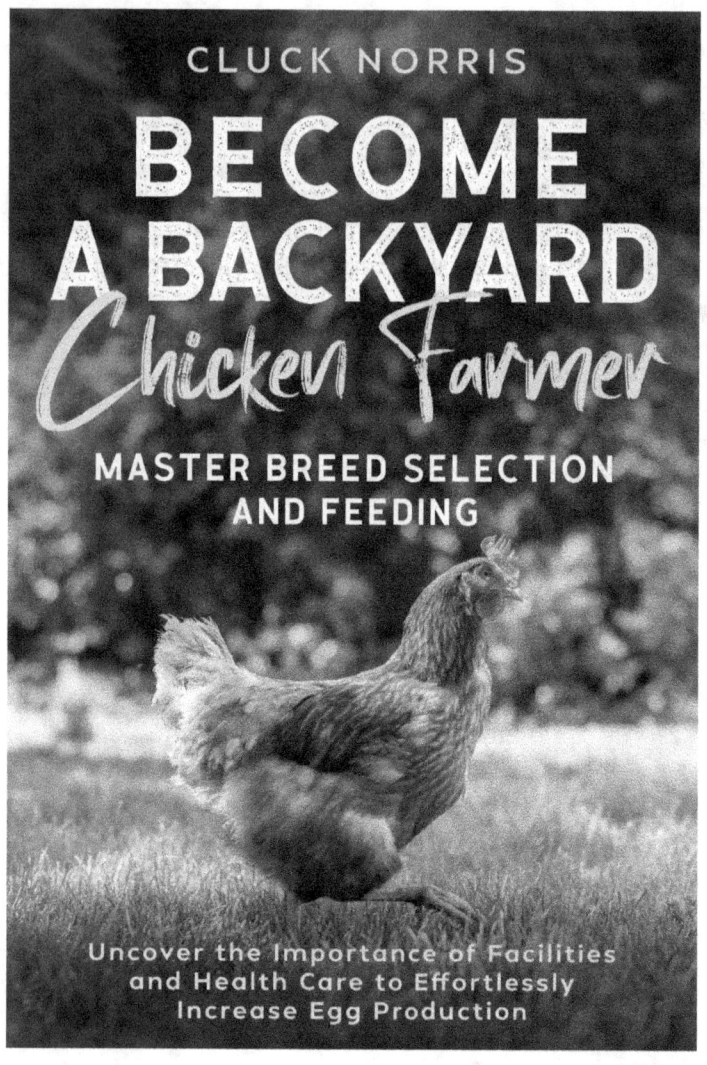

Appealing Imagery

The imagery is very eye-catching. It shows a healthy, active chicken—the kind every chicken farmer would love to raise.

Correct Hierarchy

Once again, the information hierarchy is made clear through the font sizes and widths.

Great Font Choices

The fonts used are appealing, and some words have the same lovely speckled effect as in Book #1.

Overall Comment

This book cover is perfect for this niche due to the colors, fonts, hierarchy, and crisp image. It looks professional, which lends the book a touch of prestige.

Scan the QR code to view this image in color.

Cover #3

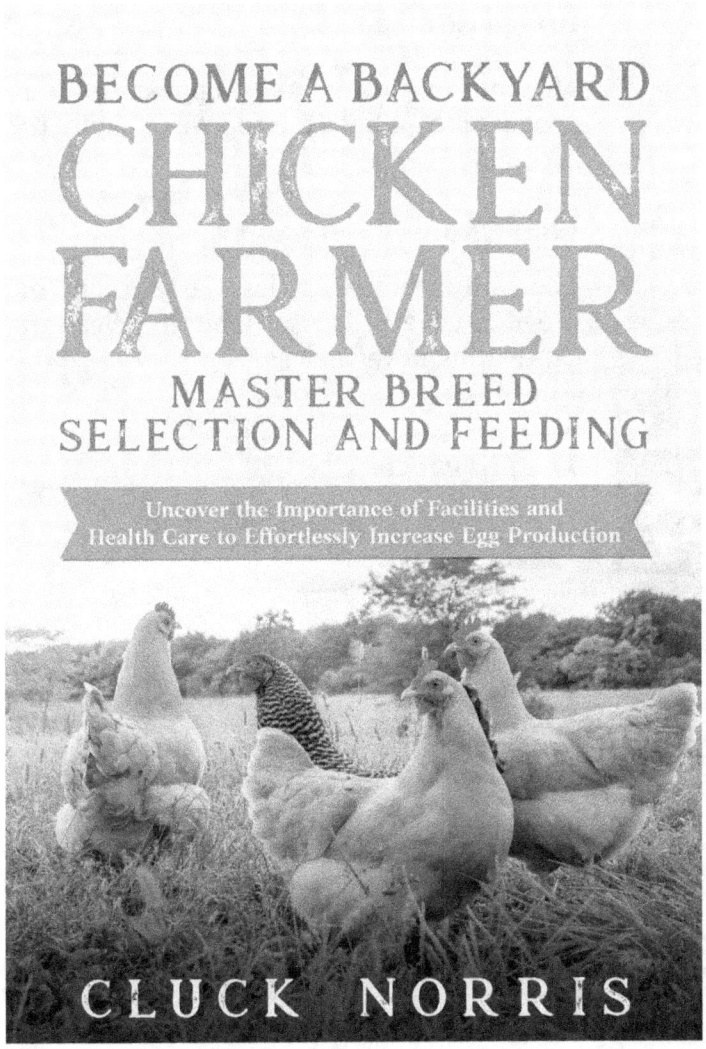

Image Choice
We love this group of happy chickens roaming freely and gathering together in the grass.

Font Choice
Once again, the font has character and is unique while still being completely legible.

The Hierarchy
The designer has aced the hierarchy of information, giving due prominence to the title and author name.

Overall Comment
This was the top choice because of how professional it looked.

Scan the QR code to view this image in color.

Cover #4

Image Choice

The chicken in this image appears to be in good health. What's not to love or aspire to?

Font Choice

The font choice is less arty than the previous covers discussed, but it is clear and captivating nevertheless.

The Hierarchy

The hierarchy is once again on point.

Overall Comment

A good choice for a book on chicken farming; no objections!

Scan the QR code to view this image in color.

Cover #5

Image Choice

This cartoon image of a chicken is super eye-catching and attractive! In this niche, it's common to see covers featuring real-life imagery such as animals, farm life, or nature. But sometimes, breaking away from these trends sets your book apart. Following what competitors are doing is a solid strategy, but it doesn't mean it's the only effective one.

Font Choice

The font choice here is ultra-engaging yet still clear to read. The diagonal lines emanating from the title upward call attention to the title. Great job!

The Hierarchy

The hierarchy is on point, too.

Overall Comment

Although we think images of real chickens are great, there is something simply unforgettable about this one—so appealing!

Scan the QR code to view this image in color.

How to Write a Brief for Your Designer

Providing your designer with a brief (a description of what you're looking for in a cover) is vital so they can ensure they're on the right track. In fact, all book cover design services require you to complete a brief. It should include the following information:

- The title
- The subtitle
- The author name
- A short summary of your vision for the cover
- A link to a Google document where you show three to nine competitor covers (Make sure your link is set to allow everyone you share it with to have viewing rights.)
- A sample, if you have a specific design in mind
- A summary of your book, which you can obtain from your book outline

We have written a sample brief so you can get a good idea of the information you will need to provide.

Sample Book Cover Brief

Title: *Become a Backyard Chicken Farmer—Master Breed Selection and Feeding*

Subtitle: *Uncover the Importance of Facilities and Health Care to Effortlessly Increase Egg Production*

Author Name: Cluck Norris

Brief:

> Hi there,
>
> I am building a brand that will contain many books in the raising chickens niche.
>
> Specifically, breed selection and nutrition are my main topics. After this book, I will write about common chicken ailments and how to spot and address them.
>
> I want strong brand recognition.
>
> Considering that this will be the first book in the series, it will set the tone for the entire brand.
>
> The cover needs to have brandable elements that can easily be transferred and manipulated with each new book to match the new topic.
>
> Besides good branding potential, I am looking for a cover that stands out from my competition. Click here to review my competitor's covers:
>
> amazon.com/dp/1612129307
>
> amazon.com/dp/1641524057
>
> amazon.com/dp/161212013X
>
> I like the fact that these covers included pictures of chickens. Many books on chicken rearing use images of eggs or barns, but I think that nothing sells the importance of smart breeding practices than the image of a healthy chicken.
>
> Please make sure that the cover doesn't look like a fiction book cover.
>
> Here is a summary of my book: This book is about empowering beginners to raise healthy, happy chickens that lay an optimal amount of eggs. It has a strong focus on nutrition, preventive health, and allowing chickens the space they need to roam and stay active.

Cover Designers Options and Recommendations

Unless you are a graphic designer with special experience in book cover design, it is a good idea to ask a specialist to design your book. The following are our top recommendations:

99designs (www.publishingservicesbook.com/99designs)

99designs comprises a global community of professional designers who can create almost anything you need, from logos to website illustrations, book illustrations, and book covers. This is our go-to choice for designing ebook covers.

Invite a Designer to Create Your ebook Cover on 99designs

Log onto the website and click **Find a Designer You Love**. Go to "What do you need designed?" and click **Book Cover**. Indicate the industry your book covers. You will see the top work of many designers and each designer's level. If you love the work of a specific designer, you can send them a brief and discuss the possibility of collaboration.

How to Run a Contest

Running a contest is a great way to choose from numerous designs. At 99designs, you can run a contest starting from $199. Go to the website and click **View All Design Categories**, then **Book & Magazine**.

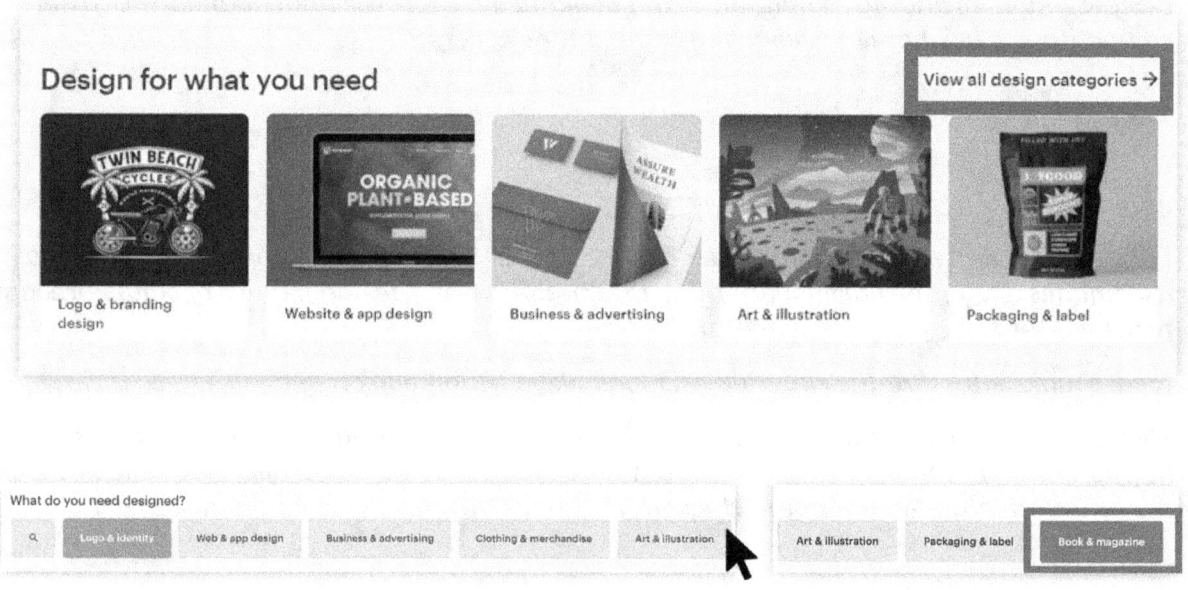

Hover your mouse pointer on the right-most option to view more.

There, you will see that you can select between hiring a designer and starting a contest. Click **Ebook Cover**, then **Get Started Now**, then **Ebook** and **Continue**.

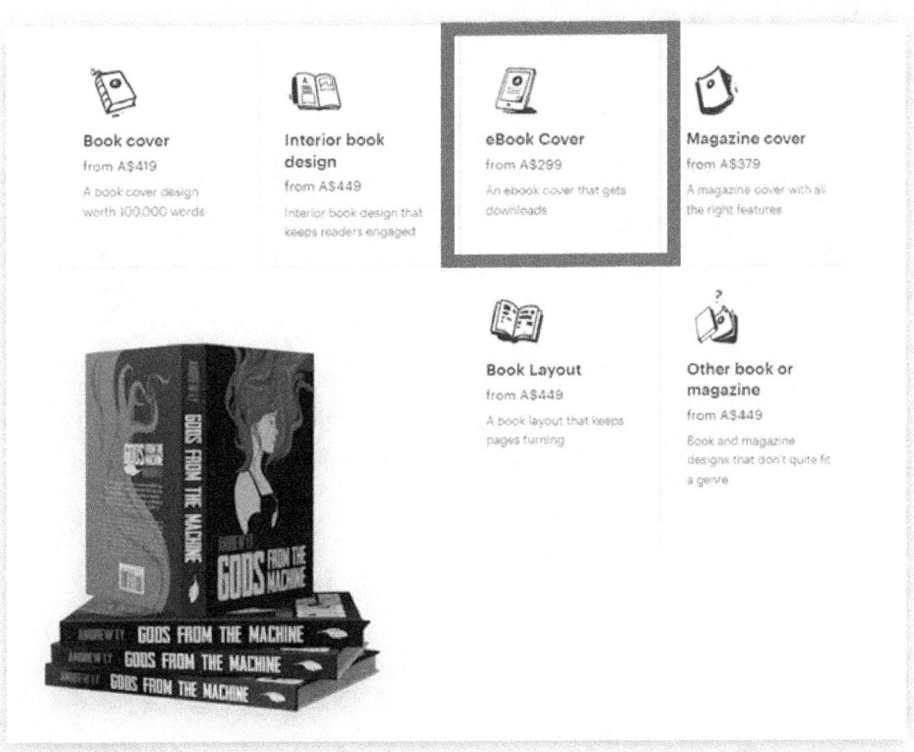

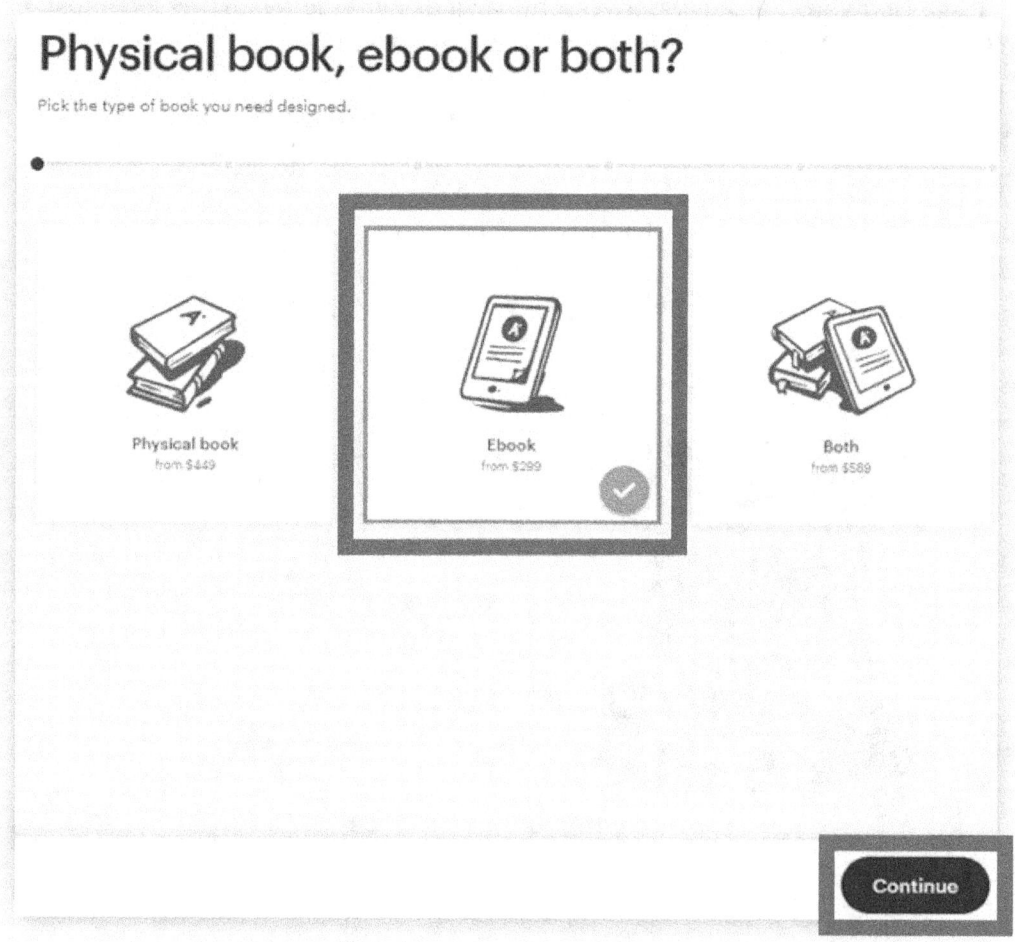

You will be shown a few designs and asked, "Which designs do you like?" You can skip this step if you like, especially if nothing aligns with your book's vision. In the next step, you will be shown various colors to explore, and you can choose the hues/color scheme you like or allow the designer to make suggestions. After that, click **Continue**, and you will be asked to fill out the "Book Cover Brief." You will be asked for the following information:

- Your email (If you already have an account, you won't need to fill this in, but if you don't, you will have to.)
- The title and subtitle of your book (You can add this information in the brief again if you wish.)
- The author's name (You can skip the "About the Author" section.)
- The genre (You can skip the "Add a Blurb." Since this is for an ebook, you will not need a back cover.)
- Information about your target audience (You can fill this in if you wish, but it isn't always necessary.)

- Your ebook: This section asks you what you would like on the first page of your ebook—i.e., your cover. Click **Title**, **Subtitle**, and **Author's Name** (Skip the box that asks, "What would you like on the last page of your ebook?" because it is not applicable.)
- Book Distributor: select **Amazon Kindle**.
- Creative vision (Choose the style options you are interested in.)
- In the box that says "Describe what you're looking for in more detail," indicate your entire brief.
- Fill in the box that says, "Is there anything designers should avoid?" (if applicable).
- Select whether or not you allow the designer to use AI-generated stock images. If you select yes, you will need to declare this when uploading your book to KDP.
- Next, click the option to allow designers to use stock images, and then click **Continue**.
- Pick the package you want. The more expensive packages feature submissions from mid- and top-level designers. The Platinum Package, which is the highest of them all, allows you to work only with top-level designers. We have had great results from selecting the **Bronze** option. The options allow you to choose from different means to promote your contest and choose the deadline for submission. The packages come with a 100% money-back guarantee and full copyright ownership of the final design.
- Note that the contest runs for several days, as follows:
    ◇ **The Qualifying Stage:** After you post the contest, the designers have 4 days to submit their designs to your contest. During this time, you can provide them with feedback about what you like and what you don't like.
    ◇ **The Selecting Finalists Stage:** You have a maximum of 4 days to pick up to 6 finalists.
    ◇ **Final Round:** This round lasts 3 days, during which you can work closely with your chosen finalists to help them revise the designs to perfection.
    ◇ **Select a Winner Stage:** You have a maximum of 14 days to pick a winner.
    ◇ **The Handover Stage:** Within a 5-day period, you have to sign the Copyright Transfer Agreement, and you will receive the final files.
- Contest title
- How you wish to promote your contest (for an additional fee, you can bump your contest to the top of the list, highlight it to make it stand out, or list your content on the company blog. You can also select to do all of these).
- Pick your contest options. (For instance, you can decide to commit to choosing a design, run a blind contest, run a private contest, and choose the duration of the contest.) We suggest ticking the **Guaranteed** box because doing so will motivate many more designers to submit covers

if you say that you will definitely award a winner and not opt out in the end. We also suggest going with a "blind" contest so that designers cannot see each other's work. One option is to click **Private Contest** so your work is not searchable. This comes at a price of $89. It has its pros and cons. The main advantage is that it is not searchable on search engine platforms like Google, so you can keep your contest private. The downside is that the designers will need to sign an NDA, meaning they cannot showcase the cover on their profile. This might deter some of them from submitting a cover, as it stops them from growing their portfolios.

- For Duration, click **Standard**. This will ensure your contest runs for 7 days.
- Finally, if you don't have an account, you will be asked to create one or use one of your existing accounts.

Pro Tip: Don't forget to give feedback to each of the designers who have submitted a design. Many will create designs you will not use, meaning they give their time in good faith. It pays to exercise kindness, thank them, and give them honest and useful feedback. As you review designs, think about updating your brief. Invite designers you like to your contest, work on building relationships with them, and guarantee the prize for your contest if you want the very best submissions. You can invite up to 50 designers every 24 hours. Take the time to do so to up your chances of receiving numerous top designs.

You can also run polls so that others can vote and rank the submitted covers. You can open as many polls as you wish. Post the link to them on your Facebook page, in relevant Facebook groups, on Reddit, or any other forums; definitely ask your friends and family for feedback!

Once your book is formatted and you have the final page count, you can get your covers for your hardback, paperback, and ACX cover done for considerably less money on Fiverr and other freelance sites. Designing the cover is the most expensive part of the process - adjusting it for various formats and platforms is not as costly.

Getcovers (www.publishingservicesbook.com/getcovers)

Getcovers is a team of book cover artists, graphic designers, and managers dedicated to making your self-publishing journey easier. It is also very easy to use and offers you access to great designs for your cover. It works a little differently from 99designs. When you click **Getcovers**, you will see a user-friendly menu at the top of the page that shows what items you can have designed (including logos, marketing materials, design help, and more). Click **Book Covers,** and you will see that they offer an unlimited number of free revisions. (Some companies cap the number of revisions you can request, so this is pretty generous.) They also offer a 100% money-back guarantee. There are three packages to choose from:

- **Basic:** For $10, you receive an e-cover design. This package does not include a back and spine. The other two packages do include them. With this package, you only get one licensed image.
- **Standard:** For $20, you receive an ebook and print-ready cover design. With this package, you get two licensed images.

- **Premium:** For $35, you get a premium ebook and print cover. The source file only comes with this package, so if you want to make design changes to the file in the future, you will need this package. With this package, you get 3-5 licensed images.

For all the above packages, you can choose add-ons, like an ad image, a cover reveal image, and more. For one-day delivery, you can simply pay $10 more. The usual turnaround time is 4 days for the basic and standard packages and 5 days for the premium package.

Once you select the package you wish, you are then asked to supply project data, including the book title, subtitle, author name, genre, whether the book is part of a series, a stock image you wish used (you can leave this choice to the designer if you wish), your brief, and more.

 **Exclusive Deal:** Use the coupon code **PS10** to get **10% off** your order on Getcovers.

Fiverr (www.publishingservicesbook.com/fiverr)

Fiverr is an online marketplace for freelance services. It connects potential clients with thousands of services—graphic design, writing and translation, video and animation, and more. To order a book cover here, simply click **Graphics & Design** on the main page. Scroll through the page, then click **Book Covers,** and you will find a host of different artists with their ratings and testimonials (as provided by clients) and the price they charge for each package. There are three packages to choose from:

- Basic
- Standard
- Premium

Each artist is free to stipulate the services included in the package, the turnaround time, how many revisions are permitted, and similar.

List of Recommended Cover Designers from Fiverr

Publishing Services team members have worked with the following designers and have had a great experience. Therefore, we can recommend them to you. Go to: www.publishingservicesbook.com/recommeded-fiverr-designers

Essential Cover Files: What You'll Need for Print and Digital

Online self-publishing companies have their own processes and use different paper in printing, meaning that design aspects may change depending on where you wish to distribute your book. For instance, aspects such as the spine width for a paperback on KDP will differ from that for IngramSpark. This means that if you wish to distribute your book in paperback, hardback, ebook, and audiobook formats, you will need the following files or versions of your cover:

- **Ebook Cover**
- **Print Book Covers**
    - Paperback for KDP
    - Paperback for IngramSpark
    - Hardback for KDP
    - Hardback for IngramSpark
- **Audiobook Cover** (We will cover more about audiobooks later on in the book)
    - If you reside in the US, Canada, Ireland, and the UK, you need an ACX cover.
    - If you reside in the rest of the word, you need to create a cover for:
        - Findaway Voices by Spotify
        - Author's Republic

When Should I Order Which Version?

Order your ebook cover while the book is being written, as you will not need a page count to do so, and you can take advantage and work on this aspect while your ghostwriter is completing your book. We will discuss trim sizes for other versions of your cover later. However, because you will be ordering your ebook cover at this stage, it pays to know that the ideal resolution for ebook cover files is 1,600 x 2,560 pixels. For all other versions, order the cover after formatting (because you will need the final page count).

What Information Should You Give Your Designer So They Can Create the Additional Versions You Need?

To ensure your designer has all they need when designing all the different versions of your cover, provide them with the following information:

- **Final Page Count:** You will have this after formatting.
- **Trim Size:** We will delve more into trim sizes later in the book when we discuss formatting.
- **Interior Type:** Publishing Services recommends black and white interior pages with cream-hued paper, which is less reflective than white paper, thus reducing glare and eye strain. Black on cream is classic and timeless and evokes a sense of tradition and quality. It is also less expensive than printing in color.
- **Back Cover Description:** This is a shorter description than what you will find on Amazon. It should be no more than 350 words long—preferably less. Publishing Services includes the back cover for free when you order a Book Outline and Description Package or a Book Description Package.

 **Pro Tip:** You may ask, "Why does the interior type matter for book cover design?" The answer is that it is important for numerous reasons, including design consistency and aesthetic harmony. Your cover design has to be consistent with the overall aesthetic and tone of the book. For instance, if your interior has a minimalist style, it would be strange if your designer used a Baroque font on the cover. Information about the interior type can also help your designer align the cover with your book's genre and audience. The interior type also says a lot about your marketing and branding strategy. The cover should complement your brand message and appeal to your target market.

Designing for Diversity, Equality, and Inclusion: Why It Matters

Ensure that your cover does not reinforce negative stereotypes and biases around gender, ethnicity, physical ability, neurodiversity, and age. If you are writing for an audience with disabilities and their families, avoid using stereotypical images. For instance, steer clear of the "puzzle" symbol to represent neurodiversity. It is seen as stigmatizing and dehumanizing by the Autism community, yet despite overwhelming opposition, it can still be found on many book covers (Crossman 2019).

If you have images or drawings of men and women, be aware of what they are doing in the image, who is leading others or doing the talking, and the body language being displayed. If you wish to draw people of different ethnicities, display them authentically, demonstrating specific people rather than mere attributes.

If you are interested in delving more into what authentically diverse, inclusive design looks like, we recommend a magnificent article by Meg Robichaud for Shopify UX, entitled "You Can't Just Draw Purple People and Call It Diversity" (2018).

The Importance of Social Media

Check out hashtags like #BookTok and #Bookstagram on Instagram and TikTok. They tell you a lot about popular design styles and expectations from your target audience. The creator of the blog *Laura's Books and Blogs* noted that in an X (formerly Twitter) survey in which she asked her followers why they bought books, almost 50% of people answered "the cover" (Smith 2021).

We hope we've got you thinking about how important a great book cover is and got your creative juices flowing. Now, let's turn to another area that will benefit from your creativity: your Facebook page.

 # Publishing Services' Book Cover Design Packages

We understand the importance of creating covers that not only look stunning but also align with industry standards and market trends. We have gathered an experienced team of book cover designers, and we now offer two specialized packages:

Book Cover Design Package

This package is perfect for authors who want a fully customized cover design from start to finish. You'll receive 5 unique cover concepts and have the opportunity to select one that resonates most with you.

From there, we'll work closely with you to refine your chosen design, ensuring it's perfect.

Once finalized, we'll deliver an ebook cover and later create print-ready covers for paperback, hardback, IngramSpark, and ACX once your book is formatted.

The package includes:

- Ebook cover (chosen from 5 unique concepts)
- KDP paperback and hardback covers
- IngramSpark paperback and hardback covers
- ACX (audiobook) cover

The turnaround for this package is seven business days, and it includes unlimited revisions until your final cover is ready.

To place an order, visit the Publishing Services website at www.publishingservices.com. Select **Book Cover Design Package**. Scroll down and download the order form. Fill it out, save your changes, and upload it in the designated section on the page. Click **Add to Cart.**

Pre-Existing Cover Resizing Package

If you already have an amazing ebook cover (designed by another professional) and only need it resized and adjusted for other formats, this package is for you.

We'll transform your existing design into print-ready covers for paperback, hardback, and audiobook formats.

This package is a time-saving solution that ensures your book can be published across platforms like KDP, IngramSpark, and ACX.

The package includes:

- KDP paperback and hardback covers
- ACX (audiobook) cover
- Optional: IngramSpark paperback and hardback covers

To place an order, visit the Publishing Services website at www.publishingservices.com. Select **Pre-Existing Cover Resizing Package**. Fill out the order form on the website, upload all the necessary files, and add the extra information we need (such as your book's trim size, interior type, etc.). Click **Add to Cart**.

The turnaround for this package is three business days.

Chapter 11

Building Your Facebook Author Page

Once you have your cover, it's time to take advantage of social media and select a winning cover from your shortlist. Start by creating an author page, as this page will be vital during various stages of your marketing efforts. An author page allows you to market and promote your book without barraging friends with this information. It also affords greater privacy and ensures only friends see your private photographs and read your personal news. Finally, Facebook has algorithms that it uses to match you with relevant content and individuals. By having a dedicated author page, you will only see industry-relevant content. By liking and commenting on this content, you can get your own news across to your target audience and other authors.

Step-by-Step Guide: How to Set Up Your Facebook Author Page

1. Go to "Create a Page" on Facebook (www.facebook.com/pages/create/).
2. Indicate your author page name using either your name or pseudonym.
3. Choose the category that best describes you. Your choices are author, writer, or publisher.
4. Check out your competitors' pages to get a better idea of interesting features—descriptions, images, covers, etc.
5. Write a description of your page. Keep it to one or two sentences, writing something similar to "I'm a marketing professional and author. I have published____."

6. Upload a profile picture and cover photo that resonates with your audience. For your profile pic, consider a professional headshot. If possible, select the same one that's published on your author website and your other social media pages.
7. Many authors use images of past books for their cover photo or a scene that is closely related to their genre. Remember the tips we provided in the previous chapter about color and style expectations for specific genres.
8. Fill in your page's "About" information. Add links to your website if you have one, and if not, add them when you do. Include your social media channels so that people can follow you.
9. Hit **Save**.

Examples of Excellent Facebook Pages

Harlan Coben's Facebook page is an effective marketing tool because it announces upcoming books and a streamed series based on one of his books.

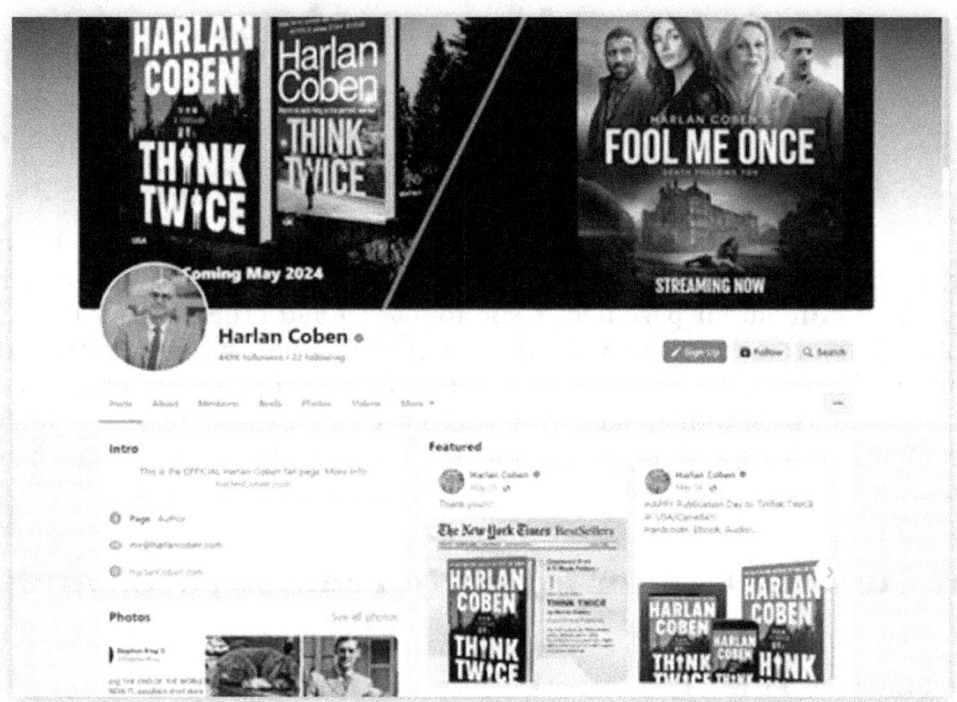

Alexandra Chan's Facebook page has a beautifully designed cover photo and a one-minute video introducing herself and her book.

Using Audience Polls to Choose Your Book Cover

Your Facebook page is a great way to help you choose from your shortlist of cover candidates. To obtain opinions from others:

- Create a picture in Canva or Paint containing 3 to 5 cover options. Include a number beneath each image. Make sure you use flat ebook cover versions, not 3D mock-ups. Below is an example of a poll for our sample chicken book:

- Make a post and ask your target audience to give you feedback and say which number (cover) they like best. We ran a poll for the above covers, stopping the ad at 44 votes. Here are the results:
    ◊ Cover 1: 2.27%
    ◊ Cover 2: 36.36%
    ◊ Cover 3: 0.00%
    ◊ Cover 4: 31.82%

- ◇ Cover 5: 9.09%
- ◇ Cover 6: 20.45%

- Run advertising on the post to target your book's audience. Simply click **Boost Post** and start by targeting the US market. You can expand to other markets once your book starts selling, but initially, it's a good idea to focus on the US as that's the biggest market.
- Indicate your target audience. For instance, if your book is on parenting, then you would target parents. You should then choose your age range. (This, once again, depends on your audience, as determined in your outline.) For your budget, we suggest spending around $100. If you obtain numerous answers, you can stop the ads when you reach, say, $40 or whatever the amount is that gets you the number of results you are seeking.
- Count up how many votes each cover got. Go with the clear winner! If there are two close contenders, keep the poll running!
- If people ask any questions about the book, engage with them. It's a great way to start building a community around your book. If anyone is interested in your book, ask them to send you a private message. Once the book is ready, you can contact them.
- Invite everyone who likes your post to like your page.

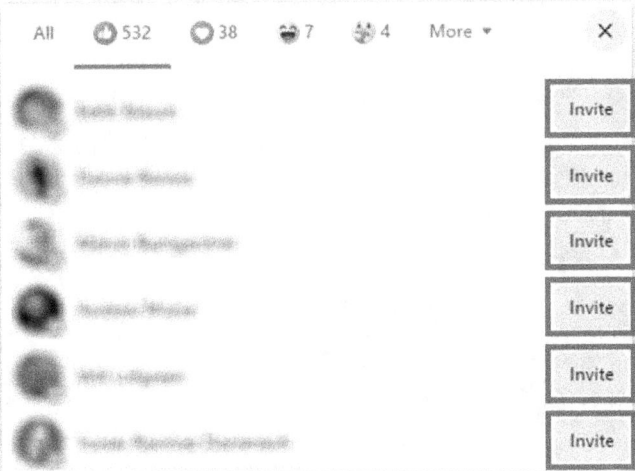

Starting your Facebook page is easy, and we guarantee it will be very fulfilling to build a community as passionate about your topic as you are. Next up, we will focus on another visual tool that can help create more engagement for your book: illustrations and graphics!

Chapter 12

Using Images and Graphics to Draw in Readers

If you're looking to engage your audience, make sure to prioritize your illustrations and/or graphics. Research indicates that 75% of all information processed by the brain is derived from visual formats. Visual information is mapped better in peoples' minds, whether presented as images, diagrams, videos, graphs, flowcharts, or infographics (Raiyn 2016). Images can also break up text and give the eyes a rest. A well-placed photograph or illustration can set the mood, inspire your readers to pause and think, and help them recall key information long after they have completed your book.

What Types of Images to Include in Your Book

It's important to ensure you have the right to include any images you choose for your book. Good choices include:

- **Stock Images:** You can find these on sites like Shutterstock (www.publishingservicesbook.com/shutterstock), iStock (www.publishingservicesbook.com/istock), and Depositphotos (www.publishingservicesbook.com/depositphotos). Most paid sites offer subscriptions that entitle you to numerous images. Some also allow you to purchase images on demand. You can also check out sites offering free images shared under a Creative Commons license like Wikimedia Commons or Unsplash. When using these sites, read the fine print. Some require you to credit photographers or limit the use of some images to editorial (noncommercial) use.

- **Your Own Photographs:** You can use your own images if you have a knack for photography and a camera that takes crisp, high-resolution images.
- **Illustrations:** You can draw or purchase illustrations from individual artists on Fiverr or Upwork.
- **Professionally Created Illustrations:** Many platforms provide these services. Below, we've listed some great options, but plenty of others are available as well.
    - Adobe Stock (www.publishingservicesbook.com/adobe-stock)
    - GraphicRiver (www.publishingservicesbook.com/graphic-river)
    - Creative Market (www.publishingservicesbook.com/creative-market)
- **Diagrams:** If you need diagrams, you can either hire a graphic designer to create them for you or try a host of free tools that help you make your own, including draw.io (http://draw.io) (a cross-platform drawing software), FigJam (www.publishingservicesbook.com/figjam) (a free online diagramming and whiteboarding tool), and Excalidraw (https://excalidraw.com/) (a free tool for those seeking an organic, sketchy look to their diagrams).
- **AI Tools:** AI tools such as Dall-E and Midjourney are making it easy to create stunning images. However, you must declare this when uploading your book to Amazon if you use AI-generated images. Because we still do not know what Amazon will be doing with this information, it is a good idea at this point to stick to free open-source or paid images.

Why Image Quality Matters

For optimal results, all images should be sized at 100%, flattened to one layer, and inserted into your manuscript file at a minimum resolution of 300 DPI (dots per inch). There is no set maximum DPI for images. However, images with excessively high resolutions may result in files timing out during processing or cause manufacturing delays. The maximum file size for upload is **650MB**.

Choosing Between Black-and-White or Color Images for Your Book

You may wonder whether color or black-and-white images are best. We suggest using color images in your book but printing them in black and white so you can significantly cut your printing costs while still having color images in your ebook. Simply select black and white when uploading your book to KDP. Only print color pictures if they are necessary for your book.

Next, let's get back to your book content, focusing on one of the most important steps to ensure your book looks professional and on-point: proofreading and editing.

Chapter 13

Refining Your Manuscript: Editing and Proofreading Basics

Do you recall reading a book or article and noticing strange or funny typos or grammatical errors? Have you ever been so confused by the incorrect use of language or awkward sentence structures that you had to read something several times to make sense of it? Has a book ever made you feel like you were on X (formerly Twitter), reading comments that confuse *it's* and *its* or *there* and *their*? It's off-putting. Nothing detracts from a book's credibility more than confusingly written sentences, typos everywhere, repetitions, and inconsistencies—which is why investing time (and, if you can, part of your budget) in proofreading and editing is vital. In this chapter, we will offer advice on how to ensure all your *I*'s are dotted and your *T*'s are crossed.

Who Should Proofread and Edit Your Manuscript?

Proofreading involves looking for spelling errors, incorrect punctuation, and inconsistencies. Editing corrects issues that are central to writing, including sentence construction and clarity. The editor may suggest removing a section of a manuscript if it is repetitive or recommend moving one or more sections to another part of the book. They may also propose a reduction of the total word count.

You can hire editors and proofreaders on many freelance platforms, such as Upwork, Fiverr, or Reedsy. There are also specialized companies that offer editing and proofreading, such as our very own Publishing Services.

Another choice is to proofread and edit your manuscript yourself. While you should always proofread and edit your manuscript, it is definitely worth the time and money to have a professional set of eyes review it before it goes to print. There are various reasons for this. If you write your book, it is incredibly difficult to identify typos and grammatical errors in your own writing.

Fun Fact: The brain "sees" words, not individual letters. Have you ever seen mirror letter games online that challenge "only geniuses" to read jumbled sentences? Here's one for you to have a go at:

"I con't woit to pudlish my first bestselling book."

We bet you probably found it easy to work out because the brain sees and processes entire words first and letters second. Your mind takes various shortcuts when reading what you have written yourself. It already knows "the final product," so to speak. Therefore, it can gloss over typos and other mistakes (Nixon 2024). Even the most seasoned writers make errors, which is why proofreading and editing should be considered essential services by those wishing to publish a quality product.

There is a second issue: spelling and meanings can vary from country to country. For instance, in the US, people say "cookies," while in the UK, they often use the word "biscuits" for the same food item. The UK saying "Bob's your uncle" (which means something is easy) might mean nothing to someone in the US, and if you used the term "ballpark figure" (an estimated amount) in the UK, they might be confused.

Countless idioms and phrases are linked to specific parts of the world, and depending on your audience and target market, you may wish to use US, Canadian, UK, Australian, or other types of English. It is crucial for the person proofing your work to have thorough and current knowledge of your chosen dialect.

Understanding the Different Levels of Editing

Editing is not a one-size-fits-all process. Depending on where you are in your writing journey and the type of assistance your book needs, different types of editing serve different purposes. Understanding these differences helps you choose the right editing level to bring out the best in your book. Below, we'll go over some of the most important and common ones.

Developmental Editing

Also known as in-depth editing, developmental editing focuses on the manuscript's overall structure, content, and concept. It involves rewriting parts of the text and, if necessary, adding sources so your manuscript flows well, is compelling to read, and provides proper citations.

Pro Tip: AI-generated manuscripts always require developmental editing because most of their issues fall within the parameters of this editing level. For example, such manuscripts often have limited or incorrect references, which can compromise the credibility of your manuscript. AI also tends to recycle phrases and repeat points, creating large repetitive sections. It cannot understand emotions or cultural context, leaving your manuscript feeling flat or superficial. AI pulls from pre-existing data, which can sometimes be outdated or outright wrong. These are all issues that developmental editors fix.

Line Editing

This stage in the editing process involves going over your entire manuscript, line by line, to find any potential mistakes and improve the flow of sentences. While it can overlap, it is best to do this sentence-level work before copyediting begins. At this stage, the focus is on phrasing and word choice.

Copyediting

This task is focused on perfecting the language, style, and overall presentation of a manuscript. Copyeditors meticulously review the text for grammar, syntax, and usage errors. They correct spelling mistakes, guarantee proper punctuation, and enhance sentence structure for clarity. Consistency in language, tone, and formatting is a key focus. They also work on improving the flow of the writing, making necessary adjustments for better coherence. Typically, while copyediting, an editor is also doing mechanical editing.

Mechanical Editing

This task centers on the technical aspects of writing. Mechanical editors thoroughly review the manuscript for grammatical errors, syntactical issues, and language mechanics to ensure correctness and adherence to language rules. They address formatting issues, such as font consistency, paragraph indentation, and overall document structure. Finally, they ensure the manuscript follows a specific style guide (The American Psychological Association (APA), The Chicago Manual of Style (CMOS), or any other guide provided by a publisher).

Proofreading

Proofreading is the final, meticulous examination of a manuscript before publication, focusing on eliminating errors and ensuring a polished, error-free document. It should be the last check the manuscript goes through before it's formatted.

Proofreaders confirm consistent use of language, style, and formatting, aligning the document with predetermined guidelines or style preferences. While it does not involve substantial content changes, it provides a final quality check to guarantee a professional and flawless presentation.

 **Pro Tip:** Even if you opt to have your book professionally proofed and edited, read it over several times before you hand it to the editor. You may spot sections that need to be moved or shortened; doing so beforehand can streamline the process.

In this chapter, we have looked into the vital role professional proofreaders and editors play. While your book is being proofread, you can focus on another key component of your book: your review pages!

 # Publishing Services' Editing & Proofreading Packages

Editing & Proofreading Package
(For non-AI-generated books)

If your manuscript has been written by a human author, this package is for you!

We've assembled a talented team of experienced editors and proofreaders who have worked on thousands of manuscripts, from debut fiction novels to non-fiction industry bestsellers.

The package is priced at $2.50 per 100 words. It includes:

- Expert copy editing, line editing, and mechanical checks
- Refinement of flow, consistency, and word choice to enhance readability
- Professional proofreading for spotless grammar, punctuation, and spelling
- Structural suggestions where needed to strengthen your narrative

The package has a 14-business-day turnaround time.

To place an order, visit the Publishing Services website at www.publishingservices.com. Scroll down and select **Editing & Proofreading Package**.

Indicate the word count of your book from the drop-down menu. You will see that you can choose from different word count categories and that the price varies depending on how long your manuscript is. Fill in the Title, Subtitle, and Author. Choose US or UK spelling, and select a style guide (CMOS or APA).

Upload your manuscript, fill in the rest of the required and optional fields, ensure you have submitted all information with the order, and indicate if your manuscript was AI-generated. (If that's the case, the AI Developmental Editing Package may be more suited to your needs.) Click **Add to Cart**.

AI Manuscript Developmental Editing & Humanization Package
(For AI-generated books)

Designed specifically for AI-generated manuscripts, this service combines developmental editing to refine structure and content with humanization to add depth and authenticity.

The package includes:

- Developmental editing and humanization
- Humanization comments and narrative flow enhancements
- Clarity, consistency, and originality checks
- Depth analysis and current content verification
- Professional proofreading
- Grammar, spelling, and punctuation check

You'll receive a fully edited manuscript (with and without visible changes) and a feedback document, giving you information on every improvement made.

With a turnaround time of just 18 business days, this package prepares your manuscript for formatting and publication.

To place an order, visit the Publishing Services website at www.publishingservices.com. Scroll down and select **AI Manuscript Developmental Editing & Humanization Package**. Indicate the word count of your manuscript and fill in the required fields, including Book Title, Subtitle, and Author. Choose US or UK spelling and opt for one of two possible style guides (CMOS or APA). Upload your manuscript, book outline, and customer research document (if it is separate from your outline).

Confirm that your attached manuscript is in Word format. Choose the tone you wish the writer to convey, confirm you have selected the correct word count, and choose any add-ons you want (a Review Page Package and/or a Book Description Package). Let us know how you heard about us, check that you have submitted all relevant information, and click **Add to Cart**.

Chapter 14

How to Create Powerful Review Pages

Review pages are exactly what they sound like—a request for your readers to leave a review of your book. As a self-publisher, accumulating a substantial number of positive reviews can significantly influence new readers to purchase your book instead of a competitor's.

Think about how often you have searched for a book (or any type of product) on Amazon. Usually, you choose one with many positive reviews and a relatively high star score. Doing so ensures you make a smart investment of your time and money.

Amazon's algorithms constantly change, and its various methods to bump books up are top-secret. However, we are aware of one—they take ratings into account, recommending higher-rated books in first-page search results.

Including review request pages in both the middle and end of your book is a strategic way to encourage readers to leave feedback. You maximize the chances of securing reviews by prompting readers at two different points.

Ensure that these pages don't seem desperate-looking or come across as too pushy or like an ad. They should offer a tip, an interesting idea, and a reason why the reader should leave a review. Sometimes, it pays to tap into your audience's altruistic side. At other times, however, it pays to be more straightforward. Striking the right tone is something a seasoned writer will know how to do perfectly. Sincerity is important.

In the end, yes, their review will help others who share their pain points, but it will also help you, and the writing should reveal that you are aware of this.

What Should Your Review Pages Include?

Ensure your reviews have all the required information readers need to leave your book a glowing review.

- **Mid-Book Review Page:** This review request goes in the middle of your book. You can choose its exact position. Generally, if your book has an even number of chapters, the page should go right in the middle. For instance, if your book has 12 chapters, a good place for it is right after Chapter 6. However, if you have an odd number of chapters, it's up to you to decide if it should go earlier or later. For instance, if your book has 15 chapters, you might decide to place the page after Chapter 7 or Chapter 8. Your Mid-Book Review should contain:
    - A headline (to capture your reader's attention and pique their interest)
    - A pertinent quote (to set a tone)
    - A short amount of text (to say a few words before you ask them to leave a review)
    - A call to action (asking your readers to leave a review on Amazon)
    - One or two more sentences to thank the reader for their support and invite them to keep reading (Let them know there's more exciting information up ahead if you wish.)
- **End-Book Review Page:** This page is much shorter than the Mid-Book Review, and it goes right before your conclusion at the end of your book. It includes:
    - A headline
    - Text (asking the reader to leave a review)
    - Something that the first review request doesn't have: a catchy image that serves as a call to action
    - Another short message thanking the reader and wishing them well

Both requests have links that lead readers to the Amazon page where they can leave their thoughts. As you will see in our sample review page, it is important to insert QR codes with your review link in the paperback version of your book and a hyperlink to your review page in the ebook version.

Create a QR Code for Your Review Pages

Creating a QR code is very easy, and it is a wonderful way to help your readers get straight to the review section of your book so they can share their opinions.

- Visit Kindlepreneur's free QR Code Generator for Books tool on www.publishingservicesbook.com/qr-code-generator, and you will see a box that states, "Enter the URL you'd like them to go to when they scan the QR."

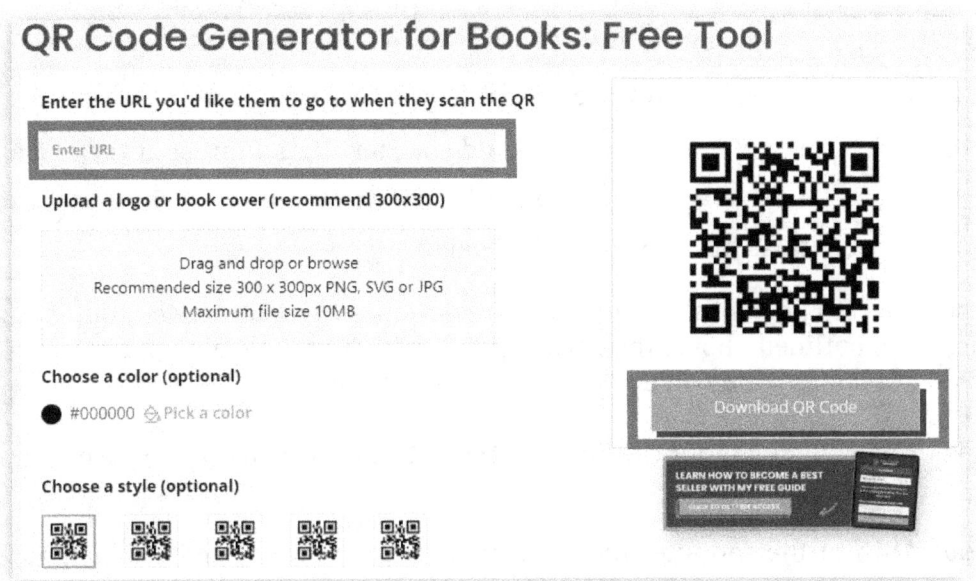

Enter the URL, upload a logo or book cover, choose a color if you wish, select a style, and download the code. The reader can then use the camera on their smartphone to scan the QR code, and they will be directed to your review page.

Other QR Code Generators

There are many more free QR code generators, including QR Code Generator (www.qr-code-generator.com), Bitly QR Codes (www.publishingservicesbook.com/bitly), My QR Code (www.myqrcode.com), and QRCode Monkey (www.qrcode-monkey.com).

How to Secure a Review Link Before Publishing

Logic would have it that your book needs to be published before you add a review link, but there is a clever hack that allows you to obtain the link prior to publication. It works this way:

1. Buy your ISBN, then turn your 13-digit ISBN into a 10-digit ISBN using the free tool on www.publishingservicesbook.com/isbn-converter.

   You can see how the tool did this in the screenshot below:

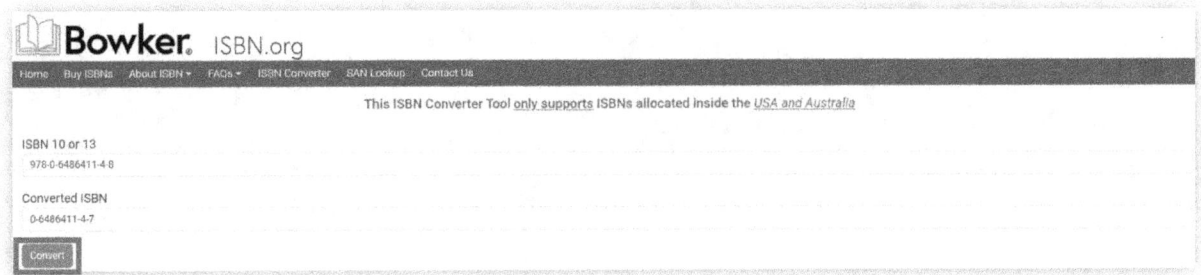

2. You will see that the converted ISBN has three hyphens. Remove them and add the 10-digit number to the end of your review link.

3. As soon as your book goes live, your review page will be active.

4. Here is the review link for you to copy: You add your ten digit number at the end after the "=" symbol. https://www.amazon.com/review/create-review/?asin=10digitnumber

5. Copy that link, and it will link to your review page.

Your book will still need to be published before the review pages can be viewed, but if you complete steps one through five outlined above, the review pages will automatically appear when your book goes live. If you do not do this, you will need to follow the steps below.

1. Publish your book first without the link and the QR code, as you only receive your ASIN once your book is published.

2. Enter your ASIN at the end after the "=" symbol: https://www.amazon.com/review/create-review/?asin=ASIN

3. Add the link and QR code to your formatted book. If Publishing Services formatted your book, you can simply email us your formatting order number and your ASIN, and we will do it for you free of charge.

4. You will need to re-upload your manuscript to KDP yourself.

Pro Tip: Because the review pages involve copywriting, we suggest that you leave the work up to Publishing Services' seasoned copywriting team. A review request can easily fall into the trap of appearing preachy or making it seem like the author is begging the reader to share their opinion. The positioning of the mid-book review is an actual interruption to the reading experience, even though it is conveniently placed in the middle of the book. Therefore, the idea isn't just to ask for a favor but to do so within the context and (most importantly) to offer the reader something new.

Below, you can check our samples for effective review pages.

Mid-Book Review Page Sample

Learn to Speak Chicken!

"The sky is falling!"

– Chicken Little (Children's fable)

The more time you spend with your chickens, the more you'll get to know their little quirks and unique personality traits. One of the first things that stood out to me with my own flock was the huge range of different sounds they make. Did you know that chickens make around 30 sounds, which they use to communicate specific messages? They use them to tell other chickens that there's food, that they've laid an egg, or that there's danger nearby (Cornish 2013).

They're very much social creatures; they'll even let each other know when they're worried or scared. They pass information on so that other flock members know exactly what's going on and whether they need to be concerned about anything. They learn about their environment and use its clues to help each other thrive, and that's such a joy to watch in action.

I remember one day when a cat was in my backyard; one of my chickens, Matilda, let out this high-pitched warning call that I'd never heard before, and the rest of them were all alerted. Luckily, they didn't have to stay alert for long because she also scared the cat, and he darted over the fence immediately!

Chickens are very much like people in this way. They help their neighbors and share information for the greater good, and I'd like to invite you to do the same thing right now. There are so many people who want to raise chickens but have no idea how to get started, and by sharing this information, we can help them begin their new chicken-raising lifestyle. You can help with this by simply leaving a review online.

By leaving a review of this book on Amazon, you'll help other people see how easy it is to raise chickens, and you'll show them where they can find all the information they need to get started.

Just as chickens make life easier for each other by sharing important information, we can help each other learn new skills by sharing what we know. Reviews help people find the information they're looking for, so while it may not seem like a lot to you, it could make a difference to someone else and their chicken-raising adventures.

Thank you so much for your support. Now, let's get back to your chickens and how to keep them safe from predators so those warning calls never mean a real disaster is coming!

End-Book Review Page Sample

Please Take a Moment to Cluck about This Book!

I hope you're feeling confident and excited about the journey ahead. I just know you're going to find raising chickens so rewarding, and as you set out on this new adventure, you're in a great position to help someone else out on theirs.

Simply by sharing your honest opinion of this book and a little about what you've learned here, you'll show new readers exactly where they can find all the information to raise a happy, healthy flock of their own.

LET OTHERS KNOW WHAT YOU THINK!

Thank you so much for your support. May your hens always be happy and your egg basket always be full!

With your review pages thoughtfully crafted to encourage feedback, the next step is ensuring your book is presented in a professional format.

In the upcoming chapter, we'll dive into book formatting—a crucial process that transforms your manuscript into a reader-friendly, print- and digital-ready product that stands out.

 # Publishing Services' Review Page Package

Our package includes two review pages that are curated specifically for your manuscript.

We do not use generic templates. Instead, the review writer reads your manuscript and pens a review request that reflects your content and is curated to your target audience.

To place an order, visit the Publishing Services website at www.publishingservices.com. Scroll down and select **Review Page Package**. Upload your manuscript and fill in the fields required, including your target audience and any additional information you wish to provide. Add on a Book Description Package if you wish. Make sure you submit all the relevant information and click **Add to Cart**.

The turnaround time is five business days.

Grab a Hammer and Help Us Break the Fourth Wall!

"Self-publishing is not just a backup plan; it's a way to take control of your career."

— Joanna Penn (Heimbigner 2024)

If you are a math person or one who tends to notice percentages and statistics, you may have looked at this book's table of contents and discovered that the topic of reviews shows up various times in this book. Chapter 14 shows you how to create review pages, and Chapter 19 shows you how to obtain verified reviews so your book sales shoot up. It is at this point that we break the wall between author and reader. We ask you to help us reach people just like you by writing a review for this book.

You know exactly why reviews are so important. They contain authentic opinions that can help new readers decide whether a book is right for them. In the introduction, we stated that our main aim is to unveil all the processes that take place in the self-publishing industry.

We want to show you how to access the many pieces that make up a top-selling work and provide you with no-holds-barred, step-by-step instructions for everything from writing a description to hiring a ghostwriter. If we have achieved this goal and got you a step closer to publishing your first book, share your opinion with new readers.

By leaving a review of this book on Amazon, you'll help others discover that self-publishing isn't a mystery; it's simply a matter of following a step-by-step procedure.

Thanks for your support. Just like all self-publishers, we need reviews to spread the word about our book, and your word can make a big difference.

To leave your review on Amazon, go to www.publishingservicesbook.com/leave-a-review or scan the QR code.

Chapter 15

Book Layout and Formatting

Up until now, you have invested a great deal of time and effort into writing a great book. The next step is to ensure your book looks professional, aligning all headings, subheadings, tables, and other design elements. There are two tasks involved in this part of self-publishing. The first is to ensure your files are complete and ready for formatting, and the second is to format the book yourself or hire an expert for the task.

Standard Book Formats

Depending on where you wish to sell your book, it will need to be in one or more of the following formats:

- **EPUB:** This format is known for its flexibility and wide-ranging compatibility with many devices (except for older Amazon Kindle models). Its reflowable text feature adjusts the layout to fit various screen sizes, making it reader-friendly. If you use Kindle Create to format your manuscript, you can format your book in files like KF8, AZW3, or KFX, which are essentially the same things as EPUBs.

- **KPF File:** KPF file stands for Kindle Create Package Format. You will not need this file if you already have an EPUB (which is the most widely used format and is compatible with various ebook readers and platforms). However, if you want to use Kindle Create to further optimize the formatting of your ebook, *specifically* for Kindle devices and platforms, you need to use Kindle Create to convert your EPUB file into a KPF file.

Publishing Services cannot help you with this task, as we format books with Vellum, not Kindle Create. To convert the file from EPUB to KPF, we would need your Amazon log-in details, which we're not legally allowed to ask for or use.

- **PDF:** PDFs maintain a fixed layout, preserving the page's original design and layout. Your printed books should be formatted as print-ready PDF files for use as paperback and hardcover books for all major platforms, such as KDP, IngramSpark, D2D Print, etc.

Differences Between Ebook and Print Formatting

Ebooks do not have fixed layouts because they are viewed on many devices—smartphones, tablets, Cloud readers, and more. Because all these devices have different screen sizes, it is impossible to standardize the layout of an ebook. Your manuscript will look different depending on the device your reader is using, the user's personal settings, and other factors.

Keep in mind that the amount of text viewable on different screens varies. On some devices, your manuscript may seem like it has pages you can flip, but that is just a tool offered by that particular device; other devices may only allow you to continuously scroll through a file.

Ebook files need to be responsive to adapt to the device's dimensions and settings. An ebook is essentially formatted as one long HTML file, so it can be read on any device your readers utilize.

This is also why ebooks don't have set page numbers or fixed pages. For example, page 24 on your e-reader might be page 54 on your friend's tablet, depending on the settings of the specific device a work is being viewed on. In contrast, PDFs/print books have specific pages because they are not viewed on screens and do not need to flow as one continuous file. Therefore, if you are opening a PDF (used for print books), a specific page (say page 5) looks exactly the same regardless of the device you use to open the file. This is not the case for ebooks.

The good news is that people using e-readers have come to expect this and understand it is their device, not the book's design, that makes it look the way it does.

In simpler terms, your ebook is like an actor performing on different stages (devices), adapting to each one's unique characteristics. If someone notices odd breaks or word hyphenations, it's not the actor's fault. Rather, it is simply the case of the script being interpreted differently at that particular stage (device).

All About Trim Sizes and Choosing the Right Size for Your Book

A book's trim size is the final size of the pages after it has been printed and cut (or trimmed) to fit the desired dimensions. It's essentially the height and width of your book when closed.

 **Pro Tip:** Select a trim size that is supported in hardback and paperback versions to avoid formatting the book in two different sizes. Check this link for more info on trim sizes: www.publishingservicesbook.com/kdp-formatting-sizes

While there are various options when it comes to sizes, we recommend the following dimensions (width x height):

- **Paperback Books:** We recommend a trim size of 5.5 x 8.5 or 6 x 9 (in inches).
  - ◊ Note: If your book is very long (60k+ words), has numerous images, or is a workbook, we recommend 8.5 x 11. In this case, you will need to format your hardback version in a different size.
- **Hardback Books:** Publishing Services recommends a trim size of 5.5 x 8.5 or 6 x 9.
  - ◊ Note: If the book is very long (60k+ words), has lots of images, or is a workbook, we recommend 8.25 x 11. In this case, you will need to format the paperback version in a different size.

Things to Consider When Selecting Trim Size

A few things to keep in mind when choosing a trim size are:

- **The smaller the trim size, the thicker the book.** This is because a smaller page size will mean less text can fit on each page, leading to more pages and a thicker spine.
- **Larger books cost more to print.** For instance, for a black-ink paperback with 24-108 pages, there is a fixed cost of $2.30 USD per book for a regular trim size and $2.84 USD per book for a large trim (over 6.12 x 9). For books that are between 110 and 828 pages, the fixed cost goes down to $1 per book, and you will be charged an additional $0.012 per page for regular trim sizes and $0.017 per page for large trim sizes. Use this tool to get an idea about the printing cost for different trim sizes: www.publishingservicesbook.com/kdp-royalty-calculator
- **It is recommended to choose a trim size that ensures your book isn't too thin.** In other words, you don't want a book with too few pages, so the customer doesn't feel like they spent their hard-earned money on a book that has little more information than a pamphlet.

Full-Page Images and Bleed: What to Consider

When you have your book formatted, you can choose to do so with or without "bleed," which is an extra area around the edges of a printed page that extends beyond the final trim size of the book.

Bleed is necessary when you want to use text, graphics, or images that go all the way to the very edge of the page. If you don't use bleed, you could end up with unwanted white gaps around the edges after trimming. To accommodate bleed, the actual page size of the book would be slightly larger (0.25 inches or 0.6cm) than the final trim size. For instance, a 6 x 9-inch book would have a file size of 6.25 x 9.25 inches.

In general, we recommend avoiding bleed because KDP is known to have issues with publishing or uploading such books.

 **Pro Tip:** Even if just one page in your interior requires bleed, your entire file should be set up with bleed. If you opt for bleed, you must also publish special rules when uploading your book to KDP. You will need to click certain categories to ensure KDP does not reject your book or report errors.

How Page Count Affects Formatting

An average 30K book with no images, tables, or complicated design elements can have between 120 and 130 pages, but it all depends on factors such as the trim and margin sizes. A formatted book may have a larger page count depending on the following factors.

- **Larger Margins or a Smaller Trim Size**: Adjusting your page size impacts how much content can fit on a single page.

- **Line Spacing**: Books typically use thicker leading (the difference between the size of the type and the distance from one baseline to the next) than standard Word documents. This enhances readability and increases the vertical space occupied by each line of text, thereby increasing the page count.

- **Fonts and Font Sizes**: Your chosen fonts and font sizes impact the number of pages your text requires.

- **Hyphenation and Justification**: Professional book formatting often involves careful hyphenation and justification of text to create a clean and polished appearance. This can affect word spacing and result in variations in the number of words on each line, influencing the overall page count.

- **Chapter and Section Breaks**: Formatting for chapter and section breaks, including additional blank space, decorative elements, or specific styles, can contribute to an increase in page count.

- **Images and Graphics**: If the book contains images, illustrations, or graphics, these elements can occupy space and contribute to a larger page count.
- **Widows and Orphans**: Book designers often avoid widows (single lines at the top of a page) and orphans (single lines at the bottom of a page) to maintain a cohesive layout. Adjustments made to avoid these can affect the overall page count.
- **Printing and Binding Considerations**: Printing and binding requirements can also impact page count. Different binding methods may require additional pages for endpapers, title pages, copyright pages, and other front matter.

Understanding Interior Margins

When reviewing your formatted book, you may notice that the right-hand margin seems to be wider on some pages, and on alternate pages, the left-hand margin is wider. The wider margins you see exist to accommodate the book's spine (the part of the book where the pages are glued or stitched together). Wider interior margins ensure that the part of the text closest to the spine isn't "eaten" or difficult for the eye to read after the book is bound. Once your book is printed, the margins will look identical because the spine will cover the excess space in the inner margin.

Below, you can see a photograph of different book spines. Some are thicker than others. The more text you have, the wider the book spine and the larger your gutter will have to be.

Making Changes to a Formatted Manuscript

If you need to make changes to your manuscript after it has been formatted and uploaded to KDP or other platforms, it is best to leave this task to a professional formatter because if you make the slightest mistake, KDP may reject your book. For instance, if you have one tiny letter that is just slightly sitting on the margin, KDP will not permit you to publish your manuscript. Theoretically, if you have an Adobe editor or an EPUB editor like Calibre, you can edit your manuscript; however, we do not recommend doing so unless you are 100% proficient with these tools and familiar with formatting. It is best to submit the book for formatting when it is 100% complete. If you have outsourced your formatting, ask the formatter for any required changes.

Re-Uploading Your Book to KDP After Making Changes

Once you receive your updated manuscript files, you will need to re-upload your book to KDP. Some people make the mistake of republishing instead of re-uploading, and this can cause them to lose their hard-earned reviews. In Chapter 20, we will explain how to upload and re-upload your book to KDP, but for now, it pays to know that there is a difference between re-uploading and republishing.

Designing Your Book Layout

The standard layout for books is as follows:

- Title page
- Copyright page
- Table of contents (TOC)
- Body chapters
    - Don't forget to include your mid-book review page in the middle of your book! Some self-publishers choose to include only one review request (either the mid- or end-book review), but we suggest using both because your reader may have the intention of helping you but forget to do so after reading the mid-book review page. The end-book review request serves as a final reminder and can help you catch any fish that slipped through the net the first time!
- End-book review page (As indicated above, this is optional.)
- Conclusion
- References
- Any additional information you wish to add (You may want to add an "About the Author" section or list other books published under your name or pen name.)

Preformatting Your Book

Preformatting a manuscript is crucial because it lays the foundation for the proper structure and layout of your document, ensuring that the final product appears consistent and professional. Formatters, whether human or automated tools, rely on certain formatting cues to understand the hierarchy and organization of the content. Skipping preformatting can lead to confusion, errors, and a disorganized final layout.

Format your headings using the heading 1 (H1), heading 2 (H2), and heading 3 (H3) presets on Word or Google Docs. To do so in Word, just select the text you wish to place in H1, H2, or H3 and select the appropriate heading in the style section of your menu. To do the same in Docs, select the text you wish to place in H1, H2, or H3 on Docs and click **Normal Text**. Then, use the drop-down menu to select the correct heading level.

Word

Docs

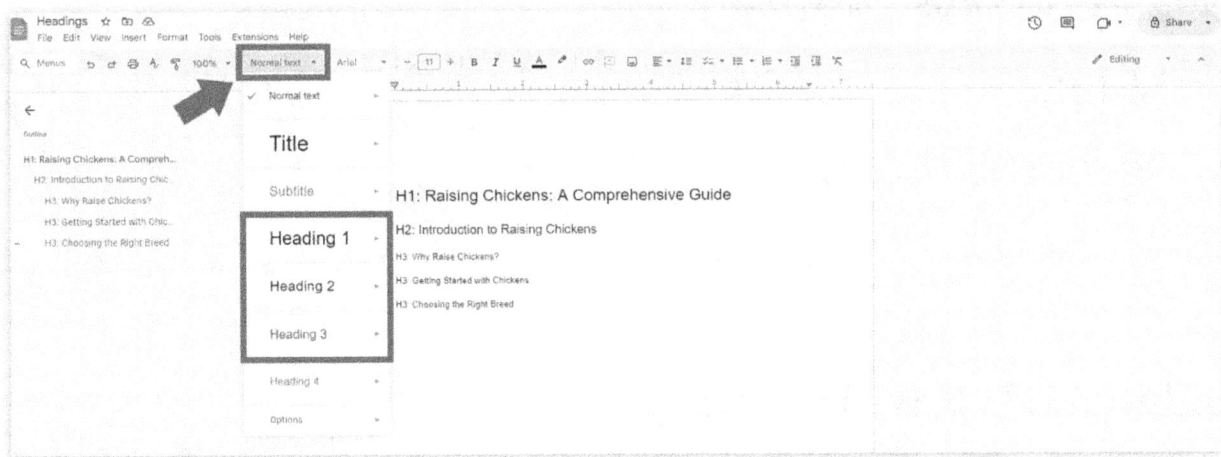

Your choice of headings should make sense and follow a clear hierarchy. Here is an example using the H1, H2, and H3 formats. Typically, your manuscript will contain:

Main Chapter Heading (use H1)
Major Subheading (use H2)
Various Sub-subheadings (use H3)

Your preformatting might look something like this:

Raising Chickens: A Comprehensive Guide (H1)

Introduction to Raising Chickens (H2)

Why Raise Chickens? (H3)

Getting Started with Chickens (H3)

Choosing the Right Breed (H3)

Housing and Care (H2)

How to Build a Chicken Coop (H3)

Materials (H3)

Equipment and Supplies (H3)

Daily Care Routines (H3)

Feeding and Nutrition (H2)

Understanding Chicken Feed (H3)

Keeping Your Chickens Hydrated (H3)

Tasty Treats for Chickens (H3)

Health and Disease Prevention (H2)

Common Chicken Diseases (H3)

Vaccinations and Parasite Control (H3)

Prevent Healthcare for Chickens (H3)

Egg Production and Breeding (H2)

How to Encourage Hens to Lay Eggs (H3)

Handling Broody Hens (H3)

Incubation Tips (H3)

 **Pro Tip:** Check your text various times to ensure that a heading has not ended up in the wrong place in your hierarchy.

Best Software and Online Tools for Formatting

Now it's time to get your book formatted! Whether you are doing the work yourself or asking a designer to do so, you will have to choose from the following software:

- **Vellum (**www.vellum.pub**)**
    - Vellum is a software that enables you to format your book or ebook and convert it into the formats you need to upload it to Amazon Kindle, iBooks, Nook, Kobo, Google Play, and any other digital distributor with the generic EPUB file option.
    - It runs exclusively on MAC, meaning if you have a PC, this choice is not available. Your Mac must be running a compatible version of macOS, with the earliest supported version being macOS Monterey (12). Check Vellum's system requirements at www.publishingservicesbook.com/vellum-faq.

    Note: Vellum does not run on an iPad since the latter uses a different operating system.

- Vellum is an easy-to-use software that practically anyone can learn very quickly. It produces clean, beautiful-looking formatting, and this is why it is used by our formatters at Publishing Services. The downside is that it is somewhat limited in layout, design, and customization options.
- It exports the following file types: EPUB, PDF, DOCX, and RTF.
- Vellum is affordable, and you can try it out for free before making a purchase. You can install it on your MAC and import your manuscript, explore styles, and preview your book. You only need to purchase when you are ready to publish your book. The cost of Vellum Press (to create unlimited ebooks and paperbacks) is $249.99. The cost of Vellum Ebooks (to create unlimited ebooks) is $199.99. The good news is that this is a one-off cost, so once you download it, you can use it for as many books as you like.

- **Atticus (**www.atticus.io**)**
  - Atticus is a web-based writing and formatting tool built as an all-in-one solution for writers and publishers.
  - Unlike Vellum, Atticus has a medium level of difficulty, and there is a learning curve when it comes to making the most of it.
  - Many users feel it isn't as intuitive as Vellum. For instance, when you upload a Word doc to Vellum and Atticus, Vellum instantly recognizes chapters and subtitles, while Atticus doesn't. It can be frustrating and time-consuming to create chapter by chapter all over again.
  - Some users complain that Atticus can be clunky and that the writing feature glitches. It often freezes and crashes, which can waste time and be frustrating.
  - It has odd features that make formatting more complicated. For instance, you cannot mark multiple headings simultaneously and bold them; you have to do so individually. This seems unnecessary at a time when software like Vellum is so user-friendly and intuitive.
  - Like Vellum, Atticus charges a one-off fee of $147.
  - It exports the following file types: EPUB, PDF, and DOCX.

- **Reedsy (**www.reedsy.com**)**
  - Reedsy is a free, web-based writing app and book production tool that allows you to write and format a piece of writing for publishing.
  - This option is very easy to use.
  - It has more limited formatting options than Vellum. When compiling your book, you have only three options for formatting. Atticus and Vellum offer several pages of

formatting options, and they allow you to format your own page. Reedsy also gives users very little control in terms of book dimensions and layout (Brockbank, n.d.).
- ◊ It does not have a preview window, so you cannot check to see how your book would look on various devices.
- ◊ It exports the following file types: EPUB and 3 PDF.

- **Kindle Create (**https://kdp.amazon.com/**)**
  - ◊ Kindle Create is Amazon's free book formatting software.
  - ◊ It works with Windows and MacOS.
  - ◊ It is very easy to use but has fewer customizable features and themes than Vellum or InDesign.
  - ◊ It exports the following file types: EPUB 3 and PDF.
  - ◊ It is not ideal for formatting books with pictures, tables, or graphics.
  - ◊ It doesn't produce the best-looking books.

- **Adobe InDesign (**www.adobe.com**)**
  - ◊ InDesign is a desktop publishing software application for creating flyers, brochures, magazines, newspapers, and books. It is considered the leading software for content creation and design.
  - ◊ It works with Windows and MacOS.
  - ◊ It is arguably one of the hardest pieces of software to master and is often the chosen tool of professional graphic designers.
  - ◊ It offers the highest degree of customization of all the tools mentioned in this section, giving you ultimate control over typography, images, and layout.
  - ◊ InDesign enables you to create intricate, visually impactful graphics for your interiors. It allows you to work in layers, make text wrap-around images, and position elements exactly where you want them on your pages.
  - ◊ It has an impressive range of typography tools and options, including kerning, leading, tracking, and paragraph styles.
    - □ Kerning refers to the adjustment of space between individual pairs of characters. This is done to achieve visually pleasing spacing and avoid awkward gaps or overlaps that certain letter combinations can produce.
    - □ Leading (pronounced "ledding") is the vertical space between lines of text, measured from baseline to baseline. It determines how the lines of text are spaced vertically.

- - Tracking, also known as letter spacing, refers to the uniform adjustment of space between all characters in a block of text.
- InDesign allows you to create master pages and templates for use throughout your book cover and related materials.
- It permits various export options, including PDF presets for print-ready files and ebooks.
- It is optimized for high-resolution printing, meaning if you opt for this software, you know your book will look crisp and sharp.
- It supports vector graphics, which you need to design marketing material like logos and illustrations.
- To use it, you will need to take out a monthly subscription. You can pay $34.49 USD per month (with the right to cancel anytime for free) or take out an annual subscription for $22.99 USD per month. (A fee applies if you cancel after 14 days.) You can also make one annual prepayment for $263.88 USD per year.
- It exports various file types, including EPUB, PDF, DOCX, RTF, and more.

Comparative Table of Formatting Tools

Software	Vellum	Atticus	Reedsy	Kindle Create	InDesign
Platform	MacOS	Web-based	Web-based	Windows, MacOS	Windows, MacOS
Cost	One-time fee of $239.99	One-time fee of $177.87	Free	Free	Subscription (from $22.99 to $34.49 per month or a one-off annual fee of $263.88)
Ease of Use	High (user-friendly)	Medium (learning curve)	High (simple)	High (simple)	Low (professional tool, more complex)
Customization	Moderate	High	Low	Low	Very High
Export Options	EPUB, PDF, DOCX, RTF	EPUB, PDF, DOCX	EPUB 3, PDF	KDP, EPUB	EPUB, PDF, DOCX, RTF, etc.

Software	Vellum	Atticus	Reedsy	Kindle Create	InDesign
Ideal for	Self-publishing authors, especially on Amazon	Authors seeking an all-in-one writing and formatting tool	Authors who prefer online tools and collaboration	Authors who are after a simple formatting tool	Professional designers and advanced users

When choosing your formatting software, consider the following:

- **Content:** If your book has numerous graphs, images, and diagrams, go for Adobe InDesign.
- **Budget:** Keep it realistic and consider the value of each option—including having a professional designer do the work for you.

 **Pro Tip:** Your cover should **not** be added to your formatted book because covers are uploaded separately to KDP.

Formatting is one of the most technical aspects of writing a book, but with a little patience and practice, you can hone techniques that can serve you well, whether you are designing your book yourself or entrusting the task to formatters. The more you know about this part of self-publishing, the clearer your instructions and awareness of your book's specific needs will be. Once your book is fully formatted, you can start thinking about how to market it in a way that makes it stand out. A+ content is a magnificent place to start.

Publishing Services' Formatting Package

We have a talented, creative team of formatters with a combined total of thousands of books under their belts.

The package includes:

- Professional book formatting in various sizes
- A unique interior layout that will make your content shine
- Clean and timeless design to enhance readability

The turnaround time for the package is five business days.

Once our team formats your book, we send you the following files:

- An EPUB file formatted with reflowable text for use on all major ebook vendors, such as Amazon Kindle, Draft2Digital, Lulu, the iBookstore, and others
- A print-ready PDF file for use as a paperback and hardcover book for all major platforms, such as KDP, IngramSpark, D2D Print, and more

To place an order, visit the Publishing Services website at www.publishingservices.com. Scroll down and select **Formatting Package**. Choose your trim size, indicate how many images and tables your manuscript includes, and select your word count. Double-check that your manuscript is completely ready for formatting.

Fill in the rest of the fields, indicating your book's title, subtitle, and author. Upload the manuscript in Word format, choose your style template, font, and block quotation style, and select which line spacing and font size you would like.

Choose optional add-ons (such as the Vellum source files, a Book Description Package, or the Review Page Package). Confirm that all relevant information has been uploaded, and click **Add to Cart**.

Comparison: DIY Formatting and a Publishing Services Formatting

DIY Formatting	**Publishing Services Formatting Package**
■ This is free or cheap, if using tools like Word or Scrivener. ■ Some advanced formatting may require a purchase.	■ The PS basic Formatting Package costs $97 (includes manuscripts up to 50k word count that contain up to 20 images/tables). ■ The price varies if the book exceeds a certain word count or includes a higher number of images.
■ It can be extremely time-consuming. ■ You must master software, learn formatting rules, and troubleshoot errors (like page breaks, headers, margins, etc.).	■ We offer a guaranteed turnaround time of 5 business days.
■ Quality will vary based on the author's skills and software limitations. ■ Mistakes (like inconsistent font sizes, incorrect margins, and poor text alignment) detract from professionalism.	■ You'll receive high-quality, polished results with consistent spacing, proper margins, chapter layouts, font usage, and enhanced readability. ■ The final product is polished and error-free.
■ Complex formatting (e.g., tables, images, footnotes, drop caps) is challenging without advanced knowledge.	■ Professionals easily manage all of these complex elements.
■ You must ensure compatibility with various platforms (e.g., Kindle, Kobo, Print on Demand). ■ Different approaches may be needed to format a manuscript for both ebook and print; issues may arise if not done properly.	■ Your book is optimized for all formats, including print and multiple ebook platforms.
■ Revisions can be frustrating to effect.	■ Unlimited formatting revisions are included in the package for free. ■ Style/content changes are subject to an extra charge, depending on the amount of work involved. ■ Minor content changes are offered at no extra cost.

Chapter 16

Maximizing Sales with A+ Content

When it comes to marketing, prioritizing the visual aspect of your content is vital. Statistics show that 91% of consumers prefer visual to written content, and articles with images are twice as likely to be shared as those without them (Cawley 2024). This is why one of the most important marketing tools for generating interest in your book is A+ content—a free marketing tool inside Amazon's Seller Central.

Why A+ Content Makes a Difference

A+ Content helps you bring your book's story to life by adding customized text, images, and other elements to your product detail page on Amazon. When optimally created, it can increase your conversion rate by 3% to 10%. The average conversion rate increase when using A+ Content is 5.6%. Essentially, this means that out of every 100 people visiting your product listing, between 5 or 6 more people will buy your book (Connolly 2024)!

To see what a typical piece of A+ Content looks like, click any bestselling book on Amazon. If it has A+ Content, you will find it by scrolling beneath the product description and looking for a section called "From the Author."

A+ Content isn't just about gorgeous imagery and engaging copywriting; it is also a sneak peek into the interior contents of your book and a useful way to help readers make more informed decisions.

Think about your own experience when you search for a book on your chosen topic. The keywords found in the titles and subtitles of various competing books in a niche may be similar. Most books provide a "Read Sample" option, but sometimes all you will find there is an introduction or a part of one chapter. Simply reading the table of contents is sometimes unhelpful as well because chapter headings are often written with metaphors or catchy language that may not necessarily tell you what the chapters are about. A+ Content is a magnificent way to let your audience know that your content will address their pain points and help them reach their end goals.

A+ Content is also a great way to create a recognizable brand and boost customer loyalty as soon as your book is live!

Goals for Effective A+ Content

From a sales viewpoint, your A+ Content is like a book description. It should follow a formula that leads your readers to buy your book. Your content should contain the following components:

- A catchy hook sentence and your book cover
- Two to three good reasons they should buy your book
- What pain points your book will address
- A statement that closes the sale

Ensure your A+ Content hits your target by doing the following:

- Prioritize the visual aspect of your content. Yes, A+ Content includes text, but by the time your audience reaches it, they will most likely have read your book description, customer reviews, and the sample you provide. Therefore, they are likely to have less patience to read the entirety of the text and be more interested in what the images tell them.
- If your book has images, diagrams, or customized illustrations in its interior, include them so your reader can envision its contents. Some authors showcase a chapter title or a page or two of the book's interior to show off their slick formatting and beautiful imagery.
- Use short, bold statements that hit your target audience's pain points.
- Show your book's main idea at first glance.
- Announce useful bonus content such as checklists, assessments, cheat sheets, and similar.
- Align your A+ Content with what your audience wants. For instance, if you are selling a coloring book for kids, effective A+ Content should contain a few of the book's most beautiful illustrations. If you're selling a self-help book on cognitive behavioral therapy, your A+ Content should reveal a couple of worksheets, quotes from authority or well-known reviewers, and a couple of key chapter headings. If you're selling a fantasy book, your A+ Content could include a map of your fictional universe, the character design of one or more characters, and quotes from reviewers. For inspiration, see what content bestsellers in your category have produced.

 **Pro Tip:** If you have published multiple books in the same niche, you can include a collage of your books in your A+ Content. This will help to establish your authority. You can also include links to these books in case your readers are interested in more of your work.

Common Mistakes to Avoid When Designing A+ Content

To ensure your A+ Content boosts your conversion rate, avoid the following:

- Huge chunks of text (Chances are, doing so will try potential buyers' patience, and they will click off the page. Use short, bold statements instead of paragraphs if possible.)
- Low-quality, blurry, or poorly styled images
- A cluttered or over-complex layout
- Inconsistent branding (Align the style of your A+ Content with your book's cover, interior, and content.)
- The use of content that violates intellectual property rights (Buy your images from a professional photographer or illustrator, or use stock images bought from Shutterstock and other leading companies.)
- The use of content restricted by KDP as stipulated in the A+ Content Guidelines section (Kindle Direct Publishing, n.d.-c) including:
    - Guarantees and reference to off-Amazon return or refund policies
    - Violations of KDP Terms and Conditions and Content Guidelines
    - Shipping details (for instance, "free shipping," QR barcodes, and personal information such as telephone numbers and addresses)
    - Quotes or attributions to people, customers, or other private figures (A maximum of four quotes or endorsements is allowed, and these should only be from well-known publications or public figures and must be accompanied by the author and, if citing a publication, the title.)
    - Reference to or comparisons with competitor products (for instance, specific names, references to "others" and similar)
    - Comparison charts to anything other than books in your KDP account
    - Pricing, promotional details, or discounts (words such as "affordable," "cheap," "bonus," and "free")
    - Language directing customers to purchase ("buy now," "add to cart," "get yours now," or "shop with us")

- ◇ Time-sensitive information (words like "now," "latest," and phrases like "on sale now," "the latest product," or "the best yet") or references to holidays
- ◇ Stand-alone symbols (Trademarks and copyright symbols are acceptable if they're of reasonable size and either already included on product packaging or always displayed as part of the logo or both. Any trademark or copyright symbols must be removed from the text.)
- ◇ Web links or language attempting to redirect to other sites inside or outside of Amazon (including your other products)
- ◇ Any content that includes hate speech, promotes the abuse or sexual exploitation of children, contains pornography, glorifies rape or pedophilia, advocates terrorism, or is deemed inappropriate or offensive
- ◇ References to off-Amazon customer service or contact information (for example, "contact us if you have problems," phone numbers, contact email)
- ◇ Images or text that attempt to mimic Amazon logos, detail page headings, or details (References to Amazon-supported programs or branded products are permitted.)

Key Features of Effective A+ Content: Examples of What Works and What Doesn't

Let's take a look at three examples of well-designed A+ Content and discuss what makes them so effective.

A+ Content #1

The colors, fonts, and layouts have been chosen thoughtfully and align with the book's cover and branding. The text summarizes all the tasks the book can help the reader with without giving too much away. The images are crisp, clear, and well-chosen. The yellow and orange hues throughout the design are warm and sunny and conjure up the joy of the outdoor lifestyle. The graphics, meanwhile, serve to call the reader's attention to the key benefits of the book.

Scan the QR code to view this image in color.

A+ Content #2

Once again, the choice of fonts, imagery, and graphics is ideal. The images of chickens, eggs, and farmers capture the joy of raising and working with farm animals. The colors are nature-inspired, with green and sunny gold text and imagery holding sway. The text clearly informs readers of the book's content. It also showcases the problems they are hoping to solve by reading the book while hinting at additional content.

Scan the QR code to view this image in color.

154

A+ Content #3

As is the case with the first two examples, this design has clear, easy-to-read text, fitting colors, and eye-catching graphics. Its modern, youthful style and informative textual information let the reader know they will find the latest techniques and information they need to raise healthy, happy chickens and harvest eggs daily.

Scan the QR code to view this image in color.

How to Design A+ Content

If you are creative and have a knack for design, you may decide to design your A+ Content yourself. If so, follow the steps outlined below.

 *Choose Your Modules*

Think of modules as different boxes you can stack on top of each other to create a poster or brochure-like work; we have included examples later in this section. Amazon offers you a total of seventeen modules; however, you are limited to seven for your A+ Content. You can combine these modules however you like or select the same module over and over again, up to seven times (except Module #1, which you can only use once). Amazon joins the modules seamlessly so they look like a cohesive design. Designers typically use around three modules to create their "poster" because effective A+ Content should not be too long.

The 17 modules (and their respective dimensions) are as follows:

Module #1: Standard Company Logo

You can only use this module once on an A+ page.

Dimensions: 600 x 180 pixels

Module #2: Standard Comparison Chart

Dimensions: 150 x 300 pixels

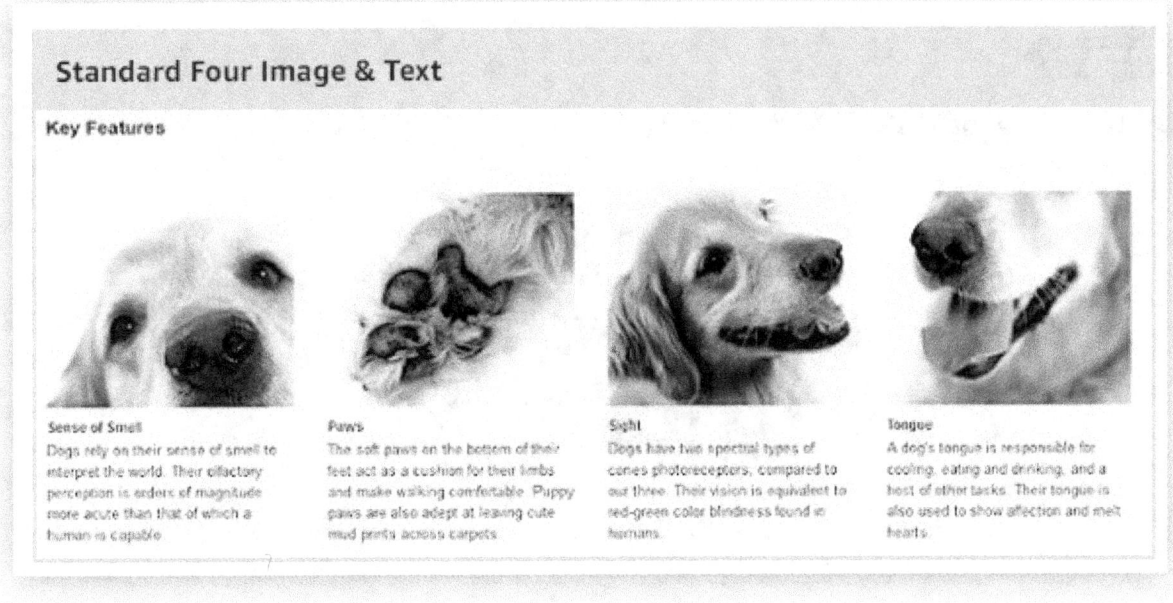

Module #3: Standard Four Image & Text

Dimensions: 220 x 220 pixels

Module #4: Standard Four Image/Text Quadrant

Dimensions: 135 x 135 pixels

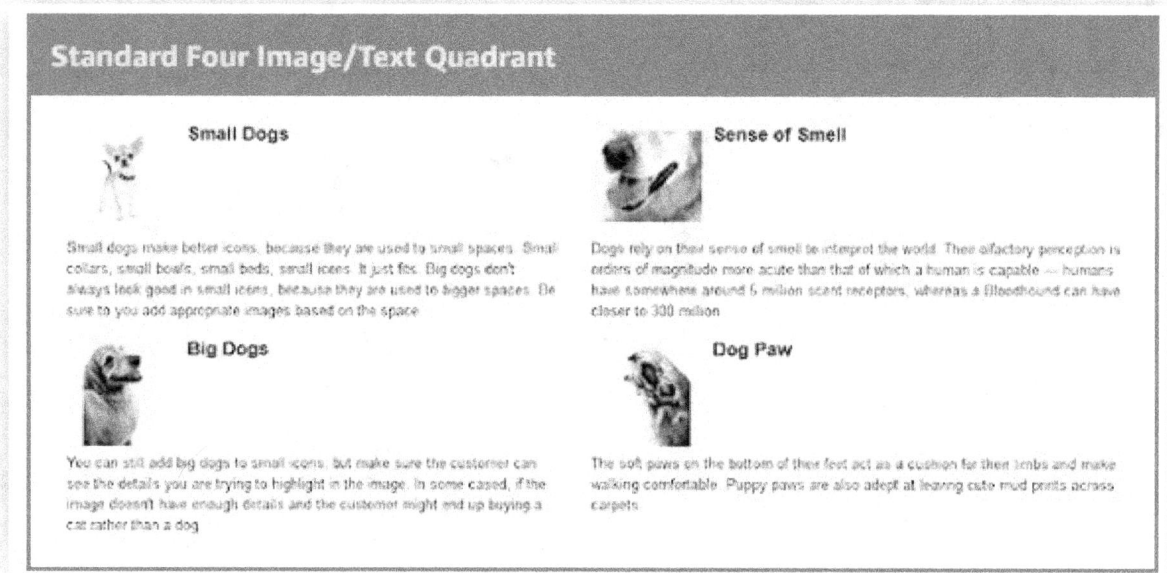

Module #5: Standard Image & Dark Text Overlay

Dimensions: 970 x 300 pixels

Module #6: Standard Image & Light Text Overlay

Dimensions: 970 x 300 pixels

Module #7: Standard Image Header with Text

Dimensions: 970 x 600 pixels

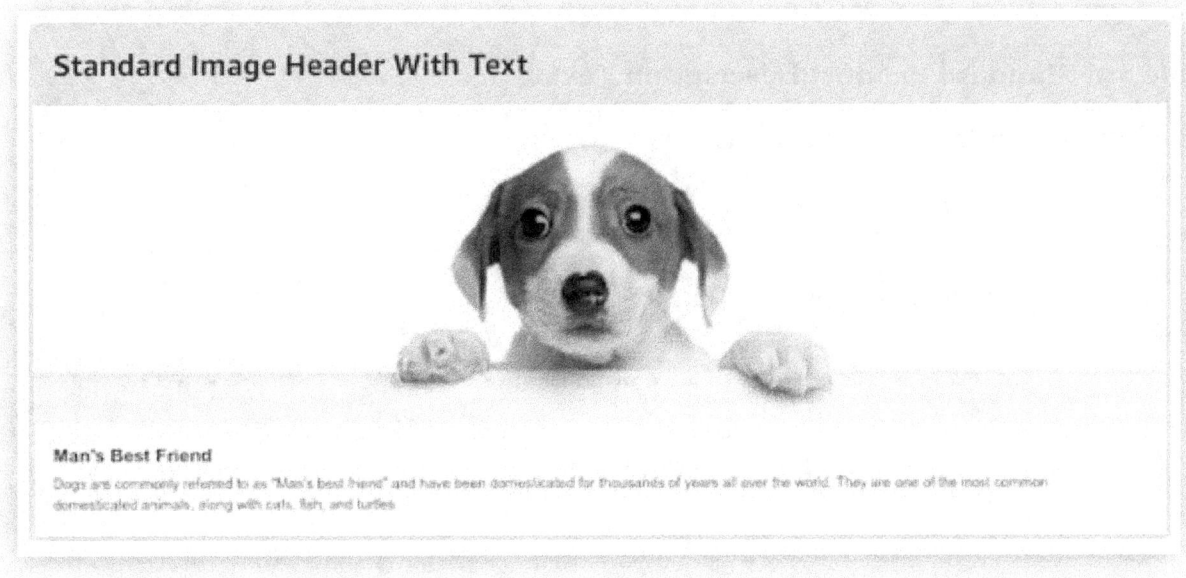

Module #8: Standard Multiple Image Module A

Dimensions: 300 x 300 pixels

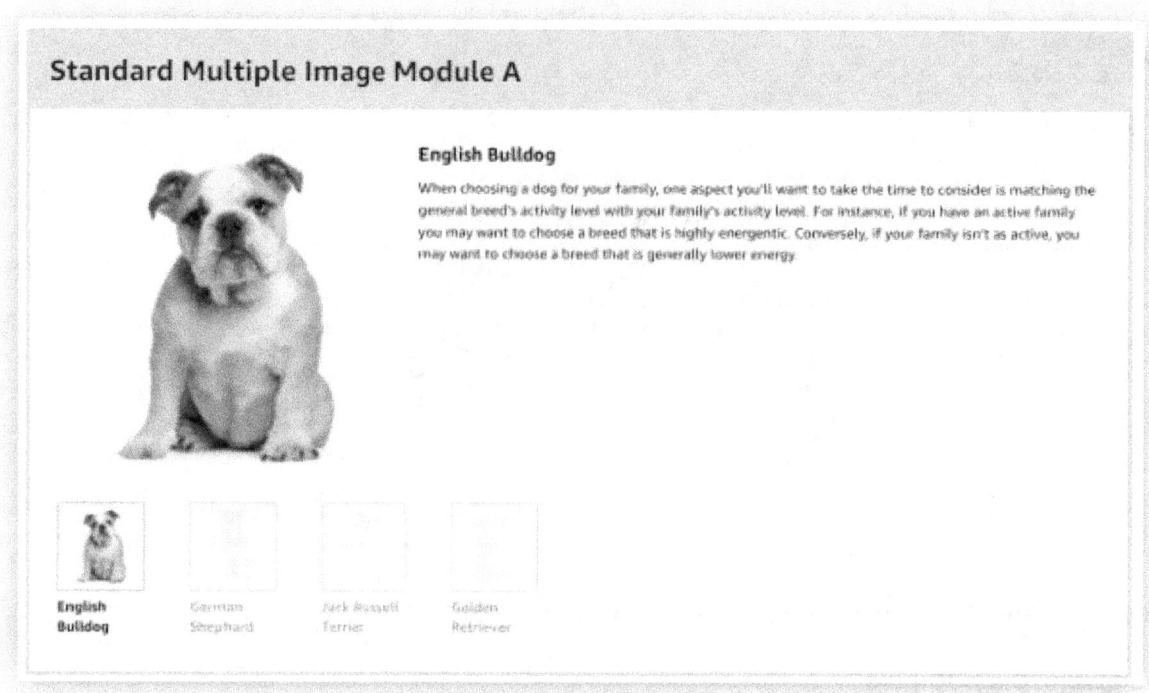

Module #9: Standard Product Description Text

This module must include formattable rich text.

Module #10: Standard Single Image & Highlights

Dimensions: 300 x 300 pixels

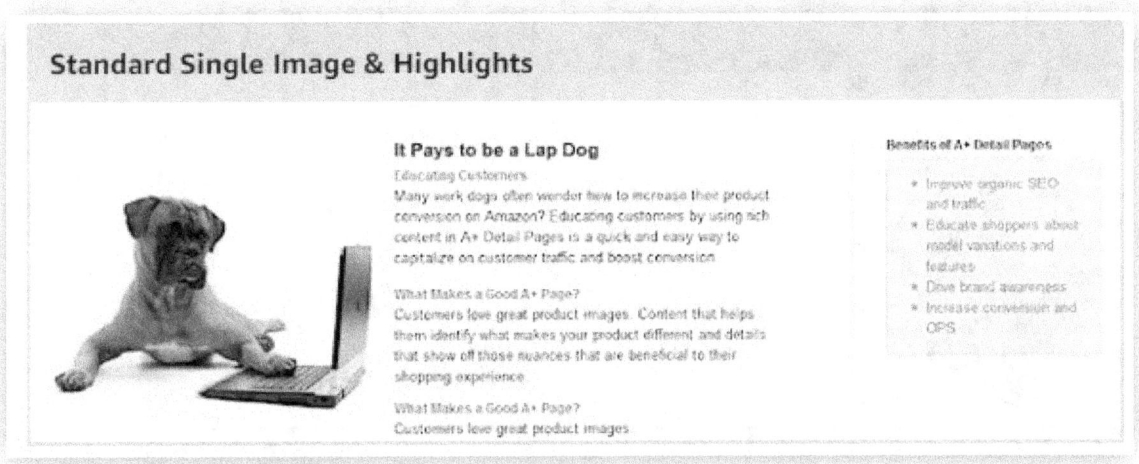

Module #11: Standard Single Image & Sidebar

Dimensions: Main Image: 300 × 400 pixels, Sidebar Image: 350 × 175 pixels

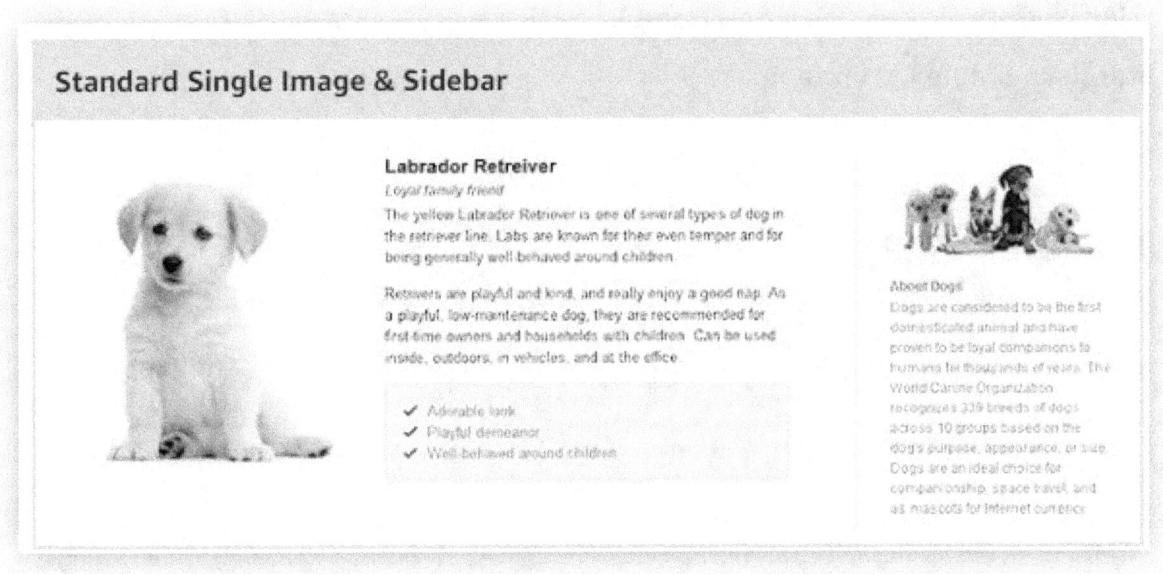

Module #12: Standard Single Image & Specs Detail

Dimensions: 300 x 300 pixels

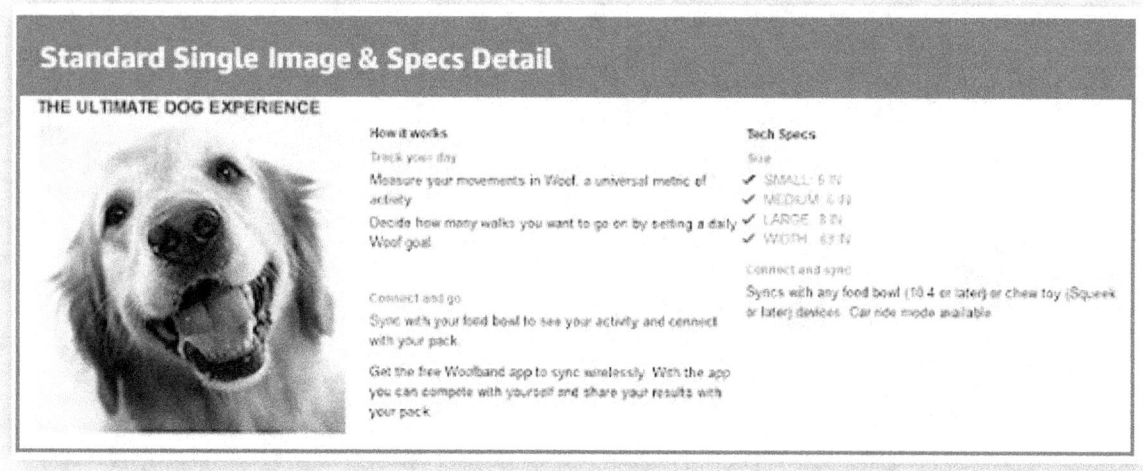

Module #13: Standard Single Left Image

Dimensions: 300 x 300 pixels

Module #14: Standard Single Right Image

Dimensions: 300 x 300 pixels

Module #15: Standard Technical Specifications

This module has no images, just a top headline with an area beneath where between 4 and 16 technical specifications with titles and definitions can be added.

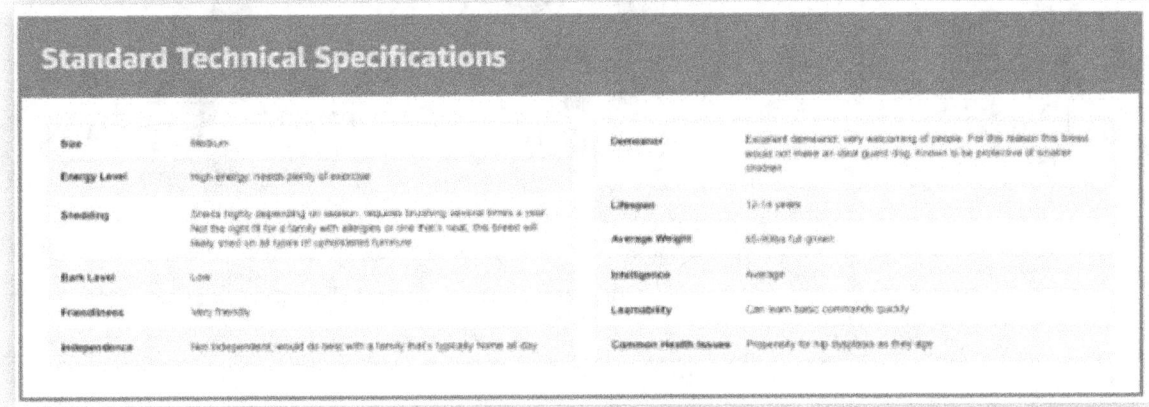

Module #16: Standard Text

This module must include formattable, rich text.

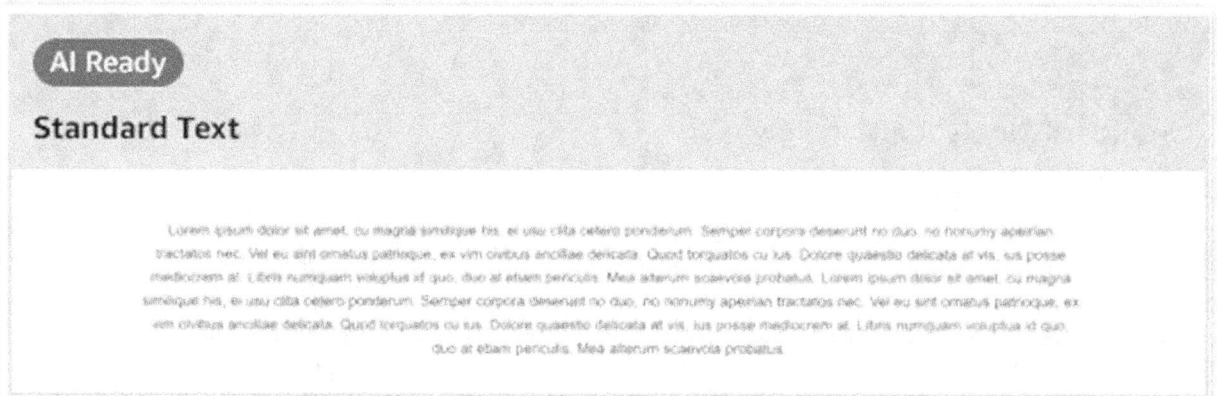

Module #17: Standard Three Images & Text

Dimensions: 300 x 300 pixels

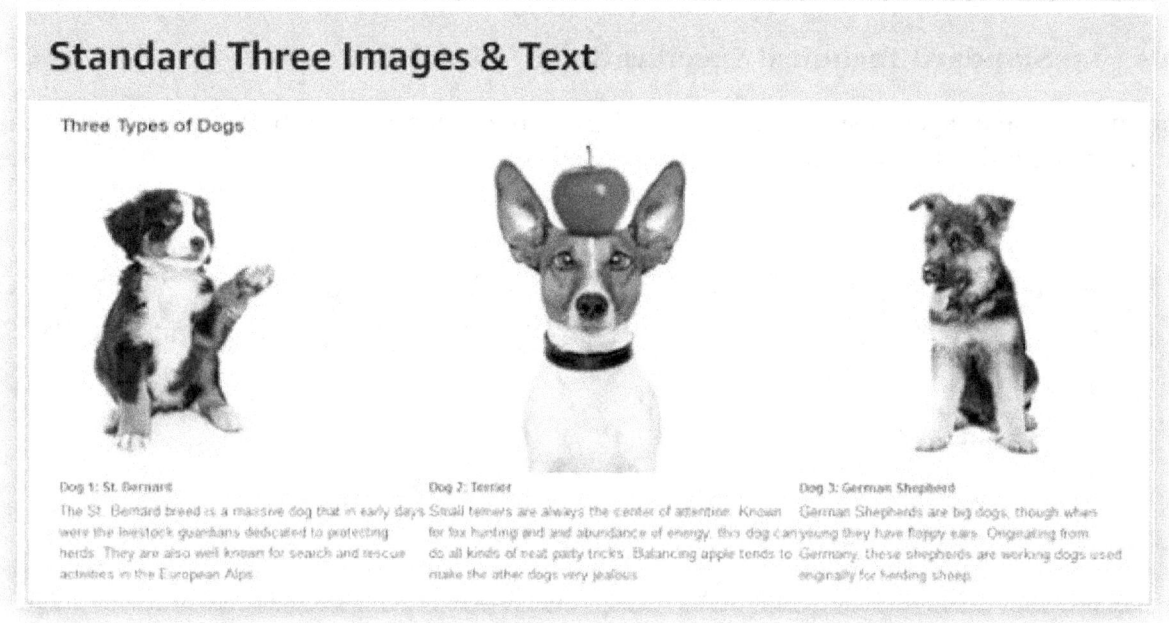

 **Get Your Visuals Ready**

Visuals can include pictures, graphs, maps, diagrams, and character designs (for fiction books). As you can see from the mock-up modules, some don't require many images at all, while others require multiple images. Remember to choose visuals that align with your brand, book cover, and interior. Note that all modules prescribe the resolution of the images required, and your images will have to comply with these requirements. The pictures need to have a resolution of 300 dpi (dots per inch).

 **Get Your Text Ready**

As mentioned above, the key to crafting winning text for this section is to keep it short and summarize what your audience can expect to find. Read the Amazon A+ Content Guidelines (www.publishingservicesbook.com/a-plus-guidelines), which provide tips that will stop your content from being rejected.

 **Upload to KDP**

Below, you will find instructions for uploading your content to KDP. The start and end procedures are always the same. What differs is the modules you wish to use. If you order an A+ Content package from Publishing Services, we will provide step-by-step instructions tailored to the layout you choose. If you create your own A+ Content, note which module sizing you use to create your content, and then select the correct module during the upload process.

Go to your KDP dashboard and select **Marketing**:

Scroll down and choose a marketplace. You will need to repeat each of the following steps for each marketplace (e.g., Amazon.com, Amazon.com.au, Amazon.ca, etc.) in which you want the A+ Content to be shown on the product page.

Click **Start creating A+ Content**.

Enter your Content name (book title).

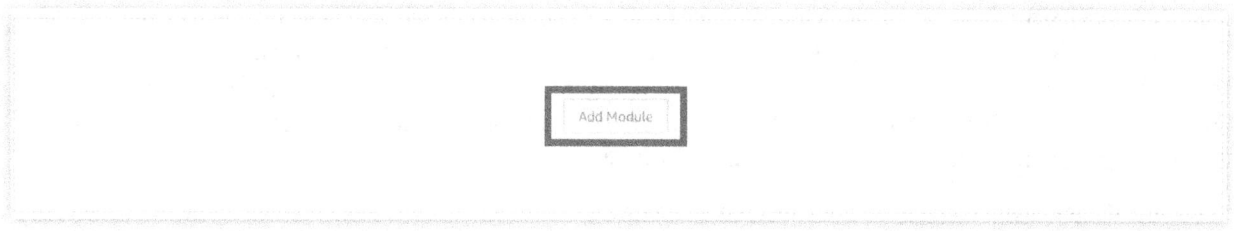

Click **Add Module**.

After you've selected a module, it's added to the content layout.

To add another module, click **Add Module** again.

After you've added modules to your layout, you can use the icons in the upper right-hand corner of the module to move a module up or down. You can also click the **X** to remove a module. If you want to remove a module, there will be a prompt to confirm that action.

To add images, click **Add Image** to drag and drop or upload an image from your computer. KDP won't resize images, so make sure the image file is sized correctly.

Finally, you should add your text unless you have embedded it in the image. In this case, leave the text boxes empty. You can type directly into the module text fields or copy and paste text from a file on your computer.

Once everything is uploaded, click **Next: Apply ASINs**.

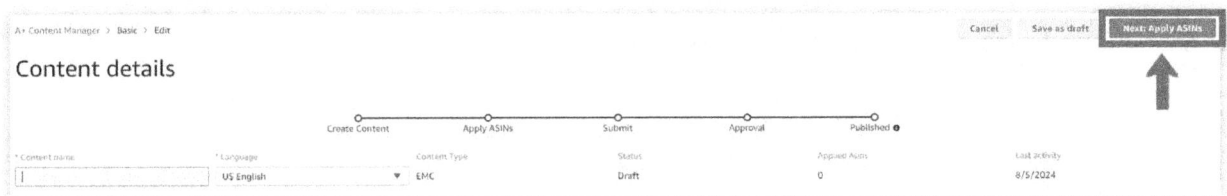

Add ASINs (one at a time).

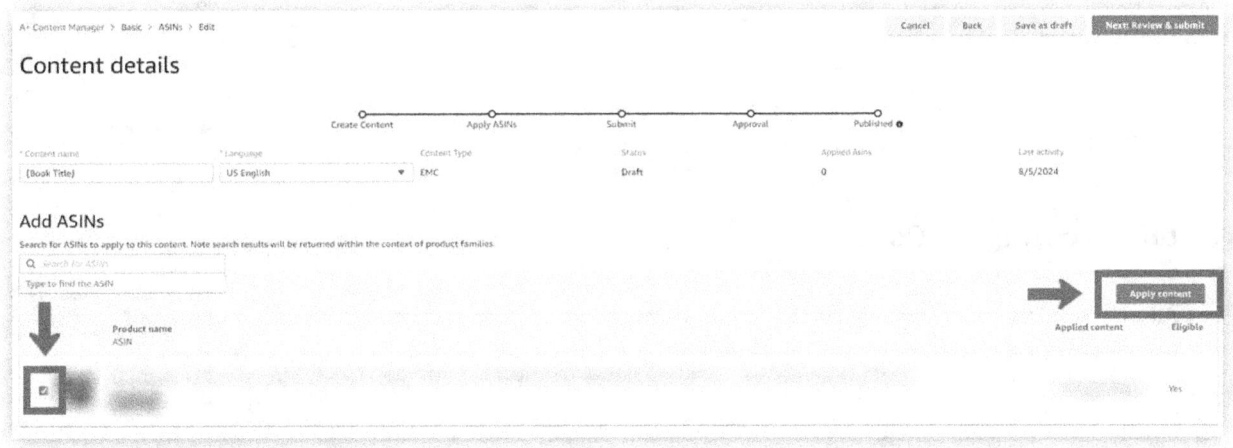

Click **Apply Content** and repeat until each ASIN is added (ebook, paperback, hardback).

Click **Next: Review & Submit**.

Once the content is reviewed and everything looks good, click **Submit for Approval**.

Go back into the KDP dashboard, click **Marketing**, and repeat the process for every marketplace.

How to Upload Your A+ Content to Non-English Speaking Marketplaces

Go to your KDP dashboard and select **Marketing**.

Scroll down and go to **Choose a Marketplace**. You will need to repeat every following step for each marketplace where you want the A+ Content to be shown on the product page.

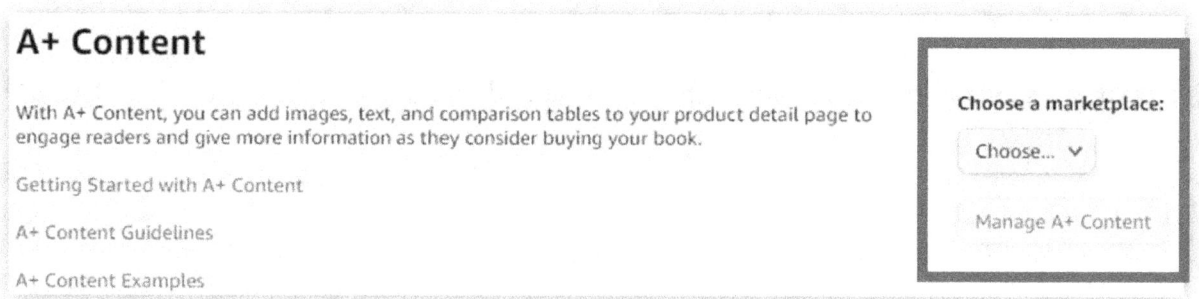

Click **Start Creating A+ Content**.

Select **English** from the Language drop-down menu.

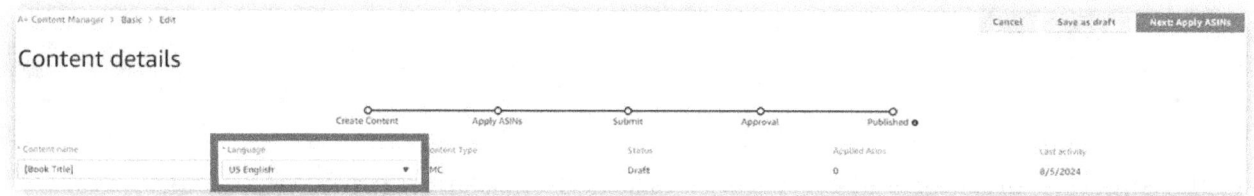

From here onwards, it is the same process as before.

Design Your Content on Canva (optional)

You can theoretically create your own A+ Content on Canva, but this should be the absolute last resort unless you are a graphic designer. Your A+ Content is a vital part of your branding strategy, and it should look slick and professional. You will need to respect the module sizes stipulated by Amazon, but you can upload a design you have already fully created on Canva. To do so, follow these steps:

- Create an account on Canva.
- Click **Custom Size**.

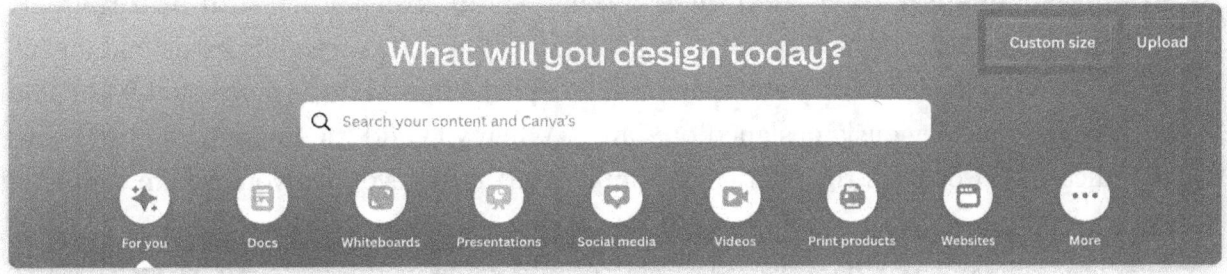

- Size it at the width and height stipulated by the modules you wish to use on Amazon. For instance, if you decide to go with four **Standard Image & Dark Text Overlay** modules stacked one on top of the other, then choose 970 pixels for width and 300 pixels for height on Canva.

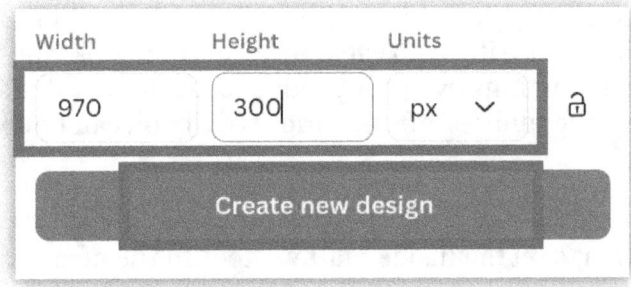

- Click **Create New Design,** and you can add as many pages as you like. Each "page" on Canva corresponds to one "module" on Amazon.
- To export your designs, go to the top right of the menu on Canva, click the Share symbol, and then **Download**. You can download the design in either JPG or PNG format. You will be asked what size you want to download it in. Start on 970 x 300 pixels, but if you upload the design and it doesn't look right, you can go back to Canva and increase the size a couple of notches. Doing so will add more pixels and most likely improve the quality.

How to Upload Your Canva Design to Amazon

- Go to your KDP dashboard and click **Marketing**. Scroll down to A+Content and choose your marketplace. If you are selling your book on various Amazon marketplaces (for instance, Amazon.com, Amazon.co.uk, Amazon.com.au, and Amazon.ca), you will have to upload your A+ Content to each individual marketplace.

- Click **Add Module**. If you are designing the module yourself, then you will simply add a headline/text/images in the indicated spots. If you choose to design your modules on Canva, then for sample #1 above, for instance, choose the appropriate sized module (in this case, **Standard Image & Dark Text Overlay,** 970 x 300 pixels). Click **Add an Image.** (You will not need to add any text because your design has already been fully made on Canva.) Do not add text to the box, and your design will be uploaded. Add three more modules to add all the images you previously designed on Canva. When you add the images, you will be asked to indicate keywords for them. You can simply type in whatever text you used in your image.

- Once you upload all your modules, click **Next,** and it will take you to the next section, which involves adding your ASINs. To obtain this number, just go to your KDP dashboard and get the ASIN of the book you want your A+ Content to apply to. Apply it to each of your book formats (paperback, hardback, ebook, etc.)

- Submit the content and wait for Amazon to approve it.

- You can always go back and edit your content if you want to change it subsequently.

Pro Tip: BookBeam (www.publishingservicesbook.com/bookbeam) has a tool called Listing Optimizer. To use it, just paste the link to your book, and it will give you a score and advice on how you can improve your product page. It provides advice on your review and ratings numbers, the number of categories your book can be found in, your A+ Content, and more.

Visuals aren't everything; what's on the inside matters, too! In the next chapter, we will enhance the quality of your content via a helpful group of people: your beta readers!

Publishing Services' A+ Content Package

Over the years, we have created hundreds of A+ Content designs. Our experienced team of copywriters and graphic designers work closely to create a winning combination of images and text for our clients' books.

The package includes:

- Exclusive banners with a custom-made mock-up of your book and catchy text (The number of banners depends on the module you choose.)
- Professionally designed images with matching text (The number of images depends on your chosen module.)

The turnaround time is seven business days.

To place an order, visit the Publishing Services website at www.publishingservices.com. Scroll down and select **A+ Content Package**. Choose the layout you like the most, then upload your manuscript, book cover, and description. You can purchase add-ons, including a Book Description Package or a Review Page Package.

Indicate your target audience and niche, as well as links to other books you have published (if this isn't your first book).

Make any special requests and share a bit about your vision if you have a specific one. If not, our team can create one for you. Tell us how you heard about us, make sure all key information has been uploaded or indicated, and click **Add to Cart**.

Comparison: DIY A+ Content and a Publishing Services A+ Content

DIY	Publishing Services
This is free.	You pay $127 for our A+ Content Package.
It may look simplistic and unprofessional.	It looks slick, polished, and professional.
The process is time-consuming.	The final product is ready in 7 days.
Your final product may contain images that do not align with your brand and target audience.	It contains professional images by professional photographers, illustrators, or designers.
It can contain text that fails to captivate an audience.	Your text is written by professional copywriters who know how to get customers to make a purchase.
The design process involves having to use software you may not be familiar with.	Our A+ Content is made by designers familiar with a wide array of software used to create stunning-looking designs.

Chapter 17

How to Connect with Beta Readers and Get Valuable Feedback

Visit Amazon's Books section, and you will see that even popular books have complaints or negative reviews.

Here are a few:

"This book is just a rehash of information that can be found in other self-help books. It's not very original, and I could have found this information myself by searching online."

"The characters are unlikeable, and the plot is unbelievable. How could anyone believe this narrative?"

"Again, people have fallen prey to influencer hype. This book is just common sense dressed up as revolutionary advice. Waste of money and time!"

"The writing is too scientific. I didn't want something that sounds this academic. I found it confusing."

"The writing is immature and too colloquial. This is a book on cognitive-behavioral therapy and the writer is supposed to be someone who has studied psychology for years. It doesn't show!"

"More typos than you could poke a stick at. The writer consistently confused "to" and "too" and it felt like I was reading a high school student's essay."

"Full of clichés."

"Full of factual inaccuracies. Michael Schumacher wasn't the driver who won the most Monaco Grand Prix races. That was Ayrton Senna."

"Could have used case studies and stories to break up the dry theory."

One thing many of these comments have in common is that they could have been avoided. But changing your book after everything has already been proofed and edited is expensive, especially in the case of printed books. This is why beta readers—test readers of unreleased work—can be invaluable. They point out things you can quickly change, especially factual errors that can hurt your credibility and result in negative reviews.

What Makes a Good Beta Reader?

Ideally, your beta reader needs to be someone who reads widely, especially in the genre you are writing for. They need to be able to provide honest, constructive feedback and identify aspects such as writing style, tone, and elements that can improve your book. For instance, if you are publishing a fiction book, your beta readers should be able to leave an opinion on the characters, plot, tone, and pace of your book. They do not need to be editors or writers or know technical terms. They simply need to be avid and patient readers. A book that is over 30K words long can take quite a few hours to get through, so they should be committed to reading your book in its entirety, not just skimming through it and leaving superficial comments.

A Questionnaire for Beta Readers

When you enlist beta readers, send them a short questionnaire to fill out after they finish reading your book.

Non-Fiction

For a non-fiction book, this might include the following questions:

1. **Overall Impressions:** What is your general view of this book? Was it engaging, or did it lag at any point?
2. **Tone and Style:** Was the tone right for the book? Was it too formal or informal in your view?
3. **Content and Structure:** Was there a logical flow of chapter content and ideas? Were any sections repetitive or unnecessary? Was there anything you think a reader might take offense to in the book?
4. **Favorite and Least Favorite Parts:** What were your favorite parts of the book? What were your least favorite?
5. **Clarity:** Were any sections too difficult to understand? Was there any jargon that needed to be explained?
6. **Emotional Impact:** Did anything in the book evoke strong emotions?
7. **Visuals and Design:** Did the visuals enhance your understanding or enjoyment of the book? Were they well integrated with the text?

8. **Suggestions for Improvement:** Do you have any suggestions for improving the book? Are there any topics that need further expansion or explanation?
9. **Audience:** Who do you think is the target audience for this book?
10. **Final Thoughts:** Would you recommend this book to other readers? Why or why not?

Fiction

For a fiction book, you can ask the following questions:

1. **Overall Impressions:** Did you enjoy the book? Were any specific parts boring or irrelevant?
2. **Plot and Pacing:** Was the plot compelling and believable? Was the flow good? Did any parts lag?
3. **Characters:** Were the characters realistic and multifaceted? Did their motivations and actions make sense? Which characters did you like the most and the least?
4. **Setting:** Did the setting feel realistic?
5. **Dialogue:** Did the dialogue between the characters flow naturally?
6. **Emotional Impact:** Did you feel emotionally connected to any specific characters? Did any events in the book bring about strong emotions in you?
7. **Suspense:** Were there moments you found exciting, so much so that you couldn't wait to discover what happened?
8. **Plot Holes:** Did you identify any plot holes or inconsistencies? Was anything confusing?
9. **The Ending:** Was the ending satisfying? Did you enjoy it, or would you have ended it differently?
10. **Favorite and Least Favorite Parts:** What were your favorite parts of the book? What were your least favorite?
11. **Suggestions for Improvement:** As a whole, how would you improve this book?
12. **Final Thoughts:** Would you recommend this book to others? Why or why not?

Where Can You Find Beta Readers?

You can ask friends and family to serve as beta readers, but don't rely exclusively on loved ones. Because they aren't approaching this as a job (as a professional would), they can have great intentions but simply lack the time to read your book patiently. Some may simply skim over the book and give you generic feedback, meaning you won't gain much from the process. You can find beta readers on many online sites, including Goodreads, Reddit, and Facebook, all with beta reader groups. Some people read books for free; others charge a price.

Upwork and Fiverr are also great places to look for beta readers. Check out Fiverr, for instance, and you will see that a beta reader charges everything from around $40 to $400 or more (depending on their experience and ratings). Upwork has similar pricing. Earlier, we wrote about the importance of starting a Facebook page. Once you have grown a following on your page, you will have access to many potential beta readers. You can also run Facebook ads for beta readers. These people can then form part of your advanced reader copy (ARC) team.

Once you receive your beta readers' feedback, make the required changes.

Pro Tip: The difference between beta readers and advanced reader copy team members is that the former usually receive an earlier copy of your book. ARC members receive a near-final version of the book and focus more on promotion and reviews.

Once your beta readers have made their helpful suggestions, it's time to set up your publishing accounts. Discover how in the next chapter!

Chapter 18

Step-by-Step Guide to Setting Up Your Publishing Accounts

In this short chapter, we will explain how to set up your KDP, IngramSpark, and ACX accounts. We will also provide instructions for alternative accounts to ACX if you are outside the US, Canada, Ireland, and the UK.

How to Set Up a KDP Account

In order to publish books on Amazon through Kindle Direct Publishing (KDP) and earn royalties, you need a KDP account, which is different from your normal Amazon account. You can use your existing Amazon account to sign up for KDP or create a separate Amazon account specifically for KDP. This can help keep your personal purchases and publishing endeavors separate.

It is completely free to set up an Amazon account.

KDP requires three different types of information to set up an account:

- Your personal information
- Your bank information
- Your tax information

To set up a KDP account, follow these steps:

 Go to https://kdp.amazon.com and click **Sign In**. You can use your Amazon login to register by signing in with your existing login. You can also create a new account if you wish.

 You will be asked to fill in your author/publisher information. At this point, you will be asked if you want to open your account as an individual or company. Check out the following table for the differences between the two options. It is advisable to check with an accountant and seek legal advice to ensure you don't pay more taxes than necessary.

Individual	Company
Easy and fast, doesn't require any paperwork	Potentially less taxed if you are in a higher tax bracket
Could end up paying more taxes on royalties, depending on employment situation (higher income = likely higher taxes on book royalties)	Limited liability—your company and personal assets are kept separate
	Gives you a business you could sell in the future if your brand is very successful
	Able to write off expenses when you file your taxes
	Extra paperwork, money, and time to initially set up the company; Will need to comply with ongoing paperwork

 **Pro Tip:** you can always start as an individual and switch to a company account once you put out your books and start making an income from your book sales. It makes more sense to start this way if you haven't published any books yet.

 You will see a section called "Getting Paid." KDP can pay you via direct deposit, wire transfer, or check. Check out the different KDP payment options at www.publishingservicesbook.com/kdp-payment-options.

KDP recommends getting paid via direct deposit because it typically has no minimum payment threshold and is fast, secure, and environmentally sustainable.

You will notice that KDP asks for your tax identification number (TIN). If you do not reside in the US, you must supply the equivalent of this number in your country.

- In the UK, this is your unique tax reference number (UTR).

- In Australia, this is your tax file number (TFN).
- In Canada, this is your social insurance number (SIN).

04 » If you do not live in the US, you will have to fill in a W-8BEN form. This is called the "Certificate of Foreign Status of Beneficial Owner for United States Tax Withholding and Reporting (Individuals)" form. It's pretty simple to fill in. Just state your name, address, and your foreign tax identification number. Once you fill this out, Amazon will inform you immediately if all the information required has been correctly submitted.

05 » Review and accept the KDP terms of service.

Once your account is created, you can access the KDP bookshelf and start publishing e-books, paperbacks, and hardback books if you wish!

Important Tax Numbers and Royalties Information for Authors

Make it a point to provide this information to KDP. If you do not have a tax number, or you do not provide it to KDP, Amazon will withhold a specific percentage from the royalties they pay out to you for tax purposes. In the US, this amounts to 30%.

Amazon KDP does not withhold taxes from US-based self-publishing authors selling on Amazon.com. However, it may do so if you are based abroad. To determine the percentage of your royalties that Amazon withholds, follow the steps below.

 Go to the free tax treaty calculator. The link below will take you to a section called "Treaty Status": www.publishingservicesbook.com/tax-treaty-calculator

 Choose your **Jurisdiction**. We have clicked the US because we hypothetically want to sell our books on Amazon.com.

 You will see a list of treaty partners for the United States and notice that all the countries have a check mark. Select **None** (to deselect all countries), then select your country of residence. We selected Australia in the example below.

 Choose your treaty status. Select **Active**.

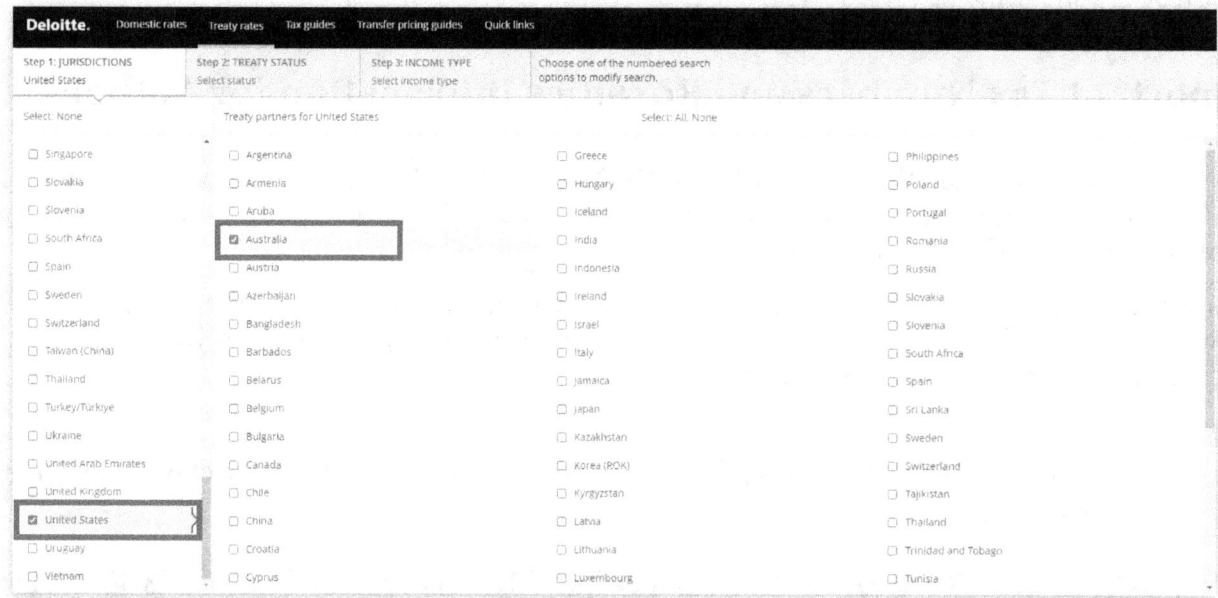

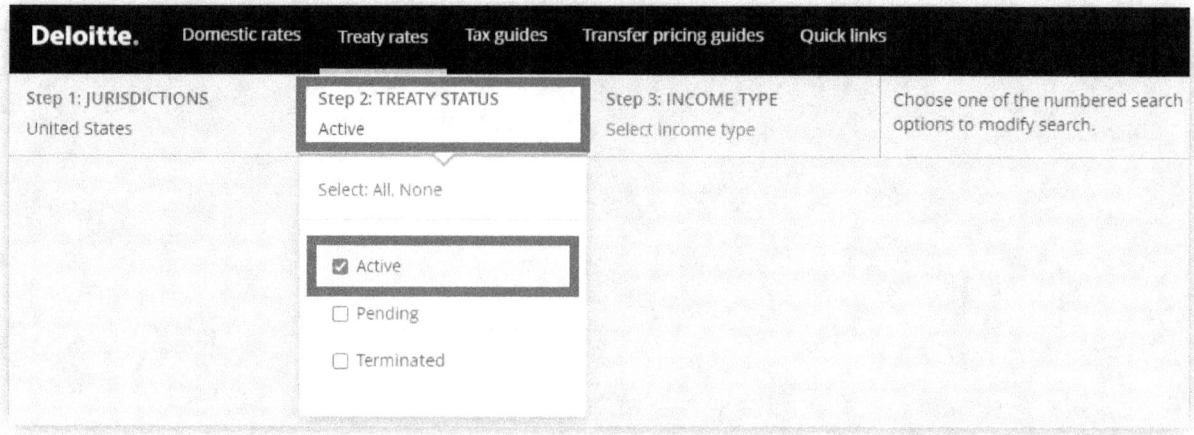

05 ▶▶ Select your income type. Choose **Royalties**.

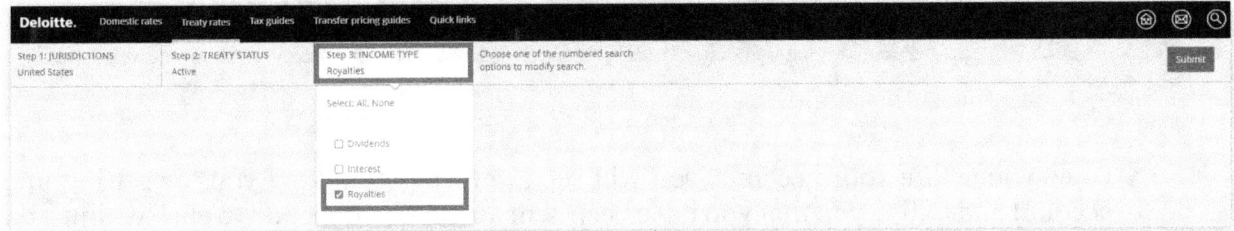

06 ▶▶ Select **Submit**.

07 ▶▶ You can see that Australia-based publishers wishing to receive royalties from KDP will have 5% of their royalties withheld for tax purposes. As stated above, the exact percentage depends on where you reside.

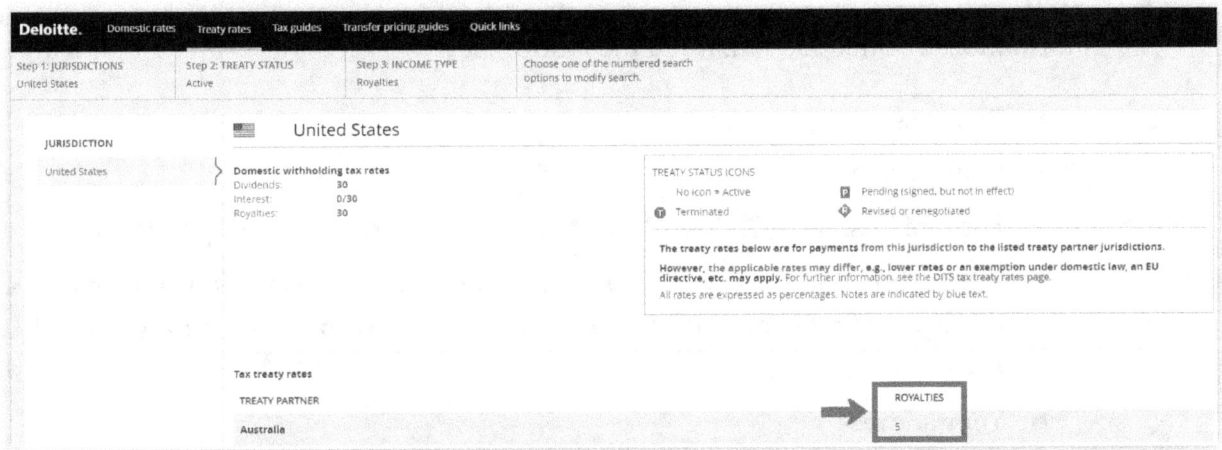

How to Set Up an IngramSpark Account

To set up an IngramSpark account, follow these steps:

01 ▶▶ Go to www.ingramspark.com and click **Create Account** next to the login.

02 ▶▶ Create your account indicating your contact name and email address, and create a password once you provide this information.

181

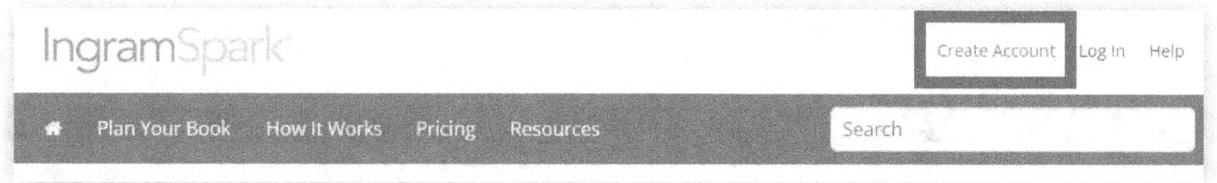

 Once you create your account, you will see a message thanking you for setting up an account and telling you that you have been sent an email with a link to click within 7 days to activate your account. Do so.

 Back on the IngramSpark page, you will see a notice that says "Policy Agreements." It will prompt you to read the agreement and click **Agree** to confirm you understand the terms.

 You will be taken to a page where you fill in various sections (business info, security, agreements, compensation, payment method, and taxes), starting with your business information. For this section, fill in the following:

- Business or legal name
- Contact name
- Form of business (Choose **Sole Proprietor** if you are a self-publisher.)
- What best describes you (Choose the appropriate description. For instance, if this is your first book, click **I've never published, but I am ready to publish now.**)
- Your address

06 ▶▶ Click **Continue**, and you will be taken to the security tab and asked to select and answer a security question. There are many questions you can choose from. Choose and answer the question and click **Save**.

07 ▶▶ You will be taken to the agreements tab. Accept their policies, use your name and title to sign the agreement, and click **Sign Agreements**.

 You will be taken to a welcome page informing you there are a few steps ahead.

09 ▶▶ Open the link to complete publisher compensation in a new tab. On this tab, choose the currency you wish to be paid in and click **Add Compensation Information**. You will be asked which payment type you wish to receive and your financial institution, country, account number, and ABA routing number. Click **Save**. There is a chat feature on this page that you can use to ask for help, so take advantage of it and ask any questions about payment.

10 ▶▶ Go back to the welcome page, refresh it, and open the link to add publisher payment in a new tab. Here, you will be asked to provide information for a valid credit or debit card.

11 ▶▶ Go back to the welcome page, refresh it, and open the link to enter tax information in a new tab. In the new tab, indicate your social security number/employer identification number (individual taxpayer identification number for resident aliens). Indicate your state. Sign in, provide your title, and click **Save**.

12 ▶▶ A W9 Form will pop up on your screen. Verify everything is correct and click **W-9 Is Correct**.

13 ▶▶ Go back to the welcome page, refresh it, and click **Finish Setting Up My Account**. The screen will then indicate "100%. Congratulations. Your Account is Complete."

How to Set Up an ACX Account

To set up an ACX account, follow these steps:

01 ▶▶ Go to www.acx.com and click **Get Started**.

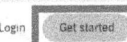

02 ▶▶ Sign in with your KDP account.

In Chapter 24, we will explore finding a narrator for your audiobook. If you are not from the US, Canada, Ireland, or the UK, you can hire audio narrators from two places: Author's Republic or Findaway Voices by Spotify. In the next two sections, we will go through setting up your account on those platforms.

How to Set Up an Author's Republic Account

 Go to www.authorsrepublic.com/register and click **Sign Up** in the top right corner. A window will open, and there you will see a statement that says, "Create your FREE account!" Fill in the boxes with the following information:

- Your full name
- Email address
- Country of residence

Then select the correct options for the two questions:

- Do you have an audiobook to distribute?
- Do you have a print or ebook?

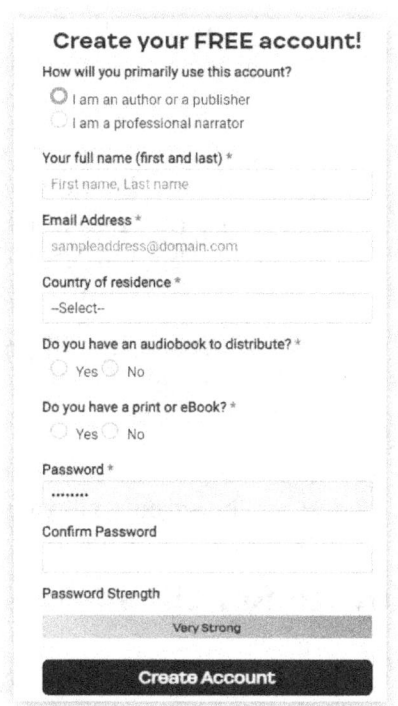

 Create a password, then click **Create Account.** You will then be led to a page in which you are invited to "Sell a Completed Audiobook" or "Produce an Audiobook."

How to Set Up a Findaway Voices by Spotify Account

 Go to www.findawayvoices.com and click **Register Free** in the top right corner. Fill in the required information, including your first name, last name, email, password, etc.

 Read and accept the terms of use and privacy policy, choose the means through which you wish to be contacted, and click **Create Account.**

Now that you know how to set up your major accounts, it's time to discover how to organize your book launch strategy.

Chapter 19

Breezing Through Your Book Pre-Launch Strategy

If you thought you wouldn't have to ask for reviews until your book was officially available for purchase, think again! As soon as the writing process has started, it's time to work behind the scenes and lean on the support from the community you build on your Facebook page and beyond. As mentioned in previous chapters, as a self-published author, your journey extends beyond writing a stellar book. If your book is going to entertain, help, or even change someone's life, they have to find it first. One of the best ways to reach your target audience is by generating excitement about your work and obtaining those juicy 4 and 5-star ratings on Amazon. You can do this by allowing a selected group of people to read your work for free before your book is actually published!

How Many Copies Should You Send to Potential Reviewers?

The answer to the above question is: "The more, the better!" In our experience, around 5–10% of the people you send your book to at this stage actually leave a review. That means if you send a copy to around 200 people, you can expect to receive around 10–20 reviews, and that's only if you do the required follow-up work. The good news is that it isn't difficult. You simply need to organize your follow-up efforts and be consistent. We will teach you how to do so.

Timing Your Book Launch

Obtaining reviews for your book is a process that should start before your book is published, but it also continues beyond publishing (until you receive a good amount of actual Amazon reviews). This is because although you cannot send the review link until your book is live on Amazon, people need to have read it and be willing to review it on the day of your book launch and forward from there. Part of your work is to send follow-up messages so that the people you sent your book to will respond and agree for you to send them the review link. What's more, you need to continue placing ads on Facebook and sending your book out until you have your desired number of reviews. So, even after your book is published, you must continue asking for reviews and following up on the messages you send.

The whole process can take 16 to 32 weeks or even longer. It depends on how long it takes you or your ghostwriter to write the book and how quickly you can obtain as many interested contacts as you are seeking. The more reviews you get, the better.

Working with Your Advanced Reader Copy (ARC) Team

Your ARC team differs from beta readers in that they read the final product of your book. The copy they review can be anywhere from two to six weeks away from going live on Amazon. Before you send out a copy of your book, make sure to watermark it. A watermark is a recognizable image or pattern embedded into a digital or physical document to identify the owner and prevent unauthorized duplication. The image is usually semi-transparent and placed over the content you wish to protect.

You can watermark your book for free on pdfFiller. (www.publishingservicesbook.com/watermark)

Watermarking ensures that no one else will post your book online. Of course, they could still theoretically do so, but the watermark clearly indicates that intellectual property rights belong to someone else.

There are both free and paid methods to obtain members for your ARC team through Facebook. The aim is to find between 1,000 and 2,000 people willing to review your book (i.e., between 100 and 200 actual reviews as a minimum). This can take weeks, so while your book is being penned, you should proactively start on your pre-launch book strategy.

How to Get ARC Readers for Free

Joining Facebook groups related to your topic is an excellent way to connect with potential reviewers, readers, and friends! When choosing your groups, go for those with a minimum of 1,000 members. Check out the group posts and ensure members are active and engaged.

Here's an example of just one category (chickens) and the potential groups that might be worth looking into:

- Backyard Chickens
- Chicken Keeping 101
- Poultry Breeders and Backyard Chickens

- Chickens, Chickens, Chickens!!
- Backyard Poultry
- Beginner Chicken Keepers
- Chicken Enthusiasts
- Raising Chickens for Beginners
- Poultry Lovers Group
- The Chicken Whisperer
- Backyard Chickens for Beginners
- Chicken Keepers Unite
- Homestead Chickens
- Backyard Chickens and Poultry
- Chicken Keeping Community
- Backyard Chickens & Farming
- Happy Chicken Owners
- Backyard Poultry Enthusiasts
- Beginner Poultry Keepers
- Chicken and Poultry Chat
- Chicken Keeping for Newbies
- Urban Chicken Keepers
- Chicken Care & Advice
- Poultry Breeding and Care
- Chicken Keepers Help and Advice
- Raising Chickens Naturally
- Backyard Chickens and Coops
- Poultry Keepers Network
- Chickens and More
- Backyard Poultry & Homesteading
- Raising Happy Chickens
- Backyard Chicken Breeders
- Chicken and Poultry Hobbyists
- Chicken Keeping Tips
- Happy Hen Keepers
- Poultry Keepers Hub
- The Poultry People
- Chicken Keeping 101: For Beginners
- Backyard Chickens Australia
- Chicken Breeders and Keepers
- Poultry and Chicken Keepers

- Chicken Owners United
- Backyard Poultry and Livestock
- Chicken Raising for Beginners
- Poultry Enthusiasts Group
- Chickens for Beginners
- Backyard Chicken Keeping
- Poultry Keepers Advice and Support
- Chicken Keepers Q&A
- Backyard Chickens & Small Farm Animals

There are two strategies you can adopt in these free groups.

Strategy 1

 Make posts in relevant Facebook groups and ask people to review your book. You will need to use your private account because most Facebook groups do not permit pages to join. Moreover, Facebook's algorithm shows posts from private accounts to more people than those from pages unless you run a paid ad.

If you are worried that your name doesn't match your author's name, don't worry. People don't seem to mind this since using pen names is a common practice. It is best practice to check with the group's admins first to ensure you are allowed to make this type of post.

 Follow the same system of writing names and sending feedback and follow-up messages, as indicated in the next section.

Strategy 2

 Join relevant groups with your private Facebook account (so that you can send people messages first).

 **Pro Tip:** Start with this strategy as soon as you have the topic of your book.

 Make a copy of our free Book Reviewers Template (**www.publishingservicesbook.com/reviewers-spreadsheet-strategy-2**). The first sheet contains the following columns:

- Group name
- Link to group
- Notes

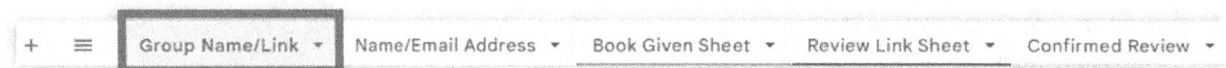

Post in these groups at least three times a week. The more you post, the better! Your posts can be anything related to your book or the group, from affirmations to bucket list ideas, gratitude posts, and more. Be as creative as you like! Below, you will find a few ideas for posts, which you can use in all the groups you are part of:

- **Book Teasers:** "I'm excited to say I have written a book on raising chickens in your own backyard! It's called *Become a Backyard Chicken Farmer—Master Breed Selection and Feeding—Uncover the Importance of Facilities and Health Care to Effortlessly Increase Egg Production*. Here's the first chapter of the book. Let me know what you think!"
- **A Poll:** "What aspect of raising chickens interests you most: egg production or companionship?"
- **A Discussion Question:** "What is the best advice you ever received about caring for baby chicks? Please share your wisdom!"
- **Personal Story:** "When I first started raising chickens, I wondered how I could ever build a sturdy and beautiful coop—after all, I had never been a great DIY carpenter! But it all became easy once I figured out that…"
- **Quote:** "I'd love to share this quote from my book with you: 'If you know somethin' well, you can always paint it, but people would be better off buyin' chickens.'—Grandma Moses (BrainyQuote, n.d.)."
- **Behind-the-Scenes:** "Ever wondered what goes into writing a book about backyard chickens? Take a look at my writing process!"
- **Book Cover Reveal:** "I'm thrilled to reveal the cover of my new book, *Become a Backyard Chicken Farmer—Master Breed Selection and Feeding—Uncover the Importance of Facilities and Health Care to Effortlessly Increase Egg Production*. What do you think of it?
- **Discussion Topic:** "Let's talk about chick health. What's your favorite care tip to ensure your chicks stay healthy?"
- **Content Preview:** "I'm working on a new blog post about sustainable chicken keeping. Any suggestions for eco-friendly practices I should include?"
- **Motivational Post:** "Remember, every great decision starts with researching various options. In just a few hours, you can decide on the coop shape and style that best works for your chickens and backyard!"
- **Survey:** "I'm planning my second book about raising chickens, which focuses more on chicken health. What topics would you like to see covered?"
- **Success Story:** "I'd love to share a success story of one of my readers, who followed my advice on egg collection."

- **Upcoming Events:** "I'm having a book signing at Bronson's Book Shop on Eggshell Lane at 9 am tomorrow. Hope to see some of you there!"
- **Photo Challenge:** "Of all my chickens, Bessie is undoubtedly the quirkiest. Here she is, squeaking her rubber chicken toy. Any cute photos of your cluckers?"
- **Fun Facts:** "Did you know chickens experience REM (rapid eye movement) sleep, indicating that they dream just like humans do?"
- **Cooking Tips:** "What's your favorite recipe made with fresh eggs laid by your chickens?"
- **A Funny Chicken Meme, Joke, or GIF**
- **A Video of You Talking About Your Book**
- **The Table of Contents of Your Book**
- **A Screenshot of a Well-Designed Page from Your Book**

04 ▶▶ Reply to every comment you receive. Send every person who comments a private message, saying something like:

> *Hi (name),*
>
> *I appreciate your comment so much. Thank you!*
>
> *I am an author, and I have a book about (topic), which will be published in (approximate time/date). I am in the final stages of finishing it.*
>
> *I would love to send you a copy for free before it hits Amazon. After you've had a chance to read it, I'd be grateful if you could leave an honest review on Amazon.*
>
> *Would this be of interest to you?*
>
> *When they say "Yes," reply: Amazing. To which email address should I send the book?*

05 ▶▶ Add the details of the people who have responded into the sheet called "Name/Email Address."

06 ▶▶ Send a message with a copy of your watermarked manuscript to those interested in reviewing your book.

 Start filling in the "Book Given Sheet."

 Comment under every single post that someone makes in the group. Engage as much as you can with people. As you make new connections, offer them the chance to review your book as soon as it is available.

Paid Method to Obtain ARC Readers (Via Facebook Ads)

To start working on obtaining reviews for your book on Amazon, follow each of the steps listed below.

First Things First

As soon as your book is watermarked and ready to be sent out, post that you want to give a free copy of your PDF book to people willing to share their honest opinions. Here's what you do:

Create a free 3D mockup of your book cover on DIY Book Design's Free Book Cover Mockups tool (at www.publishingservicesbook.com/3d-mockups).

Design a post on Canva. Use language, imagery, and fonts that align with your target audience's tastes.

Sample Canva Design

Make the post on your Facebook author page using the image you created and some catchy text (sample below).

> ***WANTED: Book reviewers for a review team!***
> *Your opinion matters and is so helpful.*
> *I am giving out FREE ebook copies of my book "Become a Backyard Chicken Farmer—Master Breed Selection and Feeding—Uncover the Importance of Facilities and Health Care to Effortlessly Increase Egg Production."*
> *I would love to get your honest feedback.*
> *If you are interested, please send me a private message.*

Pro Tip: On your Facebook post, avoid saying you are giving your book away in exchange for a "positive review." The emphasis should be on leaving an honest opinion. Amazon does not allow dishonest reviews. Also, note that you are technically not allowed to give something (in this case, your PDF) and request a review in return. Yes, you can ask for a review, but it should not appear like you are offering an exchange.

Next Steps

Run a Facebook ad on your published post, targeting your book's audience in the US.

The reason why you should limit yourself initially to the US (which is often the biggest market for self-published authors) is that to leave an unverified review (a review on an item they did not purchase), your reader needs to have spent at least $50 in the previous 365 days on the same Amazon marketplace you are requesting a review in. That means that if you want someone's review to appear on Amazon.com, they would need to have spent at least $50 on Amazon's US marketplace in the previous 365 days. If you send your book to someone who lives in Spain (for example), they are not likely to have spent $50 or more on Amazon in the US. Instead, they would most likely have an account with Amazon Spain (Amazon.es) and have spent their money in that marketplace.

Something worth pointing out before you publish the post: In our sample, you will see the line, "If you are interested, please send me a private message." If you have a Facebook page, you cannot send messages directly to people, but you can respond once they send you a message. This is why it is so important to get them to contact you privately first.

Pro Tip: You may wonder how much you need to budget for this ad. The answer is that it very much depends on the niche and how many people are likely to leave a review for your type of book. Aim to send your book to between 1,000 and 2,000 people. To obtain a list of around 1,000 people, you would most likely need to spend between $500 and $700. This amount could be less. For instance, if you get a good response from over 2,000 people early, you can stop running ads if you want to. Obviously, the more ads you can run, the better, as it increases the number of reviews you are likely to get.

 **Download our free "Book Reviewers Spreadsheet" ([www.publishingser-vicesbook.com/reviewers-spreadsheet](www.publishingservicesbook.com/reviewers-spreadsheet)).**

Hopefully, you've already been using this for your free strategies. At the bottom of the spreadsheet, you will see three separate sheets. You will see that each one is used to store different information. These three sheets help keep track of to whom you sent your book and when they are ready for you to send the review link so they can leave their review on Amazon. The first "Book Given" sheet is used once you send the book to readers. The second "Review Link" sheet is used when you send out the link so readers can leave their Amazon reviews directly. The third "Confirmed Review" sheet is used to confirm that people have actually left reviews as they said they would.

- **Sheet #1: Book Given Sheet**

- ◇ You will see in the template that this sheet lists:
    - ☐ The name of the person you sent the book to
    - ☐ The date you sent it to them
    - ☐ Notes (any pertinent things to keep in mind about the person)
    - ☐ Cells to check when you have sent up to 7 feedback messages (Send the first feedback message after 10 days, then 5, 5, 5, 5, 10, and 10 days after the previous message.)

- **Sheet #2: Review Link Sheet**

- ◇ You will see in the template that this sheet lists:
    - ☐ The name of the person you sent the review link to
    - ☐ The date you sent them the book
    - ☐ Notes
    - ☐ The date you sent the review

- ☐ Reminders (Send the first reminder 5 days after sending them the review link, and then, if necessary, 5 more reminders 5 days apart from each other.)

- **Sheet #3: Confirmed Review Sheet**

- ◇ You will see in the template that this sheet lists:
    - ☐ The name of the person who left a review
    - ☐ Their Amazon name (Some people do not use the same name on Amazon as on their social media pages, so to check if they have left a review, you will need their Amazon name.)
    - ☐ Notes
    - ☐ Their email address
    - ☐ The marketplace they used to leave their review
    - ☐ The star rating they gave your book

 **When people reach out to you via private message, send them a "Message to First-Time Reviewers" response.**

Use the Facebook messages below for an idea of what to send. Logically, your message will differ if you are sending it to someone who has never reviewed one of your books versus an "old and trusty" reviewer with whom you have already established a relationship. The number of days you give them to review the book may differ according to your niche, how technical your book is, and how many words it contains.

For your convenience, we have compiled the following templates in this link: www.publishingservicesbook.com/facebook-message-template. Feel free to copy them for your own use and adjust them as you see fit.

Sample Message to First-Time Reviewers

Hey there [first name], nice to meet you!

This is the second book I have written to help you raise healthy chickens, and I am excited to offer you the ebook in exchange for your honest opinion. My book, "Become a Backyard Chicken Farmer—Master Breed Selection and Feeding—Uncover the Importance of Facilities and Health Care to Effortlessly Increase Egg Production," outlines all the strategies you need to breed healthy, happy chickens that lay an optimal number of eggs.

The good news is, with this ebook, you will see how easy it is to transform your backyard into a happy home for chickens! This ebook is targeted at beginner breeders who are ready to commit to their chicken's health and well-being. The aim is to read it and review it on Amazon in the shortest time possible. (Most people only take about 10 days as it is only 200 pages long.)

Is this something you would be interested in undertaking?

I look forward to hearing from you,

Cluck Norris

Sample Message to Past Reviewers

Hi [first name],

It's been a while since we last spoke. I wanted to reach out because I am in the process of launching a new book.

I was wondering if you'd like to review it, too. The book is called "Become a Backyard Chicken Farmer—Master Breed Selection and Feeding—Uncover the Importance of Facilities and Health Care to Effortlessly Increase Egg Production," and it is all about how to raise happy, healthy chickens that lay eggs effortlessly.

Are you interested in reading and reviewing it in the next 10 days? I'm excited to hear from you.

Thanks,

Cluck Norris

04 ▶▶ Watch for their responses.

If the person says they are interested in reading and reviewing your book, send them the watermarked copy of your book with a message a sample of which you can read a below:

> *Hi [first name],*
> *Awesome, I am excited to start this journey with you!*
>
> *I have included a host of techniques and checklists to ensure you stay up-to-date with your tasks. The book will also help you discover potential health problems so you can quickly nip them in the bud.*
>
> *Thank you so much for taking the time out of your day to help an author and chicken breeder like myself. I will message you in ten days to give you some time to read it and see how you are enjoying it.*
>
> *Know that anyone can be a great chicken breeder if they treat their chickens with love, care, and science-backed knowledge!*
>
> *Cluck Norris*

Note: You can send your manuscript in two ways: as a link or attached as a PDF in your message. For many people, simply attaching a PDF to their message is easier. The downside of attaching files to messages is that sometimes, these attachments can no longer be accessed on Facebook and other sites a few days after they are sent. By sending a link, you can ensure the person will always have access to your manuscript.

To send the link to your manuscript, follow these steps:

1. If you don't already have a Gmail account, create one.
2. In the upper right-hand corner of Gmail, click the box with 9 dots.

3. Click **Drive**.

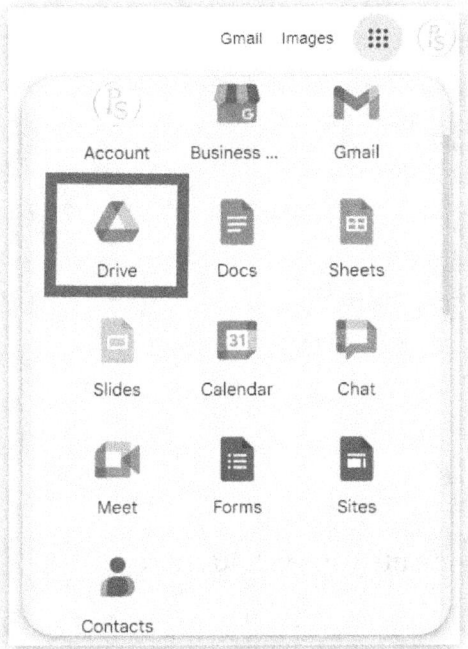

4. Click on **My Drive** and then **New**.

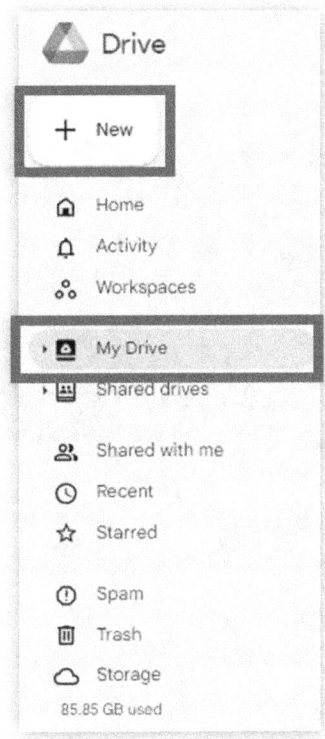

197

5. Click **File Upload**. Choose your book file and click **Upload**.

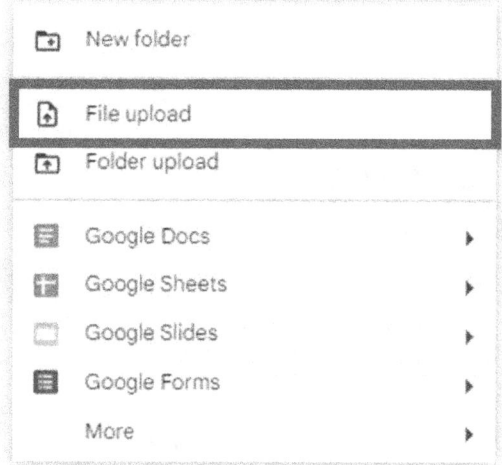

6. Click the three dots next to the file you wish to share.

7. Click **Share**.

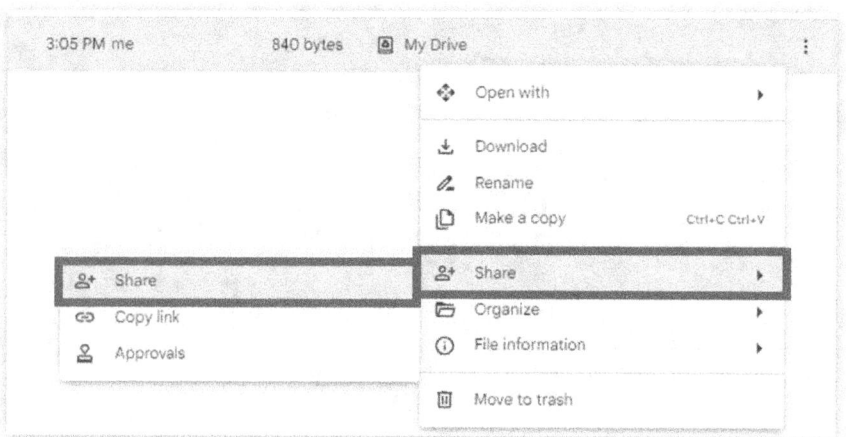

8. Click the **Down Arrow** next to "Restricted" and select **Anyone with the Link**.

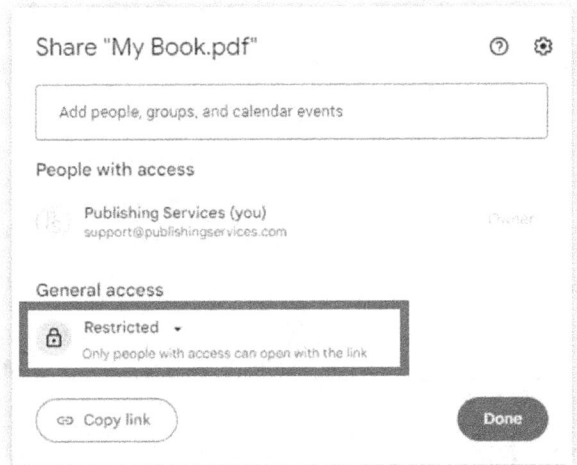 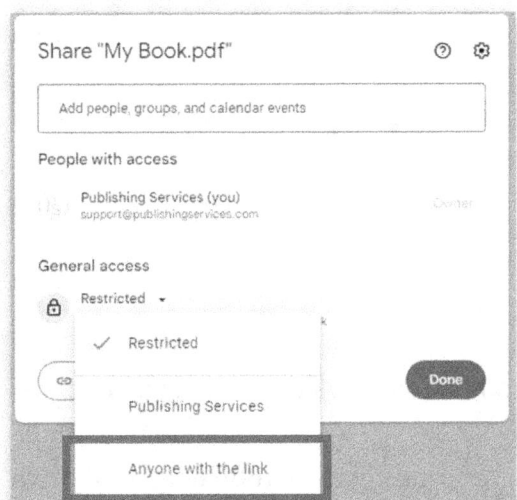

9. Make sure the **Viewer** option is selected. If it isn't, then click the down arrow on the right-hand side and swap it for **Viewer**.

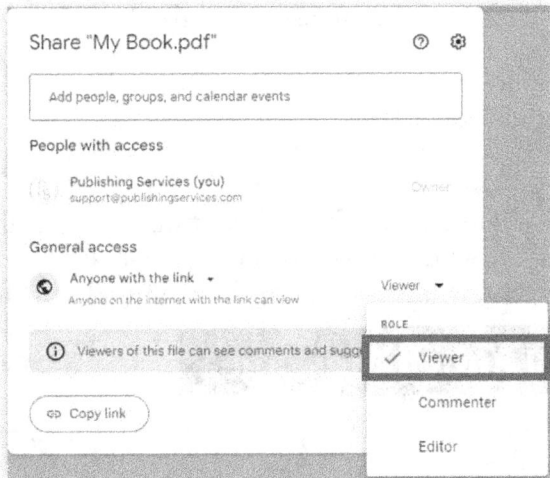

For easy access, add your book to your starred files.

1. Select the star on the right-hand side.

2. You can find your book in your drive by clicking **Starred** on the left-hand side.

*Remember you can simply send the PDF in a message. Just be aware that access to your book may expire.

Right after sending them the book, send them the following "Message After Giving Them the Book:"

> *Also, just quickly, feel free to let me know if there is anything you are unsure about, and I will be happy to clarify it for you. Happy reading!*

Remember to fill out your spreadsheet as you go to stay organized.

 **Send feedback.**

A couple of days before your book's launch date, begin the process of sending feedback messages to the people you have sent your book to. Send a pre-launch message to everyone who has had your book for at least 10 days. (Anything less, and chances are, they haven't had time to read it.)

Sample of a Pre-Book Launch Message

> *Hey [first name],*
>
> *I hope life is treating you well and that you had time to kick back and relax while getting some good strategies and tips from the book. If you have finished it, just let me know so I can give you the review link, and you can share your thoughts with other people who would love to raise chickens in their backyards. My book is going live on Amazon in two days, and I'm so excited! Hope you can lend me a hand with your review!*
>
> *Talk soon,*
>
> *Cluck Norris*

 **Launch your book on Amazon!**

 **Pro Tip: Schedule your free promotion.** When enough people are interested in reviewing your book, it is time to schedule your promotion. See the heading "Hack for Getting Verified Reviews" later in this chapter for more information.

07 **Create your review link.**

You want to send the review link with a message to everyone who has read your book and expressed an interest in reviewing it: https://www.amazon.com/review/create-review?asin=ASIN. Since you have launched by this point, you will need to replace ASIN with your actual ASIN number. Send the link along with the following message to those who have responded to you:

- **Review Link Message:**

> *Here is the review link:* https://www.amazon.com/review/create-review?asin=ASIN
> *Thank you so much for taking the time to help get the word out there to as many people as possible.*

08 **Keep sending your book out to new readers.**

After they have had at least 10 days to read your book, send them a post-launch message.

- **Post-Book Launch Message:**

> *Hey [first name],*
>
> *I hope life is treating you well and that you had time to kick back and relax while getting some good strategies and tips from the book. If you have finished it, just let me know so I can give you the review link, and you can share your thoughts with other parents. My book has recently gone live on Amazon, so I hope you can lend me a hand by leaving your opinion of my book.*
>
> *Talk soon,*
>
> *Cluck Norris*

 **Send the following feedback follow-up messages to everyone.**

- **Feedback Follow-Up Message #1:** (5 days after sending your Pre-Launch Message or the Post-Launch Message)

> *Hello again [first name]! Have you had a chance to get to the section on time management for chicken breeders yet? My readers report that it helped them balance their chicken-raising activities with other tasks, so I was excited to include it. I just wanted to touch base to ask you if you have finished reading the book so I can send the review link your way.*
>
> *Talk soon,*
>
> *Cluck Norris*

- **Feedback Follow-Up Message #2:** (5 days after the previous message)

> *I hope that everything is alright in your life and that you are embracing a few of the troubleshooting tips I included in the book. I also hope that you see the powerful link between feeding chickens the right nutrition and filling your egg basket daily! In saying that, if you have finished the book, reach out and let me know so you can get the link to review it.*
>
> *Talk soon,*
>
> *Cluck Norris*

- **Feedback Follow-Up Message #3:** (5 days after the previous message)

> *Hello [first name],*
>
> *It's me again. I am just checking how you are progressing through the book and if you have any feedback for me on it or if you are ready to review it.*
>
> *Talk soon,*
>
> *Cluck Norris*

- **Feedback Follow-Up Message #4:** (5 days after the previous message)

    If you are still reading the book, what has been your favorite part so far? Do you have any suggestions to make the next book better, or are you ready to share your thoughts with the world?

    Talk soon,

    Cluck Norris

- **Feedback Follow-Up Message #5:** (10 days after the previous message)

    So I have good news and bad news. The good news is that you are still in the running to receive future books.

    The bad news is that while I completely understand that life can hit you where it hurts when you are least expecting it, we did have an agreement that you'd read the book and help other chicken enthusiasts determine if this book had info that would help them.

    Unfortunately, my next message will be to tell you that I can not offer you any future books because you didn't hold up your end of the agreement we had.

    However, there is still time! Just reach out and let me know you are ready for the review link. Then, post the review to Amazon so that our community can grow stronger and better prepared.

    Talk soon,

    Cluck Norris

- **Feedback Follow-Up Message #6:** (10 days after the previous message)

    This is my last message, I promise, which is sad because it means that I won't be able to offer you any of my future books because, as far as I can tell, you did not hold up your end of our agreement. In saying that, I wish you all the best in your egg-collecting journey!

Take note: This process can continue as long as you like, even after your book has been published.

10 ▶▶ Follow up to ensure the person actually leaves a review.

Once you send the review link to interested readers, transfer their details from the "Book Given Sheet" onto the "Review Link Sheet" to stay on track. Send a review link message to the people on your sheet along with the review link. Send a review follow-up message 5 days after sending the review link. Every 5 days, send a new review follow-up message, sending a total of 7 follow-up messages.

- **Review Link Message:**

> *Thank you for taking the time to leave a review!*
> *The review link is here! I can't wait to hear your thoughts. Simply click the link below to get started:*
> *[Review Link]*
> *Thank you so much for your time and support!*
>
> *Best,*
> *Cluck Norris*

- **Review Follow-Up Message #1:**

> *Hi [Name],*
> *Just a quick reminder to share your thoughts on my book. Your review helps other readers discover the book and is incredibly appreciated.*
> *Here is the link again:*
> *[Review Link]*
>
> *Warm regards,*
> *Cluck Norris*

- **Review Follow-Up Message #2:**

    Hi [Name],
    Just a friendly nudge to leave your review for my book. Your honest feedback means a lot to me!
    Here is the link again:
    [Review Link]

    Best,
    Cluck Norris

- **Review Follow-Up Message #3:**

    Hi [Name],
    Your review can make a big difference for others considering the book. Any chance you could share your thoughts soon?
    Here is the link again:
    [Review Link]

    Thanks a bunch!
    Cluck Norris

- **Review Follow-Up Message #4:**

    Hi [Name],
    Your feedback is incredibly important to me, so please don't hesitate to share your thoughts. And if you've already left a review and I missed it, please let me know!

    Warm regards,
    Cluck Norris
    P. S.
    Here is the link again:
    [Review Link]

- **Review Follow-Up Message #5**:

> *Hi [Name],*
> *I really value your opinion on my book. If you haven't already, could you take a moment to leave your review? It would mean a lot!*
> *Here is the link again:*
> *[Review Link]*
>
> *Thanks a bunch!*
> *Cluck Norris*

- **Review Follow-Up Message #6**:

> *Hi [Name],*
> *This is a final reminder about leaving your review for my book. Unfortunately, as we initially discussed, I won't be able to offer you future books without your review.*
> *Here is the link again:*
> *[Review Link]*
> *Thanks for your understanding.*
>
> *Best,*
> *Cluck Norris*

- **Review Follow-Up Message #7**:

> *Hi [Name],*
> *Unfortunately, as I haven't received your review, I won't be able to offer you any future books. I truly appreciate your time and support, and I wish you all the best in the future. Thank you and take care.*
>
> *Best,*
> *Cluck Norris*

 **Pro Tip:** You can send them personal loom videos and show them how to leave a review.

11 ▶▶ **Transfer the details.**

Once the person has left a review, cut and paste their details from the Review Link Sheet to the Confirmed Review Sheet. This is an important sheet to use for the next book you write because it contains the names of dependable people you know you can count on.

12 ▶▶ **Repeat the process.**

Continue to run ads and request reviews as indicated above until you hit your target number of reviews. You should aim for 150.

Here is a little graph representing the entire process involved in the free and paid methods.

Return to this graph as you read through this chapter. As you will see, the entire process spans from before your book is even completed to after it is live on Amazon.

Outsourcing the ARC Process: A Hassle-Free Option

If the process of finding reviews is too time-consuming for your lifestyle, there is another option: outsourcing! Below, you will find a few handy tips for doing so.

Done for You KDP Reviews

There is an avenue through which you can receive legitimate KDP reviews, and in our view, it is definitely worth the investment. The company Done for You KDP Reviews, which is one of Publishing Services' affiliate partners, can ensure you will get a specific number of reviews for your book. They offer you the following:

- **100% Legitimate Reviews:** These reviews are accepted by Amazon terms. These are real reviewers who are not compensated in any way, and they are not connected to you or Done for You KDP Reviews in any way.

- **One-on-one Coaching Calls:** The team joins you for two strategy calls, where they guide you through the review services process and offer personalized publishing advice to suit your unique needs.

- **Book Launch Guidance:** If your book has not yet been launched, during the one-on-one coaching calls, the team at Done for You KDP Reviews will teach you the specific launch strategy they use to get books to the $5K to $10K per month range.

- **Verified Reviews:** This is possible while you are enrolled in KDP Select (a 90-day program that allows you to offer your Kindle ebook for free for up to 5 days to attract new readers and obtain reviews). Between 20% and 35% of the reviews from Done for You KDP Reviews will appear "Verified."
- **Full Transparency:** You can see every lead the company generates and read the messages sent to potential reviewers.
- **Non-Invasiveness:** Done for You KDP Reviews does not require access to your Facebook or KDP account. They use their own Facebook ad account to give you full access to everything that is taking place.
- **Contact Information:** After the service has been completed, you will receive the contact information of the readers who have left a review on your book.

 **Pro Tip:** KDP Select is a free 90-day program for Kindle ebooks only, but don't worry. The verified reviews you obtain via KDP Select will appear for all formats of your book.

To utilize this service, go to www.publishingservicesbook.com/dfy-kdp-reviews. You'll be able to see how Done for You KDP Reviews works.

Scroll to the bottom of the page and click **Book a Free Strategy Call Now**. You will be asked to send your book cover and manuscript. The team will need to ensure that your book is right for their service and vice-versa before they start the process. If they feel your book will be a good fit, you will be asked to choose one of three different tiers, which vary in price and depend on how many reviews you are seeking.

 **Exclusive Deal:** Use Code **PS** at the checkout to obtain a **$50 discount** for this service.

How to Get Verified Reviews: A Simple Hack

Above, we have provided you with all the steps you need to obtain reviews from people who have not purchased your book. These reviews are called "unverified reviews" precisely because they are not actual customers. As you can imagine, verified reviews (those left by people who have actually bought and reviewed your book) are more valuable. One reason is that unverified reviews only appear in the marketplace where they have been left. In other words, if a reader leaves their review on Amazon.com, then their review will not appear on Amazon.ca, Amazon.es, or Amazon.com.au.

The second reason is that verified reviews are the most objective and independent reviews possible. They are left by genuine purchasers who are interested in your niche and who simply want to let others know what they got out of your book.

The good news is that for a limited time, it is possible to obtain a verified review from someone who has not purchased your book. It goes as follows:

- Run a Facebook ad as outlined above, targeting the US market.
- When you enroll in KDP Select, Amazon allows you to run specific promotions. One promotion works as follows: Within 90 days of enrolling in KDP Select, you are allowed to run a **FREE PROMOTION** for **5 days**. The days do not have to run consecutively, but to obtain reviews, it is a good idea to do so. To ensure people leave their verified reviews on your chosen day, when you get to Step 8 above (the person being ready for you to send them the review link), send them the Amazon link and tell them, *"Hey, the book is currently free on Amazon. Can you please download it and then click the link I sent you and leave a review?"* If they do so, their review will show up as verified on Amazon, and it will show up in all Amazon marketplaces.

Pro Tip: Every time you renew your enrollment in KDP Select (every 90 days minimum), you get another 5 days of free promotion time. You can opt out of KDP Select if you want to, but if you want to stay enrolled a bit longer, the following is important information.

How to Enroll in KDP Select

To enroll your ebook in KDP select, follow these steps (Kindle Direct Publishing, n.d.-d):

To enroll your ebook draft in KDP Select, follow the steps below:

1. Go to your bookshelf.
2. Select the Kindle ebook you want to enroll, and click the ellipsis button ("**...**") under "Kindle Ebook Actions." A drop-down menu will appear.
3. Click **Enroll in KDP Select**. A pop-up will appear.
4. In the pop-up, click **Enroll**.

To enroll your published ebook in KDP Select, follow the steps below:

1. Go to the marketing page.
2. Under KDP Select, click **Enroll an Ebook**.
3. Select your ebook and click **Continue**.
4. Click **Enroll**.

You can change your Kindle ebook details (royalty options and book descriptions) without affecting your enrollment in KDP Select. You can also unpublish KDP Select-enrolled titles anytime during the term and republish them on KDP later. This will pause your KDP Select enrollment period until you republish your Kindle ebook. Remember that your Kindle ebook must remain exclusive throughout the title's current 90-day participation period.

Scheduling Your Free Book Promotion

Once your book is published, you've sent your feedback message, and you received numerous replies to these messages, it's time to take advantage of the free promotion. Don't do so before this stage because, as mentioned above, the promotion runs for only 5 days. To schedule your free promotion, follow these steps:

1. Click the three dots that appear next to your ebook.

2. Under Run a Price Promotion, select **Free Book Promotion,** then hit **Create a Free Book Promotion**.

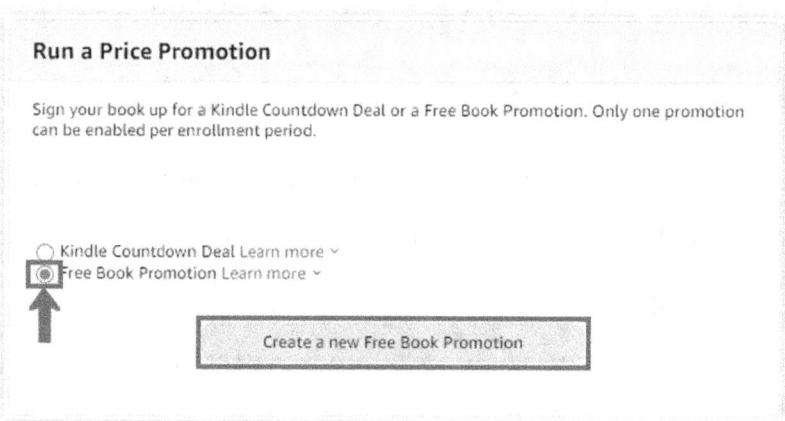

3. Select the **Start and End Date** of the promotion and then hit **Save Changes**.

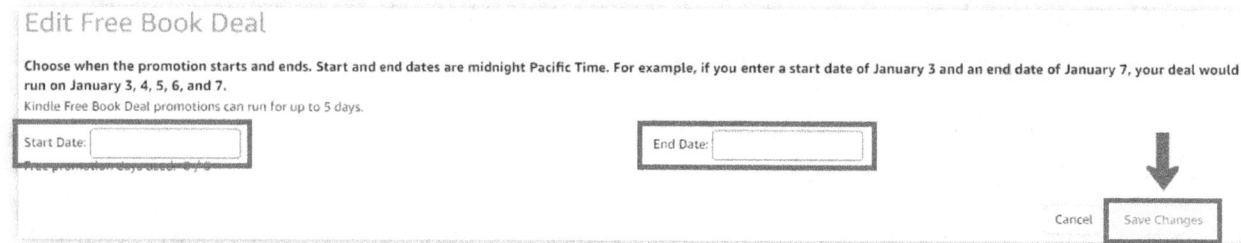

**Pro Tip:** As you build a network of followers who read your books and always leave reviews of your work, ask them for a favor! Send them a printed copy of your book and ask them to take a picture of the book or to include a video review (even better!) of your book. You cannot send it directly to them from Amazon. Instead, order author copies (which cost less) and send them to yourself or place an order as a customer would through Amazon. Once you receive the books, send them to your reviewers by mail. Doing so will ensure you abide by Amazon's regulations. Verified video reviews are the very best type of reviews you can get, followed by verified reviews with pictures, non-verified reviews with video, non-verified reviews with pictures, verified written reviews, and finally, non-verified written reviews.

Now that we've covered the strategies for preparing your book for a successful pre-launch, it's time to take the next step: actually sending your book out into the world. In the upcoming chapter, we'll go over the process of uploading your book to KDP's platform. Let's turn all that pre-launch preparation into a polished, published product!

BOOK STATUS	ACTION	TIMELINE
Book creation in progress	• Join Facebook groups and collect email addresses	Throughout the writing process
Book is 100% finished	• Send book out via emails • Start Facebook ads and send book out to anyone interested	2-6 weeks before your launch date
	• Refine email messages (remove time frame)	
	• Reach out for initial feedback	A few days before your launch date
	• Publish your book	On your launch date
Book is live	• Schedule free promotion	Until you have your desired number of reviews
	• Send the link to your free eBook to your entire review team and ask them to download your book for free • Send out review links to everyone who is ready to review the book • Keep sending your book to new readers	

Chapter 20

Uploading Your Book to KDP: Everything You Need to Know

This chapter will show you all the steps involved in uploading your ebook, paperback, and hardcover editions to KDP. Before starting, ensure you have everything you need at hand. You'll need your covers, interiors, seven backend keywords (explanation below), and metadata (any data that describes your book, including the title, subtitle, price, publication date, ISBN, and other relevant information).

Before You Begin: Key Steps to Take

Before starting, we want to cover some keyword information, give you some recommendations, and help you with pricing strategies. With all this knowledge under your belt, you'll be ready to fill in all the required details quickly. Then, we'll look at how to upload your book to KDP and how to re-upload it to KDP after making changes to it.

Publisher Rocket–What Is It and Why We Recommend It

Publisher Rocket is a valuable tool for authors that helps optimize their book listings and dominate the Amazon marketplace. It provides lifetime access to its many tools for $199, which, in our view, is a small price for all the tasks it can help with.

Its key features include:

- **Keyword Search:** This helps you find more relevant keywords and identify those needed for your book to sell.

- **Category Search:** Amazon has over 19,000 categories, but these do not appear in Amazon's short categories list on its main page. Publisher Rocket will help you find the perfect fit for your book.
- **Competition Analyzer:** This helps you discover your competitors' sales, rankings, and strategies.
- **Amazon Keywords Generator:** This aids in finding keywords. (Although, we recommend KDSpy for this task.)

You can use Publisher Rocket (www.publishingservicesbook.com/publisher-rocket) to discover the best Amazon keywords for specific categories.

Here's how:

- Purchase Publisher Rocket first; then download the software.
- When you open the program, click **Keyword Search**.
- Type in your main topic to see all other relevant keywords. For instance, for our hypothetical book, you might search for the phrase "chicken farming." You will see how often specific keywords are used, how much money publishers who use them earn (by clicking on the magnifying glass in the right-hand column), and how difficult it is to rank for those keywords. This page will also show you relevant categories for your keywords so you can find categories that will help your book reach more readers.
- Use Publisher Rocket's category search to delve into potential categories you may have missed.

KDP Select

In previous chapters, we briefly mentioned how you can use KDP Select to obtain verified reviews for your book. KDP Select is a 90-day program for Kindle ebooks that allows you to access more readers via Amazon and Kindle promotions. All authors, regardless of where they live, are eligible to use it.

The benefits of signing up for KDP include (Kindle Direct Publishing, n.d.-e):

- **Kindle Unlimited:** When you enroll in KDP Select, your book can be accessed by Kindle Unlimited readers for free. Kindle Unlimited is a popular subscription service that allows users to download free ebooks. Users pay a small amount to enjoy the service, and they have access to books enrolled with KDP Select. The pages they read are called Kindle Edition Normalized Pages (KENP), which is a measurement system that Amazon uses to track the number of pages read by Kindle subscribers. Because ebooks don't have a fixed page count, Amazon creates a "normalized" page length using a specialized algorithm. Doing so stops publishers from artificially increasing page numbers by using large font sizes and numerous images. The normalized system makes earnings fair. If you're enrolled in KDP Select, you will find your

KENP page count under the Promote & Advertise tab on your Bookshelf.

Your book becomes eligible for royalty payments under this program. Payments are based on how many KENP pages an individual customer reads from your book for the first time. Royalties vary monthly based on two factors:

- The size of the KDP Select Global Fund (how many readers sign up for the right to read Kindle Unlimited books)
- The total number of pages they have read from your book

For instance, if in a given month, $10 million in funds were available and customers read a total of 100 million total pages, then:

- An author with a 100-page Kindle ebook that was borrowed and read completely 100 times would earn $1,000 ($10 million x 10,000 pages for this author/100,000,000 total pages).
- An author of a 200-page Kindle ebook that was borrowed and read completely 100 times would earn $2,000 ($10 million x 20,000 pages for this author/100,000,000 total pages).
- An author of a 200-page Kindle ebook that was borrowed 100 times but only read halfway through on average would earn $1,000 ($10 million x 10,000 pages for this author/100,000,000 total pages).

To work out how much you would receive, go to Kindlepreneur's KENP Calculator at www.publishingservicesbook.com/kenp-calculator. This will give you an instant calculation. However, for the math lovers among you, we will share the formula for calculating your monthly royalties (Kindlepreneur, n.d.-b).

Your Royalties = Your KENP Pages Read * KENP Rate

KENP Rate = KDP Select Global Fund/Total Pages Read

If you want to know how much your book earns if someone reads it entirely from start to finish, the formula is as follows:

Your Royalties = Your KENP Pages Per Book * KENP Rate

- **Free Book Promotions:** As mentioned previously, you can offer your Kindle ebook for free for up to 5 days for every 90-day period you are signed up to KDP Select. Doing so allows you to obtain verified reviews even though readers have not purchased your book.
- **Kindle Countdown Deals (KCD):** Discount your Kindle ebook for a limited time on Amazon.com or Amazon.co.uk.
- **Amazon Literary Contest:** Amazon offers writing competitions in multiple marketplaces and languages.

Please note that when you enroll in KDP Select, you grant exclusivity to Kindle for at least 90 days. You cannot publish your ebook in marketplaces other than Amazon during this time frame.

How to Find Your 7 Backend Keywords When Uploading Your Book to KDP

Your seven backend keywords are those that Amazon asks you for when you upload your manuscript (see Step 15 below). They are added later and differ slightly from your main keywords (placed in your title and subtitle). When searching for your keywords, you want to ensure the following:

- Your book indexes for more keywords.
- Your book shows up for the best keywords in your niche.
- Amazon keeps you in your chosen categories.

It pays to know that Amazon looks for keywords on KDP via your book's title, subtitle, description, and A+ Content. For instance, in our example book, *Become a Backyard Chicken Farmer—Master Breed Selection and Feeding—Uncover the Importance of Facilities and Health Care to Effortlessly Increase Egg Production*, pertinent keywords and phrases include:

- Backyard chicken farmer
- Breed selection
- Feeding
- Facilities
- Health care
- Egg production
- Become a backyard chicken farmer
- Master breed selection
- Uncover the importance of facilities
- Effortlessly increase egg production

Once you identify the terms that Amazon will consider your keywords, it's time to help Amazon index your book for these keywords (connect your product to them) to rank your book higher (Barry KDP 2024).

To ensure your keywords are indexed:

- Choose keywords with high traffic because there is no point in using keywords that nobody searches for.
- Take advantage of long-tail keywords. These are longer keyword phrases that website visitors are more likely to use when they're closer to the point of purchase or using voice search. These keywords have a lower search volume than short or "head" keywords. For instance, a long tail

phrase in the sample book might be "backyard chicken breeding *for beginners.*"

Say you have written a book on math for kids. A short keyword term might be "algebra for kids," while a long-tail keyword term might be "algebra for kids *aged 3 to 6.*" As you can see, long-tail keywords are typically more specific and have more words. They comprise four or more words, while short keywords are made up of only 1 to 3 words.

Consider the main function of using long-tail keywords, which is telling Amazon what your book is really about. These keywords may not be searched as often as short keywords, but they are vital in helping Amazon know where to show your book and who should see it. Long-tail keywords also help you rank for short-term keywords, as they often contain short keywords within them.

In summary, long-tail keywords help you make your book more relevant so it can enjoy a higher conversion rate. Ensure the terms you use are highly relevant to the audience likely to search for your books.

 **Pro Tip:** Do not use the same words and jumble them up, as Amazon already indexes all possible combinations of these words. For instance, if one of your keyword phrases is "chicken farming for beginners," avoid also using "beginners chicken farming," as this is already covered.

Do not use too many words for your backend keywords on KDP because the more words you use, the lower your initial rankings will be (Kindlepreneur 2024).

Even though you can select relevant categories for your book when you are uploading it to KDP, Amazon can change these categories if it wishes, and it often does so based on your choice of backend keywords.

You can use keywords that are already in your book's title or subtitle if you wish for your backend keywords. However, ensure that the most important keywords are in your title or subtitle, as Amazon gives the latter far more importance than those in your 7 KDP boxes (Kindlepreneur 2024).

Also, avoid using invented words, as Amazon will not deem them searchable.

Kindlepreneur (2024) recommends that you fill in the 7 keyword boxes as such:

- **Use a specific phrase in the first 3 boxes.** These are phrases that you need to rank well with. To find these phrases, go to Publisher Rocket's keyword search and type in your words. In our example, one might type in "backyard chicken."

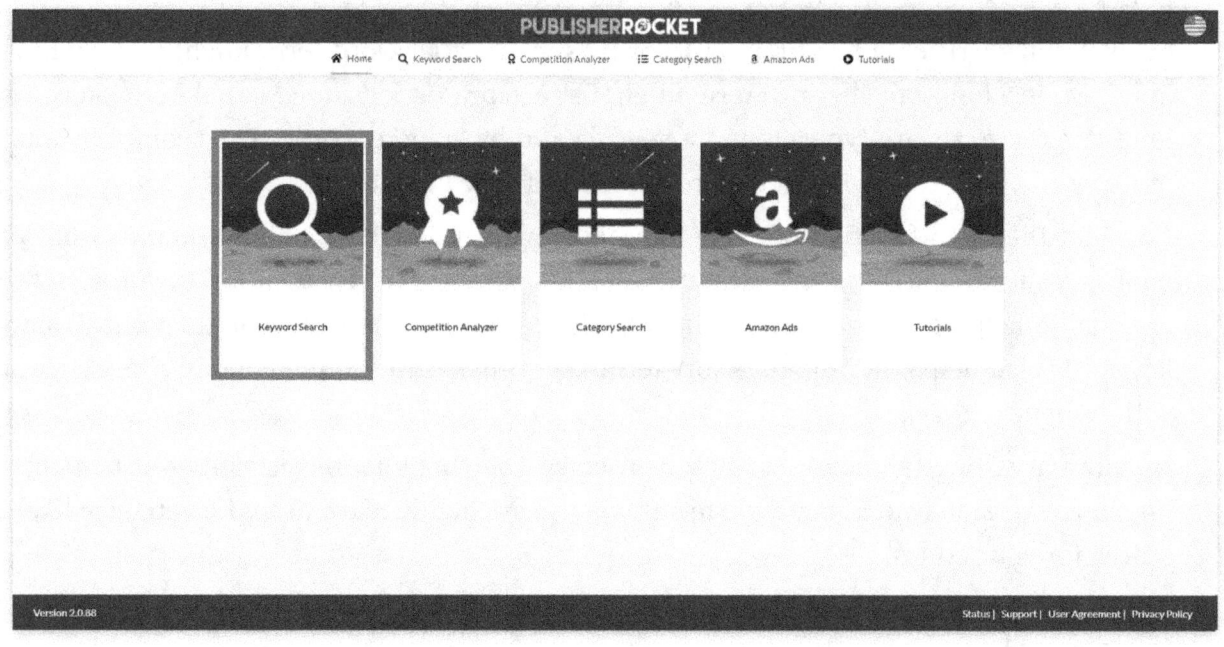

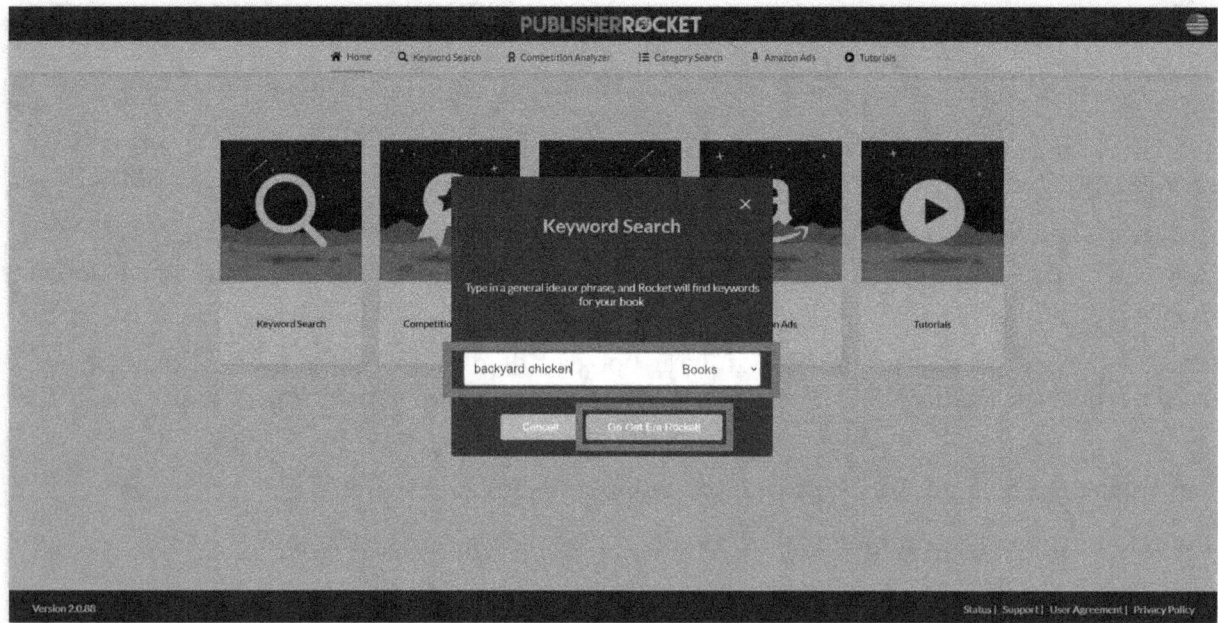

◊ Publisher Rocket will then reveal numerous keywords and let you know how many monthly searches these terms receive.

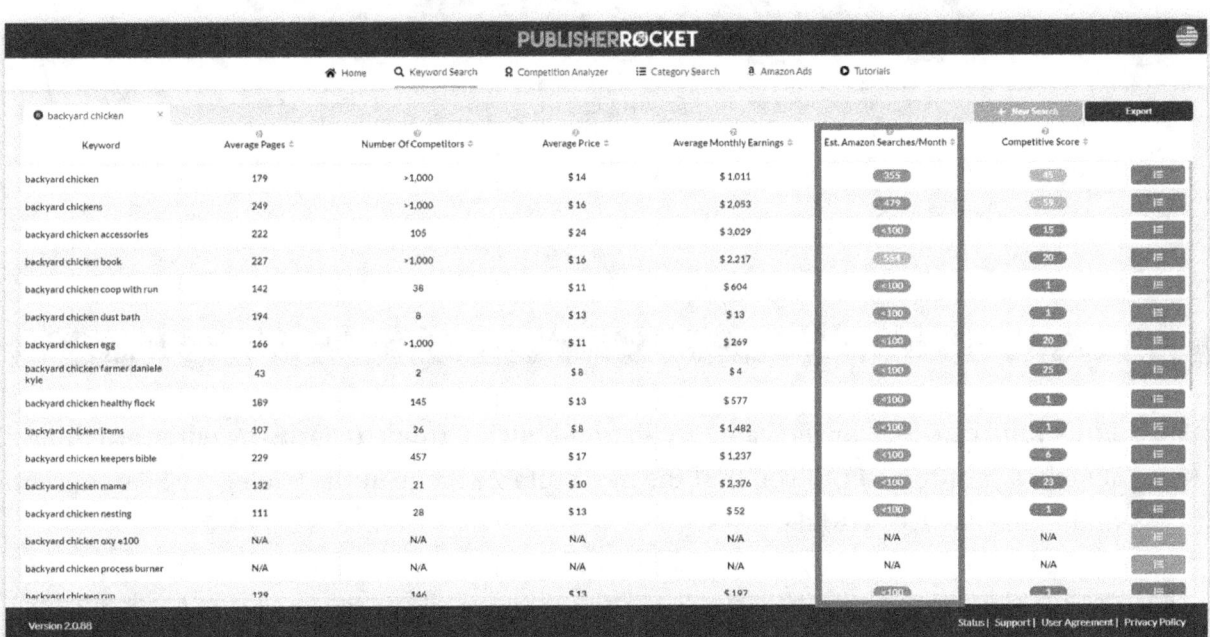

- Publisher Rocket has a handy coloring system (red, gold, and green) that will help you identify keyword terms that make sales.
- For the first 3 boxes, choose specific phrases like "backyard chicken farming," not broad ones like "chicken farming." Ensure the term is not too competitive. Terms in red are the most competitive, terms in green are the least competitive, and terms in gold are midway between the two.

- **Use the next two boxes for leftover words and phrases**. These are terms that are not as specific or descriptive as the last ones and may not have had as much traffic. For instance, "chicken farming for absolute beginners." You can use a few more words in these 2 boxes than in the first three. Avoid using commas, quotation marks, and other punctuation marks.
- **In the last two boxes, use the categories for which you want to be ranked**. This will ensure Amazon does not remove you from your chosen categories. For instance, you might use "animals" and "livestock." If you have Publisher Rocket, click **Category Search** to find good keywords for specific categories:

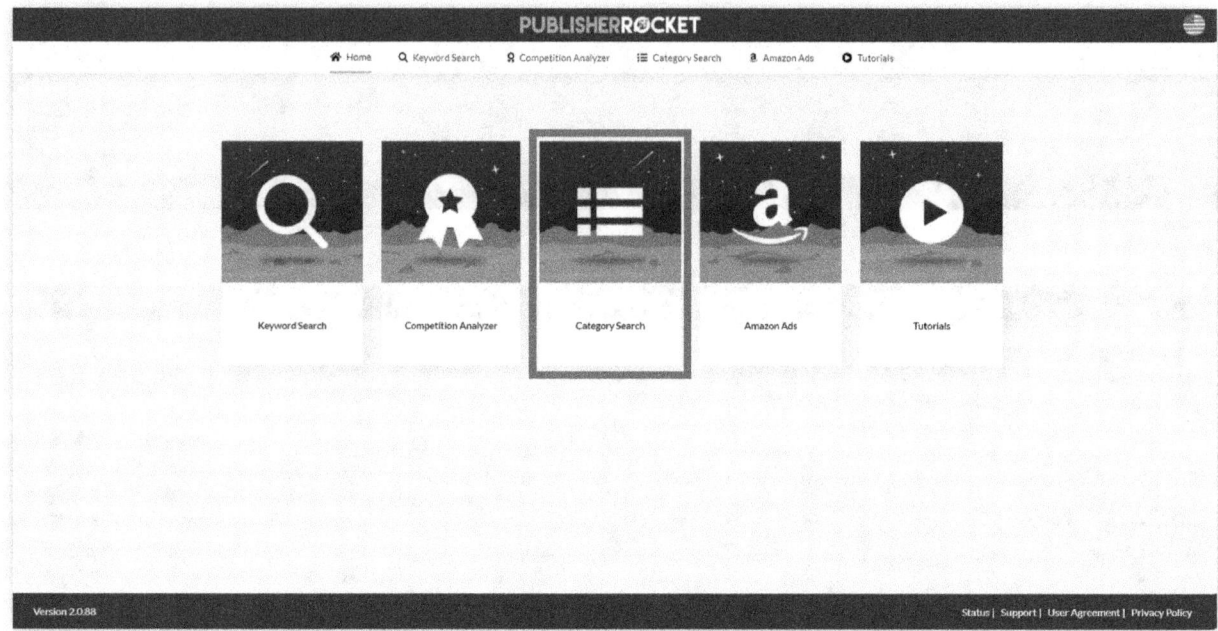

◇ Find your category in the category list and click **Check it Out,** or enter anything that matches your topic until you find the best suitable niche in the "Category Search" feature, and then click **Keywords**.

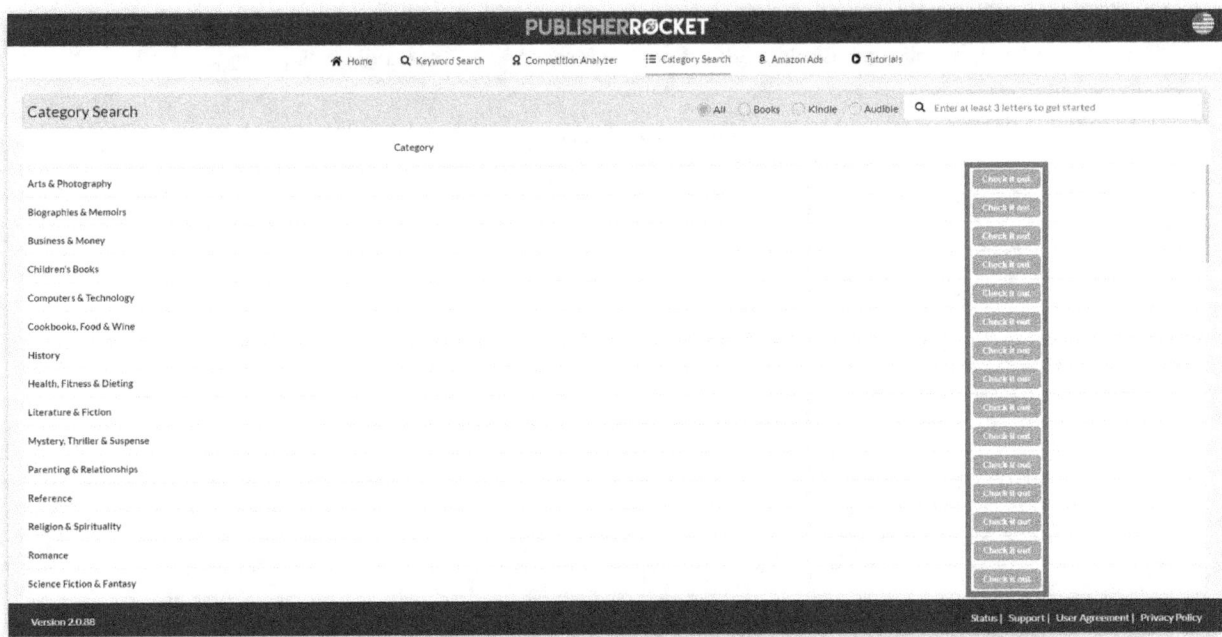

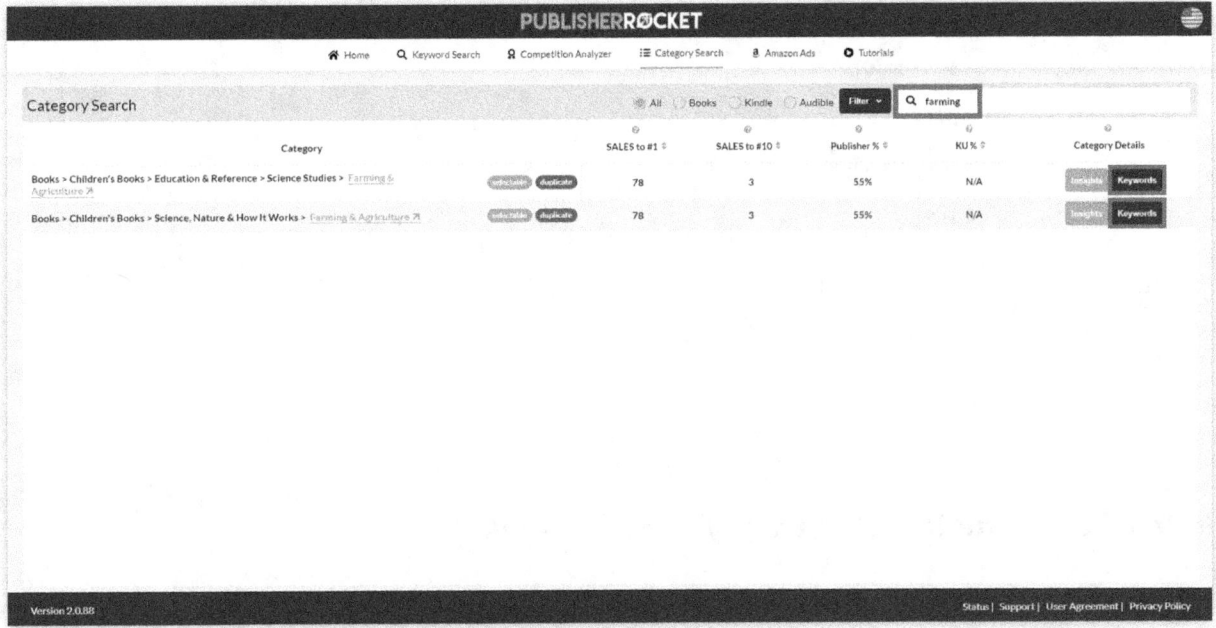

◇ Publisher Rocket will then provide you with a list of keywords that can help connect your book to your chosen category on Amazon. Choose the two that best suit your book and place them in the last two Keyword boxes. As with the previous two boxes, these can be filled with more words than boxes 1 and 2.

221

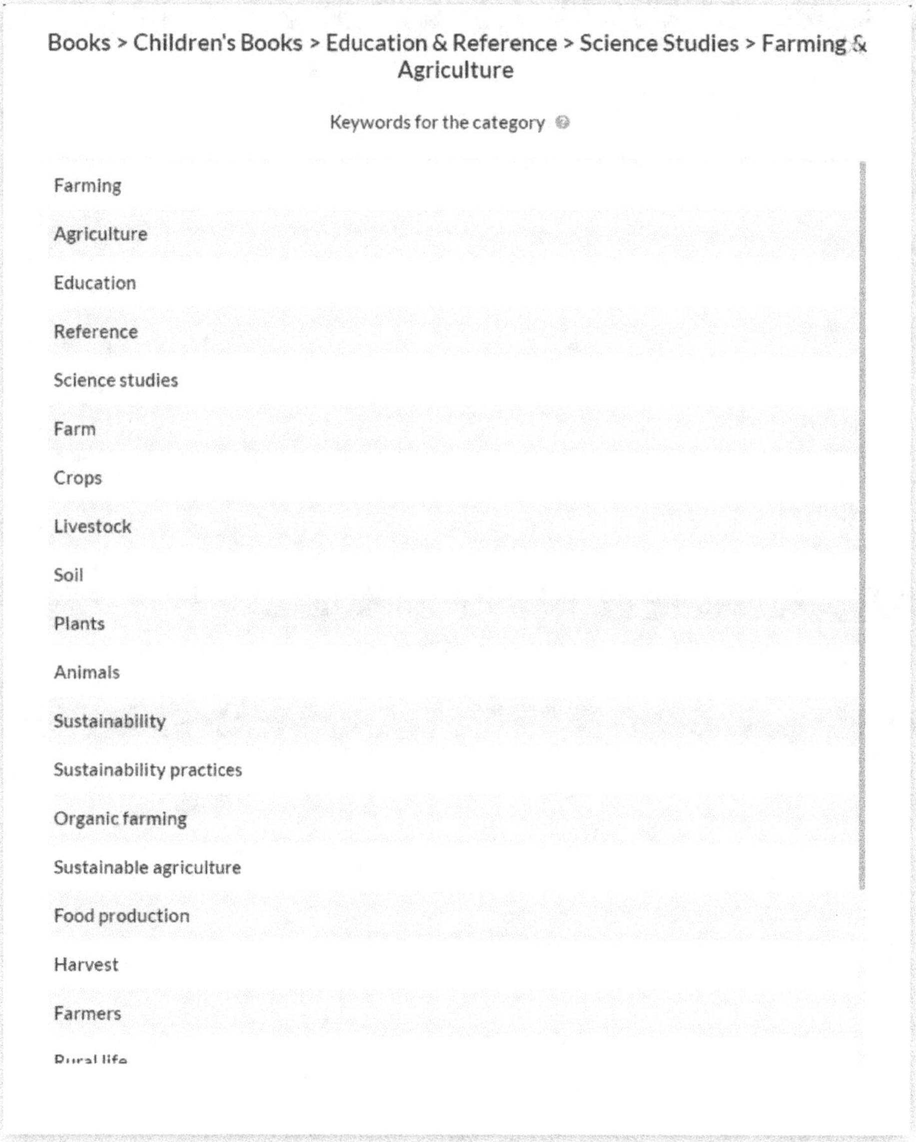

> Books > Children's Books > Education & Reference > Science Studies > Farming & Agriculture

Keywords for the category

- Farming
- Agriculture
- Education
- Reference
- Science studies
- Farm
- Crops
- Livestock
- Soil
- Plants
- Animals
- Sustainability
- Sustainability practices
- Organic farming
- Sustainable agriculture
- Food production
- Harvest
- Farmers
- Rural life

How to Choose the Right Pricing for Your Book

We recommend the following prices for your different book formats. All prices supplied are in USD:

Ebooks

- During the launch period/review collection time, PS recommends $0.99.
- After hitting 100+ reviews, adjust your price to $2.99 and keep going until you notice that sales decrease. Then, go back to the last price where you had good sales. Go no higher than $9.99.

Paperback

- During the launch period/review collection time, PS recommends $9.99.
- Once you start running Amazon ads (at least 20 reviews), increase your price to $14.99.
- Check your competitors' prices and then set your price accordingly. Your book doesn't have to be the cheapest book on the market, but it shouldn't be *much* more expensive than that of your competitors.

Hardback

- Check competitor prices and set your price accordingly.
- Make sure your hardback is more expensive than your paperback.

 **Pro Tip:** When setting a price for your book and looking at competitor titles, think about three things: the length of their book (page count), the trim size, the number of reviews they have, whether their book is selling well (BSR), and when their book was published.

You may find this table useful.

Format	ebook	Paperback	Hardback
Book Launch	$0.99	$9.99	Compare
When you start running Amazon ads	No change	At least $14.99	Compare
30 days post-launch	$2.99	At least $14.99	Compare
When you have 100+ reviews	Compare	Compare	Compare

How to Upload Your Book to KDP

This section will be divided into three parts:

- Part I: Uploading your ebook
- Part II: Uploading your paperback
- Part III: Uploading your hardback

Part I: Uploading Your Ebook

Let's upload your ebook first!

 Sign into your KDP account and click the **+ Create** button.

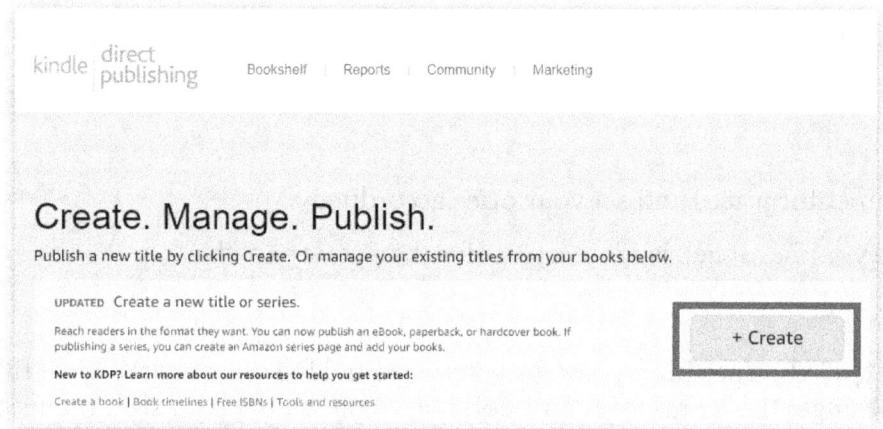

 Select **Create Ebook**.

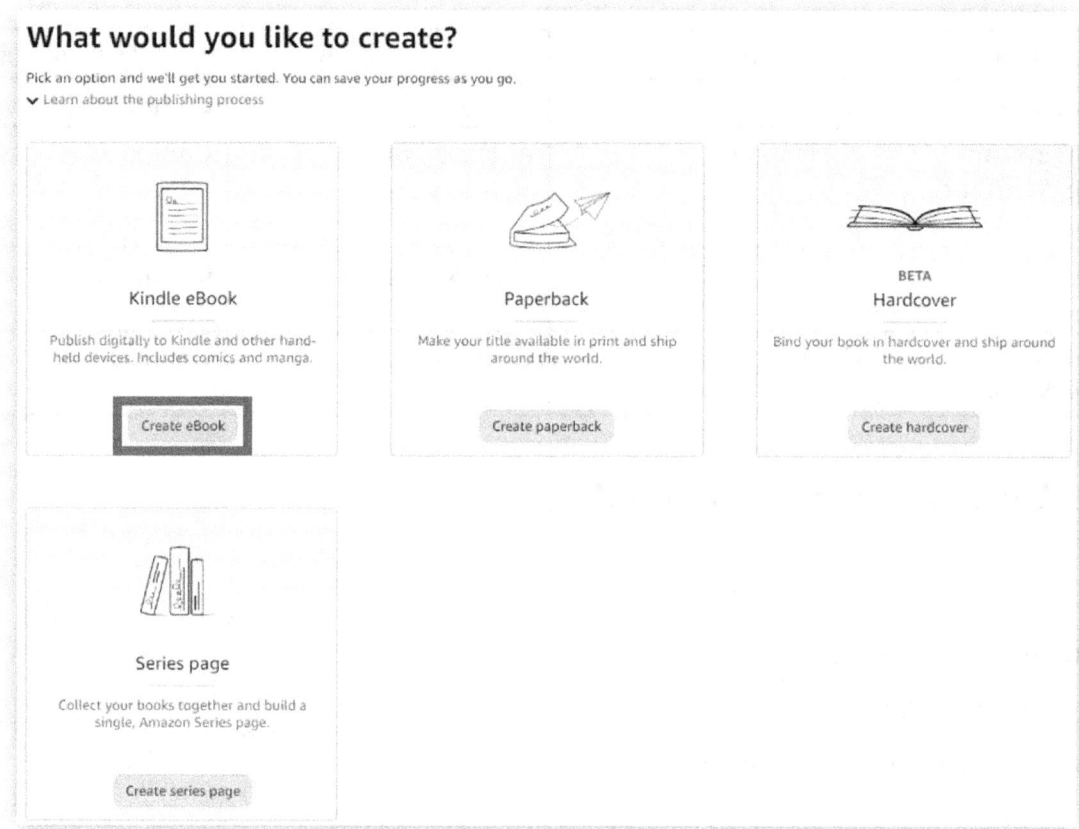

03 ▶▶ Fill in your ebook details, including your language, book title, and whether your book is part of a series. If your book is part of a series, click **New Series** or **Existing Series**, then choose if your book is your main content or a related work. For example, a workbook or a short story spinoff is considered a supplemental or related work.

> **Language**
> Choose the primary language your book is written in. Supported languages
>
> [English ⌄] ⬅
>
> **Book Title**
> Enter your title as it appears on the book cover. If you add a subtitle, a colon will be inserted between the title and subtitle. Before continuing, check your spelling since this field cannot be updated after publication. Book title guidelines
>
> **Book Title**
> [   ]
>
> **Subtitle** (Optional)
> [   ]

04 ▶▶ Don't add to a series and leave the edition number field blank.

> **Series**
> If your book is part of a series (or will eventually be), you can add it now. Alternatively, you can add it later using the options on the Bookshelf. Learn how to start a series
>
> If you create a series, it'll build a product detail page on Amazon, showcasing all books in the series. Linked formats of your books will be automatically added to the series.
>
> [Add to series]
>
> **Edition Number**
> The edition number tells readers whether the book is an original or updated version. Note: This cannot be changed after the book is published. What counts as a new edition? ⌄
>
> **Edition Number** (Optional)
> [   ]

05 ▶▶ Indicate your author's name. Leave the contributors field blank unless it is applicable.

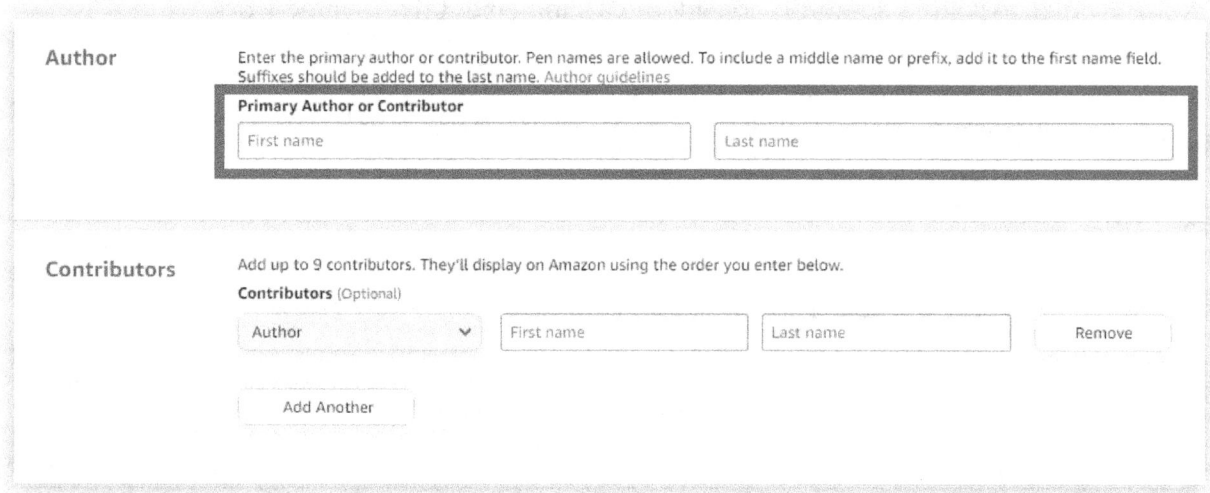

06 ▶▶ Insert your HTML description. Your description can contain up to 4,000 characters, and you can format your text in bold type, italics, bullet points, and similar.

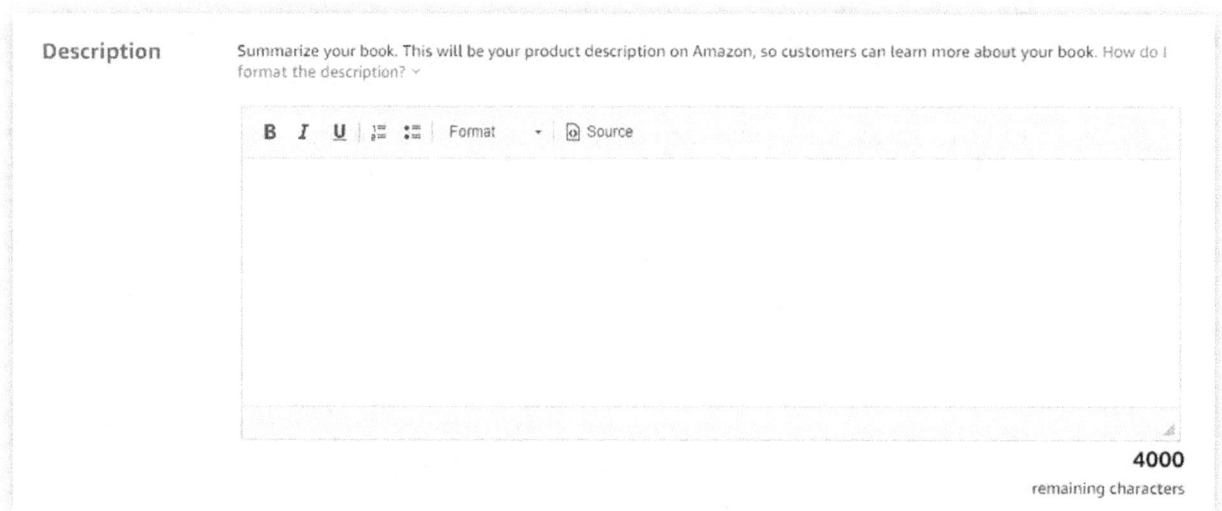

07 ▶▶ Indicate if you have publishing rights or if the book is a public domain work (a work that is not protected by intellectual property law and is therefore owned by the public).

 Indicate if there are sexually explicit images on the cover or interior or if the title has this type of language. Set the reading age if pertinent. This is particularly useful for children's authors or books containing content for readers aged 18+.

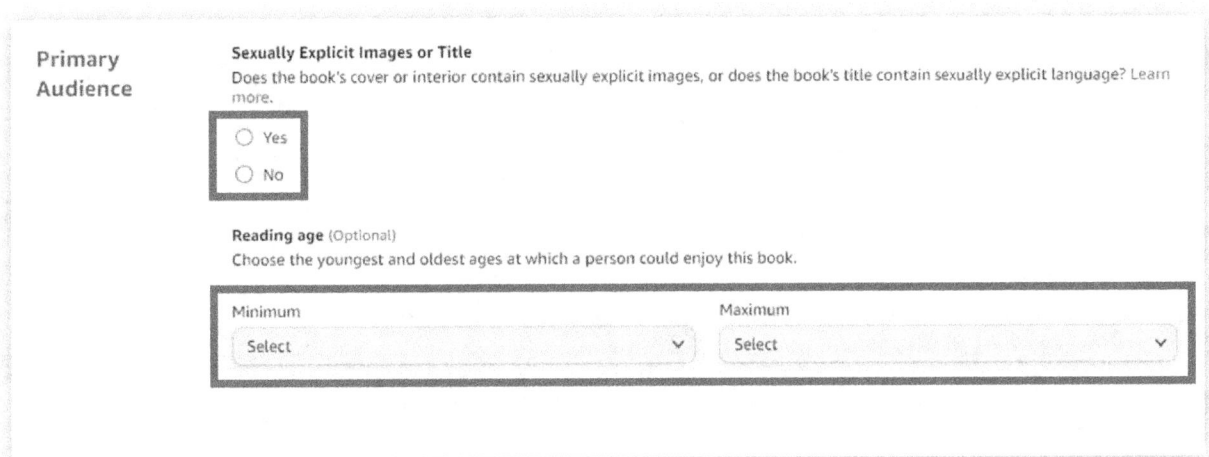

09 Choose your primary marketplace. For instance, if it is the US, choose **Amazon.com**.

10 Select up to three categories that best describe your book.

 Fill in up to 7 keywords. You are permitted up to 50 characters for each entry.

 You can then choose to release your book immediately or set a release date up to 12 months later (i.e., set a pre-order). If you decide to sell pre-orders, KDP will provide you with a product page you can use for this purpose. All your files and updates must be ready at least 72 hours before your book goes live on Amazon.

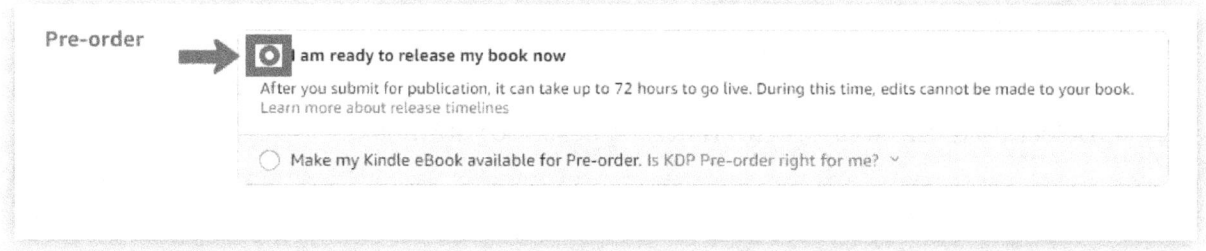

 **Pro Tip:** We do not recommend setting your release to "pre-order" status because if you do so, KDP will expect you to upload everything at least 72 hours before your scheduled publication date. If you fail to do so or cancel the pre-order, you will be banned from creating another pre-order for a full year. KDP does give you one "reset" period so you can change the date of your pre-order, but after that, you will be penalized for canceling or changing the date.

There is a second disadvantage of selecting a "pre-order" release date. As of the date of writing this (March 2025), pre-orders are not available for print books on Amazon. Technically, IngramSpark permits pre-orders for print books, but it's not worth going for this option because although the pre-order will show up on Amazon, IngramSpark will be responsible for setting up your sales page. That means you won't get to choose your Amazon categories, optimize your sales page, or access the book via KDP. Essentially, you will have less control over your book.

Finally, pre-orders can impact your sales negatively if you don't sell loads of books during the pre-order stage. This is because Amazon considers the pre-order stage to work out if your book is popular. If you aren't making solid sales during this time, it will take a massive effort post-launch to combat the earlier slump.

 Lastly, click **Save and Continue**.

 Now it's time to upload your "Kindle ebook Content," starting with your manuscript. We recommend uploading your manuscript as an EPUB file because this file type is responsive. As mentioned previously, this means it can automatically adjust the layout of your manuscript to fit different sizes and orientations. It also supports features that enhance the reading experience, such as adjustable text sizes and dark mode. You will see that KDP recommends uploading your manuscript using the Kindle Packaging Format (KPF). However, we advise against this for the following reasons (Booth 2019):

- KPF files are designed for use on Kindle e-readers. If your book is formatted as a KPF file, you cannot sell it on alternative marketplaces like Apple Books or Barnes & Noble.
- Kindle Create is not well-suited to books with images, tables, or non-standard fonts.
- When you upload a KPF file, Amazon conducts a quality check. If there are any formatting errors, the file is rejected, and you must start the formatting process again.
- The Kindle Previewer, which allows you to see your book's appearance, is sometimes inaccurate. This means that sometimes you don't spot formatting mistakes until your book has been published.
- KPF files can be harder to revise and update. They also lack advanced features that some authors enjoy including in their work, including embedded media and interactive features.

* Note that if you choose to upload your manuscript as a KPF file, you cannot undo it.

** Click **Add Digital Rights Management (DRM)** to stop people from accessing or copying your work unlawfully.

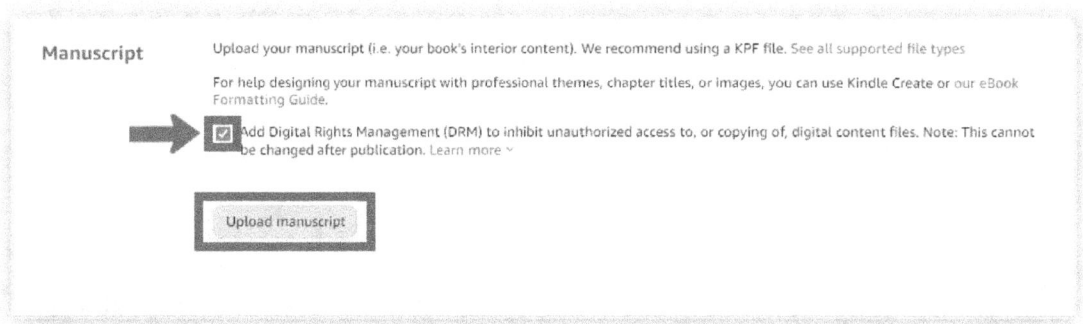

15 ▶▶ Upload your cover file. Remember that covers should not be added to the formatted book because they are uploaded separately.

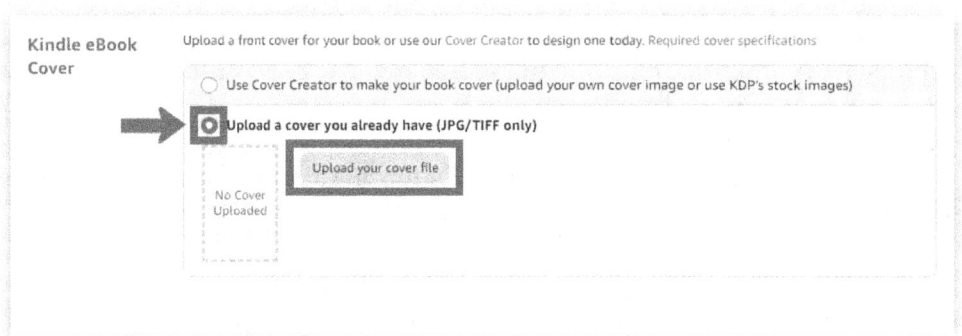

16 ▶▶ Fill in the "AI-Generated Content" section, indicating if you used AI tools to create texts, images, or translations in your manuscript. Indicate the degree to which you used AI for any translations in your book. There is a difference between AI-assisted and AI-generated work. AI assistance includes using AI to correct spelling or grammar mistakes. On the other hand, AI generation involves using AI to create actual content, **even if you edit it afterward**. If you have not used AI in any way, then select **No**.

230

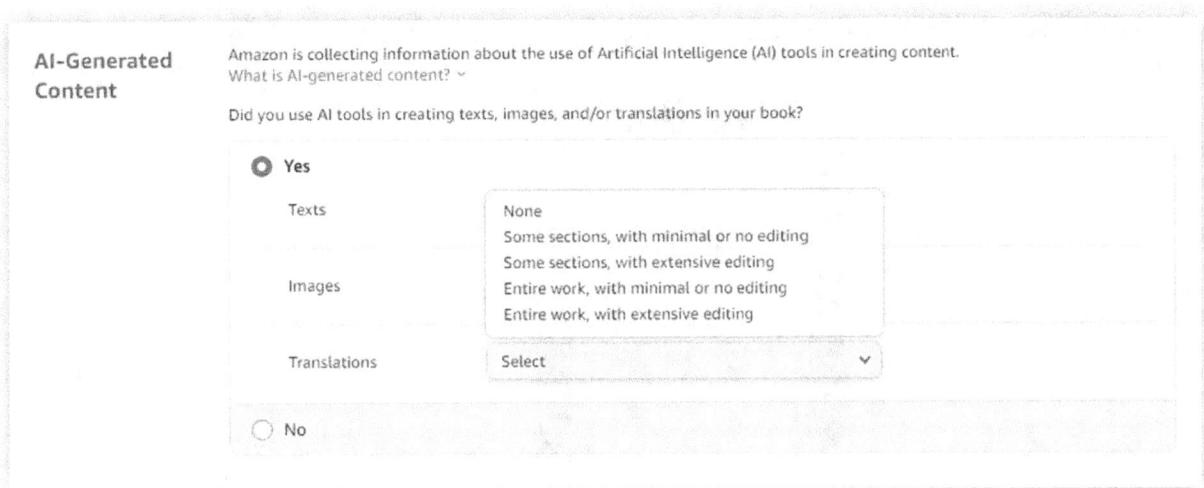

17 ▶▶ Click **Launch Previewer** to check out how your manuscript will look once published.

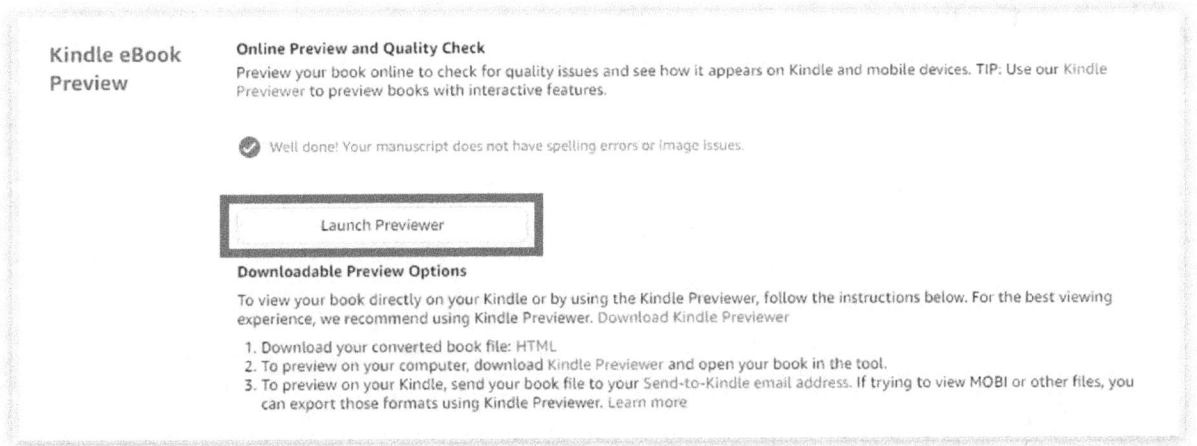

18 ▶▶ On the upper right of your screen, you will see that Amazon indicates any "Quality issues" it finds. You can ignore or fix these issues as you wish. Click through the entire manuscript, and if everything looks good, click **Back** in the top left-hand corner.

19 ▶▶ Skip the Kindle ebook ISBN section unless you have an ISBN for your ebook. Click **Save and Continue**.

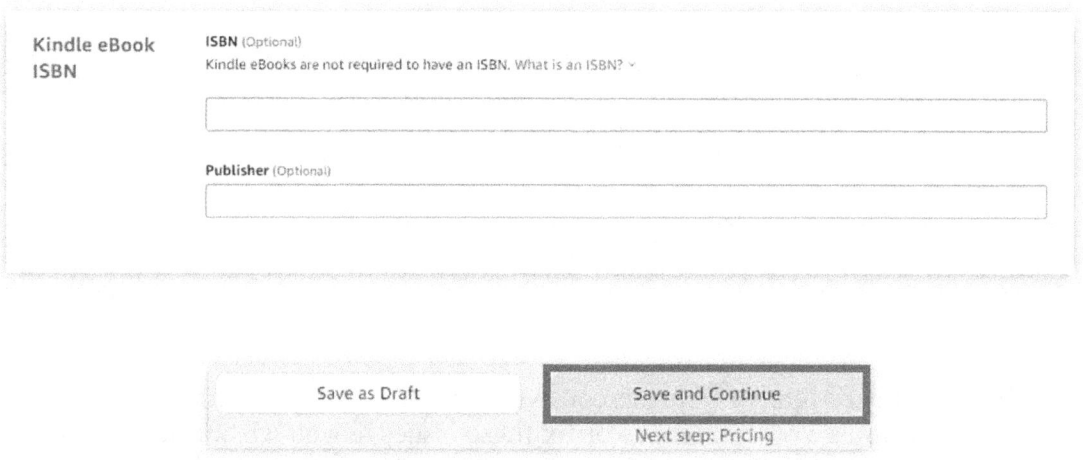

20 ▶▶ You will then start filling out the pricing tab. Choose if you wish to enroll your book in KDP Select.

 Select **All Territories (Worldwide Rights).**

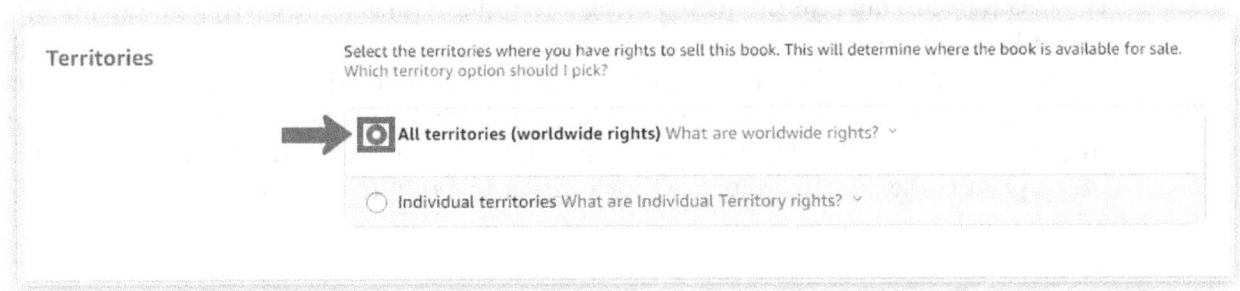

 Fill in the pricing, royalty, and distribution sections. When you first publish your book, set the price at $0.99. You will need to switch to 35% royalties for this. Once the 30-day launch period is over, go back into the listing and adjust the price. Set it to 70% royalties. This will enable you to choose a price between $2.99 and $9.99.

As mentioned earlier, we recommend setting a price just below the dollar (for instance, $5.99). Once you set your price in your primary marketplace, you will be shown a list of price conversions for other Amazon marketplaces. You have the option to manually adjust them or leave them as they appear.

Click **Publish Your Kindle Ebook.**

Part II: Uploading Your Paperback

 Once your information is all set, a pop-up notice will appear instructing you to "Publish your book as a paperback."

 The first relevant tab is entitled "Paperback Details." You will notice that all the metadata you indicated for your ebook will automatically appear. You will, however, still need to choose at least three relevant categories for your paperback since the previous categories you chose were only for your ebook. Indicate if your book is a low-content book or a large-print book. Examples of low-content books are journals, notebooks, and planners. Large-print books, meanwhile, are those with a 16-point (or larger) text.

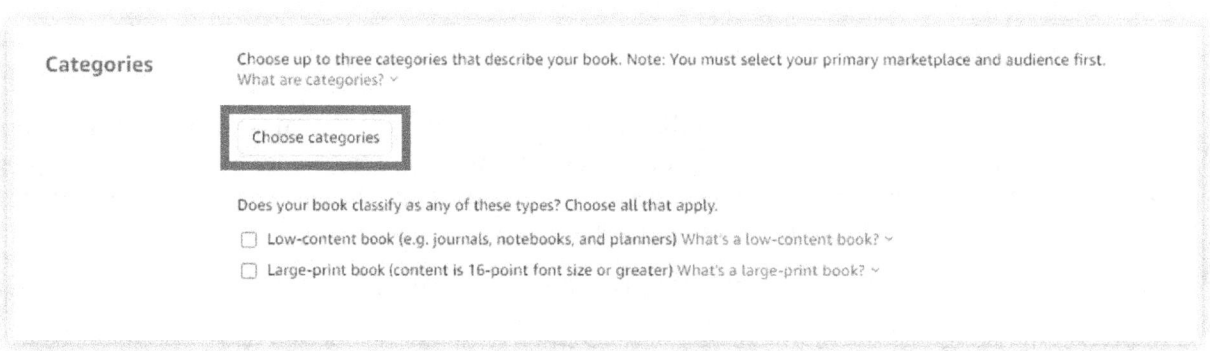

 Choose up to 7 keywords for your paperback version (as in Step 15 above). Pick different keywords from those selected for your ebook to potentially appear in more searches.

 Indicate your book's publication date, letting Amazon know if your publication and release dates are the same or if your book has been previously published. (This might be the case, for instance, if you bought the rights to a previously published book.)

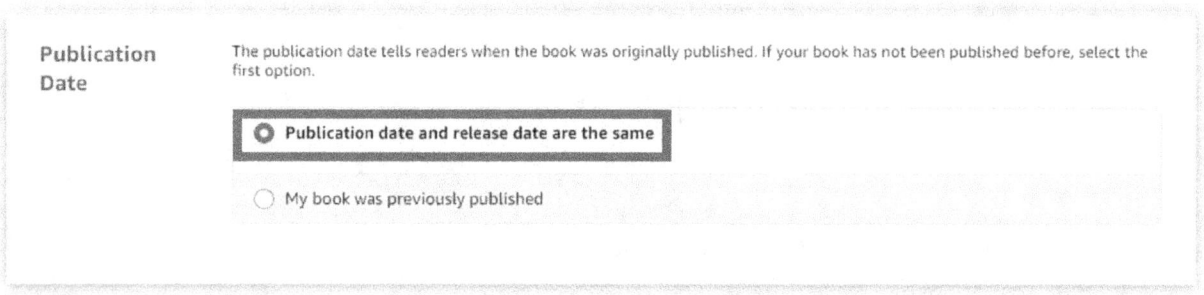

 Choose your release date, selecting **Release My Book for Sale Now** if you're ready and set to go, or schedule your book's release date. You can then order author's copies if you wish before your launch date. However, your product page will not appear until your scheduled launch date.

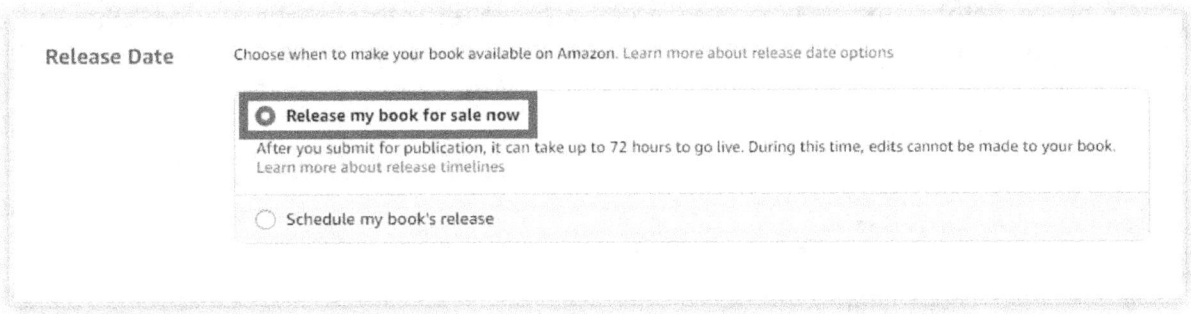

06 ▶▶ Click **Save and Continue**.

07 ▶▶ Start filling in the information required on the "Paperback Content" tab. First, choose to either get a free KDP ISBN or use your own. As mentioned previously, we recommend that you purchase your own.

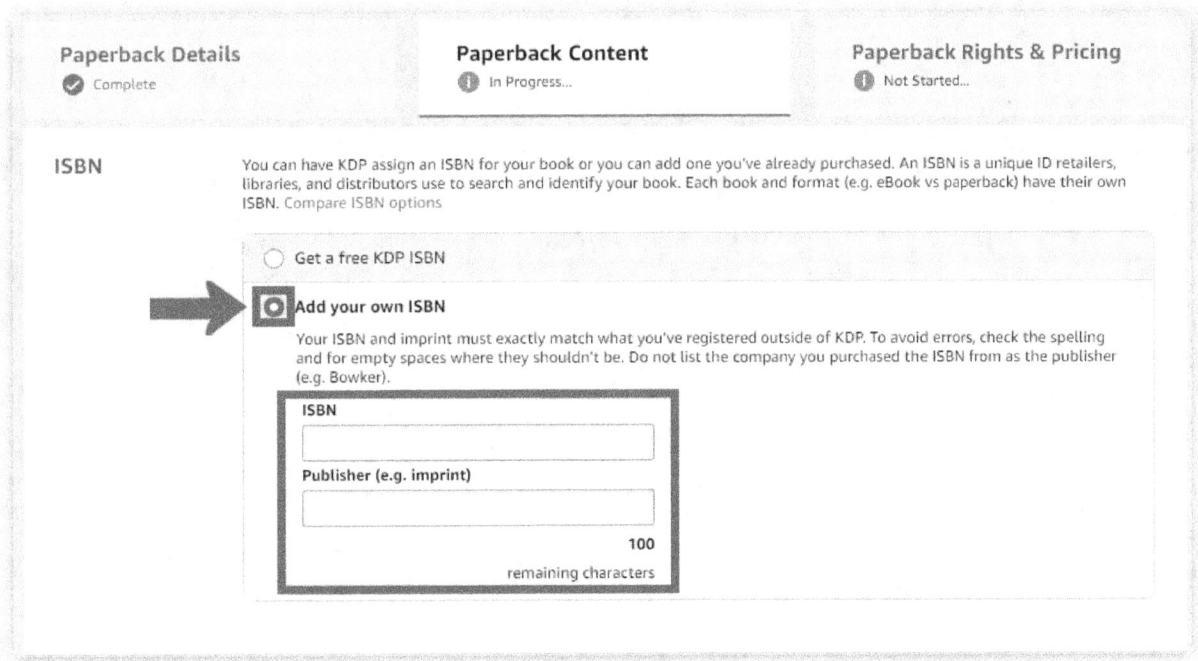

08 » Next, choose your print options, including the ink and paper type, trim size, bleed settings, and whether you prefer a matte or glossy finish for your paperback cover. Choose **Bleed** if your book has content that extends beyond the margin of your interior pages.

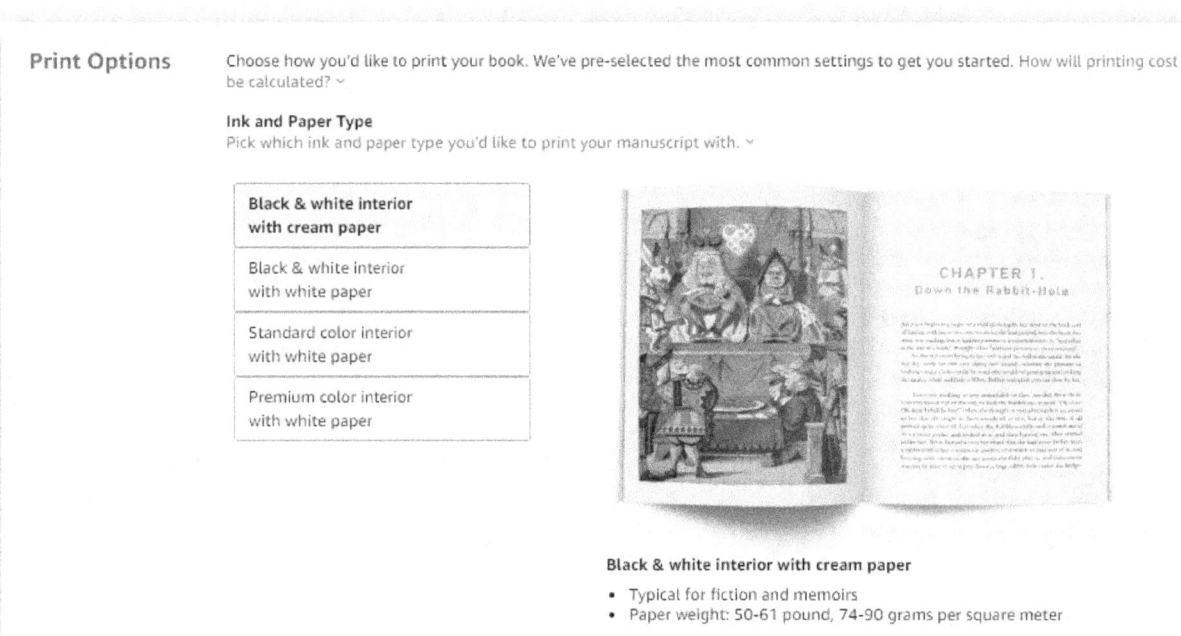

236

09 ▸▸ Upload your paperback manuscript. You will see that Amazon recommends utilizing a PDF file, and we agree for the same reason indicated above. PDFs are simply the best for preserving your layout, fonts, images, and other design elements. Using this type of file ensures that your book looks exactly as you envisioned!

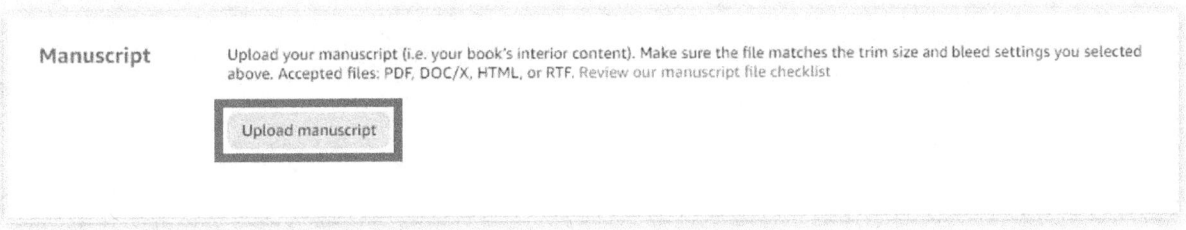

10 ▸▸ Upload your PDF cover file.

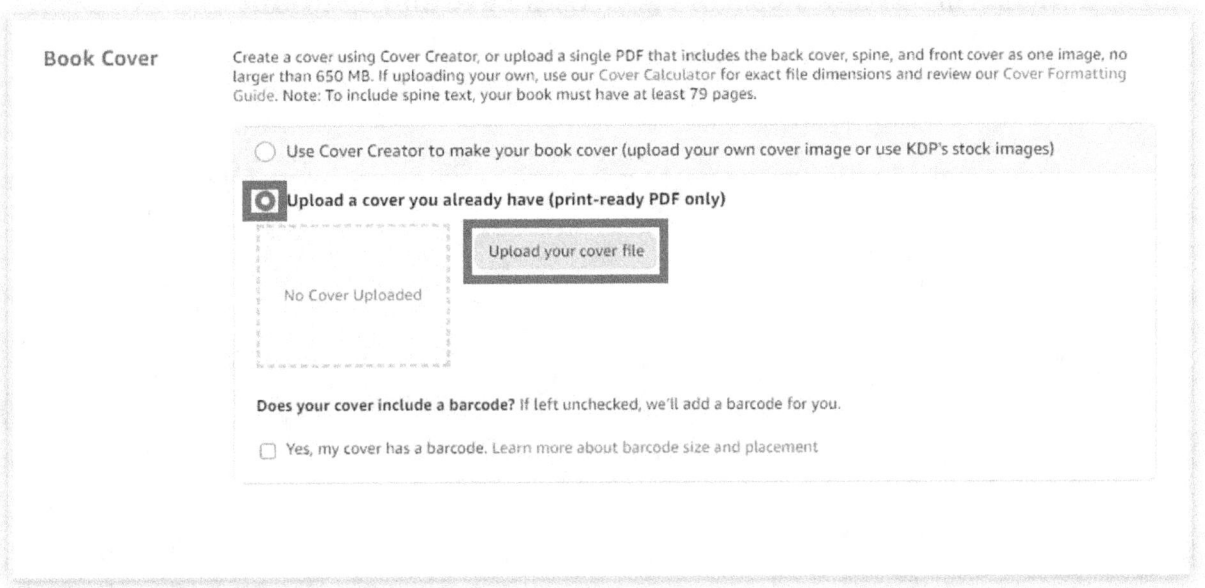

11 ▸▸ Fill in the "AI-Generated Content" section, as in Step 20.

12 ▸▸ Select **Launch Previewer** and make sure everything looks great. Amazon will demonstrate any errors it finds in the "Quality Check" box, which will appear on the left-hand side of your preview. For any problems that are perplexing you, you can contact KDP support for clarification. Click **Approve** once you are pleased with what you see.

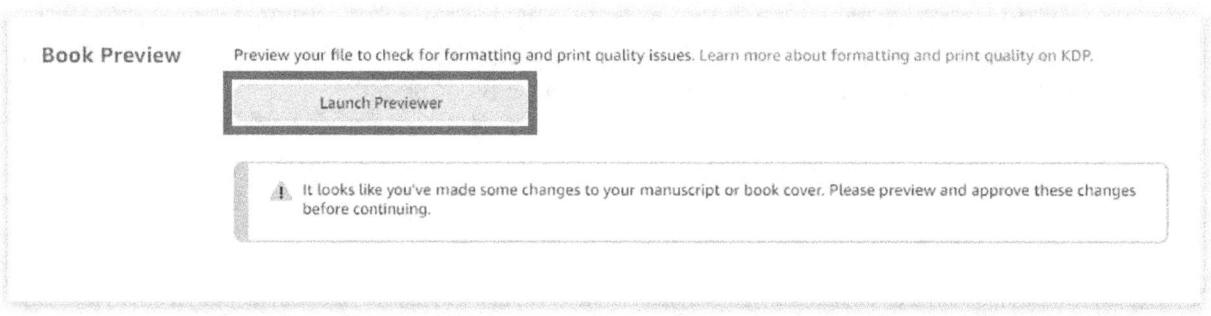

 Next, turn to "Summary," where you will be informed of your printing cost per book. You then obtain 60% of the price per book beyond the printing cost. For instance, if your book is priced at $10, but the printing cost is $2.30, you would get 60% of $10 minus the printing cost. The calculation would be $10/100*60 = $6 minus $2.30 for printing. Your royalties, in this case, would be $3.70. Click **Save and Continue**.

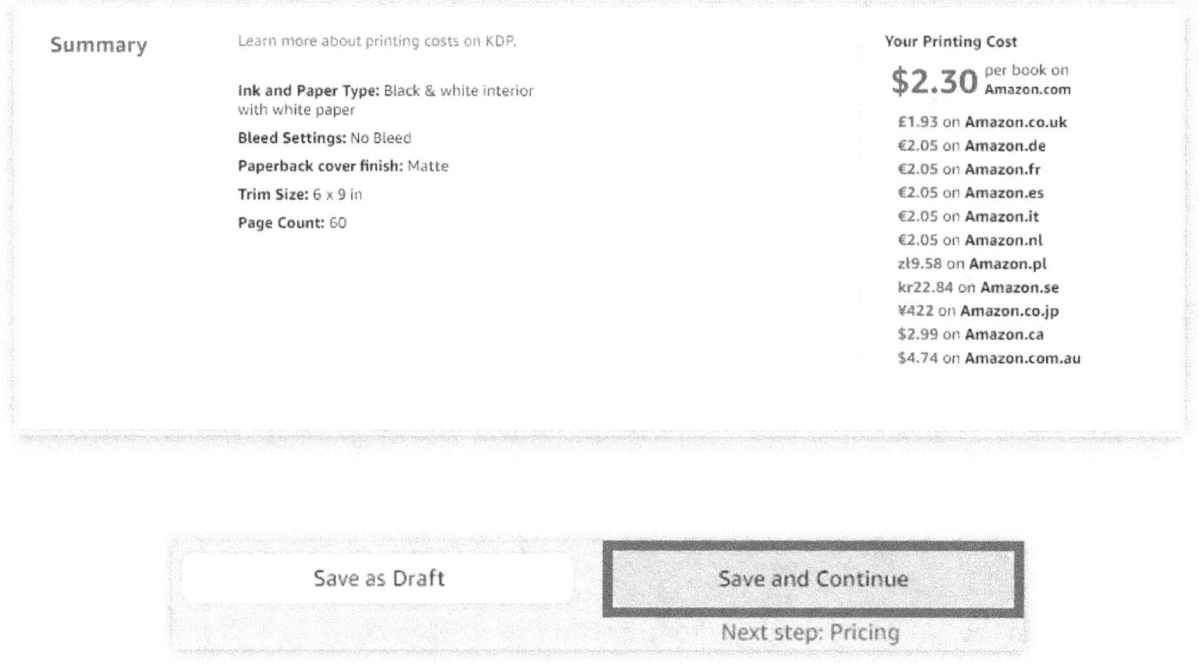

 Choose your distribution territories (we recommend **All Territories**), your primary marketplace, and your pricing, as you did for your ebook. Do not select **Expanded Distribution** if you also publish your book through IngramSpark.

[Screenshot of KDP Pricing, royalties, and distribution page showing Amazon marketplace pricing table with list prices, printing costs, royalty rates, and royalties for Amazon.com ($14.99 USD), Amazon.co.uk (£11.41 GBP), Amazon.de (€13.53 EUR), Amazon.fr (€13.53 EUR), Amazon.es (€13.53 EUR), and Amazon.it (€13.53 EUR).]

15 ▶▶ Choose whether to save everything as a draft or to publish your paperback book. If you are preparing for your launch day, click **Save as Draft.** If your launch day is today, click **Publish Your Paperback Book.**

16 ▶▶ You will be informed that your paperback has been submitted. Click **Done** and prepare to fill in all the information you need for your hardback book.

239

Part III: Uploading Your Hardcover

 Click **Hardcover** and select **+ Create Hardcover**. You will find that most pertinent details have already been filled in. You won't have to indicate new categories or use new keywords, but if you have any keywords in your list that you think might be beneficial, then you can use them in the keywords panels. Once again, schedule your release date and click **Save and Continue**.

You will need to use a different ISBN for the hardback version of your book.

Choose your print options.

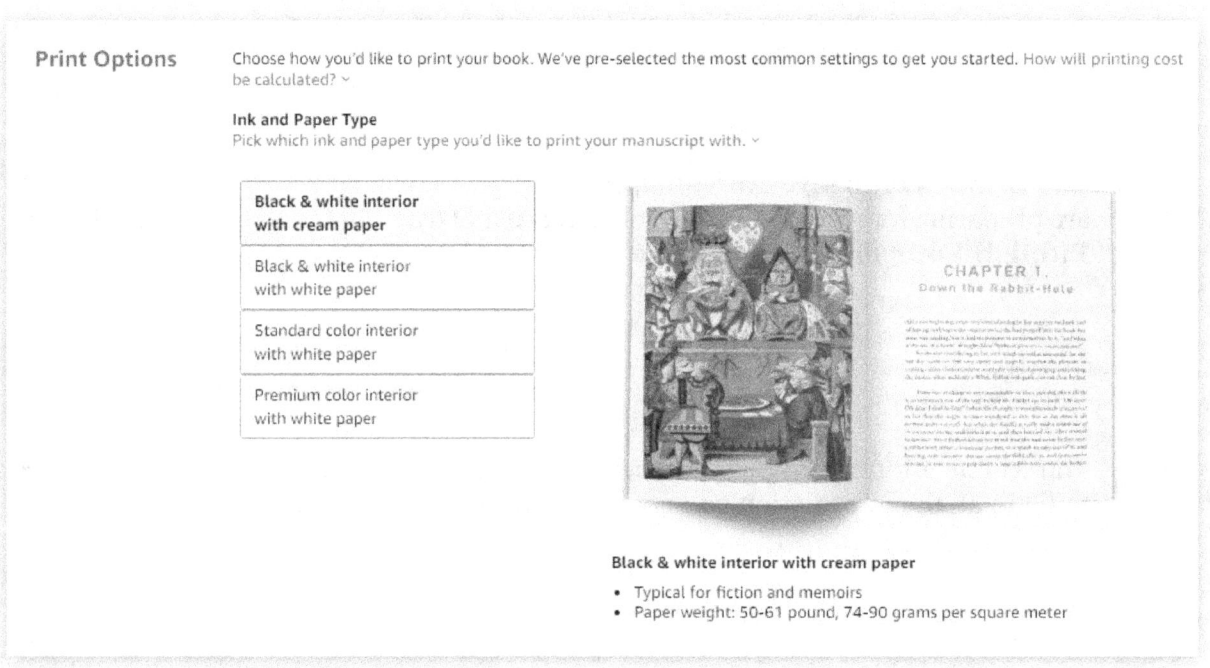

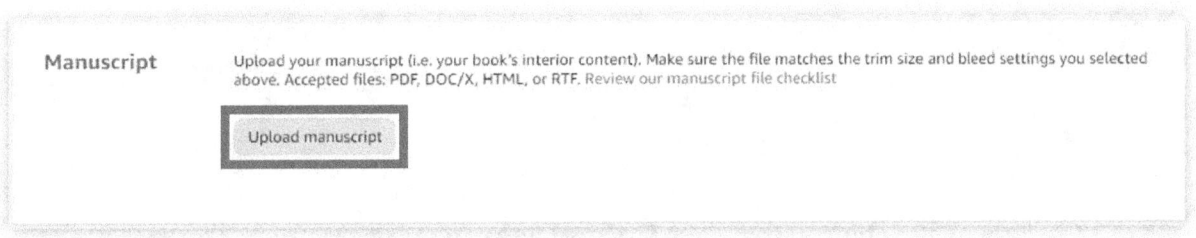

04 ▶▶ In the manuscript panel, click **Upload Manuscript**. You can use the same interior, but you will need to upload a different cover for your hardback manuscript since the sizing will be different.

05 ▶▶ Declare any AI-generated content as you have for your ebook and paperback, launch your preview, read the quality check (on the left-hand side of the page), and once you are ready, click **Approve**. Click **Save and Continue**. Again, select your territories, set your pricing, and adjust regional prices to keep amounts below the dollar. Note that you cannot select extended distribution for hardbacks.

06 ▶▶ You can skip "request proof" if you have done a thorough check while clicking through the preview.

07 ▶▶ Click **Save as Draft** or **Publish Your Hardcover Book**. Your ebook will most likely be ready in a few hours, while your paperback and hardback copies will most likely take up to 24 hours.

 **Pro Tip:** Upload everything before the launch date so all of your work can be ready for sale as soon as you decide! This way, if there are any issues, you will have more than enough time to fix them, and you won't need to postpone your launch date. For example, if you find a formatting issue or your cover is not properly sized, you can fix these problems and ensure everything is perfect on your big day!

How to Re-upload Your Book to KDP After Making Changes

Sometimes, you may wish to make changes after uploading your manuscript. To re-upload your new manuscript, return to your original listing on your KDP Bookshelf.

 Click the three dots on the right side and select **Edit Ebook Content**.

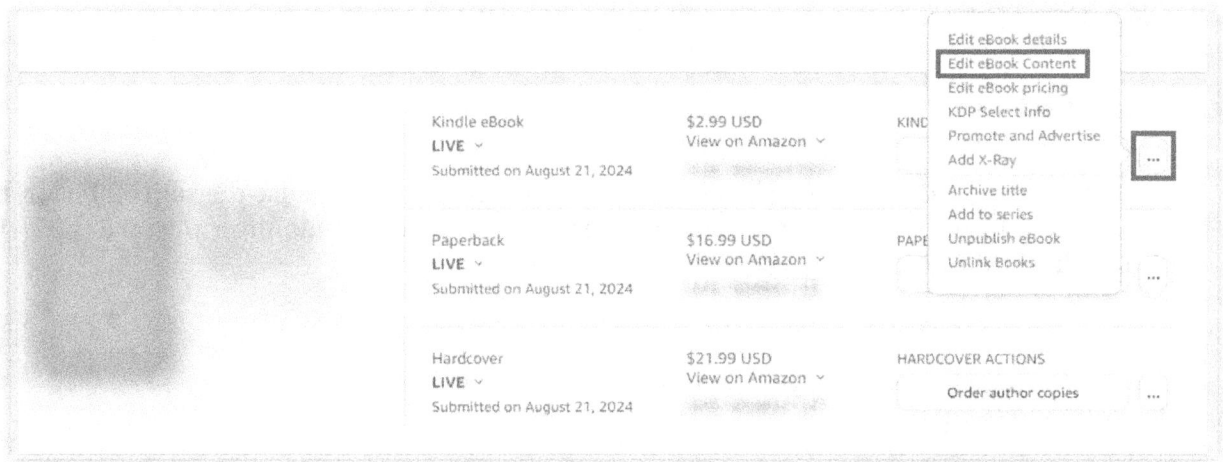

 Click the yellow button that says **Upload Manuscript**.

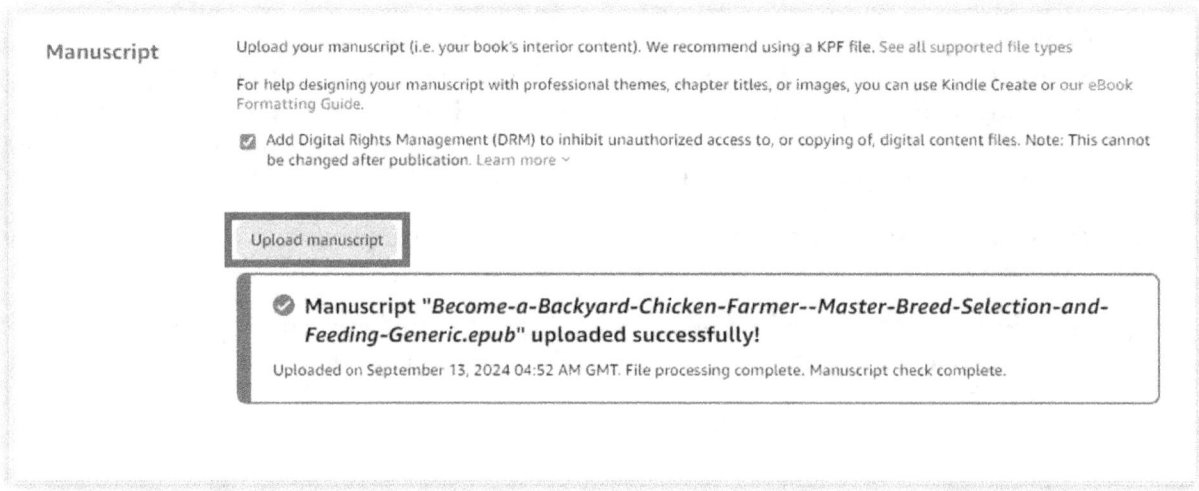

03 ▶▶ Once your new manuscript is uploaded, you can review it by clicking **Launch Previewer.**

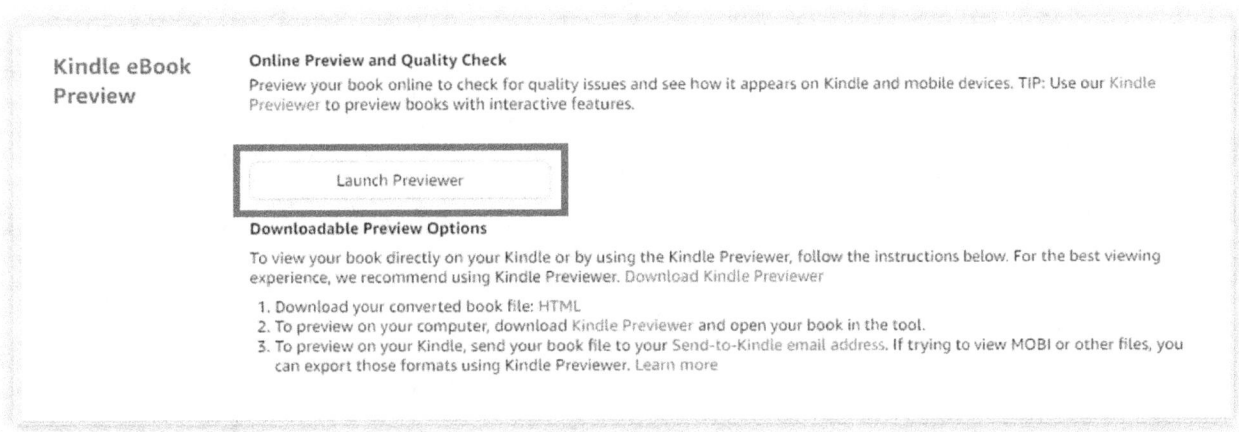

04 ▶▶ Once reviewed, scroll down and click the yellow box to **Save and Continue**.

05 ▶▶ It will bring you to the pricing page. Scroll down to the end of the page and click the yellow button, **Publish Your Kindle Ebook**.

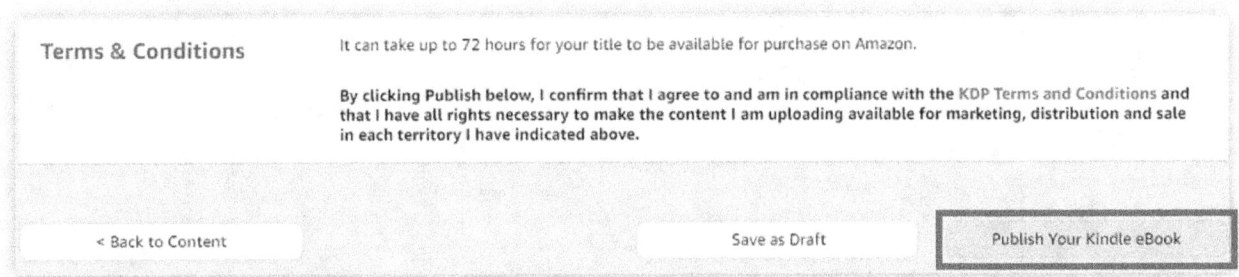

Now that you've learned how to upload all your key files to KDP, it's time to take things a step further. In the next chapter, we'll focus on avoiding common mistakes with KDP—especially those small mistakes that could lead to big consequences, like putting your account at risk. Let's ensure your publishing journey stays smooth and trouble-free!

Chapter 21

Preventing KDP Account Issues

If you are active in online self-publishing forums, you may have encountered publishers saying they have been "banned from KDP." Some authors have had their accounts terminated without any reason or previous warning. Do the best you can to avoid getting banned, but if you do, there are avenues you can take to reinstate your account. Remember that whatever you say or do on KDP should *contribute to a positive customer experience* (Dollwet 2023).

How to Avoid Account Termination

We recommend avoiding the following actions with your KDP account:

- **Publishing the Same Book Twice with a Different Cover:** Some publishers of no-or low-content books have tried to trick the system by publishing the same content and switching up the book cover. Whether your work is a coloring book or a self-help book packed with content, it is never a good idea to publish identical content and make it look like a different piece of work. Doing so means that a reader could potentially pay twice for the same product, which isn't a fair practice.

- **Using Online Templates Without Editing Them:** Users are not allowed to obtain a template from Creative Fabrica or Canva and publish it as though it were their original work. Just think about it: If a dozen other people uploaded the same information, then your content would be identical to theirs, and a reader could, once again, pay money for content they have already purchased. Note: this does not mean you cannot "bundle" your works and sell them as a new product. Selling book bundles is perfectly legal because you clearly state that your new product comprises a specific set of your previously published works.

- **Engaging in Keyword Stuffing:** KDP will not accept work that displays keyword stuffing. They specifically look at your book's title, subtitle, and author name. For instance, if your published author name is "Top nutritional advice for backyard chickens" instead of an actual name, it is evident that you are merely trying to get more keywords into KDP. Your author name should be a real name or pen name. Your account could also be terminated if you stuff keywords into your subtitle and excessively use words like "book" or "gift" in your title. You can also get banned if you use the same keywords in the title and subtitle. An example of keyword stuffing might be:
  - *Become a Backyard Chicken Farmer—Master Breed Selection and Feeding for Chickens, Poultry, Hens, Roosters, Layers, Free-Range Chickens, Organic Chicken Farming—Build Facilities, Coops, Chicken Houses, Pens, Ace Health Care, Veterinary Care, Chicken Health, Disease Prevention, Feed Types to Effortlessly Increase Egg Production, Egg Yield, Egg Quality, High Egg Production*

- **Making False Promises in the Title:** For instance, if you say your book will offer treatments for numerous chicken diseases, ensure your content actually does what you said it would. If you only provide information about one chicken disease and how to treat it, your title's promise could be construed as false.

- **Using a Subtitle that Isn't on Your Cover:** Your cover and metadata have to match.

- **Publishing Your Ebook in Other Marketplaces if You're Enrolled in KDP Select:** The KDP Select program has an exclusivity clause that says your ebook must remain exclusive to Amazon. This means you can't sell it anywhere else, including your own website, while enrolled. If your ebook is in Kindle Unlimited, you're in the KDP Select program, and the same exclusivity applies.

- **Offering Nonexistent Bonuses, Gifts, or Boxed Sets:** Do what you promise; give what you said you would.

- **Having Multiple KDP Accounts:** You may wonder how many KDP accounts you are legally entitled to have. The simple answer is that it is best to have just one account. We recommend using your personal account. If you wish, you can open up an LLC and then change the details in your personal account from personal to LLC, but you should NOT have two accounts. Ensure you have the following:
  - Legal name
  - Tax ID

- Telephone number
- E-mail address
- Bank account

- **Stealing Ideas:** You are not permitted to have a book cover design, title, or author name that is too similar to that of another work. This is the case even if the book being copied from is not trademarked or copyrighted. Do not use the exact same design style, font, and colors a competitor title has utilized. If it is deemed too similar, your account may be suspended.
  - Essentially, KDP does not tolerate what it deems attempts at "tricking" readers. For instance, if you are writing a similar book to an iconic work like Harriet Lerner's *The Dance of Anger* (2014), which is a bestseller with over 3 million copies sold, you cannot publish a book about anger management titled *Dancing with Anger*, as someone searching for Lerner's book might buy yours thinking it is the bestselling classic. KDP might also deem it unconscionable to use a pen name that implies authority one does not have. For instance, if you wrote a book called *Anger Management* and your pen name was Harry Lerner, it could be inferred that you are attempting to create a connection with this author that does not exist.
  - Publishing summaries of other people's work, creating companion guides for these works, and publishing others' workbooks without obtaining their approval is not tolerated.

- **Claiming Irrelevant Categories:** It is not okay to place your book in random categories on KDP to improve your chances of receiving a bestseller badge if these categories have nothing to do with your book. This is considered metadata manipulation and could lead to a negative customer experience.

- **Publishing Plagiarized Content:** Run every chapter of your book through a plagiarism checker. Grammarly has a plagiarism checker, which comes with Grammarly Premium. The latter costs around $30 per month for a monthly subscription or $12 per month with annual billing. There are also free checkers like Duplichecker, but these only check a small amount of text (around 1,000 words) at a time.

- **Obtaining Fake Reviews:** Tools like BookBeam help you analyze book reviews, showing you how many reviews were posted on given dates. Using this tool, it is very easy to see if reviews have been obtained organically. For instance, if a book receives 600 reviews in a day, chances are that these are fake, and KDP will delete them. Buying reviews or participating in review swaps is not permitted, either.
  - As we mentioned before, asking friends and family members to review your books isn't a good idea. Your friends and family are not necessarily the target audience for your book. If you receive numerous reviews from friends and family, Amazon will

recommend your book to people with similar profiles, and they may not be your target market, either. Low interest from these people in your book may lead Amazon to think your book will not be a great seller. If so, they will reduce the frequency with which your book is exposed via the "You may like these books too" suggestion generated by the algorithm.

- ◇ Some self-publishing authorities suggest that algorithms may be used to remove reviews left by your social media contacts. You could still have friends and family review your book because more reviews tend to make people want to buy your book, but it is unknown whether Amazon will take these reviews down.
- ◇ Although Amazon has *not* officially confirmed whether its algorithms check or consider authors' social media connections, it *has* confirmed the following information:
  - **Shared Addresses or Payment Methods:** If multiple Amazon accounts use the same shipping address or payment method, Amazon could deduce that these accounts belong to close connections, such as family members.
  - **Wishlists and Gift Registries:** Public wish lists and gift registries can reveal which users are connected, especially if friends and family members purchase items from each other's lists.
  - **Amazon Prime Household:** Amazon's Prime Household feature allows multiple accounts to share Prime benefits. Amazon deems all accounts availing of this service as closely connected.
  - **Purchase Patterns and Account Links:** If accounts are linked via addresses, payment methods, or frequent purchases for each other, Amazon might deem these accounts to be close contacts.

- **Turning No- or Low-Content Books into Ebooks:** If you publish a book such as a coloring book or journal (which is unsuitable for use as an ebook), don't publish it as an ebook. As Kindle Scribe grows in popularity, this rule may change since users will be able to fill in journals or create artwork on their screens.
- **Using Trademarked Terms:** Words such as "Harry Potter," "Google," "Marvel," "NFL," or "Star Wars" are not yours to use. Check the USPTO's Trademark Electronic Search System (TESS) before publishing your book.

 **Pro Tip:** Avoid writing books about well-known brands such as Disney or video games such as Fortnite, as these are trademarked.

- **Using Copyrighted Materials Without Permission:** KDP has strict guidelines against publishing content that includes copyrighted material without proper authorization. This means you can't use text, images, or other intellectual property owned by someone else unless you have explicit written permission. Copyright infringement is taken seriously because it exposes KDP to legal risks, so always ensure that any material you use in your book is either your own, in the public domain, or properly licensed.
- **Publishing Low-Quality Content:** Books that continually get one-star reviews will most likely cause the KDP account that publishes them to be shut down. Low-quality books include those translated into another language using Google Translate.
- **Failing to Send Accurate Tax Information Requested by KDP or Non-Compliance with Tax Regulations:** As a KDP publisher, you're required to provide accurate tax information for compliance with international tax laws. If KDP requests specific forms or updates to your tax details and you fail to provide them—or if the information you submit is inaccurate—your account may be suspended or terminated. Always ensure your tax details are complete and up-to-date to avoid complications.
- **Publishing Work That Is 100% AI-Generated:** While using AI to help you research and create some content is okay, you should take the time to edit or rewrite AI manuscripts that are obviously computer-generated. Consider that if people identify your book as machine-generated and get bored by exaggerated metaphors, repetition, and lack of originality, they will most likely give your book a low rating. As such, using AI will save on ghostwriting in the short term, but you will pay dearly in the long term if your book is reviewed poorly or banned from KDP.
- **Violating KDP's Terms of Service:** Failing to comply with KDP's terms of service — violating publishing rules or participating in banned activities—is a no-go.
- **Violating KDP's Community Guidelines (www.publishingservicesbook.com/community-guidelines):** Actions such as hate speech, abuse, and other illegalities may result in an account being banned (Kindle Direct Publishing, n.d.-f).

As a whole, you can avoid having your account terminated by creating authentic quality for your readers, respecting the intellectual property rights of others, and operating within legal limits. The good news about termination is that KDP does not take you by surprise. Instead, users are given numerous warnings before their accounts are terminated. If your account is suspended, contact KDP immediately and fix the issue causing contention.

How to Avoid Account Banning on KDP

Before filling you in on the steps to take if your account gets banned, we will explain the difference between a warning, suspension, and termination.

- **Warning:** When Amazon spots something that violates its terms, it sends you a notification email so you can fix the problem before Amazon takes further action.
- **Suspension:** Amazon temporarily freezes your account, so you cannot publish or effect changes until the problem is resolved.
- **Termination:** Amazon permanently closes your account, and all your books are removed from its store.

Pro Tip: It is important to note that in most cases, account actions are triggered by Amazon's automated system and not by individuals working for the company. Amazon's algorithm analyzes various factors and creates a risk score for all accounts. If your score surpasses the threshold, the system issues a warning or suspends or terminates your account. This algorithm explains why some self-publishers are seemingly punished without doing anything wrong, while others seem to get away with more serious infractions.

Steps to Take If Your Account Is Suspended or Terminated

If you discover that your account has been suspended or terminated, follow these steps:

01 Read Amazon's notification to determine the exact reason why your account is under threat.

02 Collect any evidence or documentation you need to prove your case.

03 Write a concise, professional appeal addressing the issues Amazon has notified you about.

04 Be ready to wait for a response, as Amazon deals with multiple appeals on any given day. Many authors have reported that it takes upward of three months to get their accounts restored (Roberts, n.d.).

05 Consider hiring an Amazon account specialist if you aren't getting anywhere. This professional has a profound understanding of Amazon's policies, and they can give you tips you may not otherwise have access to. Some authors have also found it helpful to contact the Alliance of Independent Authors (www.publishingservicesbook.com/alliance-of-independent-authors). This group is based in the UK and is run by independent authors. As a last resort, you can seek legal advice so a lawyer can draft an official appeal to Amazon on your behalf. This process is undoubtedly costly, and even with a lawyer, it can take around three to six months to reinstate a terminated account (Hamilton 2023).

Now that you've mastered the process of uploading your book to KDP and ensuring your account is safe, it's time to explore another vital platform for self-publishing: IngramSpark. In the next chapter, we'll guide you through the steps of publishing your book on IngramSpark, discuss how it differs from KDP, and explain why this platform can be an important part of your distribution strategy. Let's get your book into even more hands!

Chapter 22

The Complete IngramSpark Publishing Process

We have mentioned IngramSpark briefly throughout the book, but now is a good time to explain a bit more about why it is a useful service when you are a self-publisher. IngramSpark is a service that guarantees publishers reliable print book and ebook distribution from one self-publishing entity. When you publish your book with IngramSpark, you plug into one of the industry's largest global book distribution networks and you obtain access to over 45,000 independent bookstores, chain stores, libraries, ebook retailers, online stores, and universities (LLC, n.d.).

IngramSpark distributes books to established companies like Amazon, Apple, Kobo, Barnes & Noble, and Walmart.com in the US and Canada. However, it also covers numerous online and physical stores in the UK, Europe, Australia, and New Zealand. When you publish your book on IngramSpark, you make it available to a much larger audience than if you limited yourself to Amazon. You can consult IngramSpark's global distribution network on its website: www.ingramspark.com.

IngramSpark's parent company is Ingram, which is the owner of the book catalog most bookstores use to order their stock. When you publish your book on IngramSpark, your book makes it to these catalogs and makes it easier for bookstores to find and distribute your work. Doing so also guarantees you automatic inclusion on Bookshop.org—a competitor of Amazon that allows buyers to choose which bookshop they would like to donate 10% of the book's profits to.

There are small differences from Amazon that also make IngramSpark an attractive choice. Amazon prints book interior pages at 55lb for black and white and 60lb for color. IngramSpark allows you to choose between 50lb and 70lb options. Keep in mind that in practical terms, it is hard for most readers to tell the difference between the paper quality of Amazon and IngramSpark books.

IngramSpark books have higher printing costs on average (around $1 to $2 per book) than Amazon, and shipping costs are also higher (Hill, n.d.). However, IngramSpark is all about taking advantage of the market that Amazon doesn't serve. It doesn't cost anything to upload the book to this platform (except for the cover resizing and the ISBNs). You'll only set it up once and never touch it again.

Most sales you make with your publishing business will come from Amazon, but this platform can create more exposure and a little extra income.

Why Publishing Services Recommends IngramSpark Only for Printed Books

When you enroll your ebook in Amazon's KDP Select program, you grant Amazon exclusive rights to distribute your ebook. This exclusivity allows your ebook to be available on Kindle Unlimited, where readers can access it and you earn royalties based on the number of pages they read.

However, there's an important restriction: if your ebook is enrolled in KDP Select, Amazon strictly prohibits you from selling the ebook on any other platform. Violating this rule can result in serious consequences, including having your account banned by Amazon.

For this reason, Publishing Services recommends using IngramSpark only for your printed books, ensuring there are no conflicts with Amazon's exclusivity requirements for ebooks.

IngramSpark: Not a Replacement for Amazon

You may wonder why you need to upload your book to KDP if IngramSpark includes Amazon in its distribution list. This is because books distributed to Amazon by IngramSpark may sometimes show up as being out of stock.

Also, your readers can end up waiting for weeks before their books are shipped. Another reason is that you need to be enrolled in KDP to upload your A+ Content.

How to Upload Your Book to IngramSpark

Paperback

 Get the following files ready so that uploading your book to IngramSpark is a breeze:

- Your manuscript
- The book cover
- Your book description in HMTL
- Your ISBN

 Open an account with IngramSpark. You will simply need an email and password. You will be asked to finish setting up your account by providing your account info (your name and address) and then clicking **Continue**. You will be sent to the Verification Tab, where you will be prompted to fill in a 6-digit verification code sent to your smartphone. Next, you'll see a list of Agreements to sign. Sign the "Print On Demand Agreement/IngramSpark Agreement," which is obligatory. You can click the **Target.com Addendum** if you

wish. Click **Sign Agreements,** then **Finish Setting Up My Account**. Enter your Payment Information (your currency and how you want to be paid, PayPal, for instance), provide the email address linked to your PayPal account, and continue. You will be asked to provide your credit card information. Fill it in and click **Continue**. In "Enter Tax Information," fill in your federal taxpayer number and your state, initial the document, and click **Save**. On the pop-up form, check that the information you have provided is correct and click **W-9 Is Correct**. Click **Continue,** and you're done!

03  Go to **Titles** on your dashboard and click **Add Title**.

04  Choose **Print Book Only**.

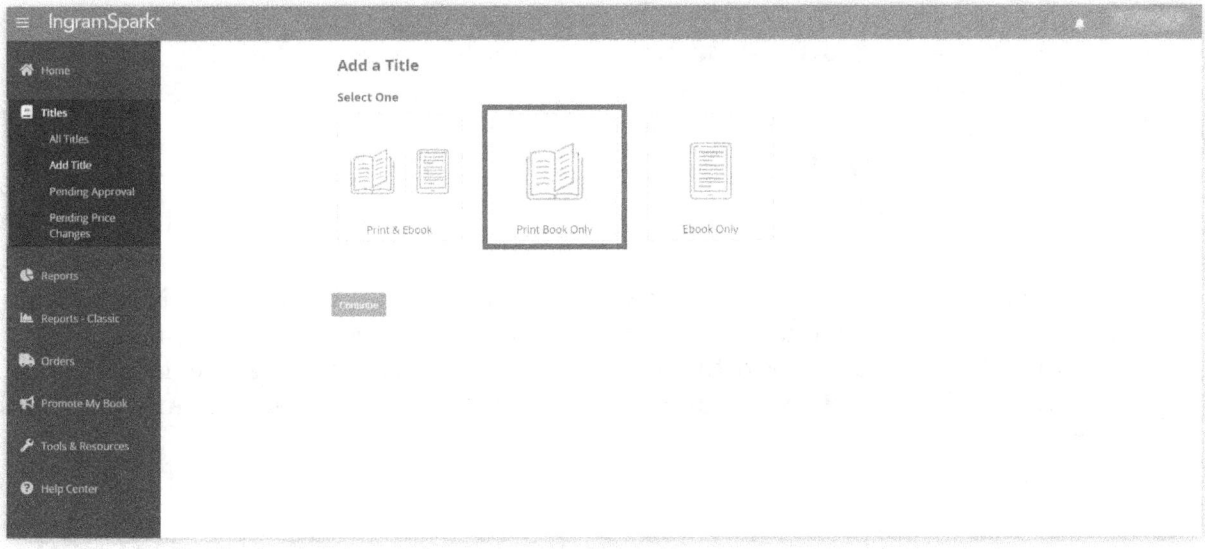

255

 Beneath, you will see the question, "Do you have files ready to upload?" Click **Yes, all my files are ready**. Tick the boxes saying you have your print jacket, cover, and interior, and click **Continue**.

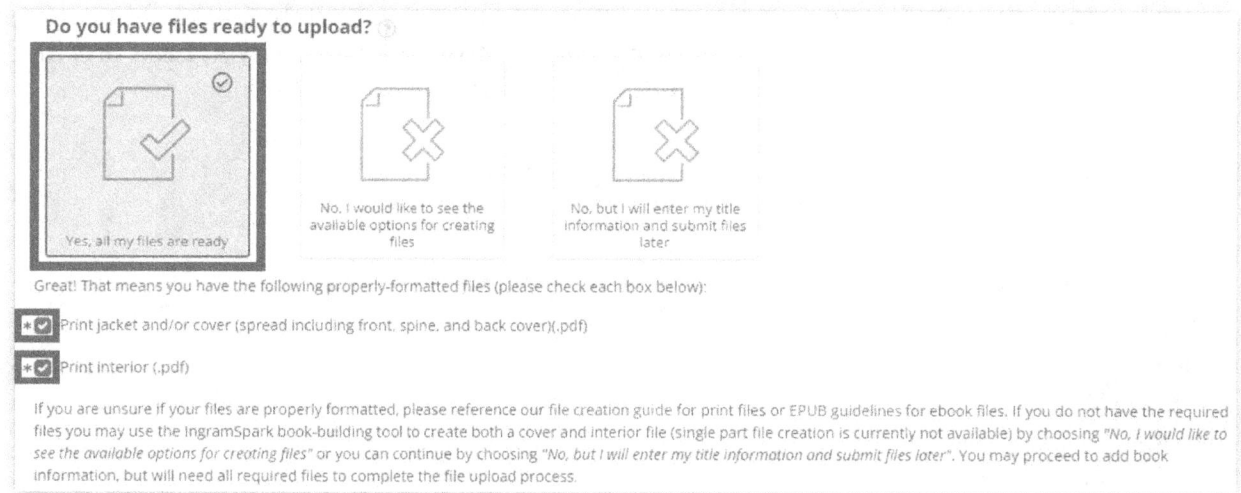

 Answer the question "What would you like to do?" by clicking **Print, Distribute, and Sell Book** and then click **Continue**.

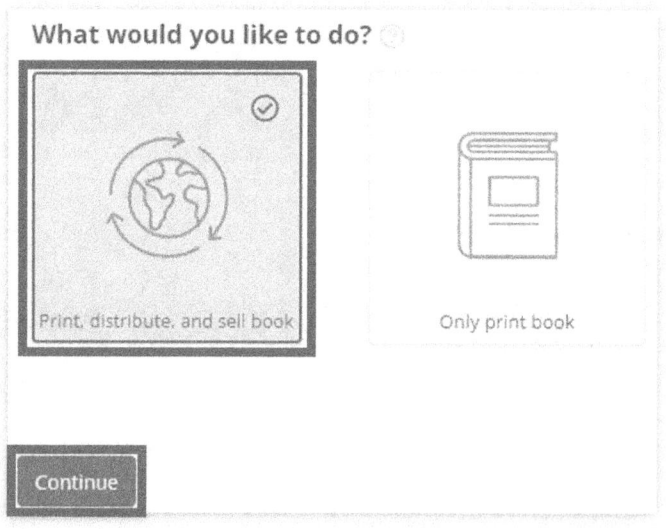

 Fill in the "Title Info" tab, indicating your book's title, language, print ISBN, and copyright information. (You can use the same ISBN you purchased for your Amazon paperback book.) If you have followed the instructions in this book thus far, then you'll own the copyright. Therefore, tick **I own the copyright or hold necessary publishing rights**.

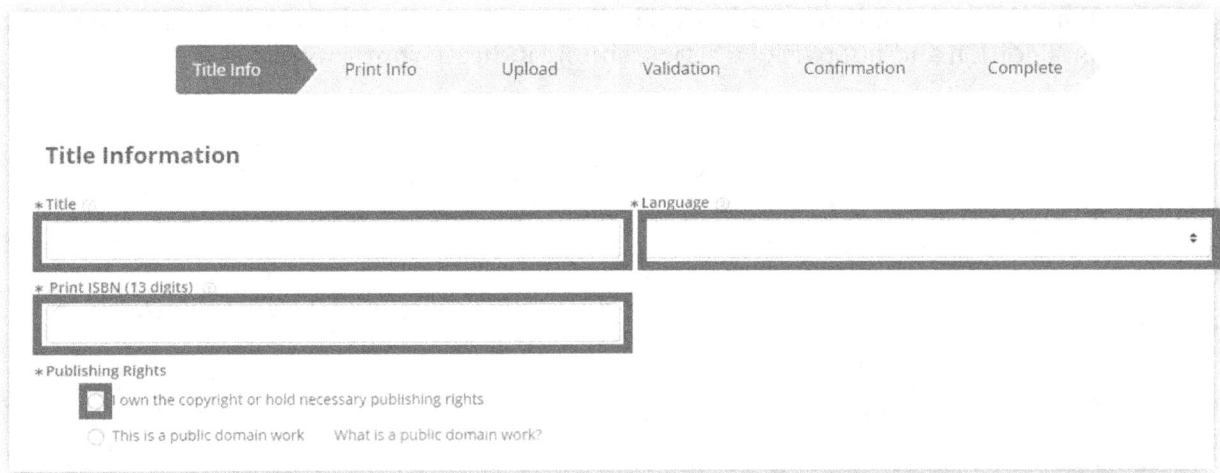

 A pop-up will appear asking you to indicate that your title does not include information such as trademarks, famous brands, or misleading information. Click **No, my title does NOT include any of the above** and then click **Ok**.

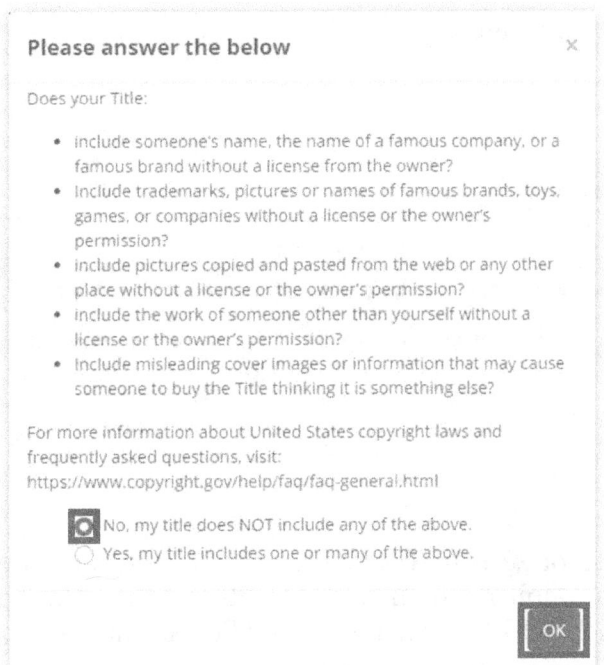

 For the question, "Has Artificial Intelligence been used in the creation of this work?" Select **No** unless you have used AI to produce your book.

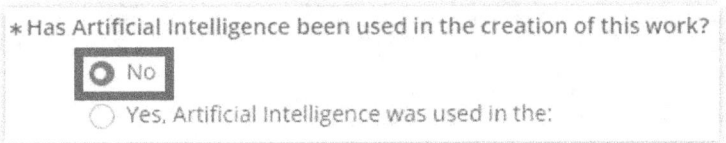

 Click the dropdown menu that says, "Show more fields to improve book optimization." Fill in the required information, including your subtitle, edition name, and more. If it's a first edition and not part of a series, simply indicate your subtitle.

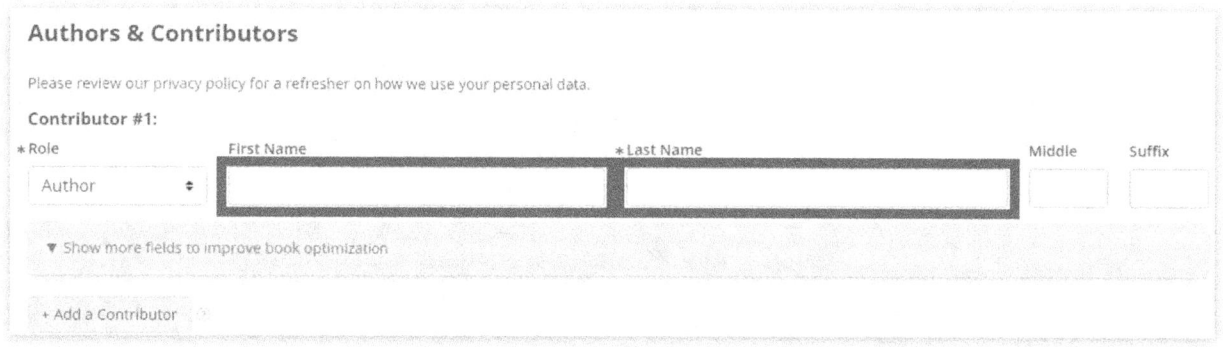

 Fill in your author's name.

 Fill in the "Categorize Your Title" information. Select an imprint. The imprint name is displayed as the publisher on most retail sites. If your desired imprint is not listed in the drop-down, click **Add Imprint.** (It could be your name, your pen name, or an LLC, for instance.)

13 ▶▶ For the subjects of your book, IngramSpark has a handy search and suggestion tool that will help you choose three categories for your book. Click **Find Subjects** and then either use the search bar or click through each category until you find the right fit. Click **Add Subjects** when you find a matching category and repeat until you have listed your book in three relevant categories.

14 ▶▶ Select the audience that best describes your readership.

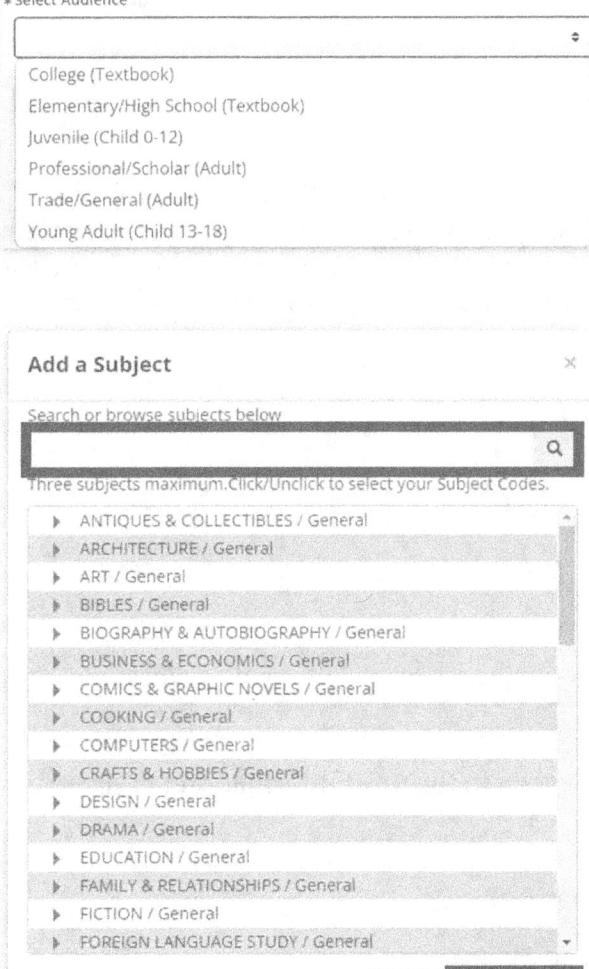

 Paste the HTML of your book description in the title description box.

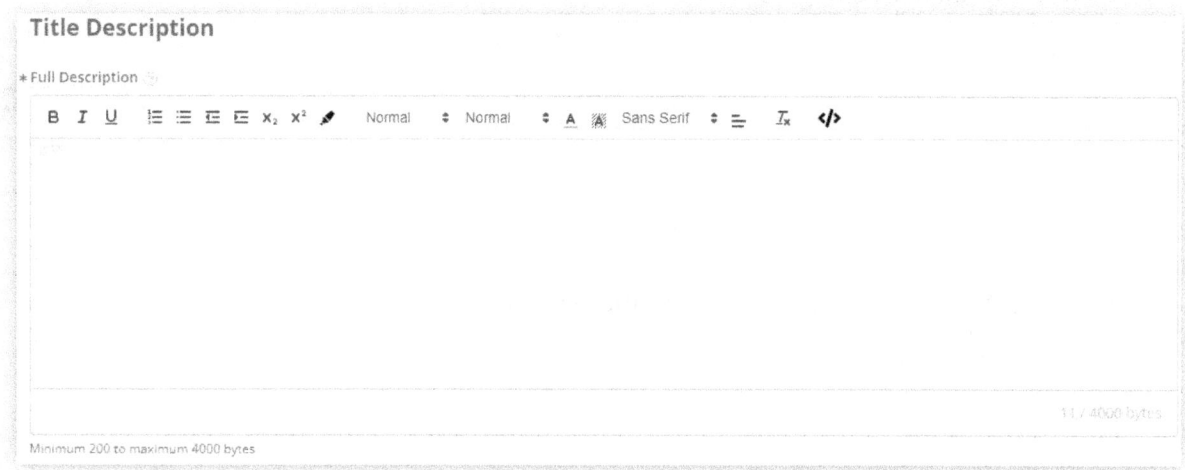

 Type your keywords in, separating them with semicolons. You should provide at least seven keywords or phrases that potential customers might search for. To find these, follow the tips we suggested in "How to Find Your 7 Keywords When Uploading Your Book to KDP." After typing in your keywords, click **Continue**.

 You will then be taken to the print information tab. Here, you will be prompted to select your trim size.

 Choose your interior color and paper (black and white or color). We recommend that you choose **Black & White** and **Creme** paper.

19 ▶▶ For your binding, choose **Paperback** and **Perfect Bound**.

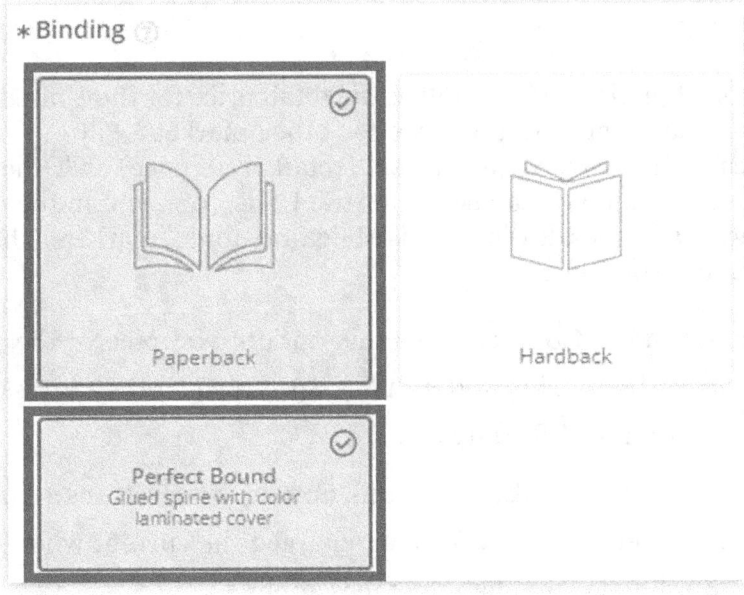

 Choose your cover finish (**Gloss** or **Matte**) depending on your preference.

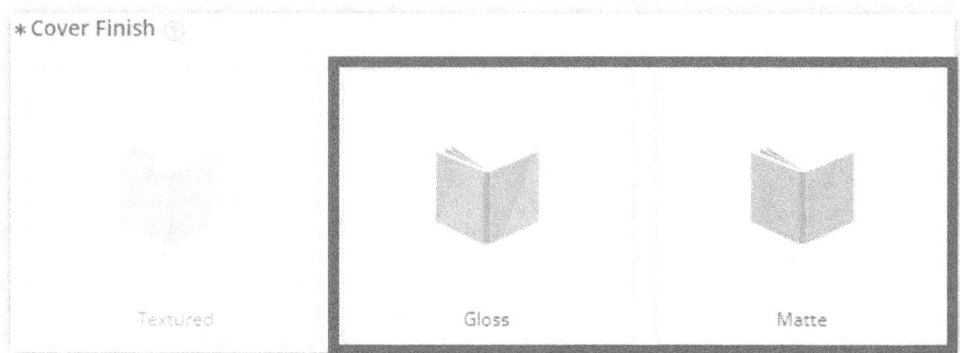

 Fill in the additional book information. Select **No** for "Dubplex Enabled." Add your total page count. Leave the market as the United States. Once you fill in this information, the print cost will pop up to the right.

 Go to the print pricing section. Fill in the retail price for the United States, and the table will automatically indicate the price for other markets. Fill in the wholesale discount box. You can either choose "55% trade" (retail preference) or "Other" (between 40% and 54%). The minimum you can select for the US is 40%, and in the rest of the world, it is 35%. Offering a wholesale discount is obligatory for all markets. The box called "Return" allows you three options:

- **Yes-Deliver Costs:** Under this option, you receive the physical copy of any returned book. This option has a $3 return to US addresses charge and a $20 charge for non-US addresses.

- **Yes-Destroy Costs:** With this option, your returned books are sent back to Ingram and destroyed. You are charged the current wholesale cost of the book, but no shipping and handling fees apply.

- **No or Non-Returnable:** Choose this option if you don't want to allow any returns. This is our recommended option.

Select the two checkboxes (confirming that you have selected **No** and that the prices above are correct).

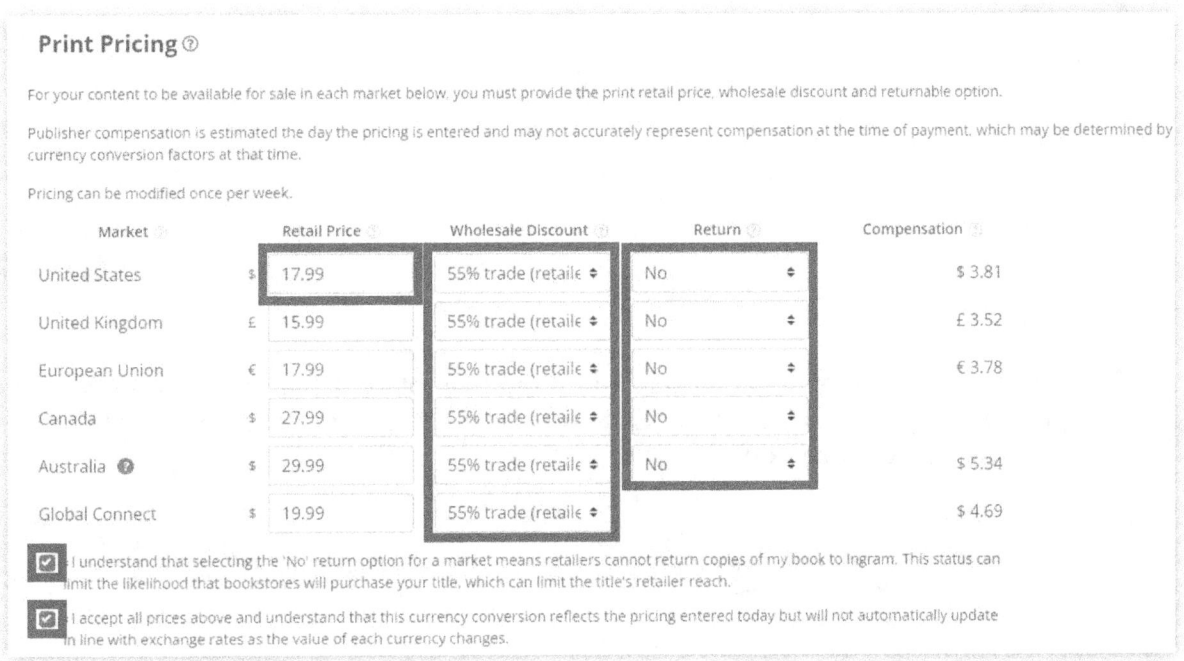

 IngramSpark allows you various printing options. Choose if you want to enable readers to get a sneak peek of your book ("Enable Look Inside the Book") and if you wish to have a large text edition. We recommend allowing your readers a sneak peek. Don't tick the "Right-to-Left Content" box unless your content is meant to be bound and read in reverse (for instance, if it's written in Arabic).

 Choose your publication date and click **Continue**.

 Upload the PDF of your manuscript and the PDF of your paperback print cover in the specified boxes. You can simply drag and drop them into these boxes. When they are uploaded, click **Continue**.

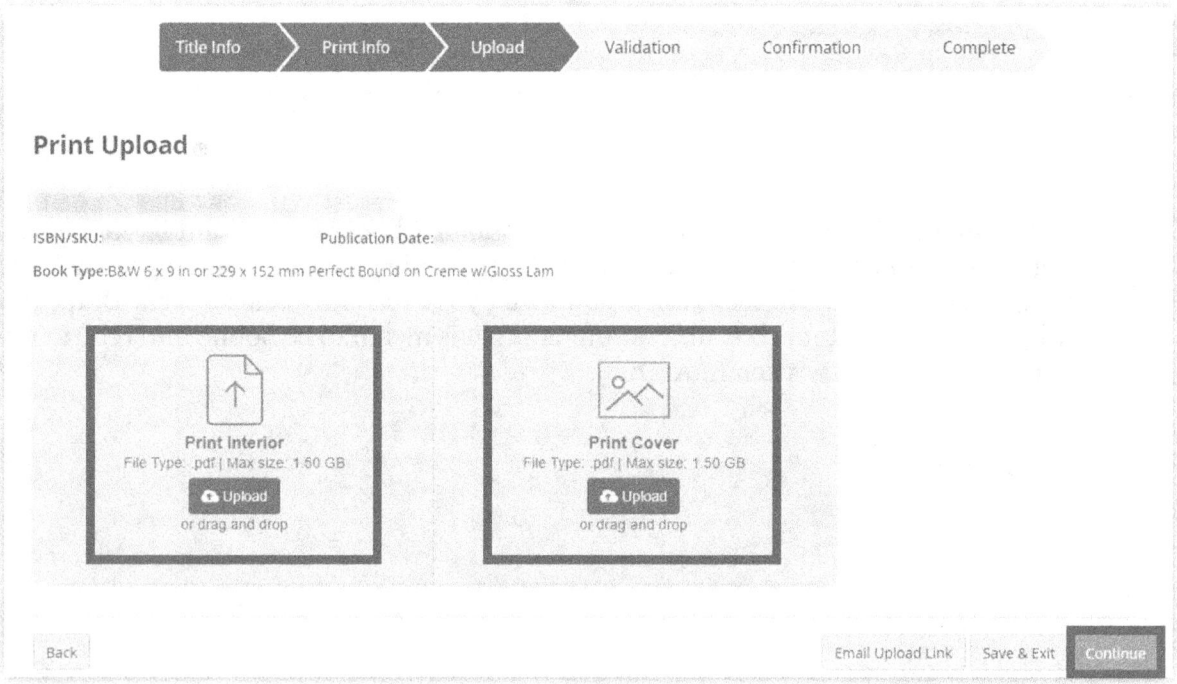

26  Wait for your title metadata and content files to be validated and click **Continue**.

27 Confirm your book's information and click **Complete Submission**.

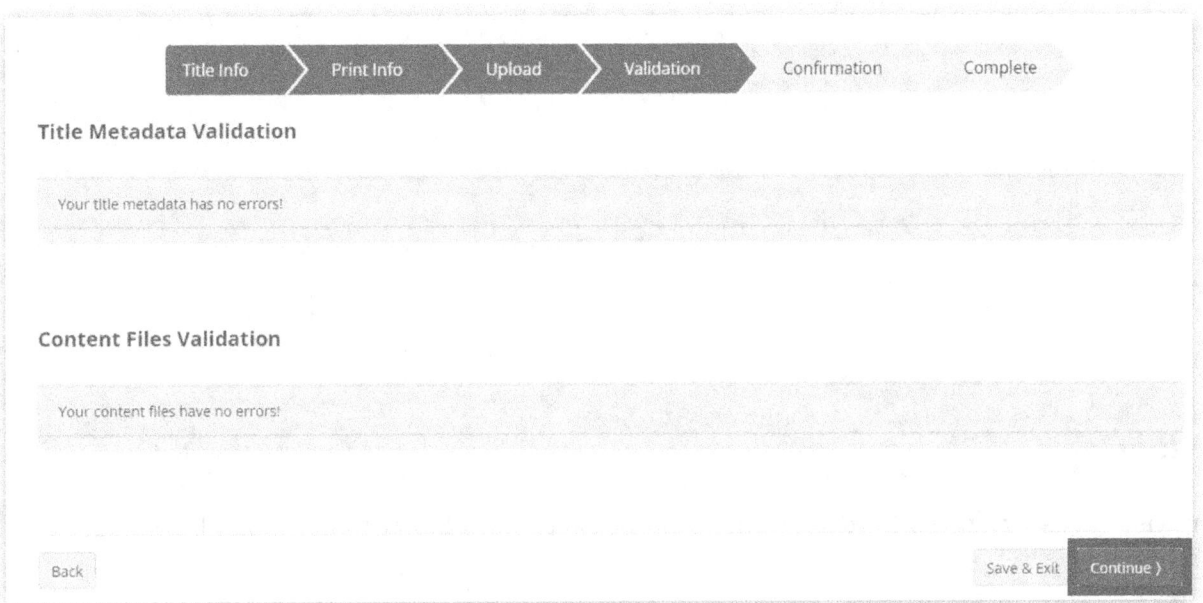

You're all done!

Hardback

If you wish to also upload a hardcover, the process is very similar, with a few small changes.

 Go back to your titles. Choose the title you wish and click **Duplicate**.

 Fill in the title info tab using your hardback's unique ISBN.

 Go through all the same steps as above until 16. You will see that most of the information is automatically included, including your author name and book description. When you reach Step 16, click **Hardback** instead of Paperback and select **Case Laminate**. Also, select your cover finish (gloss or matte).

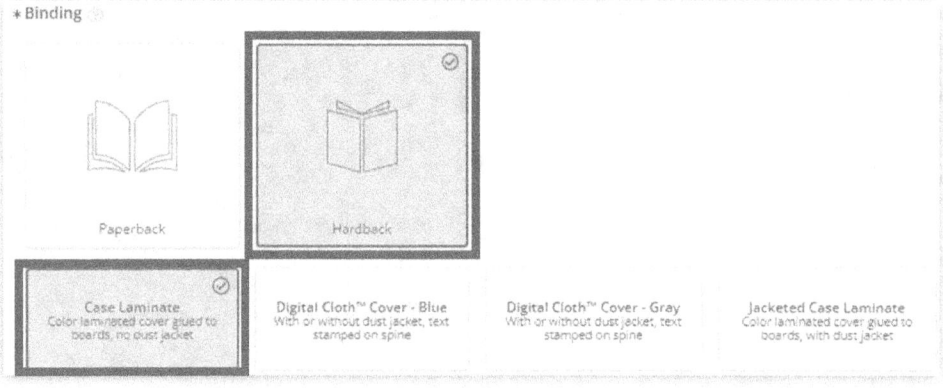

04 ▶▶ Complete the same steps as indicated above until Step 22. In the case of hardbacks, you need to upload your print interior and hardback cover. Both of these are PDF files.

05 ▶▶ Follow the rest of the steps until completion.

Between 3 and 5 days after you submit all your information, IngramSpark will send you an email notifying you that your work is ready for approval.

01 ▶▶ Open the email and click **Approve Eproof**.

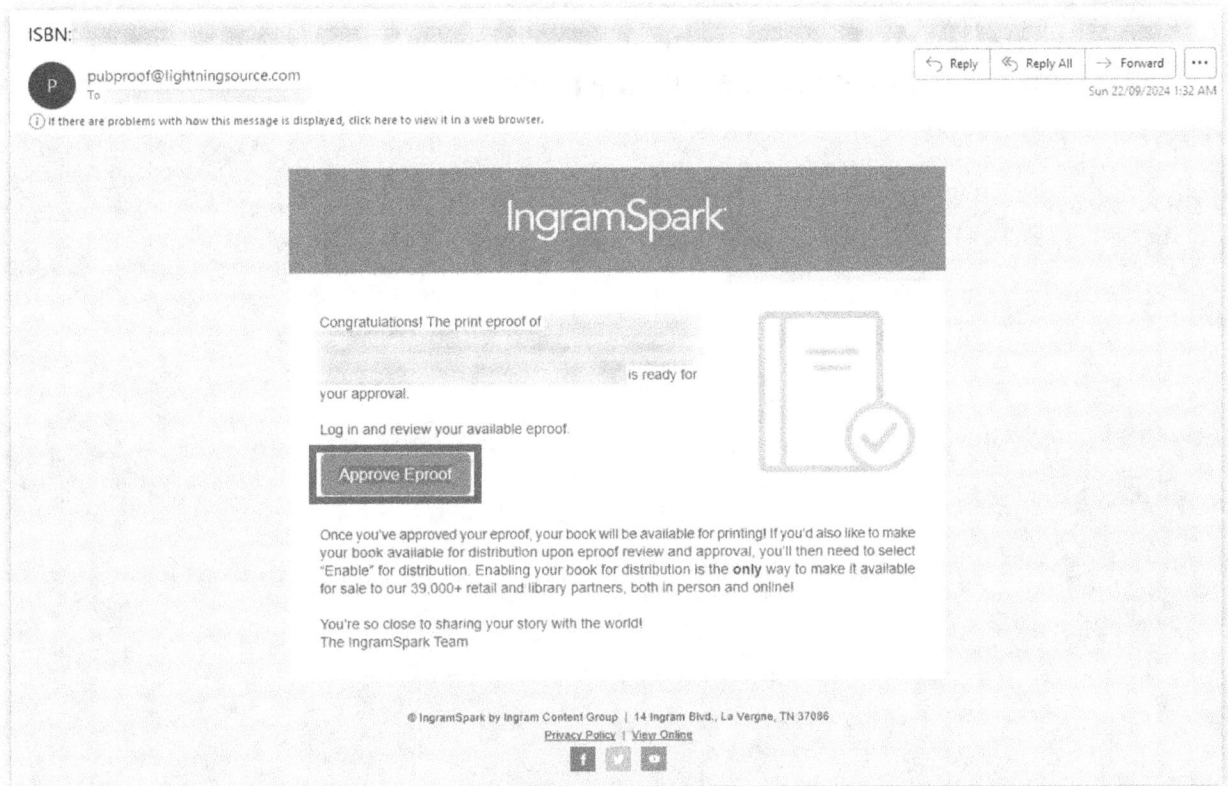

02 ▶▶ A page will open that lists all your titles pending your approval. Select the title that you wish to approve.

267

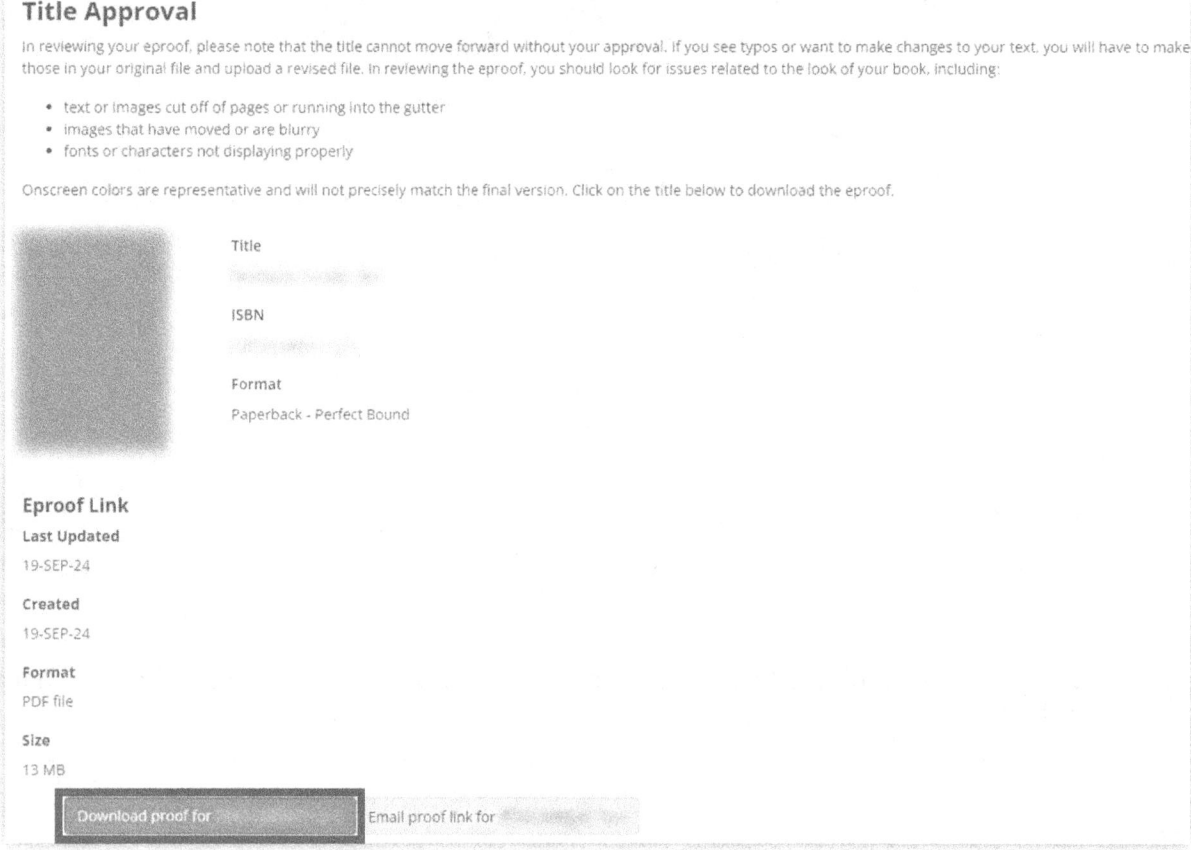

03 >> Click **Download Proof for [Your ISBN]**.

 Review the downloaded file page by page and ensure that everything looks good.

 If you are happy with the book, select **[Your business name] approves this title for printing, distribution, and sale from orders placed by my account and/or retailers** and click **Continue**.

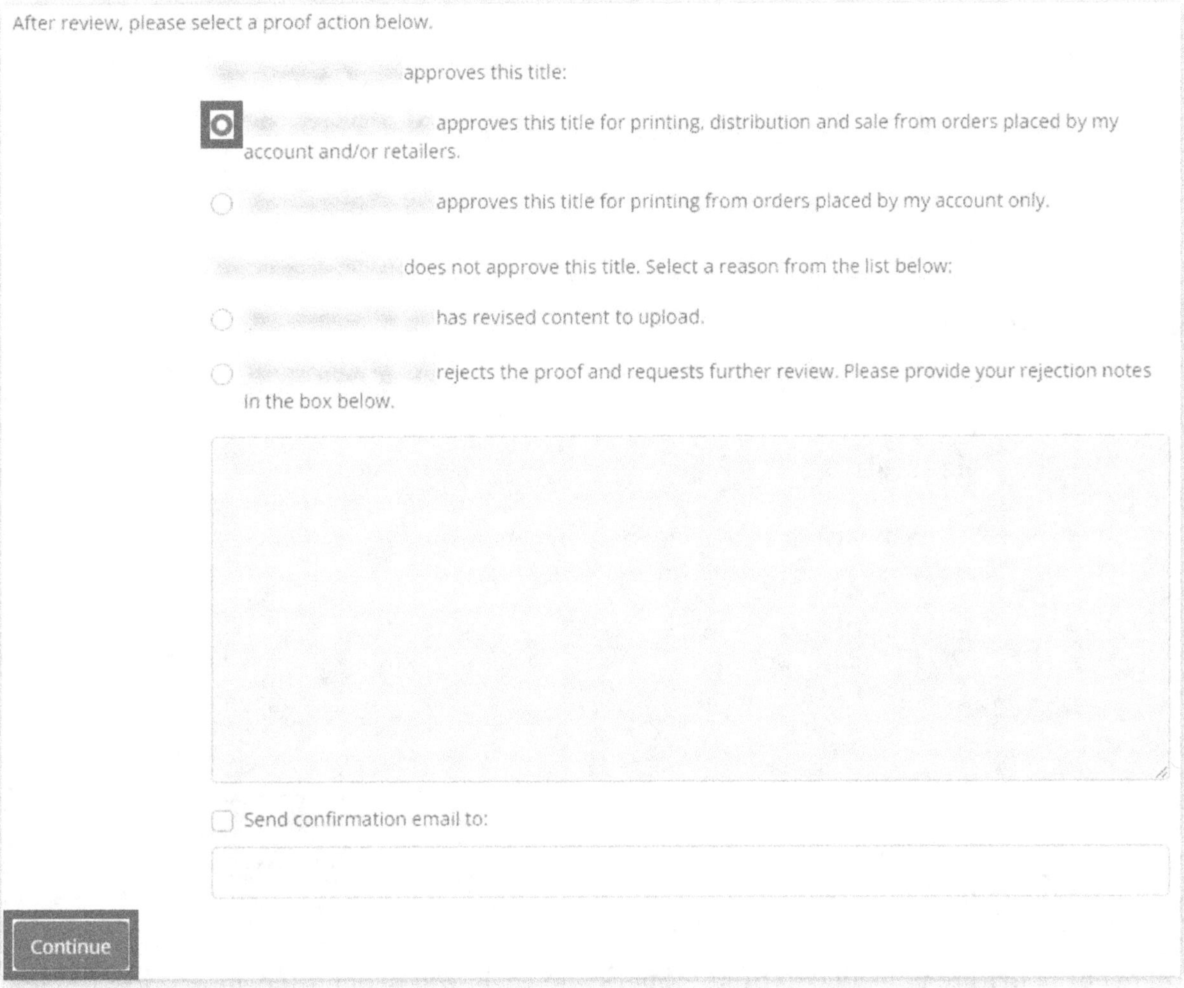

 A window will pop open that allows you to promote your title. We have had more success with other means of promotion, and therefore, we recommend that you click **No**, but some may like to try this out, in which case you would need to select **Yes**.

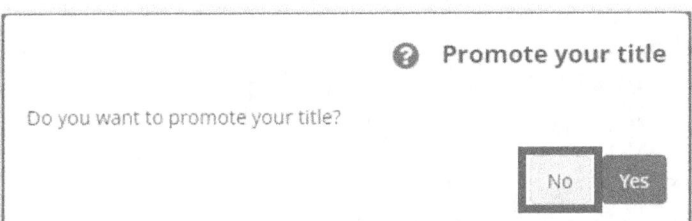

Re-Uploading Your Book

If, for any reason, you need to re-upload your book, the steps are as follows:

Click **Titles** -> **All Titles** -> Find the book you want to re-upload -> Click **Upload New Files** (see the screenshot below) -> Confirm that you are happy with the $25 charge (see the screenshot below) -> **Reupload Files**.

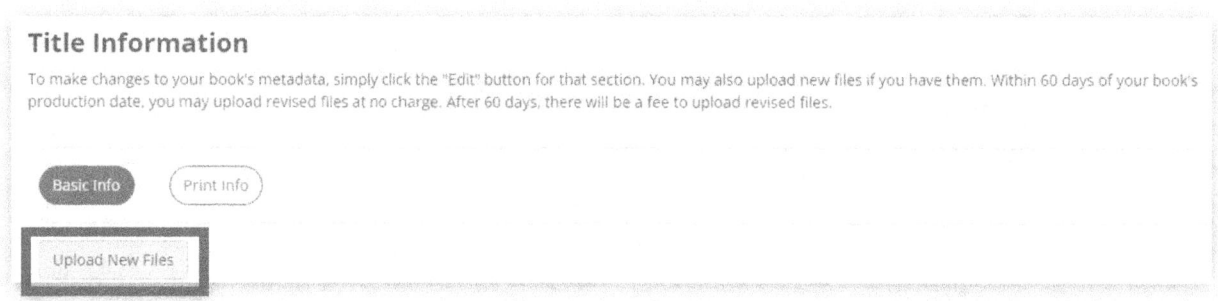

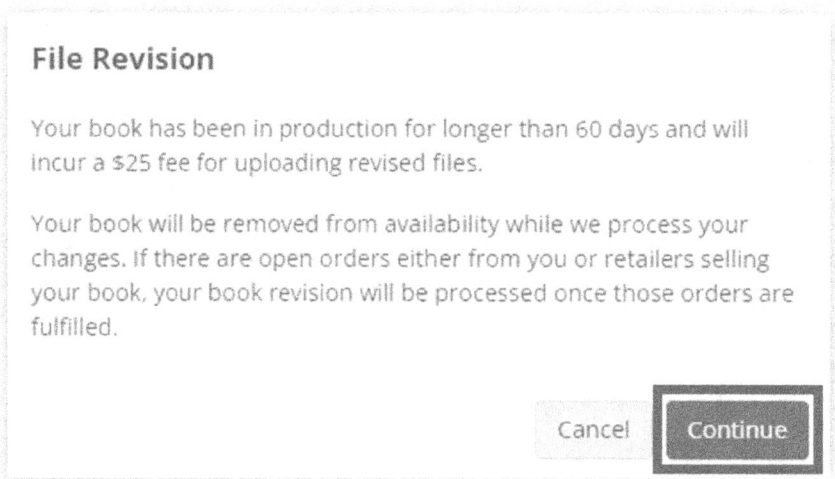

Now that your books are uploaded to IngramSpark and KDP, you're definitely much closer to reaping the rewards for your hard work! The next chapter will feature a brief discussion of alternative distribution channels, which you might consider an extra boost for your book sales.

Chapter 23

Exploring Alternative Book Distribution Channels

KDP, IngramSpark, and ACX aren't the only places to distribute your books. Earlier in this book, we covered KDP, IngramSpark, ACX, Author's Republic, and Findaway Voices. In this chapter, we will discuss a few alternatives for your print, ebooks, and audiobooks.

Print (Paperback & Hardback) Distribution Channels

Barnes & Noble (https://press.barnesandnoble.com/)

Barnes & Noble's self-publishing platform, called Barnes & Noble Press™, allows independent publishers and authors to publish both print and digital books. To take advantage of this service, just upload your book and make it available for purchase on BN.com, on NOOK devices, and in stores. There are no delivery fees or production costs, making it free to use throughout the process. The platform gives you instant access to millions of readers at BN.com and NOOK.com, as well as customers with NOOK® devices and those who use free NOOK reading apps.

The process is pretty easy. Just create an account and choose whether to create a print book or an ebook. B&N will help you format your cover files and interior. Once you click on **Publish**, your book will appear on BN.com within 72 hours.

The pros of publishing your book with B&N include attractive royalties. Authors can earn up to 70% of the list price for ebooks and 55% for print books minus the per-book printing cost. In addition, B&N does not require exclusivity. The site is user-friendly, you can print on demand, and you will find a host of marketing tools, including resources on author pages, promotions, and the company's dedicated affiliate program.

On the downside, Barnes & Noble Press has a much smaller reach than Amazon, its formatting options are somewhat limited, and Barnes & Noble Press only distributes books to B&N stores and their online site (Haynes 2023a).

Lulu (www.lulu.com/)

Lulu, an online self-publishing book & ebook company, has existed for around two decades. It boasts over one million titles and allows users to publish, print, and sell their books internationally. Uploading your work to Lulu is similar to the process involved for other channels. You will need a PDF for your paperback and an EPUB for your ebook. Lulu isn't free; it has a range of publishing packages ranging from beginner to premium level and charges a higher rate for printing than other channels do (including Amazon). Lulu has additional services, such as cover design and marketing, which you can access by paying additional fees. To sell your books on this platform, you need to set up a storefront, select your distribution channels, and promote your books. Like Barnes & Noble, Lulu has a print-on-demand service, which allows you to cut your print costs. Books are priced higher, and royalties can be a little lower than those of its competitors. On the downside, some self-publishers have found that Lulu can have formatting issues and have experienced difficulties using the templates provided by this company (Baird 2023). Other publishers have noted that commission prices (around 20% of the book's net profit) are unreasonably high (Haynes 2023b).

Ebook Distribution Channels

Apple Books (https://authors.apple.com/)

Apple Books is a self-publishing platform with a host of benefits, including 70% royalties on all ebooks regardless of price, no limitations on offering free books to customers, no payments for preferential store placement, and more. This platform provides you with information on how to design a captivating cover, create attractive page layouts, and properly format your files. By publishing your book on this platform, you will have access to readers in over fifty countries and regions worldwide.

Draft2Digital executive Dan Wood recently identified Apple Books as a marketplace that seems to attract a younger crowd (primarily females in their mid-20s to early 40s). Therefore, if your target market comprises younger women, this channel may be particularly interesting.

Apple Books offers users affiliate codes (which they can use freely). What's more, unlike Amazon, it factors pre-orders into your sales rank as they happen, counting presales cumulatively on launch day in your sales rank. The publishing process is also relatively simple, and you have greater control over your metadata. That is, Apple allows you to choose the exact categories for your listing, access detailed reporting, and enjoy greater flexibility in setting discounts on your pricing.

On the downside, Apple Books only has a 10% market share worldwide, and users require an Apple ID to preview their books (Tortora, n.d.-a).

Draft2Digital (www.draft2digital.com/)

Draft2Digital is an aggregator offering distribution services to authors whose books are not exclusive to Amazon. Instead of uploading your ebooks one by one to sellers like Barnes & Noble, Kobo, and Apple, you simply need to upload them once, and Draft2Digital will take charge of the rest. If you are enrolled in KDP Select, you will not need this service, as it caters more to authors wishing to sell their books across a wider range of stores. Although the company's main service is distribution, it offers independent authors and publishers many additional resources, including print-on-demand and help with tasks such as formatting, sales tracking, and promotion.

It takes just a couple of minutes to sign up for the service. Once you create an account, you are prompted to add your book and provide relevant information and a cover if you have one. (If not, you can add your cover later.) As with KDP, you will be prompted to choose keywords and categories. You will also be asked to upload your manuscript and description, check your layout, and select from different template style options for your formatting. Finally, you can set your price and pick your distributors. You don't have to pay a monthly or annual fee to use Draft2Digital. The company simply takes a 10% fee of the retail price of any book you sell (Chesson 2023b).

Kobo (https://kobowritinglife.com/)

Kobo (or Kobo Writing Life) is a free self-publishing portal that allows authors and publishers to create, edit, and upload ebooks to the Kobo platform. It has localized storefronts in over 40 countries and 25 retail partners. Books distributed on this platform reach millions of readers in over 200 countries. Signing up is easy; you simply have to create an account, set up your bank account details, and upload and publish your ebook. The process is very similar to that of Amazon or IngramSpark. If your book is already published on another aggregator, you can make your books available on Kobo. There is also Kobo Plus, a monthly subscription-based service available to subscribers in the US, the UK, Canada, Australia, New Zealand, and many more countries.

The benefits of publishing your ebook on Kobo include the fact that Kobo Plus requires no author exclusivity. It pays authors from a shared pool based on the number of minutes readers spend on your book in each specific country. Kobo has an impressive market share and pays authors a 70% royalty rate for ebooks, offering high visibility for ebook boxed sets sold exclusively by the company. For boxed sets, it offers a 60% royalty rate. When publishing your book directly to Kobo Writing Life, you are offered the chance to be included in exclusive promotions. Kobo also has a popular pre-order service; all you need is a placeholder file, and you are free to change your publication date if needed.

Kobo is particularly popular among romance, thriller, and serialized book readers, so if your book falls within these categories, it may be worth ensuring your book is available on this portal.

The downsides of Kobo include the greater popularity of Amazon and Apple Books in the US (and of Apple Books in Australia and New Zealand). Moreover, non-fiction works don't sell as well on Kobo as fiction books and series. Kobo also lacks author pages, so interested readers won't have a chance to learn more about you. Finally, there is a minimum earnings threshold for receiving monthly payments (Tortora, n.d.-c). Right now, the minimum is 50 CAD.

Kobo also allows you to upload audiobooks onto its platform. As is the case with your printed books, you can enroll your audiobooks in Kobo's subscription service, Kobo Plus.

Audiobooks enjoy all Kobo's top benefits, including freedom from exclusivity, the chance to reach new audiences in countries like Belgium and the Netherlands, and the ability to track your sales and performance on Kobo Plus via the Kobo Writing Life dashboard (Bidilică 2024).

An Updated List of Book Distribution Channels

Below is a list of major book distribution channels. Keep track of new channels as they arise here: www.publishingservicesbook.com/book-distribution-channels

Print (Paperback & Hardback)

- Barnes & Noble Press (https://press.barnesandnoble.com)
- IngramSpark (www.ingramspark.com)
- KDP (https://kdp.amazon.com)
- Lulu (www.lulu.com)

Ebook

- Apple Books for Authors (https://authors.apple.com)
- Barnes & Nobel Press (https://press.barnesandnoble.com)
- Draft2Digital (www.draft2digital.com)
- Google Play Books (https://play.google.com/books/publish)
- Gumroad (https://gumroad.com)
- IngramSpark (www.ingramspark.com)
- KDP (https://kdp.amazon.com)
- Kobo Writing Life (www.kobo.com/au/en/p/writinglife)
- Lulu (www.lulu.com)
- PublishDrive (www.publishingservicesbook.com/publishdrive)

Audiobook

- ACX (www.acx.com)
- Author's Republic (www.authorsrepublic.com)

- Findaway Voices by Spotify (www.findawayvoices.com)
- Kobo Writing Life (www.kobo.com/au/en/p/writinglife)

Having perused the many additional channels for distributing your book, it's time to discover how to create and publish your audiobook!

Chapter 24

Publishing Your Audiobook: From Script to Sound

The global audiobook market is thriving, and by 2032, it is expected to reach a worth of $39.1 billion (Pangarkar 2024). Thanks to the rise of ever-present connectivity, smartphones, and earbuds, many more readers are interested in consuming great books while on the go.

Just think about the times you were on a long drive wishing you had something entertaining to do. Audiobooks are a great way to enjoy a novel, receive useful advice, or simply find information to help you achieve personal and professional success.

Finding the Perfect Narrator for Your Book

Choosing the right narrator is a priority for most self-published authors, and rightfully so. When you listen to a powerful performer narrating a dystopian novel or the gentle rhythm of a narrator giving self-help tips, the experience can transform an audiobook from good to unforgettable. Take time to find the perfect narrator, one who can express the key messages in your book and connect with your target audience through their tone, timing, and understanding of the book's contents.

Before you even hop onto ACX or another platform to find professionals, imagine the perfect voice for your book.

Questions to ask yourself include:

- Are they male or female?
- Is their voice high, low, or somewhere in the middle?

- Does the voice sound older or younger?
- If your work is a fiction book, will you require several voices or just one?
- Is your narrator willing to take part in a Zoom call with you so you can discuss character traits or other specifics that are important for them to know?
- How quickly can they deliver the finished product? Depending on the length of your book, the process could take anywhere from a couple of weeks to a month.
- What is your budget for the book? How would you like to pay for it? Do you wish to pay by milestone (VoiceOverAngela 2021)?

Keep your audience in mind when making these choices. Note that some authors narrate their own books. If you wish, you can simply use your audio files, ensuring that they meet your chosen platforms' audio submission requirements. However, we recommend a seasoned professional narrator to ensure the audio sounds as polished as possible. It costs just a few hundred dollars to have a polished product created for you, and producing a manuscript can also involve a little editing. Therefore, unless you are experienced in this field, leaving it to the professionals is best.

Where to Find a Narrator

To find a quality narrator at an affordable price, try the following:

ACX

ACX has thousands of narrators, many of whom provide samples of their work so you can listen to them and decide if they are right for your book. On ACX, narrators are called "producers" because they produce retail-ready audiobooks in addition to narration. You can search the site and find your ideal narrator/producer or have interested professionals audition for your audiobook project. You can narrow down your choice based on factors such as age, gender, and accent. You may have to speak with many narrators to find a perfect match. For instance, you may want your book read in a specific accent, and those who can perform this task may happen to be booked, charge higher prices, or demand upfront payment. Just keep searching and negotiating until you find someone with the talent and dedication to bring your audiobook to life.

To find a narrator, take the following steps:

1. Go to www.acx.com and click **Get Started**. Sign in with your Amazon account details.
2. Register for ACX by indicating your personal information, location, account role, and eligibility.
3. Choose **Create a Title Profile** and describe your book and the type of narrator you wish to contract. You will also have to post a one- to two-page excerpt from your book, which will serve as an audition script for interested narrators.
4. Post your book to receive auditions, or listen to sample narrations and invite a few producers to audition for your book.

5. If you are interested in a specific narrator, click **Send Message** on their profile and ask them to audition for your title. Include a link to your title profile.
6. Review auditions from interested producers.
7. Select **Make Offer** on their profile if you're ready to make a binding offer.
8. If the producer accepts your offer, get started. Your producer will record and upload a 15-minute checkpoint of the audiobook so you can approve it and provide feedback. Once you approve the sample, your producer will start recording the whole book.
9. Listen to the entire recording to ensure that everything sounds perfect.

 **Pro Tip:** Use headphones or earbuds to cancel out background noise.

10. Distribute your audiobook. ACX will distribute your audiobook via Audible, Amazon, and iTunes. You can grant ACX exclusive or non-exclusive rights. If you opt for a non-exclusive contract, you can distribute your audiobook through additional channels.
11. Use the "Promote Yourself" section of ACX to ensure your audiobook reaches your target audience.
12. Earn royalties on your audiobook sales and track your progress on ACX's sales dashboard, which you can access through your account.

Narrators Hub

Narrators Hub has a team of high-quality voiceover and dubbing actors and a skilled team of translators who can translate both fiction and non-fiction books. The company offers audiobook narration in multiple languages, and all work completed complies with the technical requirements demanded by the leading distribution platforms. See https://narratorshub.com/ for further details.

Upwork

Upwork is where you can find a host of talent for all things creative—including audiobook narration. Click www.upwork.com/hire/audiobook-narrators/ to find narrators, each of whom stipulates their price per hour and additional information (including their language/s and accent/s). To hire an audiobook narrator, take the following steps:

1. Write a project description. Indicate the scope of the work and the skills and requirements you are seeking. Also include the project length and your budget.
2. Open an account on Upwork and post the project description. When posting a job, include the following information:

- **A Job Post Title:** Create a simple title that clearly indicates what you are looking for. Use keywords you think your candidate might also use to find your project. Examples include:
    - "Audiobook narrator with a general American accent needed for a new book on raising chickens"
    - "Narrator needed with a Manchester accent for my book"
    - "Looking for a narrator for my self-help book for young adults"
- **Your Project Description**
- **Additional Requirements:**
    - Experience narrating self-help books
    - The ability to speak in an engaging and lively way
    - Clear diction
    - The ability to stick to the agreed-upon deadline

3. Once proposals start coming in, create a shortlist of professionals you wish to interview.
4. Interview the narrators and choose the one you think best fulfills your requirements.

Author's Republic (www.authorsrepublic.com)

Author's Republic has a roster of professional audiobook narrators from whom you can request auditions. This company has the following easy, three-step system to help you turn your manuscript into an audiobook:

1. Prepare your ebook manuscript, ensuring it is well-edited, clear, easy to read, and in the right format (EPUB or PDF).
2. Upload your ebook manuscript, metadata, and a sample script into the "Author's Republic Studio."
3. Audition interested narrators, or privately request auditions and hire the best narrator for your book.

How Much Will a Narrator Cost You?

Each narrator can freely set their own price. Most charge per hour of completed audio (this is also referred to as "per finished hour" or PFH). On ACX, for instance, beginning narrators usually charge between $10 to $100 per finished hour. On Upwork, they charge anywhere from $20 to $30 to upwards of $200 per hour. On Author's Republic, narrators charge anything from $40 to $400 or more. When calculating your budget, bear in mind that the average narrator reads an average of 9,300 words per hour (Author's Republic 2022). In our experience, most self-published authors pay between $150 and $450 for a three-hour (30K) book.

Avoid Giving Narrators a Royalty Share

Some sites may allow you to pay narrators a royalty share on the sales of your book. We strongly advise against it, as doing so could result in a loss of thousands of dollars. As mentioned above, you can easily get your book narrated for around $50 to $150 per hour. This means that a three-hour book (30K) would cost you between $150 and $450 one time. A royalty share means you pay forever!

How to Prepare Your Manuscript for Narration

As mentioned above, when hiring a narrator, you must present your manuscript in the format required by each platform or narrator. If you have formatted the book yourself, make a copy of your source files. Next, adjust your manuscript, removing images, any visual text that doesn't translate well to audio (including graphs and charts), and any text you do not wish the narrator to read.

If you have not formatted the book yourself, ask the narrator to make the following adjustments:

- Replace phrases like "In this book …" with "In this audiobook."
- Adjust the review page to say, "Review this audiobook," and remove the reference to Amazon.

In addition to working on the actual manuscript, do as much as you can to give the narrator a good idea of the setting, cultural context, and timeframe of the book. Provide notes if you think they will be useful. For instance, if you have written a book about ancient Rome, it might help to give the narrator a bit of information about the major events your book is focused on. If you are using any unusual jargon, character names, places, or foreign words your narrator may struggle with, provide them with a pronunciation guide.

What Should the Narrator Include in Their Reading?

The narrator's reading should include:

- Opening and closing credits
    - Opening Credits:
        - Title
        - Subtitle (if applicable)
        - Written by [name of author]
        - Narrated by [name of narrator]
    - Closing Credits:
        - The end "This has been [Title of audiobook]."
        - Subtitle (if applicable)
        - Written by [name of author]
        - Narrated by [name of narrator]

- The introduction
- Body chapters
- Review pages (adjusted so that the text states "audiobook" rather than "book")
- The conclusion

What Should the Narrator NOT Include in Their Reading?

- The title page
- The copyright page
- The table of contents
- References

Choosing the Right Distribution Services for Your Audiobook

Below is a list of top distribution services to consider. We will briefly discuss each one and present a comparative table beneath them to demonstrate their respective royalty rates, distribution channels, and more. We at Publishing Services recommend ACX as the number one place to publish an audiobook. Anyone not eligible to publish on ACX because of their location should publish their books on Author's Republic and Findaway Voices.

ACX (www.acx.com)

ACX is a distribution service for Amazon. As mentioned earlier, only authors who reside in the US, Canada, Ireland, and the UK can publish their books on ACX. Those residing in other countries can rely on Author's Republic and Findaway Voices by Spotify.

Exclusive and Non-Exclusive Distribution on ACX

When you opt to have your book distributed by ACX, you can choose between exclusive and non-exclusive distribution. According to ACX, "Exclusive distribution means that your audiobook will only be available on Audible's channels, which currently include Audible, Amazon and iTunes (ACX, n.d.)." You cannot distribute or sell your audiobook in any other format on any site or store outside of Amazon, Audible, or iTunes. Audiobooks published and distributed exclusively earn a 40% royalty.

If you opt for non-exclusive distribution, you can distribute your audiobook or print book via other distributors, but if you do so, you will only earn a 25% royalty. If you choose the non-exclusive distribution, you can also sell and distribute your completed audiobook in other physical formats, such as on CD, wherever you choose. Non-exclusive projects may not be published as a royalty share project and must be completed as a pay-for-production or uploaded directly to ACX.

So, which option should you go for? It's a matter of weighing the pros and cons. If you choose ACX exclusive, you earn more per book, but your book isn't available on every platform. ACX exclusive does not distribute to libraries or bookstores. What's more, Audible retains the sole discretion to set the price of the audiobooks it sells. On the other hand, Audible makes up about 41% of *all* audiobook sales (Mongeau 2022). Spotify sales are currently on the rise but aren't quite a threat to ACX yet. Therefore, we recommend going for ACX exclusive if you can.

Author's Republic (www.authorsrepublic.com)

Author's Republic allows you to distribute your audiobook to 50+ retail, library, and streaming channels and offers an attractive 70% royalty of net profits. Consider Author's Republic as a kind of middleman. It sets up agreements with different platforms, each of which has different royalty rates. It then keeps 30% of whatever revenue comes in while you keep 70%. Author's Republic has three different distribution options:

1. **Distribution via Audible, iTunes, and Amazon:** If you choose this option, you get 75% of the 25% royalty share offered by ACX.
2. **Preferred Sales Channels:** Channels that are exclusive to Author's Republic include Audiobookstore, Audioteka, BookBeat, Book Walker, Divibib, Behear, Speechify, and more (The Self-Publishing with Dale Podcast 2024). Some can also be accessed through Findaway Voices.
3. **Music Channels:** This includes options like Spotify Streaming, Deezer, Napster, Apple Music, YouTube Music, and more.

Findaway Voices by Spotify (www.findawayvoices.com)

Findaway Voices by Spotify also allows you to reach a global audience thanks to its extensive retail and library partners. You can choose your own pricing and select your availability from a wide selection of its partners, including Spotify, Audible, Amazon, Hoopla, Tune In, Rakuten Kobo, and more. What's more, you get to keep 100% of your royalties on all sales made via Spotify!

Comparison of Audiobook Distribution Channels

Feature	ACX	Findaway Voices by Spotify	Author's Republic
Royalty Rate	40% (exclusive) / 25% (non-exclusive)	100% of royalties on Spotify 80% of net royalties everywhere else	70% of net royalties
Pricing Requirements	ACX does not give you the option to determine the prices of your books. They decide the price based on the length of your audiobook. The ACX website indicates that regular pricing on Audible is as follows: **Under 1 hour:** under $7 **1 - 3 hours:** $7 - $10 **3 - 5 hours:** $10 - $20 **5 - 10 hours:** $15 - $25 **10 - 20 hours:** $20 - $30 **Over 20 hours:** $25 - 35	You can set your own price, but when you distribute to Audible, the prices are adjusted in line with ACX's guidelines.	You can set your own price, but when you distribute to Audible, the prices are adjusted in line with ACX's guidelines.
Exclusivity Options	Exclusive or Non-Exclusive	Non-exclusive	Non-exclusive

Distribution Reach	Audible, Amazon, and iTunes	38 channels, including Audible, Apple, Google, Kobo, and libraries	50+ channels, including Amazon, Audible, Apple, Google, and Spotify
Redemption Codes (will be further discussed in this chapter)	Rights Holders will automatically receive 25 codes per marketplace (US and UK) for Audible upon publication of their title. It can take up to one hour for Promo codes to be redeemable by customers on Audible. Additional codes: Once your audiobook has received 10 Promo code redemptions and 100 qualified sales overall, you can generate an additional 25 codes per marketplace per title, up to a total maximum of 50 codes per marketplace.	You receive 100 free codes for Spotify per audiobook. Codes will appear after the click of one button.	You can request codes if you have selected them from the distribution list. It will take 1-2 weeks to receive the codes. The codes you receive on Author's Republic can be redeemed on Audiobooks.com.
Production Services (Narrator Marketplace)	Available	Not available	Available

 **Pro Tip:** If you publish on Author's Republic or Findaway Voices, it is a good idea to follow ACX's pricing strategy. It is based on a sound principle. A longer book should logically be priced higher than a shorter one since the former takes more time and money to produce.

How to Obtain Reviews for Your Audiobooks

Getting reviews for audiobooks is a little easier than for your print books since you can find other authors who wish to swap codes or reviews. This differs from what KDP allows, so only do it for your audiobooks!

All three of the above-mentioned distribution platforms offer redemption codes as follows:

ACX

- ACX offers you redemption codes for every audiobook distributed on its platform. Rights holders automatically receive 25 codes per marketplace (US and UK only) for Audible upon publication of their title. It can take up to one hour for promo codes to be redeemable by customers on Audible.

- Once your audiobook has received 10 promo code redemptions and 100 qualified sales overall, you can generate an additional 25 codes per marketplace per title, up to a total maximum of 50 codes per marketplace.

- Audible is the best place to redeem your codes because of the platform's immense reach.

Findaway Voices by Spotify

- Findaway Voices by Spotify offers you 100 free Spotify codes per audiobook. The codes appear after the click of one button. They are only redeemable on Spotify. Although the latter's share is constantly growing, Audible codes are still more valuable.

Author's Republic

- You can select promo codes through your Author's Republic dashboard. You can receive as many as you like by clicking **Promo Codes** on the marketing tool tab on your dashboard. Click **Promo Codes** and then **Request Promo Code**. Choose the title for which you are selecting codes and enter the number of codes you need. Click **Send Request**. Author's Republic's website states that it takes 1 to 2 weeks to receive the codes. While promo codes are always valuable, Author's Republic promo codes are less valuable than the other two options because they can only be redeemed on Audiobooks.com.

Using Bookblaze to Receive Reviews

We have previously discussed Bookblaze (www.publishingservicesbook.com/bookblaze), explaining that it allows users to obtain reviews for audiobooks, offering you the chance to receive an unlimited number of verified reviews. We recommend using this service to garner excitement around your audiobook!

As you wrap up the publishing your audiobook, it's time to shift gears and focus on what happens next.

Launching your book effectively is the key to turning all your hard work into success. In the next chapter, we'll explore how to streamline your book launch strategy—combining timing, promotion, and outreach to make the biggest impact possible.

Chapter 25

Streamlining Your Book Launch Strategy

In previous chapters, we provided detailed instructions for all the steps you need to take during your book's pre-launch stage. You may recall that we recommended strategies for obtaining reviews and generating a buzz around the arrival of your book.

 **Pro Tip:** To ace your launch strategy, start by uploading your book to KDP a few days before your launch to ensure it is completely ready and you are happy with how it looks and reads. However, don't click **Publish** just yet—only review your book with a Launch Previewer to ensure everything looks good.

Kindle eBook Preview

Online Preview and Quality Check
Preview your book online to check for quality issues and see how it appears on Kindle and mobile devices. TIP: Use our Kindle Previewer to preview books with interactive features.

✓ Well done! Your manuscript does not have spelling errors or image issues.

[Launch Previewer]

Downloadable Preview Options
To view your book directly on your Kindle or by using the Kindle Previewer, follow the instructions below. For the best viewing experience, we recommend using Kindle Previewer. Download Kindle Previewer

1. Download your converted book file: HTML
2. To preview on your computer, download Kindle Previewer and open your book in the tool.
3. To preview on your Kindle, send your book file to your Send-to-Kindle email address. If trying to view MOBI or other files, you can export those formats using Kindle Previewer. Learn more

Once you publish and your book goes live, however, prioritizing the performance of your book during the first 30 days is just as vital. During this period, Amazon analyzes your sales and determines whether your book is of interest to readers and if it should remain ranked (Ken Self-Publishing Secrets 2023b). Try to ensure your book obtains as many sales from multiple sources as possible, including downloads from your free book promotion, ebook sales, and paperback sales.

Free Book Promotion on Amazon: How to Get Started

Once your book is launched, take the following steps to create a free book promotion:

1. Set the price for your ebook to $0.99 and your print book to $9.99 if it is a high-content book.
2. Run a free promotion to increase traffic during the first week of your launch. You can run this promotion so long as your book is enrolled in KDP Select for a maximum of 5 days of each 90-day KDP Select enrollment period. On your KDP dashboard, click **Marketing,** and you will see a section called "Run a Price Promotion." Click **Create a Free Book Promotion**. Choose your book and click **Continue**. Indicate the desired start and end date, ensuring the end date does not coincide with the last day of your KDP Select term. Click **Save Changes**. Note that you can run your free promotion for 5 days straight or select five individual days. The earliest you can launch your free book promotion is the second day of your KDP Select enrollment timeframe. The scheduled start and end dates are normally midnight Pacific time (Kindle Direct Publishing, n.d.-g).
3. When you hit between 10 and 15 reviews, run ads at the price you can afford. We will give you the full rundown of how to advertise your book on Amazon in Chapter 31.

Remember to select the right keywords and ensure there is a demand for your book, that you target your audience's pain points effectively, that you have chosen appealing A+ Content for your book, and that you have at least ten reviews for a high-content book.

As mentioned, high-content books are those containing a considerable amount of text and information. They are meant to be read from cover to cover. Examples include novels, self-help books, textbooks, and biographies. Low-content books are those with either no or minimal content. Examples include coloring books, puzzle books, diaries, journals, calendars, etc.

Additional Book Promotion Services to Boost Your Launch

You don't have to rely exclusively on Amazon to promote your book. Book promotion sites (paid and free) can help promote your book via social media channels or emails. Essentially, these sites let their followers know about your book, offering readers the chance to download it and boost its popularity. Some book promotion sites charge for this service, but many others offer it for free. In case you're wondering what's in it for them, the answer is that they have affiliate links to your book. This means that they get a small percentage when someone buys your book within 24 hours of clicking on the link on their site (Corson-Knowles, n.d.). Amazon pays this percentage, and it has no effect on your royalties.

Have a good look at our list of suggested book service sites to determine which you think might be right for you. Note that the number of platforms each site promotes your book to (and how many times it does so) varies. Some work only with specific book genres (say, mystery, thriller, or science fiction). Some require that your book have a particular number of reviews and a specific minimum rating, while others only admit books with high-quality covers.

When Should You Schedule Your Book Promotions?

The timing of when you promote your book is just as important as the service you choose. Follow these tips to ensure that your scheduling is on point (Chesson 2017):

- Observe your KDP dashboard and avoid scheduling book promotions on the days when you make the most sales. This might be a Saturday or Sunday, but it could be any other day of the week. Instead, schedule the promotions right before your biggest-selling days so you can create momentum and get more people to purchase your book. If your book is new and you don't have an established pattern yet, the general rule of thumb is that books usually sell more on weekends than weekdays.

- Remember the 5 days' worth of free promotion you get under KDP Select for every 90-day period? Divide those 5 days up into two sets (one of three days, one of two days) and schedule them just before your top-selling days. Say your top sales happen on a Saturday. Schedule three of your five free days from Wednesday to Friday one week, then on the following week, schedule the two remaining free days on Thursday and Friday. That way, readers will have to pay for your book on the top-selling day.

- Remember that the first 30 days post-launch are one of the most critical periods for marketing your book. If you rely on a book promotion service, ensure your chosen company promotes your book during the 5-day free Kindle ebook promotions you run via KDP Select. Bear in mind that each book promotion service has different notice periods. Some will ask you to contact them a couple of weeks in advance before they promote your book. Read the conditions of each service in detail so your timing is perfect.

- In addition to the free book promotions, KDP Select also offers Kindle Countdown Deals (KCD), which allow you to run limited-time discounts only for Kindle ebooks on Amazon.com and Amazon.co.uk. You can run this promotion once you have published your book, and you can only run a free book promotion or a Kindle Countdown Deals promotion per enrollment period. To set up the promotion, click the three dots that appear next to your ebook.

- Under "Run a Price Promotion," select **Free Countdown Deals**, then hit **Create a Free Book Promotion**.

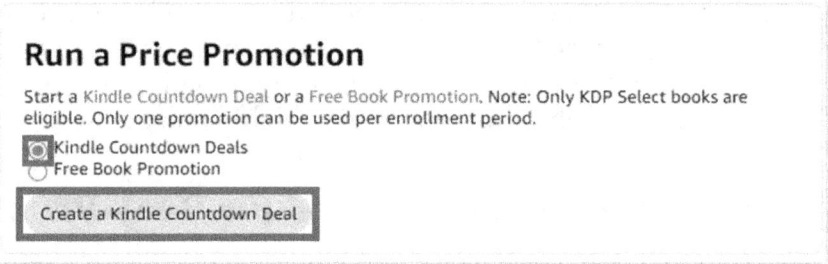

- Select your book and click **Continue**.

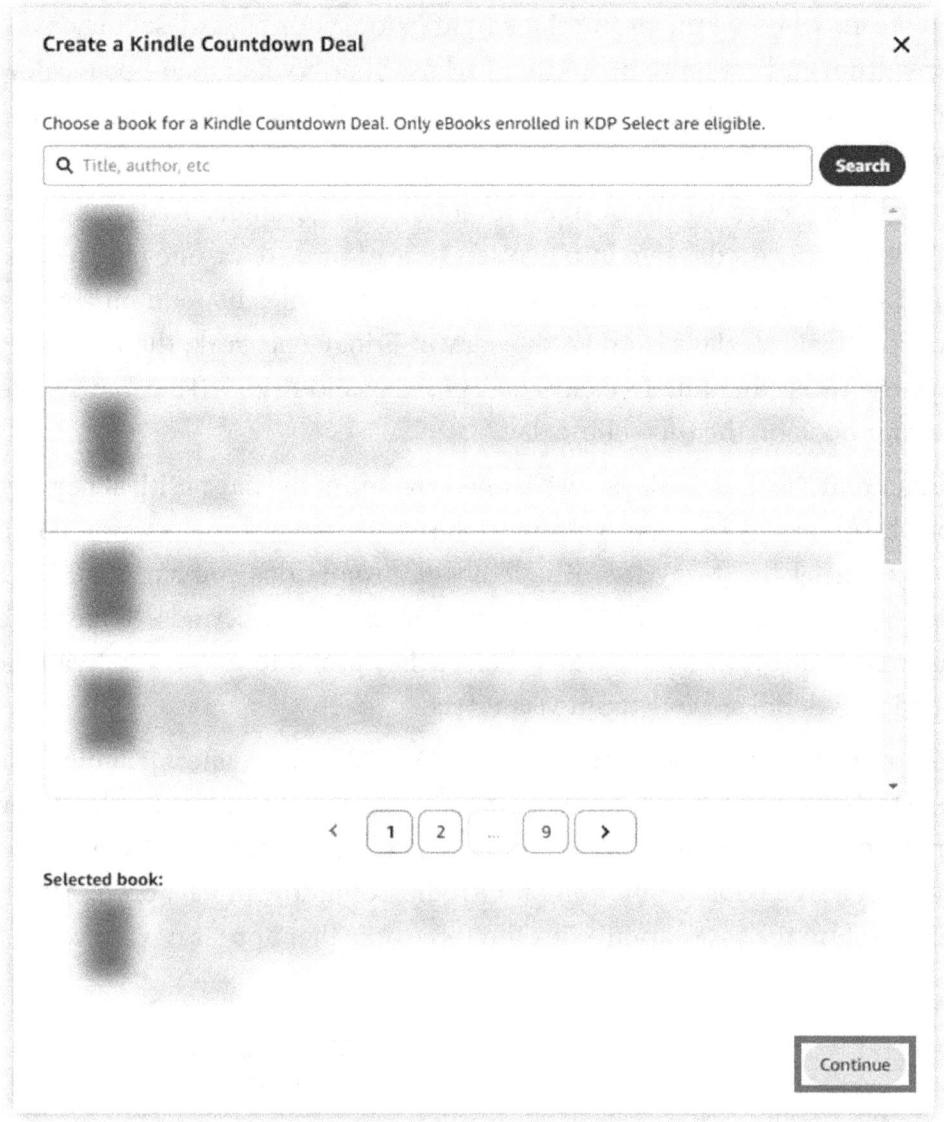

- Indicate the marketplace, start and end date, number of price increments, and starting list price of the promotion, and then hit **Save Changes**.

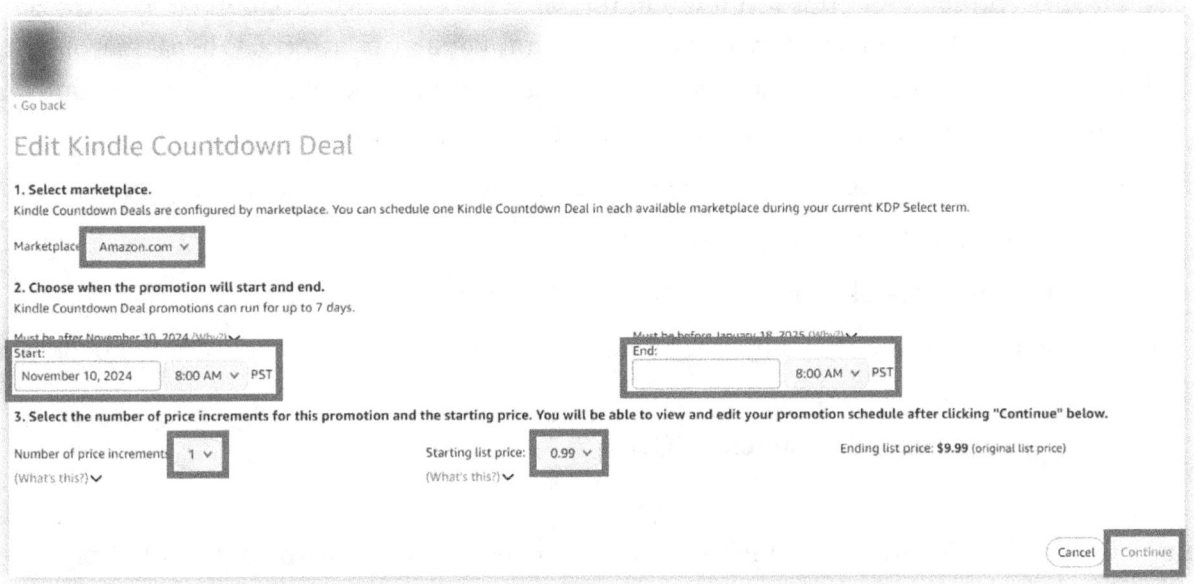

- Do all you can to promote your book in the days leading up to and during the promotion. Let people on your social media channels and Facebook groups know they can download the book without spending a cent. The good news is that they can leave a verified review if they download the book during KDP Select's free 5-day promotion. Contact people via direct message, asking them to download your book and follow up with review requests.

- Only rely on our recommended list of book promotion sites to ensure your book reaches actual readers who are likely to download and read your work. Some book promotion sites claim to have thousands of followers but actually rely on inactive emailing lists.

Promotion Sites Vetted by Publishing Services

You can find a list of trusted book promotion sites with vital information regarding what each organization offers and what their requirements are at www.publishingservicesbook.com/promotion-sites.

How to Make the Most of Promotion Websites

To ensure your promotion strategy hits its target, aim to:

1. Stack your promotions so you run numerous ones within days of each other. This triggers an effect that Kindlepreneur refers to as the "Amazon Popularity Effect." When Amazon notices that a book is selling well, it increases the number of keywords that can be used to find it and raises the book's ranking for those keywords (Chesson 2022c).
2. Test the effectiveness of any book promotion sites you use. Track factors such as:
   - The amount spent on the promotion
   - How many books you sold the week after the promotion
   - How much money your series made the week after the promotion (if the book is part of a series)
   - Your return on investment (ROI)

Obtain your ROI by dividing how much you earned by how much you spent and multiplying that amount by 100% (Chesson 2022c). For instance, if you earned $200 and you spent $50 on a book promotion site, then your ROI is 200/50 x 100 = 400%. Compare the different ROIs you achieve from different promotion sites.

How to Market Your Book on Facebook

You have seen how Facebook can help you start working on finding readers to leave reviews for your book once it is launched. However, not all ends there, as it can also be a useful tool when your book is already launched. By this stage, you will most probably form part of a thriving community and be a member of many groups in your genre, as well as those centered on self-publishing. You should also already have your author page.

Create a post about your book launch and include links so readers can purchase your book. Once your audiobook is ready, post an audiobook sample and include the link to purchase the full audiobook. Keep posting about the book. Every time you have interesting news to share, create a post and let your followers know about it. For instance, consider creating a post when you receive a bestseller tag, during your book promotion, if someone interviewed you, if someone created a blog or post about your book, and similar.

Example Post

> 🔖 Exciting News! 🔖
>
> The wait is over! 📖 My new book, "Book Title," is now LIVE on Amazon!
>
> For the first two weeks, you can grab the ebook for only $0.99 and the paperback for just $9.99! 📱📖 Don't miss out on this special launch price! ⏳
>
> Click the link below to secure your copy now! 🔥
>
> [Amazon Link to US page]

Building Your Following

Once your page is up and running, use your personal Facebook page and other social media channels to invite friends and followers to like your author page. Send an email to a select group of contacts, asking them to follow you. Once you have a good following, use your page to offer promotions like book giveaways, free chapters, merchandise, and more. Check your page daily and be active and responsive. Comment and like other pages, and if someone comments on your post, make sure to comment back, invite them to like your page (if they haven't already), and answer any queries they may have.

You now have many handy tips to market your book once it is launched. In the next chapter, we will cover legal matters by diving into copyrights.

Chapter 26

How to Copyright Your Book

Copyrighting your book ensures you have exclusive rights to it and enables you to sue for copyright infringement if someone attempts to steal characters, plot, and any other likenesses from your book. It is imperative to obtain your copyright, whether your book is fiction or non-fiction. Once your book is registered with the copyright office, you can freely share it without fearing that someone else will use its contents without your permission.

The Copyrighting Process: Everything You Need to Know

There are three required steps for copyrighting your work:

1. Creating the copyright
2. Providing a copyright notice
3. Registering your copyright claim

We will discuss each step in detail below.

Creating the Copyright

Even before you register your book, you already own the copyright to it. In fact, your rights begin as soon as you start writing the book. By simply working on your book, you obtain the right to all its contents.

However, this is true only if a human created the work. If your book was generated by an AI tool, the situation is different. Copyright law recognizes the rights of human authors but does not extend those rights to AI-generated content. While you may hold the copyright to the specific way you've edited, organized, or supplemented the AI-generated material, the content itself may not qualify for copyright protection in the same way human-authored work does.

Providing a Copyright Notice or Page

You can review an example of a copyright notice at the beginning of this book. There, you will find our claim to the rights to this book. A copyright notice must contain the following elements:

- The copyright symbol, which looks like this: ©
- The year of publication
- The name of the copyright owner
- The rights retained by the copyright owner (Komnenic 2023)

You can also use our free copy-and-paste template. Simply go to www.publishingservicesbook.com/copyright-page and make a copy of the template.

Registering Your Claim

Now it's time to officially register your copyright with Copyright.gov. This applies regardless of where in the world you reside. It is a relatively easy process that will take just a few minutes to complete.

01 Go to www.copyright.gov/registration. This will take you to the registration portal.

02 Click the blue bar entitled **Log in to the Electronic Copyright Office (eCO) Registration System**.

 Open an account/register with the site by clicking "**If you are a new user, click here to register**."

299

04 ▶▶ Fill in the information required in the boxes and click **Next**.

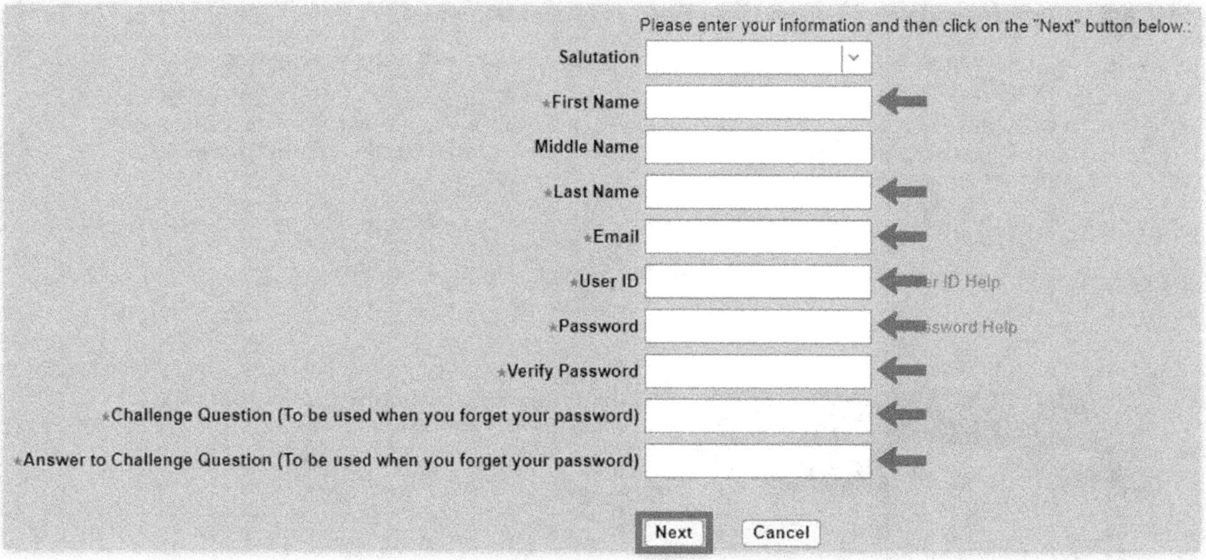

Please enter your information and then click on the "Next" button below.:

- Salutation
- ✱First Name ←
- Middle Name
- ✱Last Name ←
- ✱Email ←
- ✱User ID ← User ID Help
- ✱Password ← Password Help
- ✱Verify Password ←
- ✱Challenge Question (To be used when you forget your password) ←
- ✱Answer to Challenge Question (To be used when you forget your password) ←

[Next] [Cancel]

05 ▶▶ Fill in the required information and click **Next**.

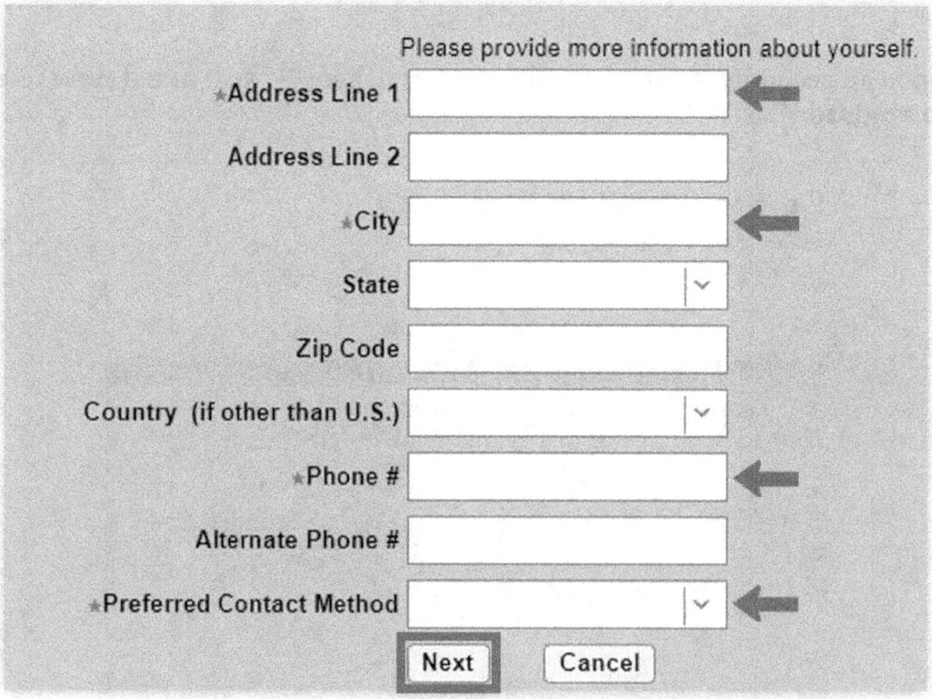

Please provide more information about yourself.

- ✱Address Line 1 ←
- Address Line 2
- ✱City ←
- State
- Zip Code
- Country (if other than U.S.)
- ✱Phone # ←
- Alternate Phone #
- ✱Preferred Contact Method ←

[Next] [Cancel]

06 ▶▶ Click **Next**.

300

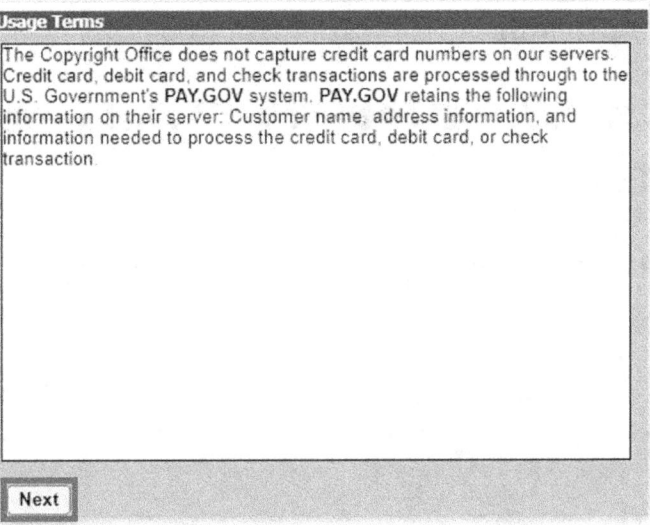

 Click **Finish**.

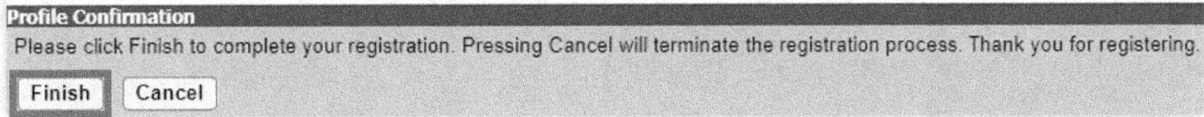

 You will be taken to a personal dashboard, where you can see any works you have that are already listed with Copyright.gov. Click **Standard Application**.

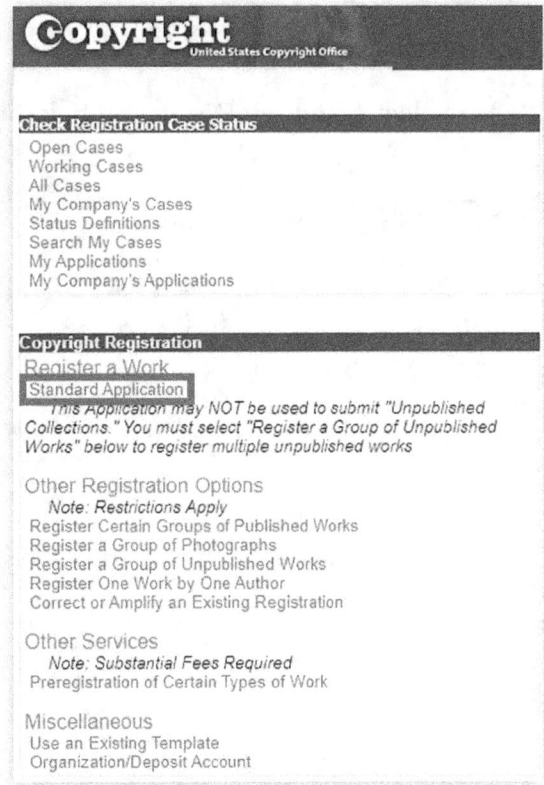

09 ▶▶ Click **Start Registration**.

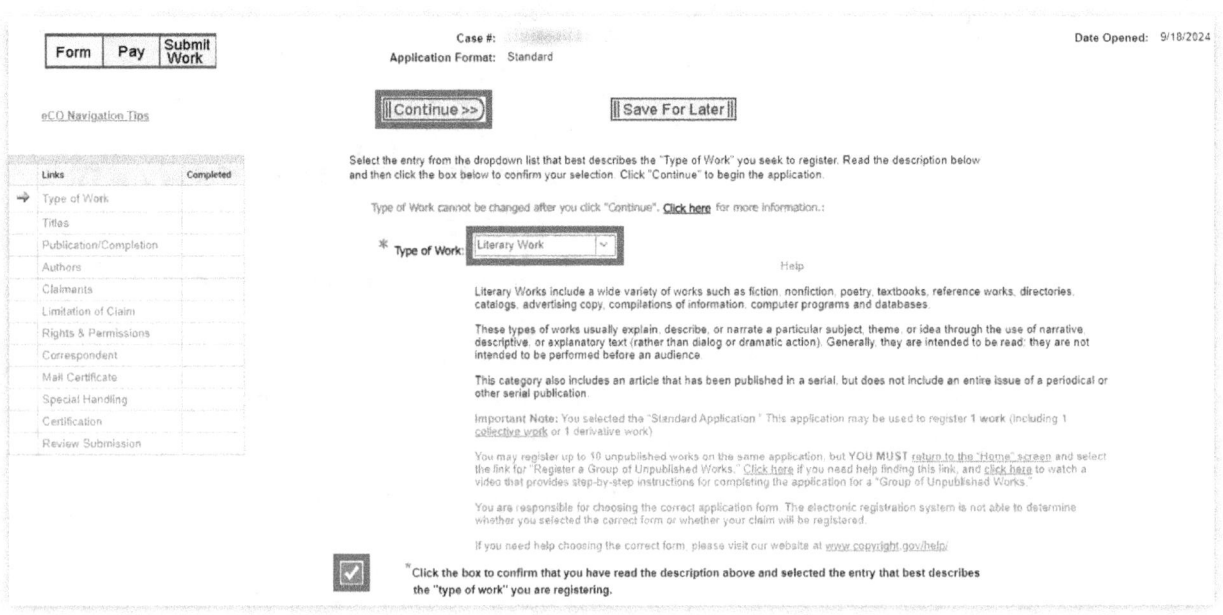

10 ▶▶ Select **Literary Work** and tick the confirmation box, then click **Continue**.

11 ▶▶ Next, you will be taken to "Titles." This is where you have to fill in the title of your work. Click on **New**.

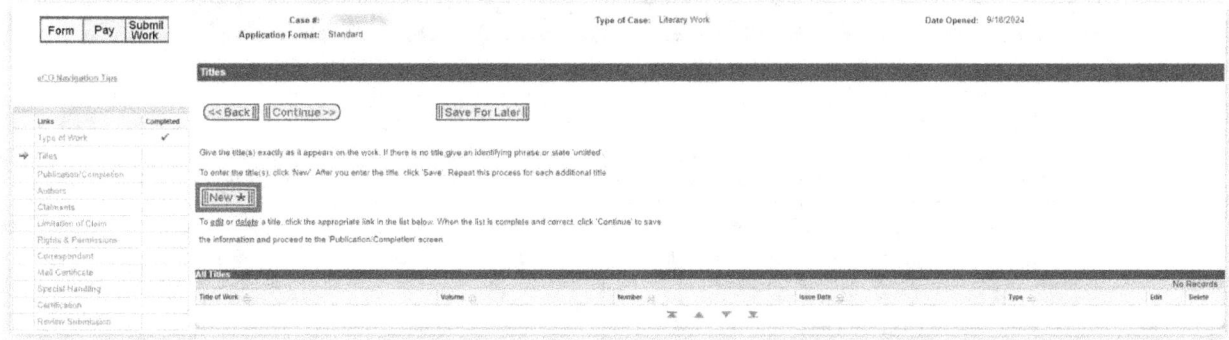

12 ▶▶ Select **Title of Work Being Registered** and enter your book title into the appropriate field. Then click **Save**.

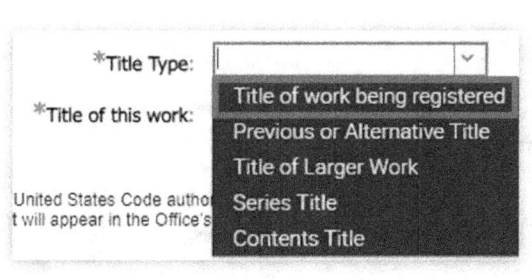 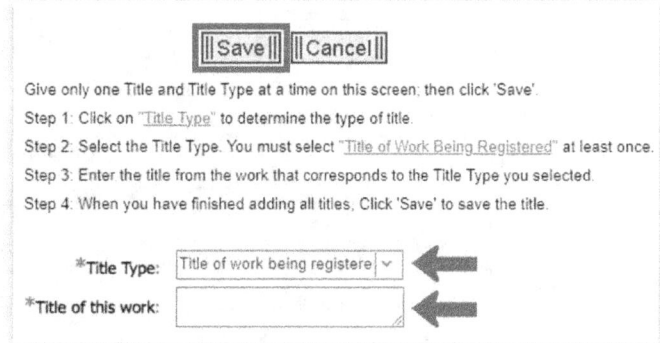

13 ▶▶ Your book will now show up under "All Titles." Click **Continue**.

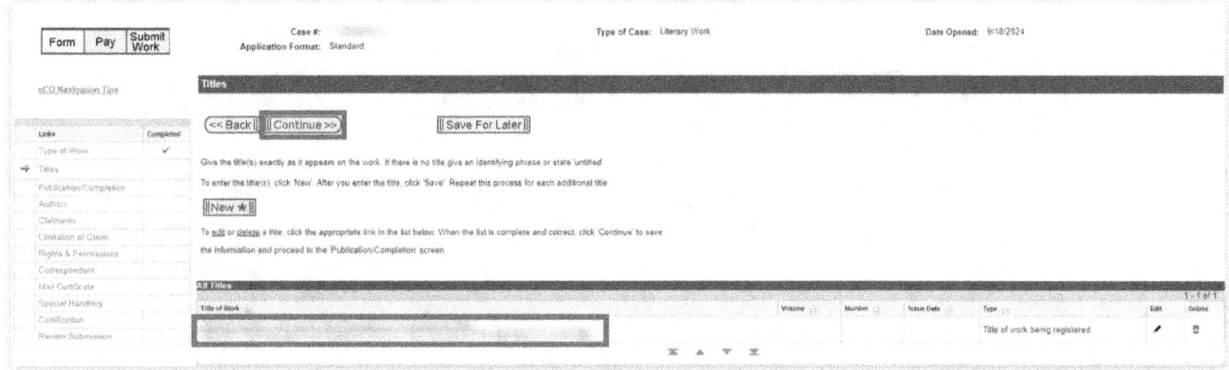

14 ▸▸ Next, you will be taken to "Publication." Select **Yes** or **No** from the drop-down menu to indicate whether your book has been published or not.

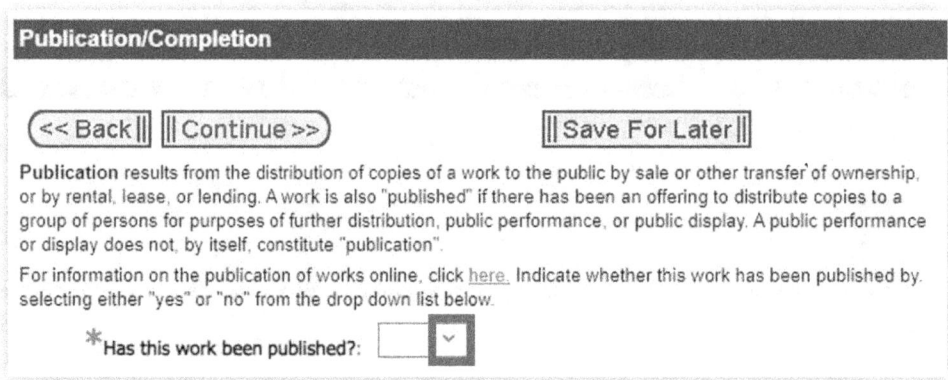

15 ▸▸ If you select **Yes**, enter the year of completion, date of first publication, and nation of first publication; then click **Continue**.

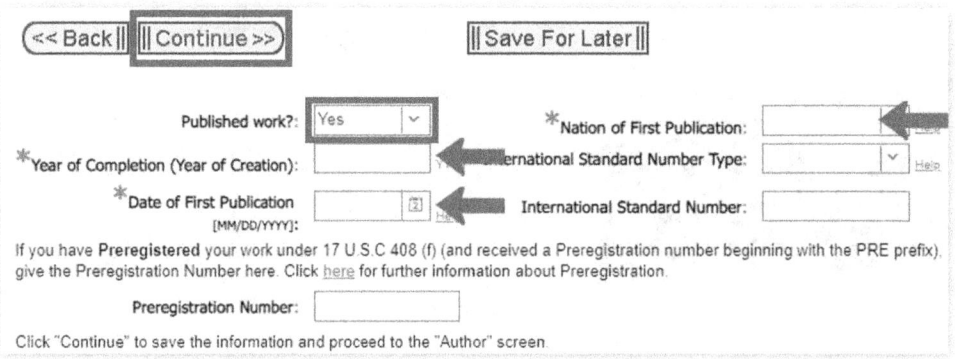

16 ▸▸ If you select **No**, fill in the year of completion and click **Continue**.

17 ▶▶ Next up is the authors tab where you can list your name and that of any additional authors. Click **New**.

18 ▶▶ You can choose to add a person (Option A) or an organization (Option B). If you choose Option A, fill in the first name, middle name if applicable, last name, and citizenship. If you choose Option B, enter the organization and the domicile. Then, click **Save**.

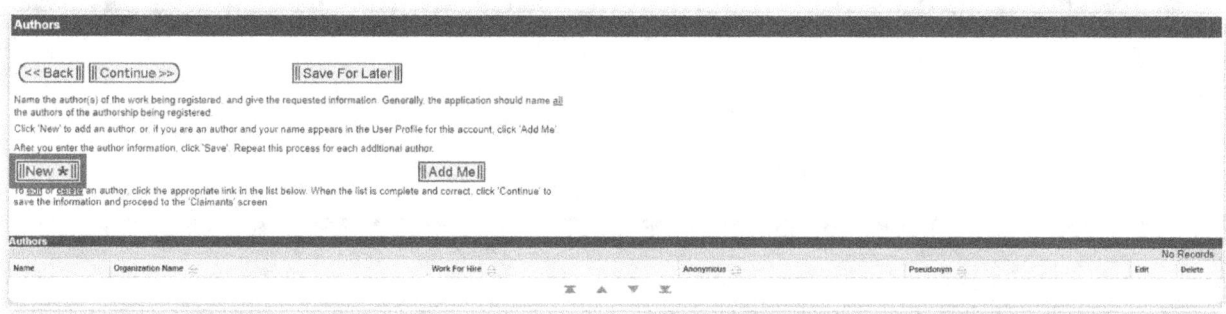

19 ▶▶ Check the box next to text and click **Save**.

 Your author will show up under "Authors." Click **Continue**.

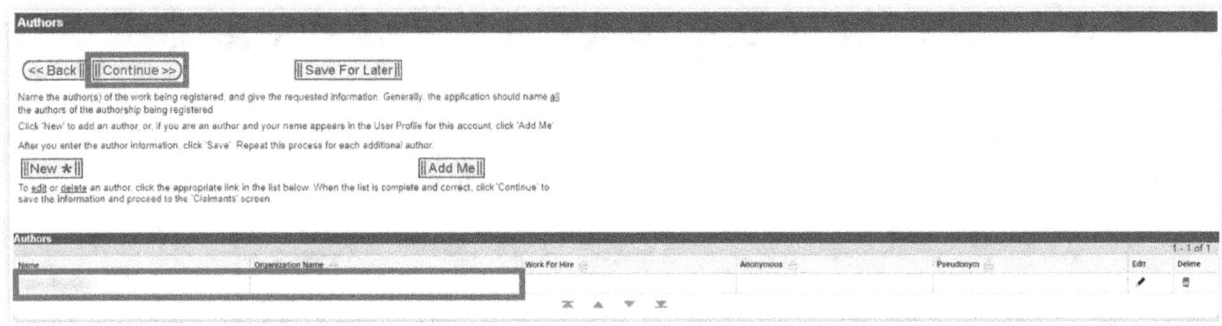

 The next section, entitled "Claimants," is where you can indicate any person or organization to whom or which copyright has been transferred. A claimant can be you, the author of the work, or a person or entity who has obtained ownership of the company, such as through a contract or purchasing it from the author. If you have set up the account under the same name as the person/organization that is requesting the copyright, select **Add Me** and then **Continue**. If the copyright should be for a different person/organization, select **New**.

22 You can choose to either enter an individual or an organization as the claimant. Only fill in one or the other and click **Save**.

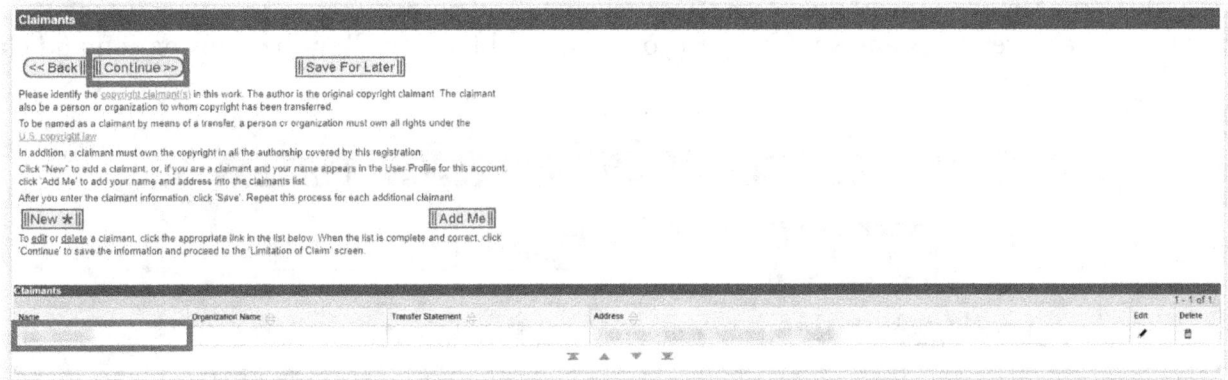

23 Your chosen claimant will show up under claimants. Click **Continue**.

24 Next is the "Limitation of Claim," where you can limit copyright or exclude specific material from the claim. If you are not excluding anything, leave all fields blank and click **Continue**.

25 ▶▶ In "Rights & Permissions," you can include contact information so you can be contacted regarding copyright management or permission to use your work. This is not a requirement, so it is up to you. Leave it blank or fill in the information and click **Continue**.

308

 In the correspondent section, you simply have to give the copyright office your contact details in case they have any questions about your application. Fill in all required fields and then click **Continue**.

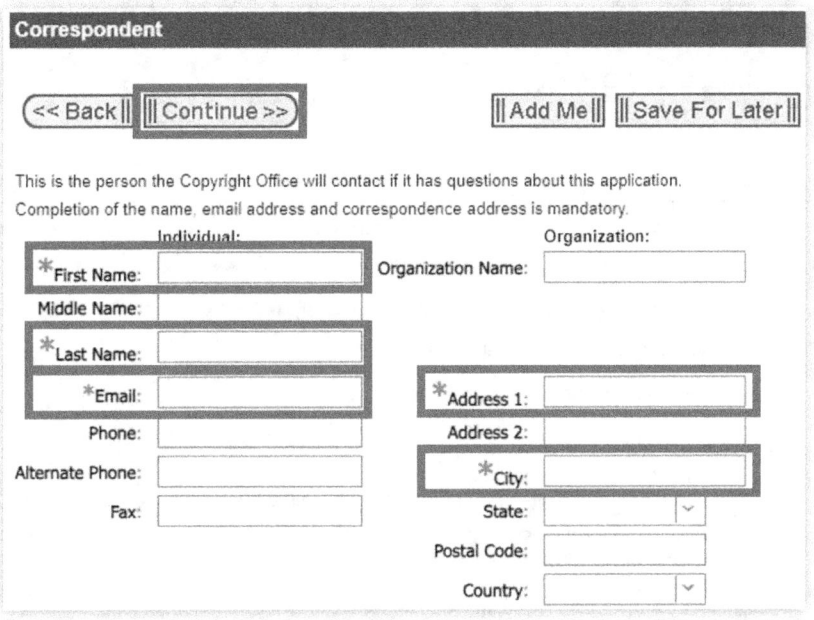

 Under "Mail Certificate," indicate the person and address to which the registration certificate should be mailed. You can choose an individual or an organization. You will need to fill in the address fields in both cases. Then, click **Continue**.

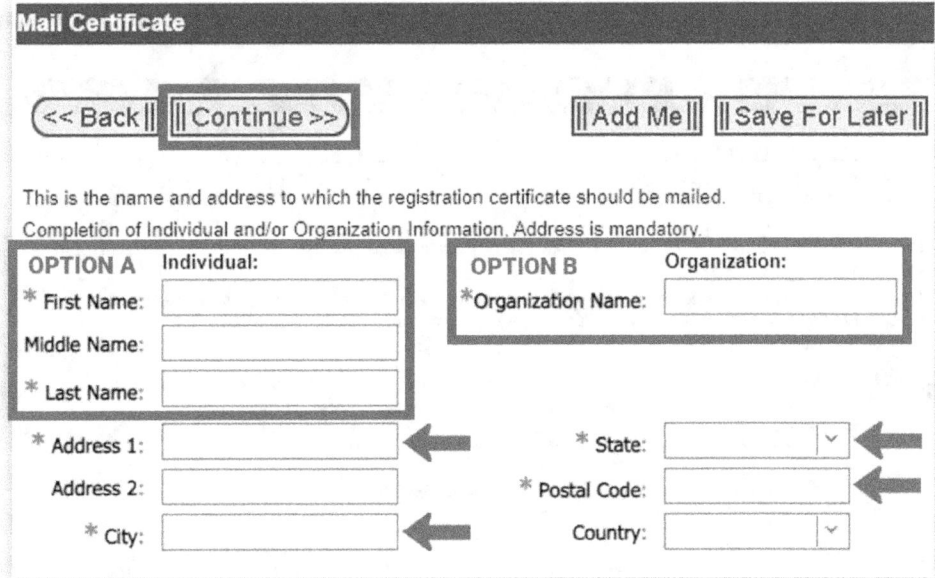

 Special handling is a service that is only for people with compelling reasons, such as pending or prospective litigation. If this doesn't apply to you, leave everything blank and click **Continue**.

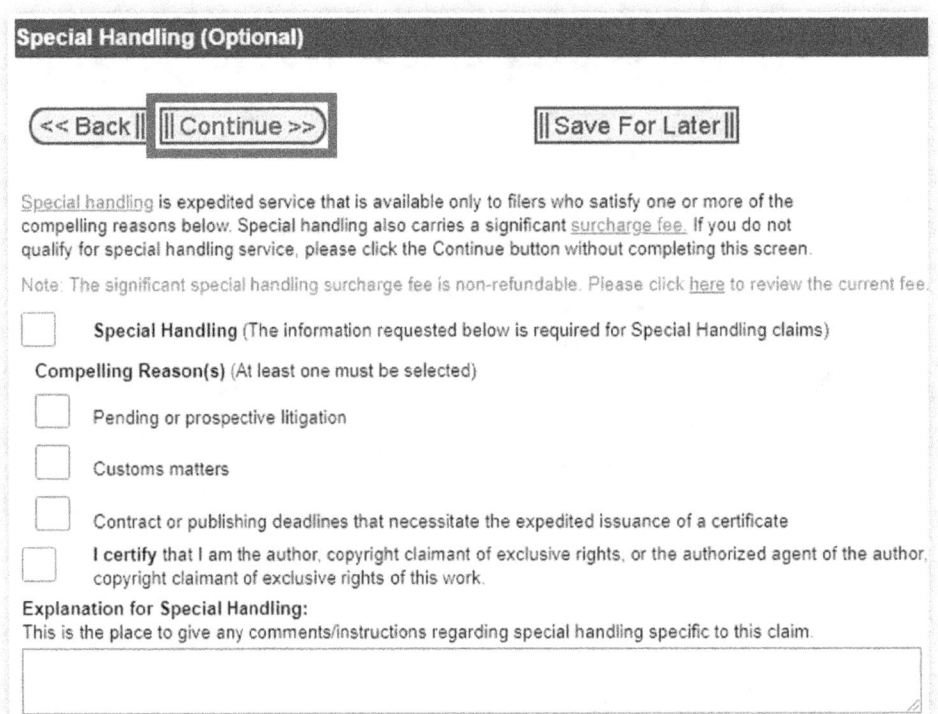

 In the certification section, you will be asked to certify that you are the author, copyright claimant, or owner of exclusive rights or similar and assure that the information you have given is true. Check the tick box, enter your name, and click **Continue**.

 Finally, you will be asked to review your submission to check that all the information you indicated is correct. If everything looks good, click **Add to Cart**.

 Next, you simply have to pay for copyright registration. Select if you want to pay via a deposit account or credit card. The registration price might change in the future. On the day this book was printed, the price for a standard application was $65.

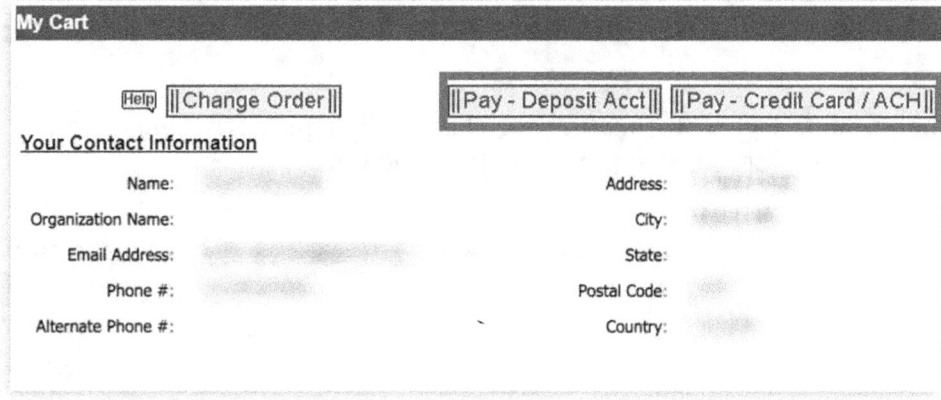

32 After successful payment, click **Continue**.

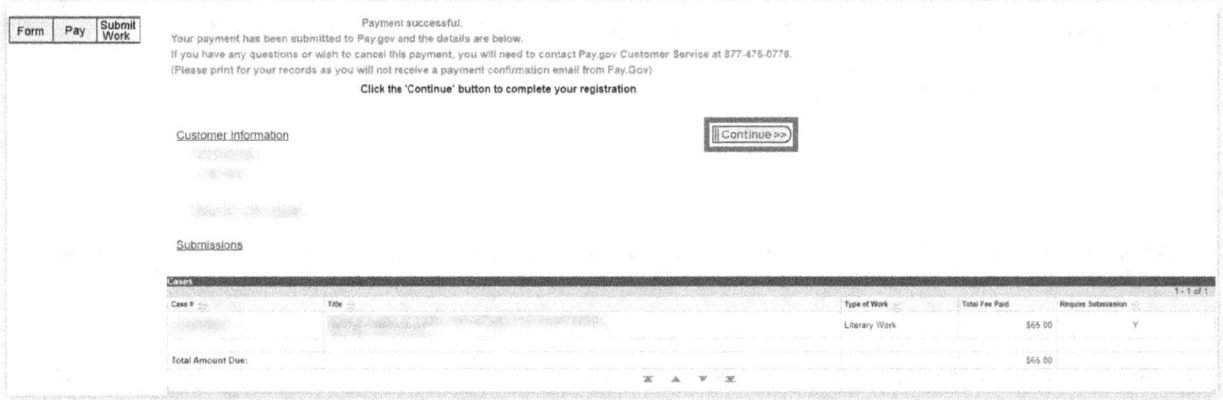

33 Click + **Select Files to Upload**, locate your PDF print book and your book cover on your computer, and click **Start Upload**.

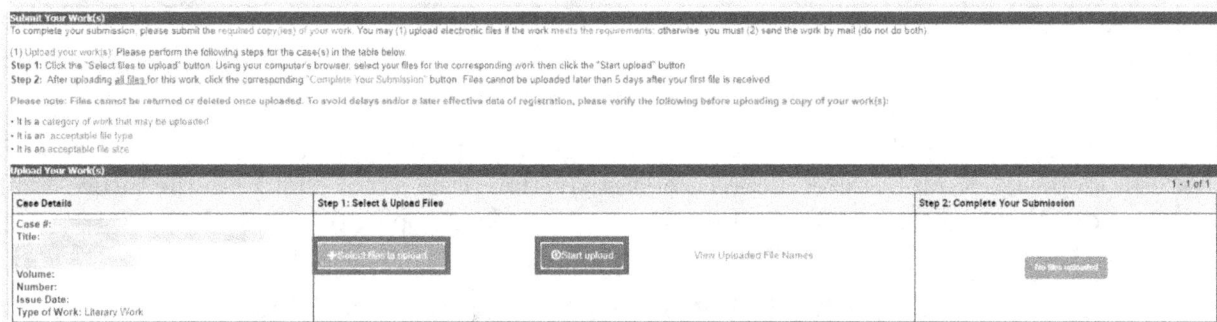

34 Finally, submit your work, and your claim will be properly filed once you choose **Click Here** to complete your submission after uploading all files.

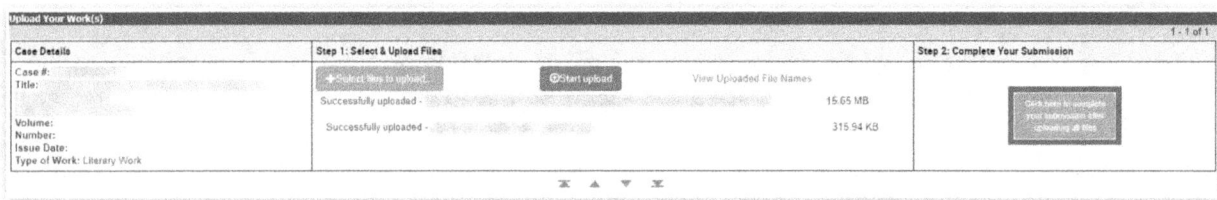

35 ▶▶ You are all done!

Upload Your Work(s)			1 - 1 of 1
Case Details	Step 1: Select & Upload Files		Step 2: Complete Your Submission
Case #: Title: Volume: Number: Issue Date: Type of Work: Literary Work		Claim submission completed: no further action required Click here for more information View Uploaded File Names	

You now have all the information you need to protect your work against copyright infringement. Note that there are special rules when it comes to copyrighting AI material, and they will be explained in a later chapter dedicated specifically to AI-generated work. In the next chapter, we will turn to another useful document to have on hand: your Author Bio.

Chapter 27

How to Write Your Author Bio

Most successful authors take time to craft a professional author bio, one that builds their credibility, lets others know why their work is worth reading, and connects them to their target audience.

When writing your author bio, we recommend creating two versions: a "full" version (of 150-200 words) for your Amazon Author Page and website and a shorter version (around 100 words maximum) for marketing purposes and the back cover of your book. Most websites will only want a short author bio when you market your book. In your bio, you can share a bit about yourself and why you are an authority in your niche. The suggested method is to write the longer version first and reduce the word count for your second version.

Fulfilling the Wants and Needs of Your Target Audience

Before starting the writing process, create a target audience persona in your head. Keep their pain points in mind, and think about how your bio can convince them that you are qualified and capable of helping them overcome their pain or find entertainment, advice, or ideas. (This will differ depending on your book genre.) Go back to your outline and read the audience research section, keeping your readers' ages, online behavior, and interests in mind. Your bio should speak to a specific, not a generic, audience.

Author Bios: Fiction Versus Non-Fiction

Author bios differ depending on whether you are a fiction or non-fiction writer. For fiction writers, the main goal should be to create an engaging, unique, and exciting persona. If you have any writing qualifications or have won any prizes for your writing, include these facts in your bio.

For non-fiction books, a writer's experience and qualifications are vital, as they must be strong enough to address specific pain points effectively. Be careful about including false claims such as qualifications or experience you do not possess. For instance, if you are writing a self-help book, steer clear of claims that you are a qualified psychologist, doctor, or therapist if this is not the case. Instead, let your readers know why you are passionate about a subject or that you are a keen researcher in the field. If you are writing a book about overcoming anxiety, you might share any facts that would make you interesting to listen to. Your book might be a distillation of all the research you conducted that helped you overcome your anxiety. There are many creative yet honest ways to show your audience why your book can help them quell their pain or fulfill their needs.

Tips for Reaching Your Audience

The following scenarios can help you with what type of content your readers may be interested in:

- If you are writing a book about real estate investment, your bio should reveal experience in the sector and include projects you have worked on or achievements you have made.
- If your book is a romantic comedy, your audience will likely resonate with you if your bio includes a couple of comedic touches that let them know they're in for a light, fun read.
- When writing a college textbook, a bio with too much personal information or a light, conversational tone may be deemed inappropriate.
- If you are writing a book for older teens about to leave home for the first time, your persona and language should resonate with this crowd so it doesn't feel like they're being "nagged."
- If you are writing a book about the occult, keep it dark and mysterious instead of discussing your interest in baking muffins.
- Make sure to include keywords that will help readers find your book.

What to Include in Your Author Biography

Author biographies should be written in the third person and include:

- Your current publication and the names of any previous works published under your author name (Keep it to two or three maximum if the author has penned many books.)
- Your work experience, especially any experience that pertains to your niche
- Your specialty, if appropriate
- Your educational qualifications, if appropriate

- If desired, a sentence or two about your personal life (where you live, a bit about your family life if you wish, your hobbies, and similar)
- Links to your social media channels (only for the extended version)

Author Bio Samples

We have provided two samples of author bios below. These samples include the full and short versions for you to review.

Cluck Norris: Author Bio (Full Version) - Sample

Renowned poultry scientist and chicken breeder Cluck Norris is the author of *Become a Backyard Chicken Farmer—Master Breed Selection and Feeding—Uncover the Importance of Facilities and Health Care to Effortlessly Increase Egg Production.*

Cluck has been a successful chicken breeder for 20 years, and his chickens have garnered many prizes at the nation's most prestigious poultry competitions—including the National 4-H Poultry & Egg Conference and the American Poultry Association National Meet. Cluck has extensive knowledge and experience in chicken health and breeding. He has dedicated his life to raising happy, healthy chickens and has empowered numerous families to raise chickens sustainably.

Cluck's academic background includes a bachelor's degree in animal science and a master's degree in poultry science from North Carolina State University, where he graduated with honors. He also holds advanced certifications in avian health and sustainable agriculture.

Born and raised in rural North Carolina, Cluck grew up surrounded by chickens and developed a passion for farming from his early years. He now resides in North Carolina with his wife, Henelope, their son, Eggbert, and a lively flock of heritage breed chickens. Outside of his work, he enjoys cosplay, breakdancing, and yodeling.

Cluck Norris: Author Bio (Short Version) - Sample

Renowned poultry scientist and chicken breeder Cluck Norris is the author of *Become a Backyard Chicken Farmer—Master Breed Selection and Feeding—Uncover the Importance of Facilities and Health Care to Effortlessly Increase Egg Production.*

Cluck has been a successful chicken breeder for 20 years, and his chickens have garnered many prizes at the nation's most prestigious poultry competitions—including the National 4-H Poultry & Egg Conference. Cluck is passionate about raising happy, healthy chickens and empowering families to produce their own fresh, sustainable eggs.

Cluck's academic background includes a bachelor's degree in animal science and a master's degree in poultry science from North Carolina State University. He also holds advanced certifications in avian health and sustainable agriculture.

 **Pro Tip:** When writing your author bio, it's important to mention key achievements, experience, and qualifications, but make sure it doesn't sound like you're bragging so that readers can relate to you.

Now that you've crafted a compelling author bio, it's time to put it to work. In the next chapter, we'll show you how to set up your Amazon Author Central account and create an interesting author page that will help readers connect with you, explore your other works, and establish your presence as a professional author.

 # Publishing Services' Author Bio Package

The **Author Bio Package is** a top choice if you are seeking an impactful bio that resonates deeply with your audience. The package includes both the short and long versions with a turnaround time of five business days.

Our talented copywriting team can catch your target readers' eyes and make them remember you. They can craft an excellent persona for pen-name authors, too.

To place an order, visit the Publishing Services website at www.publishingservices.com. Scroll down and select **Amazon Author Bio Package**. Fill in the fields required, including your author name, their professional credentials, the theme of their work, why the author is qualified to write about the topic, whether they are an expert, and any personal information. Upload your manuscript, let us know how you heard about us, make sure all the information has been supplied, and click **Add to Cart**.

Chapter 28

How to Set Up and Optimize Your Amazon Author Central and Author Page

Amazon Author Central is a handy marketing tool that anyone with an ISBN can access. In this section, you publish your author page and inform your readers of book launches and other news. It is also a place where readers can find all the books you have written available for purchase on Amazon.

Key Features of Amazon Author Central

In Amazon Author Central, you can do all of the following:

- Add books to your author page.
- Add a biography in multiple languages.
- Manage all your books (and keep the information in your descriptions and Editorial Reviews section up-to-date, all from one handy place).
- Control your author profile on Amazon and Audible and in Kindle books.
- Check your BSR.
- Read reviews from your readers.
- Add editorial reviews (more on this in the following chapters).

- See how many Amazon followers you have. (Amazon has a follow button that can be found on your author page in Amazon Author Central.)
- Find BookScan sales information (a US-only feature that allows you to track the sales of print books, relying on sales figures obtained by Amazon, Barnes & Noble, and other booksellers).

Setting Up Your Amazon Author Central Account

To create your Author Central Account, follow these steps:

1. Go to https://author.amazon.com/ and click **Join for Free**.
2. Sign in with your regular Amazon username and password. If you don't have an account yet, click **I Am a New Customer** and fill in the required information.
3. Enter your author name, and a list of books will appear. Select any one of them to create your account. You can also search for your book via their ISBN or title.
4. Amazon will send you a confirmation email so you can complete the process. This can take anywhere from 3 to 7 days to obtain.
5. Once your account is confirmed, ensure all the versions of your book are on your author page (including your audiobooks, ebooks, paperback, and hardcover versions). To add books, go to the books tab, go to the bottom of your bibliography, and click **Add a Book**. Find your selected books via your author name or their titles or ISBN. Beneath your book/s, click **This Is My Book**, and it will be added to your list of books.

Setting Up Your Author Page

To set up your page, get your Amazon Author Bio ready and log into Amazon Author Central. Next, follow these steps:

1. Click the **Profile** tab.
2. Copy and paste your Amazon Author Bio into the space provided. The biography should be at least 100 words long to meet Amazon's requirements.
3. Click **Preview biography** to check your work. When you're happy with it, click **Save Biography**.

4. Add a photograph to your profile, selecting a photo that will resonate with your readers. For instance, Cluck Norris might upload a picture of himself holding one of his prize chickens. Meanwhile, a writer of a book on finances might choose to have a professional-looking headshot as their profile pic. Ensure your photo is square and at least 300 x 300 pixels. To upload the photo, click **Upload New Photo**. If you already have an image you wish to replace, click the blue pencil icon and upload the replacement pic by selecting the pic and clicking **Open**. Click **Publish**.

5. Make sure you can see the **+Follow** button under your profile pic and name so that your readers can stay up to date with your latest news.

Pro Tip: If you want to edit your bio in the future, click **Profile** and then **Edit** on Amazon Central. Effect your changes or paste a new bio if you wish.

How to Create an Amazon Author Page for a Pen Name

If you are using a pen name, you will need a separate Author page for all the books you write under this pen name. To create this page, follow these steps:

1. Go to Amazon Author Central and click the **Books** tab.
2. Click **Add It Now**.
3. Enter your pen name, title, or ISBN to search for your book, and then click **Add This Book**.
4. You will see [Author name] is my pen name. Click **Continue**.
5. Once Amazon verifies that you are the author of your chosen books, an additional author page will be available for all the books written under that pen name. You can access it any time in the drop-down menu next to your name in the upper right corner of Amazon Author Central.

Pro Tip: If you co-author a book, you and your co-author can concurrently claim the book under your accounts. You can help each other out by providing a link to your co-author's bio page on your own.

You now see what a useful marketing tool your Amazon Author Central section can be. Now, let's focus on every publisher's bread and butter: reviews.

Chapter 29

How to Obtain Amazon Editorial Reviews

In earlier chapters, we discussed the importance of reviews, the difference between verified and unverified reviews, and strategies for gathering unverified reviews through social media and other methods. Now, in the upcoming chapters, we'll focus on how to secure editorial and verified reviews.

A key distinction exists between the "normal" reviews (verified or unverified) and editorial reviews. The main difference between them lies in who writes it, the purpose, and how it's presented:

Normal Review

- **Written By:** Regular readers or customers who've purchased and read the book
- **Purpose:** For readers to share personal opinions and experiences with the book, often subjective
- **Style:** Casual, reflecting the reader's perspective and personal preferences
- **Where it Appears:** Customer reviews sections on Amazon and other platforms
- **Impact:** Offers social proof; potential readers use it to gauge the book's general appeal

Editorial Review

- **Written By:** Professional reviewers, journalists, or industry experts
- **Purpose:** To provide a critical analysis of the book's content, style, and quality
- **Style:** Formal, in-depth, and structured, often highlighting key strengths and weaknesses
- **Where it Appears:** In publications, websites, product pages, or as part of the book's promotional materials
- **Impact:** Adds credibility to the book, especially for marketing, as it signals a professional endorsement

Reviewers can include prominent authors, magazine writers, or book reviewers from dedicated review sites. Amazon gives you plenty of freedom with this section, so make the most of your right to include content that can boost your sales rate.

Benefits of Editorial Reviews

Editorial reviews are important for the following reasons:

- They come from authority or respected sources. Sometimes these sources are other writers or specialists in your field.
- Your reviewers don't require proof of purchase to leave a review that appears on all marketplaces.
- You posted them, not the buyer. You can, therefore, choose the very best reviews from the most authoritative or influential reviewers possible.
- They appear in a dedicated section, separate from reviews by customers.

Where Are Audiences Looking?

Kindlepreneur conducted an experiment on Amazon editorial reviews and found that customers pay attention to them. The experiment involved using heat maps to track the eye movements of users who visited book pages. The results showed that customers give more importance to the reviewer as a person than what they said. This study also showed that between six and ten editorial reviews are the perfect number for an editorial review section. If you have fewer than six, your customers will likely gloss over the section; if you have more than ten, they tend to disregard it. Moreover, when done correctly, these reviews influence shoppers to purchase books at a noticeable rate (Chesson 2022a).

What Makes a Good Review?

To publish an editorial reviews section that hits the mark, add a fact to the name that makes the reviewer an "authority" or person whose opinion is worth taking into account. Take a look at these two examples to see what a difference specifying what makes an author an authority can make:

> Example 1: *"This was an amazing book that will have families all over America cooking healthy meals with their kids on weekends."*—**Al Dente**

> Example 2: *"This was an amazing book that will have families all over America cooking healthy meals with their kids on weekends."*—**Al Dente, Executive Chef of Michelin-starred establishment Slice, Slice Baby**

As you can see, the first review isn't quite as meaningful as the second, which shows exactly why Al Dente is a figure who knows what he is talking about.

Other examples of reviews backed by "authority facts about the author" are:

> *"A book that will make passing primary school math a breeze."*—**Matt Ricks, author of *Math Adventures: Journey Through Numbers***

> *"An easy yet powerful introduction to cognitive-behavioral therapy."*—**Dr. Mindy Matters, Behavioral Psychologist**

> *"A great read that will teach small business owners how to boost their sales."*—**Jasper Julep, Editor, *Finance Whiz* magazine**

Where Can You Get Editorial Reviews?

There are a few places where you can look for editorial reviews. We discuss several in detail below.

Pro Tip: In addition to everything listed below, you may also be able to find reviewers from among your existing followers or the people you interact with online. Find out what they do, and if you think they have a background that would lend authority to your Editorial Review section, pursue the connection and ask them for a review.

Other Authors in Your Genre or Niche

Kindlepreneur's Dave Chesson (2022b) recommends that self-published authors target one very well-known author, three to five authors who represent where they want to be, and five or more authors just like them. You can find other writers in local author groups or online exchange critique groups (where you agree to critique someone else's work in exchange for them doing the same for you). Sites where you can find critics include:

Critique Circle (www.critiquecircle.com) (for stories only)

- **What They Offer:**
  - Critique Circle is an online writing community where authors can share their work and receive feedback from other writers. It operates on a credit system, where users earn credits by critiquing others' work and then use those credits to submit their own work for critique. It offers various tools like writing workshops, storyboarding, and submission tracking. Critique Circle supports writers across multiple genres, providing a collaborative environment for improving their writing skills.

- **Price Range:**
  - **Free Membership:** Users can participate in critiquing and receive critiques on their work by using the credit system. Basic tools are available for free users.
  - **Premium Membership:** A fee of $4 per month (or $40 annually) provides access to additional features like private queues, enhanced privacy settings, the ability to post more stories at a time, additional tracking tools, and increased storage.

Scribophile (www.scribophile.com)

- **What They Offer:**
  - Scribophile is an online writing community that allows writers to share their work and receive detailed feedback from other writers. It operates on a "karma" system, where members earn karma points by critiquing others' work and use those points to post their own writing for critique. The platform also offers writing contests, forums for discussion, and educational resources on writing and publishing. Scribophile is widely known for its high-quality, in-depth critiques, making it popular among serious writers.

- **Price Range:**
  - **Free Membership:** This level offers access to the basic features, including earning and spending karma points by critiquing and submitting work, participating in forums, and entering contests. Free users can post up to 2 works for critique at a time.
  - **Premium Membership (Scribophile Premium):** A fee of $11 per month or $65 annually includes additional perks such as:
    - Unlimited submissions for critiques
    - Access to private writing groups and queues

- Enhanced privacy settings (such as the ability to post work privately)
- More detailed manuscript analysis tools and statistics
- Priority placement in critique queues

BlueInk Review (www.publishingservicesbook.com/blue-ink-review)

- **What They Offer:**
  - BlueInk Review provides professional reviews of self-published books. Authors can submit their books to receive objective, in-depth critiques from experienced reviewers, many of whom have written for mainstream publications. The service aims to help indie authors stand out in a crowded marketplace by providing high-quality reviews that they can use for marketing and credibility.
- **Price Range:**
  - **Standard Review:** $445 (completed in 7–9 weeks)
  - **Fast Track Review:** $545 (completed in 4–6 weeks)

BookLife (https://booklife.com)

- **What They Offer:**
  - BookLife is a free resource from Publishers Weekly that assists indie authors with book marketing and self-publishing advice. It offers tools for authors to submit their self-published books for potential review in Publishers Weekly. BookLife also provides guides on various aspects of book production, marketing, and promotion.
- **Price Range:**
  - **Free:** Users can submit books for possible reviews in Publishers Weekly.
  - **Premium:** Editorial services, like book editing and marketing, may come at an additional cost, but pricing isn't directly listed on the website.

Chanticleer Book Reviews (www.chantireviews.com)

- **What They Offer:**
  - Chanticleer Reviews offers book reviews, writing competitions, and editorial services. It is focused on discovering outstanding new talent in the indie publishing industry. Chanticleer hosts various awards for different genres, with winners receiving

promotional opportunities and industry recognition.

- **Price Range:**
    - **Standard:** A fee of $495 offers a book review in six to nine weeks.
    - **Expedited:** For faster service (three to five weeks), the fee is an additional $150.

City Book Review (https://citybookreview.com)

- **What They Offer:**
    - City Book Review is a platform that operates several local book review outlets, including San Francisco Book Review and Manhattan Book Review. They offer paid review services for authors who want to reach a wider audience. They cover a wide variety of genres and provide marketing services alongside reviews.

- **Price Range:**
    - **Basic:** $200–$349 (depending on the chosen turnaround time)
    - **Premium:** $250–$399 (depending on the chosen turnaround time)

Feathered Quill (https://featheredquill.com)

- **What They Offer:**
    - Feathered Quill is an online review site that caters to independent and self-published authors. It provides detailed book reviews, author interviews, and promotional opportunities. The site also offers various book awards and services that help authors gain visibility.

- **Price Range:**
    - **Spotlight Review:** Only five books at a time are given this spotlight placement every week for $149.
    - **Featured Review:** This service includes a review placed on the high-traffic main page of your book's genre for $125. It will be prominently displayed above the links to reviews of other books and be featured for at least one week.
    - **Standard Review:** For $85, a review will be placed on a page created for your book, with a link from the genre-specific page.

- **Children's Book Review:** There is a special rate of $50 for children's books that are full-color, 32 pages or less, and 1,000 or fewer words. It includes a review that will be placed on a page created for your book.

Foreword Reviews (www.forewordreviews.com)

- **What They Offer:**
  - Foreword Reviews focuses on independently published books, including self-published and small-press titles. The platform offers professional book reviews, industry insights, and interviews with authors and publishers. It's a trusted source for readers, librarians, and booksellers looking for new voices in indie publishing.
- **Price Range:**
  - **Professional Review:** A Foreword review costs $549. They have also partnered with BlueInk Review (www.publishingservicesbook.com/blue-ink-review) to offer you a special two-review package for the discounted price of $745.
  - **Premium Options:** Rapid turnaround or enhanced promotional features are available at an additional cost.

IndieReader (www.publishingservicesbook.com/indie-reader)

- **What They Offer:**
  - IndieReader is a review service and discovery platform for independently published books. It offers professional reviews, the IndieReader Discovery Awards, and various editorial services aimed at helping authors improve and market their work. IndieReader reviews are often used by authors to gain credibility and reach a larger audience.
- **Price Range:**
  - **Basic package:** $299 (completed in seven to nine weeks)
  - **Rush package:** $399 (completed in four to six weeks)

Online Book Club (https://onlinebookclub.org)

- **What They Offer:**
  - Online Book Club is a community-based platform where members can participate in discussions about books, submit reviews, and receive free books in exchange for

reviews. The site features a mix of professional and user-generated reviews. It also offers authors opportunities to get their books reviewed by its large community of readers.

- **Price Range:**
    - **Standard Review:** This is free but only if selected by the community.
    - **Paid Review:** These prices range from $97 to $297, depending on the speed of review and promotional options.
    - **Featured Book of the Month:** These promotions can cost more.

Readers' Favorite (www.publishingservicesbook.com/readers-favorite)

- **What They Offer:**
    - Readers' Favorite offers free and paid book reviews for indie and traditional authors. It hosts an annual book award contest and provides various promotional tools to help authors reach their audience. The platform is known for its large reviewer base and focus on giving exposure to both emerging and established authors.

- **Price Range:**
    - **Free:** This is on a limited availability and subject to wait times.
    - **Express:** A fee of $59 guarantees your book will be reviewed in 2 weeks.
    - **Multiple Review:** A fee of $129 nets you multiple reviews for a true consensus on its quality.

Review Blogs or Sites

Some sites are specifically dedicated to reviewing books. Some bloggers or writers charge for these services, while others do so for free. Because these are not Amazon reviewers, you can pay them to review your work if you wish, and you can use words from their reviews in your editorial review section. We previously mentioned Fiverr as just one place where you can pay for beta readers. You can also find people willing to leave words for your editorial review section.

Websites in Your Genre

Numerous websites focus on specific genres, especially fiction. Contact the editors or administrators of these sites. Check out this list of book review blogs on Kindlepreneur (Chesson 2023a) www.publishingservicesbook.com/book-review-blogs.

Bookstragrammers and BookTokers

Look up the hashtags #Bookstagram and #BookTok on Instagram and TikTok. Check out influencers with a good following and active followers and ask them if they will review your book.

Press Release Outcomes

If you wrote a press release for your book, see if any media outlets have published it or commented on it. If they have, you may be able to get a good sentence or two for your editorial review section.

 **Pro Tip:** If the review comes from a review site or company, credit the site or company rather than the specific reviewer, as readers are more likely to have come across the names of the sites or companies than the individual reviewers.

How to Obtain Written Permission for Editorial Reviews

Once you get people on board to contribute to your editorial review section, ask for their written permission to publish their reviews. You should not edit or rephrase their review without their written consent.

How to Format Editorial Reviews

Use basic HTML tags to bold and italicize your editorial reviews. To enhance the authority or interest of your reviewers, *italicize their review* and **put the reviewer's name and fact of interest/profession in bold**. This makes the most eye-catching part of the review stick out more.

You have three options when it comes to formatting your Editorial Review, as outlined below.

Option 1

The easiest option when it comes to formatting reviews is to use the free Kindlepreneur book description generator tool. Go to Amazon Editorial Review and apply bolding and italics where you see fit. Click **Generate Code**.

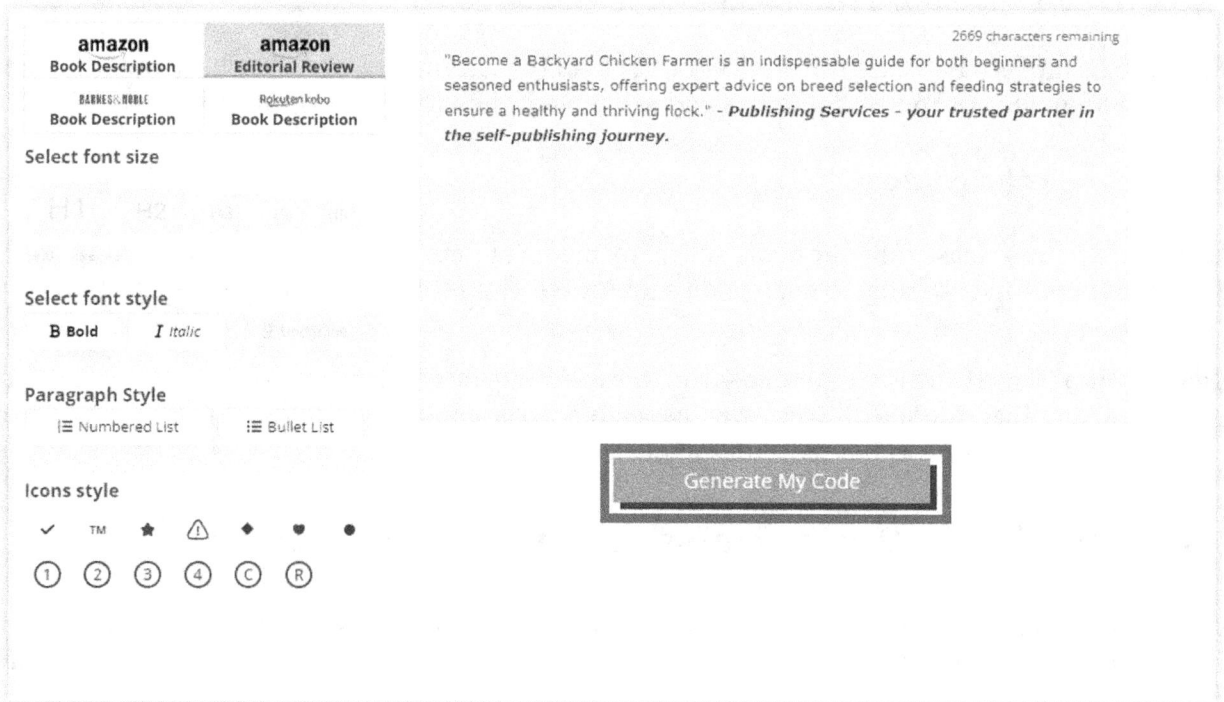

Option 2

Write the review directly on Amazon, then apply your bolding and italics. Do not copy from Word or Google Docs. You can only do so from plain text editors like Notepad.

Option 3

If you know how to apply HTML coding to text, click **Source** (in the upper right) and write your review in HTML, or copy and paste the HTML from the Kindlepreneur tool directly into Amazon once **Source** is checked.

Key codes recognized by Amazon include:

- Italics = <i>text goes here</i>
- Bold = text goes here
- Line break =
- Unordered (bulleted) list = <ul><li>List item 1</li><li>list item 2</li><li>And so on</li></ul>
- Ordered (numbered) list = <ol><li>List item 1</li><li>list item 2</li><li>And so on</li></ol>

Uploading Your Editorial Reviews on Amazon Author Central

To create this section, follow these steps:

01 ▸▸ Log into your author central page.

02 ▸▸ Click on the **Books** tab at the top of your page.

03 ▸▸ Choose the book you want to add the editorial review to. If you have more than one edition, you will have to add the reviews to each one. Then click **Edit Book Details (US-only)**.

 In the editorial reviews tab, click the **Add Review** button.

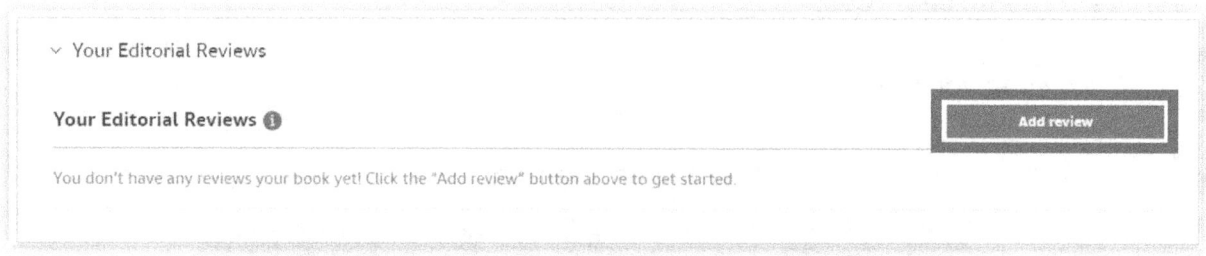

 Add your editorial reviews in HTML following Amazon's guidelines in the text box provided, and click **Preview**.

- Keep reviews to around one or two sentences instead of including full, lengthy reviews.
- Do not include URLs, contact numbers, time-sensitive comments, promotional material, or obscene or profane content.
- Keep the total character limit to 20,000 characters, with each review having no more than 4,000 characters. Amazon recommends using no more than 3,000 characters per individual review (Tortora, n.d.-b).

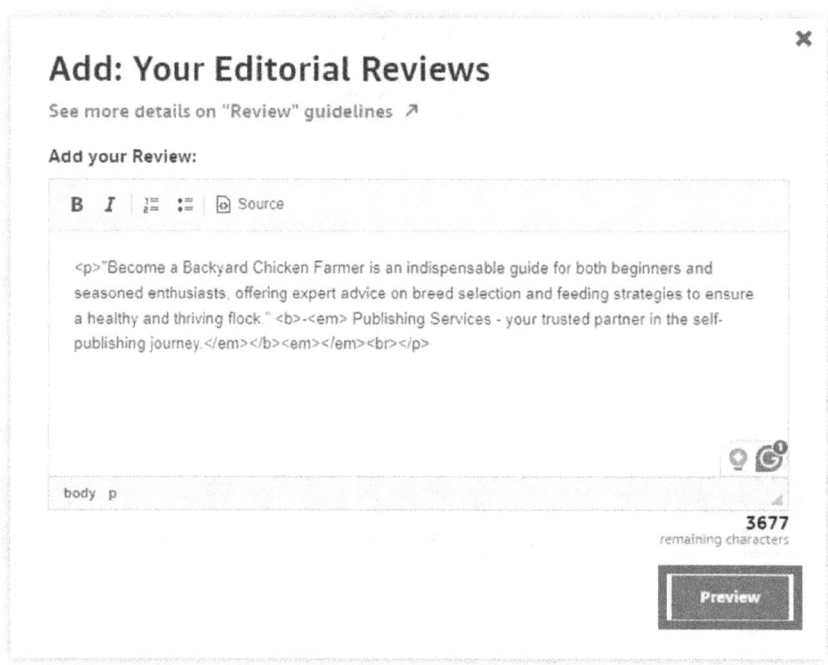

 Your text will still show up in HTML format. Don't worry about this; it will be displayed without the code on the Amazon product page. If you are happy with the text, click **Submit**.

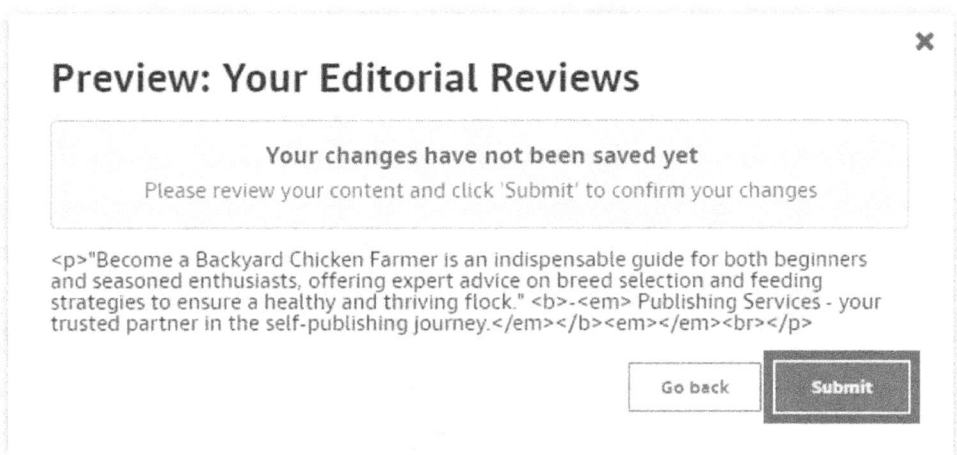

Now that you know how to secure Amazon Editorial Reviews to add credibility to your book, it's time to focus on obtaining verified reviews.

These reviews carry extra weight with potential readers and can significantly boost your book's visibility. In the next chapter, we'll explore how to get those all-important verified reviews to strengthen your book's presence in the marketplace.

Chapter 30

Obtaining Verified Book Reviews

Now that we've covered how to obtain unverified and editorial reviews, it's time to dive into verified reviews—the gold standard for building trust with potential readers. In this chapter, we'll explore what makes verified reviews so impactful, where to find them, and strategies for obtaining them to boost your book's credibility and sales.

Once your book is published, keep working hard to obtain as many reviews as you can.

Remember, more reviews = more sales = more money. Ensure your book has at least 100 reviews before moving on to your next book.

Who Can Review Your Book?

We mentioned earlier that authentic readers (rather than friends and family) should review your book. Having friends and family review your book is against Amazon's terms, and we previously explained that it is very easy for Amazon to work out who your close contacts are.

A genuine review comes from someone with no personal connection to you who is not paid for their opinion. You have three options to obtain these: your ACR team (covered in previous chapters), review services, and organic reviews (those that come naturally from people who buy your book and leave their opinions on Amazon).

Review Services

You can use review services like Bookblaze (formerly known as Bookbite) (www.publishingservicesbook.com/bookblaze) and Book Bounty (www.publishingservicesbook.com/book-bounty) to obtain verified reviews and increase your visibility.

Your sales will improve significantly if you can obtain between 5 and 20 reviews per month. Therefore, the amount charged by these services is definitely a worthwhile investment.

Bookblaze connects authors with real readers who agree to review books for coins, and in turn, they can use those coins to get reviews for their books. You upload your book to their platform, and readers interested in your genre can review it. It's like a matchmaking service between authors and reviewers, making it easier to get honest feedback.

You can receive reviews on your ebook, print, and audiobook (if your audiobook is published through ACX).

Book Bounty is a review platform where you earn "bounties" by reading and reviewing other authors' books. Then, you use those bounties to request reviews for your own book. It's a give-and-take system that is great for generating ebook and print book reviews.

Even though these are paid services, all they do is connect you with people willing to leave a genuine review based on what they think of your book—this doesn't go against KDP's rules, and the method is 100% legitimate.

Below, we'll go over both platforms in more detail and explain how to use them to their maximum potential.

Pro Tip: Make sure to only use one of these platforms. Using both Bookblaze and Book Bounty to generate reviews simultaneously violates Amazon's review policies. Amazon prohibits any activity that may appear as a coordinated effort to generate reviews. For example, if you review one author's book on Book Bounty and the same author reviews your book on Bookblaze, Amazon would consider this a review swap—which is not allowed and might lead to reviews being removed and your account terminated.

Bookblaze (www.publishingservicesbook.com/bookblaze)

Bookblaze allows users to obtain reviews for low-content books and audiobooks as well as for high-content books, which is great news considering that audiobook sales rely heavily on social proof.

The platform works on currency. By reviewing other authors' books, you earn currency you can then use to have your book reviewed. Once you submit your book and its staff approves it, Bookblaze offers you the following:

- An unlimited number of reviews
- The chance to choose between verified and free book reviews
- Full control over who gets to review your book since the company operates on a "request to review" functionality (Bookblaze asks interested readers numerous questions to ensure they have a genuine interest in your book and that they won't spam or troll you.)

- A standard turnaround time of around four days or a fast turnaround option of two days
- The chance to match your free book promotion from KDP with its services
- A convenient dashboard where you can find present and past reviews for your books and audiobooks
- The chance to include your book in Bookblaze's library, where readers can request the chance to read or listen to the book for free
- The choice of which Amazon marketplace you wish the reviews to appear on
- A 14-day free trial

Bookblaze has four monthly and four yearly payment options starting from $4.99 monthly. The top-tier plan (Unlimited Books and Audiobooks) costs $29.99. It allows you to upload an unlimited number of books and audiobooks, obtain an unlimited number of reviews, and receive a 2,000-coin bonus. The yearly fee starts at $47.99, and the most expensive plan costs $300 yearly (Unlimited Books & Audiobooks). All plans can be canceled at any time.

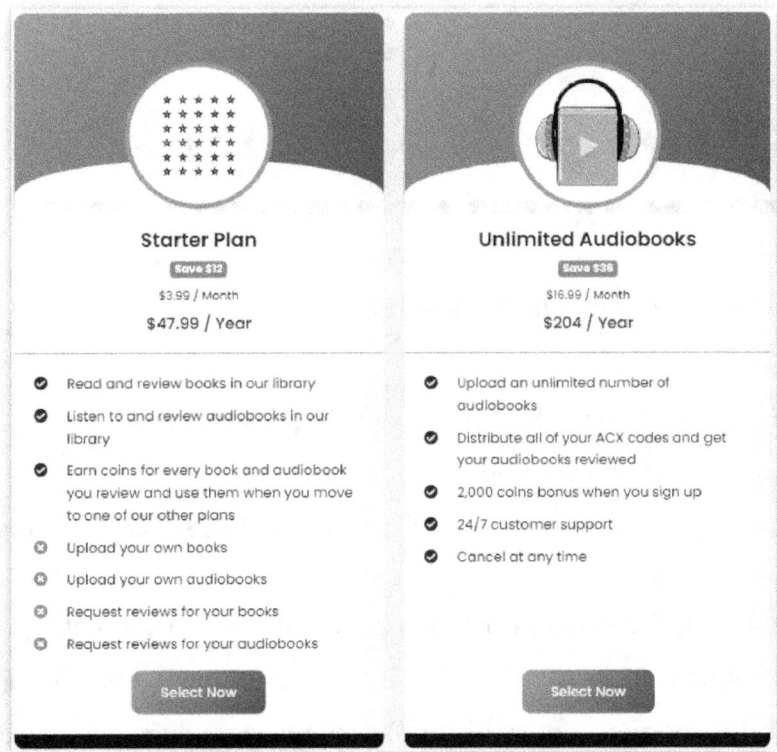

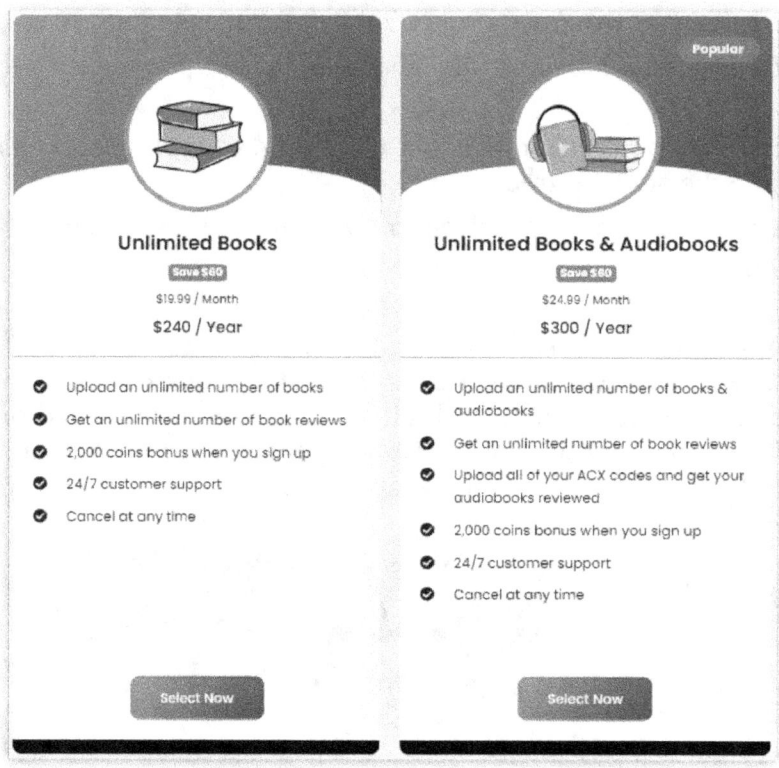

How to Obtain Verified Reviews on Bookblaze

To obtain verified reviews on Bookblaze:

1. Create an account, choosing the best pricing plan you can afford.
2. Go to the dashboard and add your books and audiobooks.
3. To earn the currency, go to "Book Library" and select **Verified Purchase** in "Choose Your Reader."
4. Choose the genre from fiction, non-fiction, or low content/no content.
5. Once you have enough coins, go to "Books" in your main menu and click **Find Reviewer**.
6. Choose **Verified Purchase**, enter the number of reviews you would like to receive, and fill in the author note tab if you have anything you'd like to say to your readers.
7. Click **Find Reviewer,** and you can select the person you wish to review your book.

Book Bounty (www.publishingservicesbook.com/book-bounty)

Book Bounty is a community-based service sustained by the efforts and support of fellow authors. Authors have the following review options:

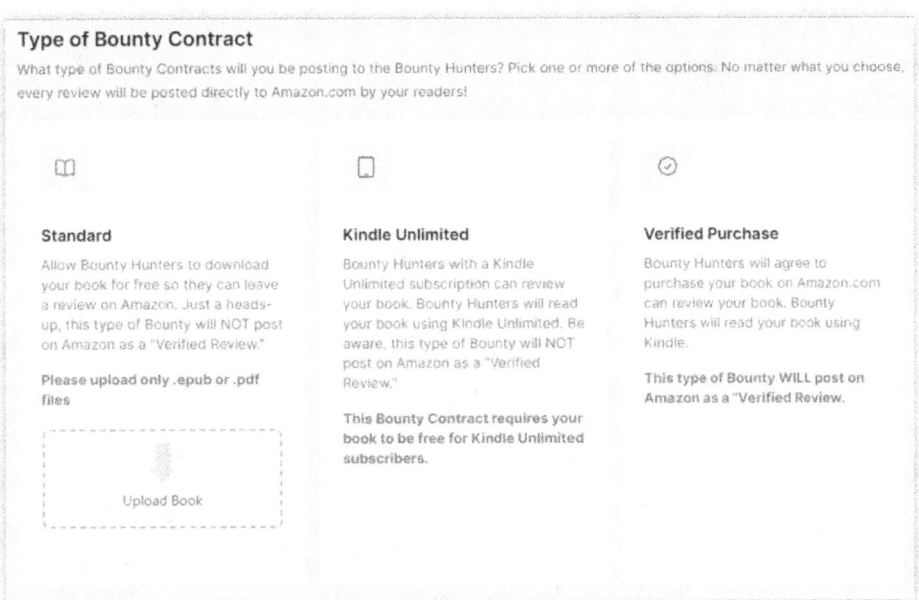

You can obtain reviews by earning Book Bounty's internal currency, "Bounty Points." To earn Bounties, you simply need to review other members' books. You can build up your Bounty quotient and exchange them for reviews of your books when ready.

When you sign up for Book Bounty, you will receive 1,500 or 2,500 Bounty Points (depending on whether you have chosen a monthly or yearly plan) once you review your first book, which is enough to obtain at least one review. These reviews appear on your Amazon book listing since reviewers post their opinions directly.

Book Bounty has the following offer:

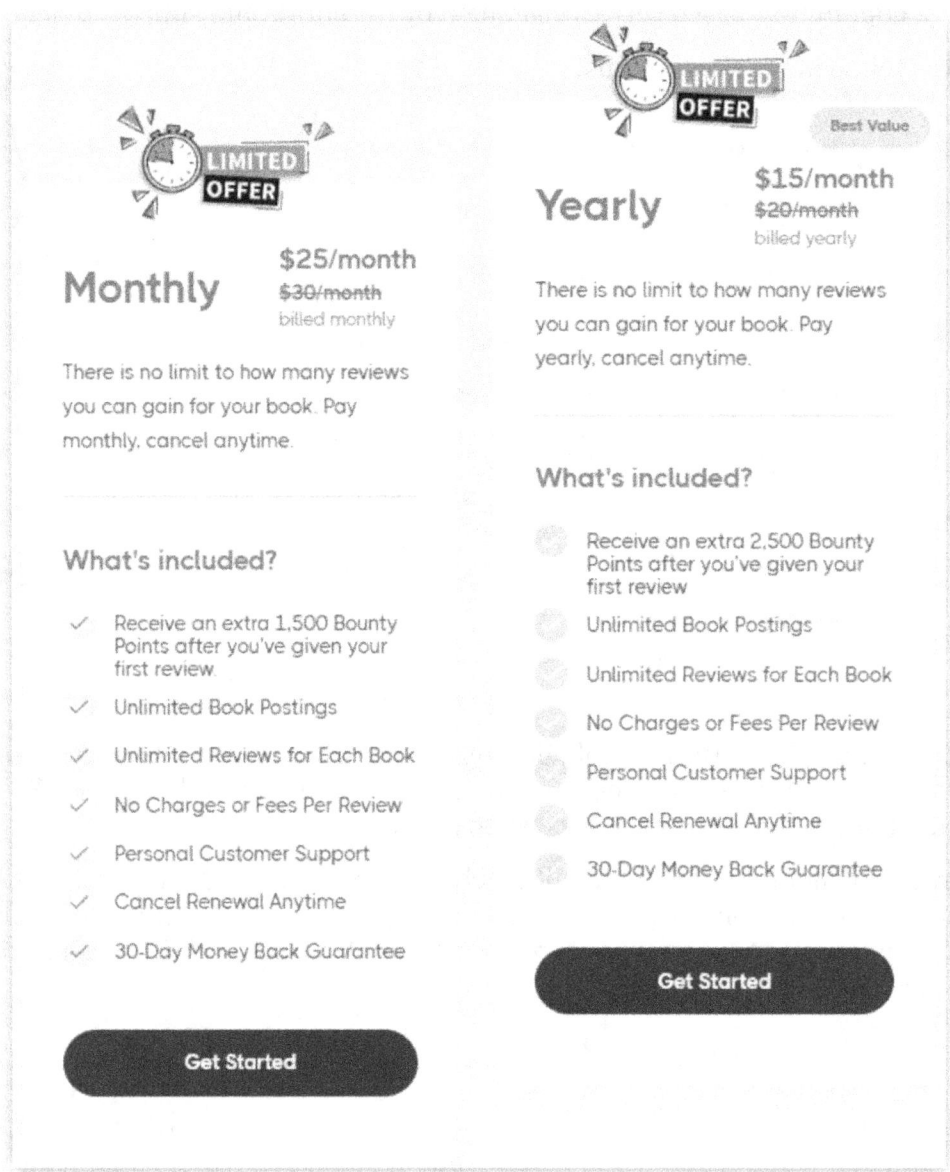

How to Start on Book Bounty

1. Create an account, choosing the best pricing plan you can afford.
2. Go to the dashboard and click **+ New Book** to add as many books as you want.
3. Fill in all required information.
4. Click **Submit for Approval**.

5. Click **Bounty Library** and select a book you'd like to review to earn Bounty Points. You can filter it by genre, free downloads, highest bounties, and other criteria.

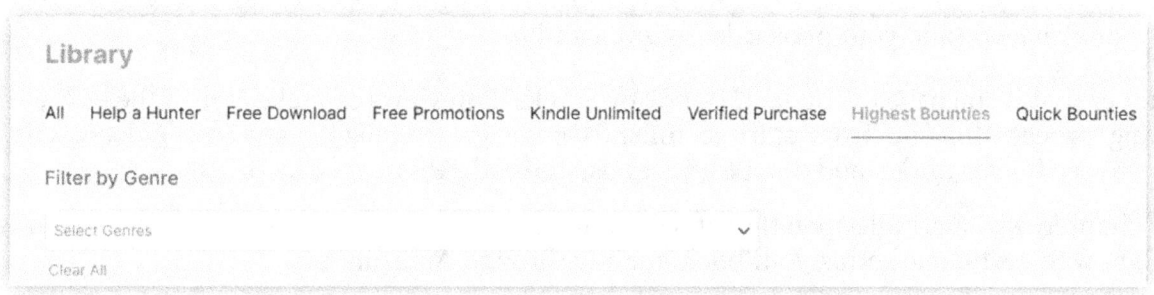

6. Now, turn your collected Bounty Points into book reviews.

Tips for Using Book Review Services Wisely

When using book review services like Book Bounty and Bookblaze, it is important to follow a strategy. We have compiled a few helpful tips below:

1. We must repeat this because it's so important: **Use only one of these platforms** to avoid issues and potential KDP account termination. We recommend Bookblaze because it offers audiobook reviewing.

2. Do not review too many books to earn bounties or coins. Aim to read one book every other day at most. Purchase a new book to review the day after you leave your review on the last book you read so your activity looks genuine. Otherwise, Amazon may deem your activity suspicious and remove your right to review books. Note that this does not mean your account will be suspended. You simply will not be permitted to leave reviews of others' books, and that will bring your Book Bounty or Bookblaze journey to an immediate end. Note that Book Bounty and Bookblaze may tempt you to download more books. Don't do so to ensure your activity is not flagged as suspicious by Amazon.

3. Attempt to actually read the books you review. When reading them on an e-reader, avoid clicking madly through the pages. Click at a normal pace and review the book properly. Skim reading is okay, but aim to spend genuine time on the sections you are most interested in.

4. Buy the books you will be reviewing if you can. You can buy great books for between $0.99 and $4.99, marking you as a genuine reviewer. After all, it is unlikely a customer would buy a book they weren't interested in. By contrast, if Amazon sees that you have reviewed hundreds of books without buying a single one, your activity may once again seem suspicious.

5. Only request verified reviews, even if both Book Bounty and Bookblaze allow you to choose a "free option." Verified reviews appear on all marketplaces, while free reviews only show on the marketplaces you write them on. That means that verified reviews can expand the reach of your reviews (and your book sales) significantly.

Remember that if you have the budget, Done For You KDP Reviews can take care of the entire review-obtaining process for you from start to finish. Go to www.publishingservicesbook.com/dfy-kdp-reviews to see how it works, and don't forget to use the code **PS** to get $50 off.

In this chapter, we have built upon the information from previous chapters on how to obtain reviews. We will now focus on marketing your book, mainly through Amazon Ads.

Chapter 31

Create Winning Amazon Ad Campaigns

Of the many advertising options open to you as a self-publisher, one you should prioritize is Amazon Ads. Amazon's advertising revenue has experienced explosive growth over the past few years, surpassing $30 billion in 2023 and showing no signs of slowing down. Industry analysts predict that Amazon Ads' revenue can potentially reach $40 billion by 2025. Currently, Amazon's average conversion rate for sponsored product ads stands at 9.47%, considerably outperforming other e-commerce platforms. Its high conversion rate can be attributed to its ability to target customers with high purchase intent, as users often visit the site ready to buy. Its ROI is also impressive, with advertisers enjoying a $4.20 return per dollar spent. Some niches have an ROI as high as 10:1 (Metz 2024).

Amazon Ads: The Basics

Amazon Ads is a pay-per-click (PPC) advertising service that Amazon offers all of its sellers, including publishers, to help them improve their sales. PPC ads allow you to only pay for your ads when someone clicks on them.

Amazon ads boost your organic ranking and sales by helping more people find your books. They also enable you to see the results of your ads and obtain key information about your audience's behavior—including how long they take to buy your book, their interests and search history, and more. Ads can, therefore, help enlighten you on new reader groups you may not have previously considered.

When Should You Start Running Ads?

The ideal time to start running ads is when your book has obtained 20+ reviews so potential buyers can see the "social proof" others have read and enjoyed your work. Before launching your ad campaign, ensure your A+ Content is uploaded so interested readers can gain more information about you and your book.

Important Terms to Know

Before we delve into a deeper analysis of Amazon Ads, it pays to define a few additional key terms.

- Your **advertising cost of sales (ACoS)** is the percentage of your sales that you spend on advertising. To calculate your ACoS (and see how effective your ad spending strategy is), follow this formula:

    ACoS = Your ad spend/Your ad sales

    - **ACoS Percentage Guide:** The following guide will let you know if your campaign is successful.
        - 10% is excellent
        - 20% is very good
        - 30% is good
        - 40% is a pass
        - 40-50% indicates your campaign is just breaking even or is unprofitable
    - Aim to keep your ACoS between 20 and 35% (Ken Self-Publishing Secrets 2023c).
- An **ad group** is a collection of ads within a campaign that share the same targeting and bids.
- A **bid** is the maximum amount you wish to pay for a click on your ad.
- Your **breakeven ACoS** is a calculation you use to gauge whether your ad spending is profitable. To calculate your breakeven ACoS, use the following formula: *Breakeven ACoS = The royalty of your book/The price of your book x 100*. For instance,
    - The selling price of your book is $14.99.
    - The royalty you earn is $5.83.
    - Your breakeven ACoS is 38.89%.
        - If your campaign ACoS is > your breakeven ACoS, your ad campaign is not profitable.
        - If your campaign ACoS is < your breakeven ACoS, your ad campaign is profitable.

- A **campaign** refers to a set of ads that focus on a single message and are the product of the same strategy.
- Your **click-through rate (CTR)** is the number of clicks your ad receives divided by the number of times your ad is shown. For example, if your ad has 100 impressions and 10 clicks, your CTR is 10%. The average click-through rate (CTR) of Amazon ads is 0.35% (The Badger 2024). Ensure that your CTR is no higher than around this percentage. If it is much lower, it could mean your ad isn't compelling enough to convince readers to click on your content. In this case, you would need to improve your keyword targeting or your listing as a whole.

  The formula for calculating a CTR is as follows: *CTR = Total clicks/Total impressions*.
  - Total clicks = the total number of clicks your ad gets and
  - Total impressions = the total number of times your ad is viewed
- **Conversion rate (CVR)** is the percentage of clicks that result in a sale. To calculate the CVR, use the following formula: *CVR = (Conversions/Clicks) x 100*.
- **Cost per click (CPC)** refers to the amount you pay Amazon every time someone clicks on your ad. To calculate your CPC, use the following formula: *CPC = Total cost of your campaign/ The number of clicks*.
- **Keywords** are the words your target audience would use to find your book.
- **Negative keywords** are the keywords for which you do not want your ads to appear because they are irrelevant and can result in a waste of your ad money.
- **Product attribute targeting (PAT)** is when you target ads based on specific attributes (including the price, brand, and range).
- **Return on advertising spend (ROAS)** is the revenue you earn for every dollar you spend on advertising. To calculate your ROAS, follow this formula: *ROAS = Revenue/Your ad spend*.
- The **search term report** is a report demonstrating the actual search terms customers used before they clicked on your ads.
- **Sponsored brands** are customizable ads featuring your brand logo, a custom headline, and multiple products.
- **Sponsored displays** are ads that target audiences both on and off Amazon based on purchasing behaviors.
- **Sponsored products** are ads that promote individual product listings.
- **Top of search impression share (ToIS)** is the percentage of your ads appearing at the top (a coveted spot) of the results page. (Your ad can appear in many places—the top, middle, or bottom of the page.) The top of the page is the best spot as it ensures greater visibility.

Three of the most important terms to remember are *ACoS*, *Breakeven ACoS*, and *Top of Search Impression Share*.

Which Marketplaces Should You Target?

The more target marketplaces you run your ads on, the better. If you have an unlimited budget, run ads in the US, Canada, the UK, and Australia. If you have a limited budget, stick to the US until you can afford to expand your target market.

Why Quality Matters in Amazon Ads

Before advertising your book, ensure it is a top-quality product that customers want to read. This is because when it comes to Amazon ads, the amount you spend won't guarantee that your ad obtains an optimal placement. Think of Amazon ads as mini-auctions in which various people bid for the best placement (for instance, at the top of a page). It's not enough to bid high to win. Your book should also already be garnering interest and have many clicks for the Amazon algorithm to take notice. Speaking of this algorithm, it is a mysterious and ever-changing thing, so there is no clear-cut way to guarantee optimal placement. Most experts agree, however, that the following qualities can help:

- Good keywords with a high demand and low competition
- An eye-catching cover
- A winning title that targets your audience and lets them know you can solve their problems
- Having over 20 reviews (to show that your book is already generating interest)
- A well-designed product page with stunning A+ Content, a well-written description, and a well-crafted author bio (Ken Self-Publishing Secrets 2023c)

The 4 Phases of Your Amazon Ads Strategy

Amazon ads help readers find your book in two main ways. The first is by searching for the type of book they're looking for in Amazon's search bar—typing in keywords that match your book. The second is by visiting other books (products), which may cover the same niche or category as your book. When they click on these books, they may see one of your ads. As such, your Amazon strategy needs to target these two components: keywords and products.

There are 4 phases of a winning Amazon ads strategy:

- **Phase 1** involves running three test campaigns to find two important pieces of information. The first is running an automatic campaign. In automatic campaigns, Amazon matches your ad with keywords and products that are similar to your products. You can use your test results to find the keywords that will bring the greatest number of readers to your book. The second test is carried out by manually searching for the list of keywords that will bring the greatest number of readers to your book. The third test is to find the list of competitors' books (products) whose pages you can use to advertise your own book.

- **Phase 2** uses the data obtained in Phase 1 to create a list of winning keywords and products.
- **Phase 3** involves creating a winning campaign using these keywords and products.
- **Phase 4** focuses on optimizing your ads.

Let's go over all of them in more detail!

Phase 1: Creating Your Automatic, Manual Keyword, and Manual Product Test Campaigns

 **Creating an Automatic Campaign**

- Go to your KDP dashboard and click **Marketing**.

- Click **Amazon Ads** and choose a marketplace. (Choose the US to start with.)

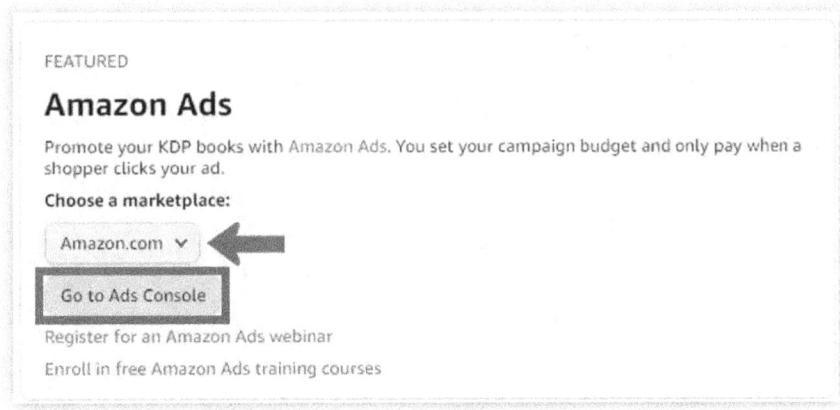

- Click **Create Campaign**.

351

- You will be prompted to choose your campaign type from two options: sponsored products and sponsored brands ads. Click **Continue** in the sponsored products box.

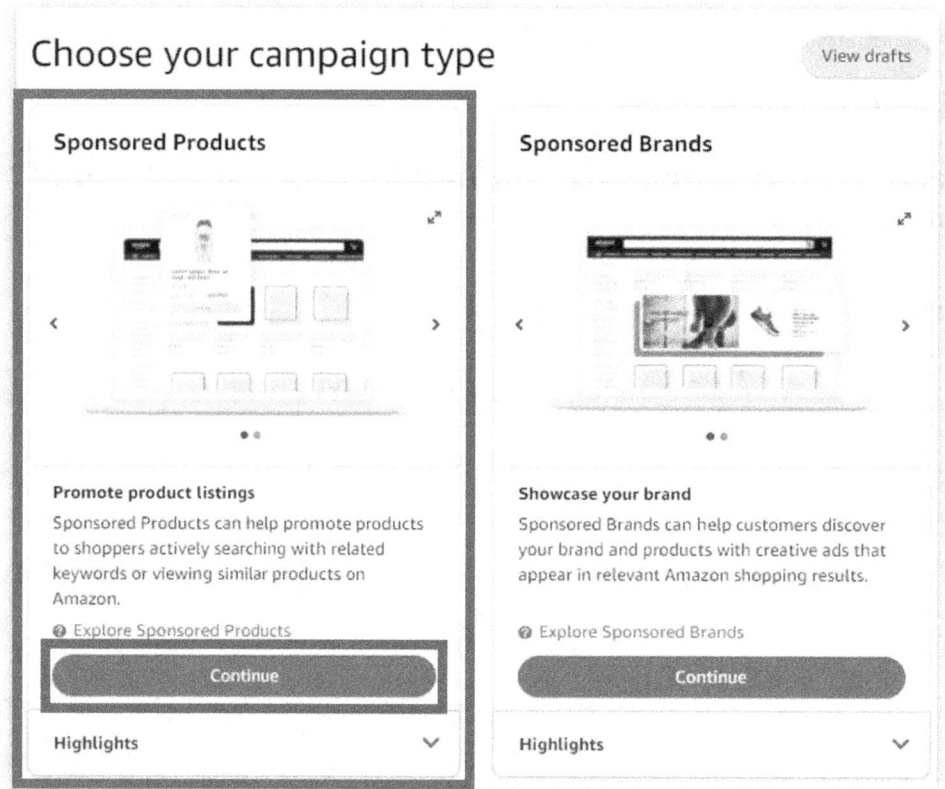

- Click **Standard Ad**.

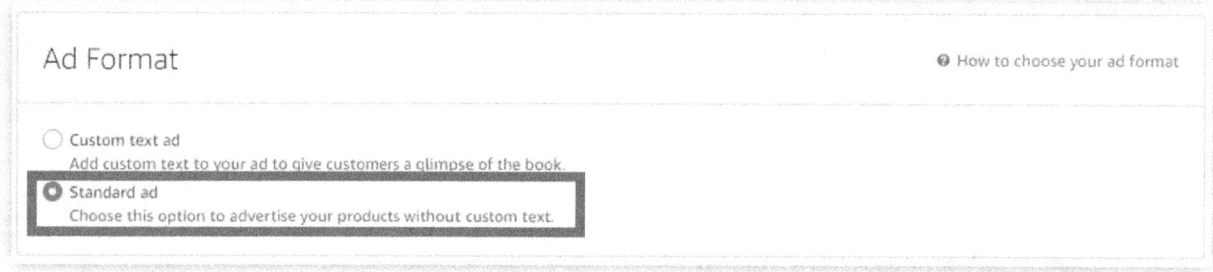

- Name your ad group "[Book Title] - Automatic Campaign."

- Go to products and select the book for which you wish to run the ads. Choose your paperback rather than your ebook version since paperbacks bring in more money than ebooks do.

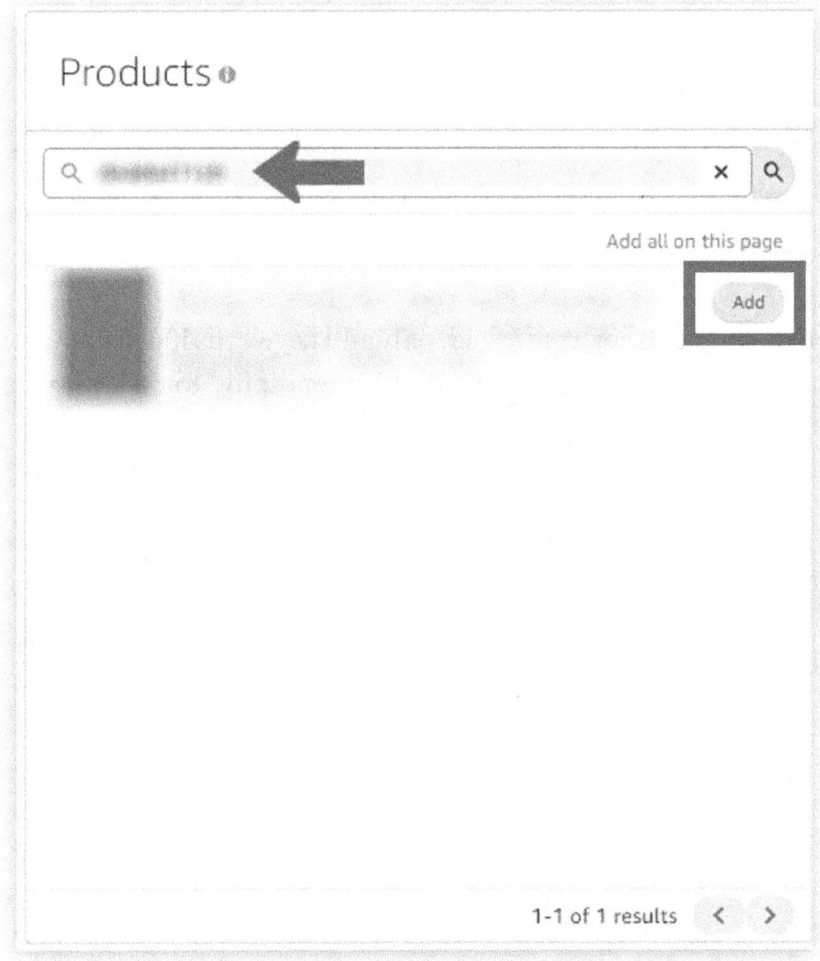

- Go to targeting and click **Automatic Targeting**.

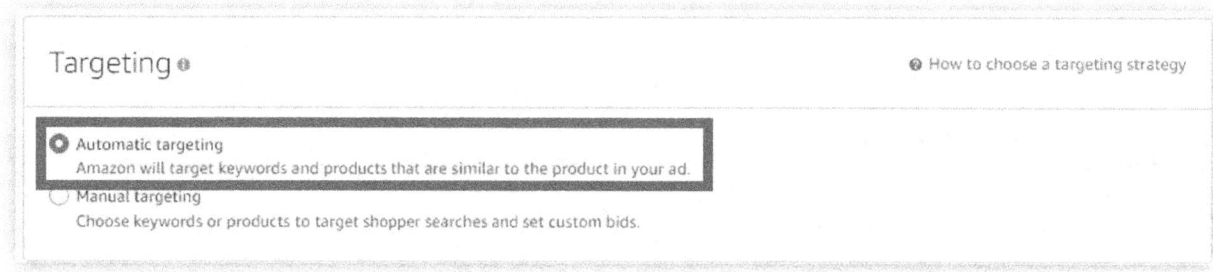

- Go to automatic targeting and leave the **Default Bid**.

- In the negative keywords field, only add keywords if you know for sure that Amazon might be targeting keywords that have nothing to do with your book. Otherwise, leave it empty.

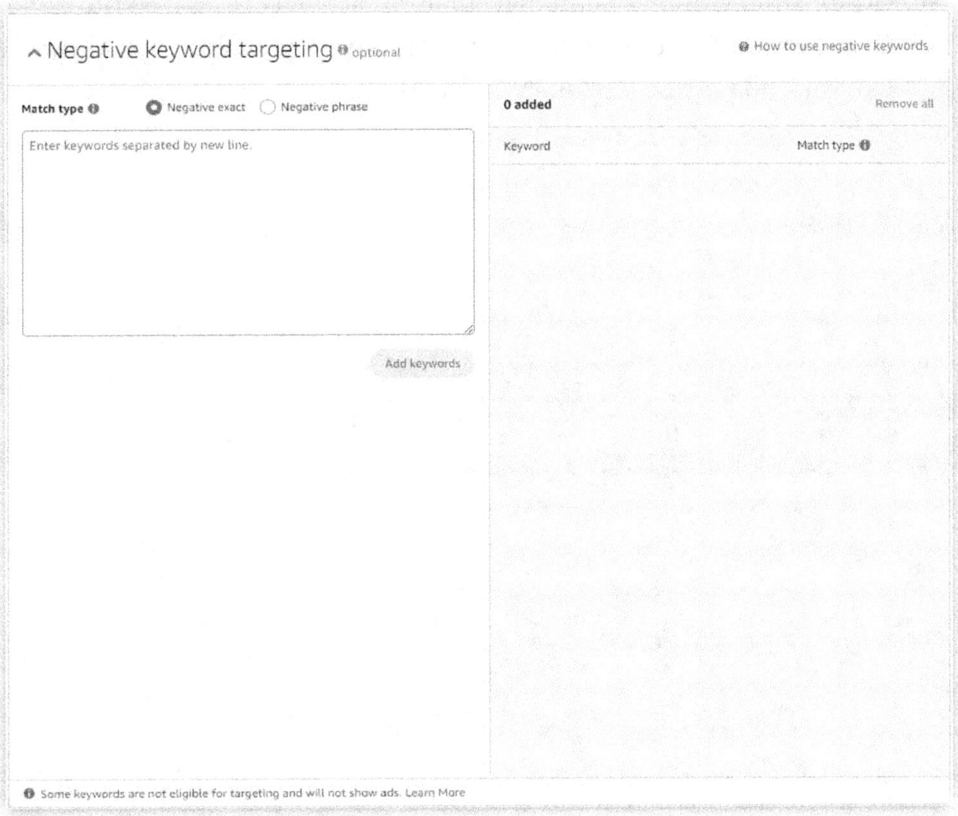

Negative keyword targeting *optional*

How to use negative keywords

Match type • ◉ Negative exact ○ Negative phrase

Enter keywords separated by new line.

Add keywords

0 added — Remove all

Keyword | Match type

• Some keywords are not eligible for targeting and will not show ads. Learn More

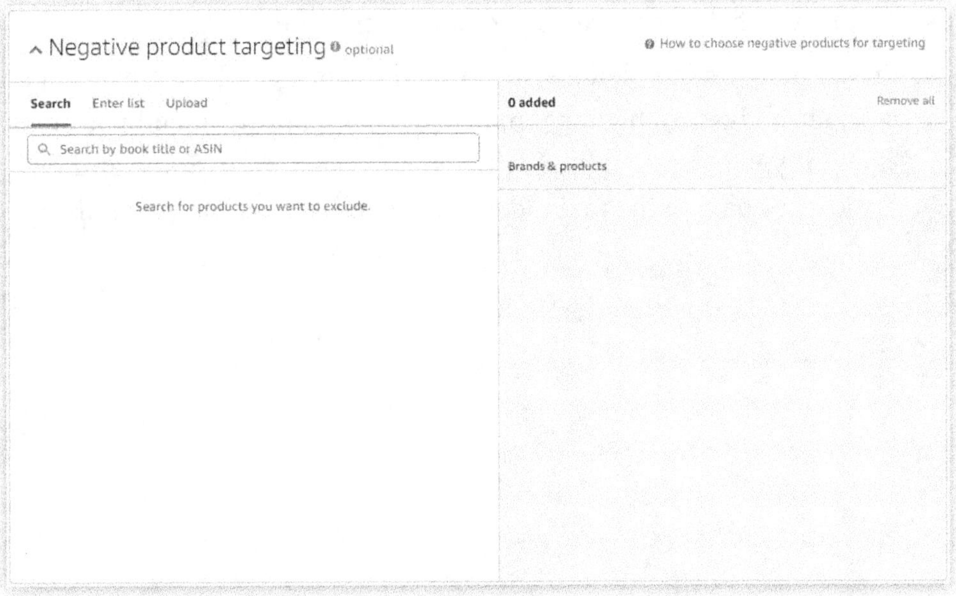

Negative product targeting *optional*

How to choose negative products for targeting

Search | Enter list | Upload

🔍 Search by book title or ASIN

Search for products you want to exclude.

0 added — Remove all

Brands & products

- Go to campaign and campaign bidding strategy. Click **Dynamic Bids—Down Only**, which will ensure that Amazon lowers your bid in real time when it looks like your ad may be less likely to convert to a sale.

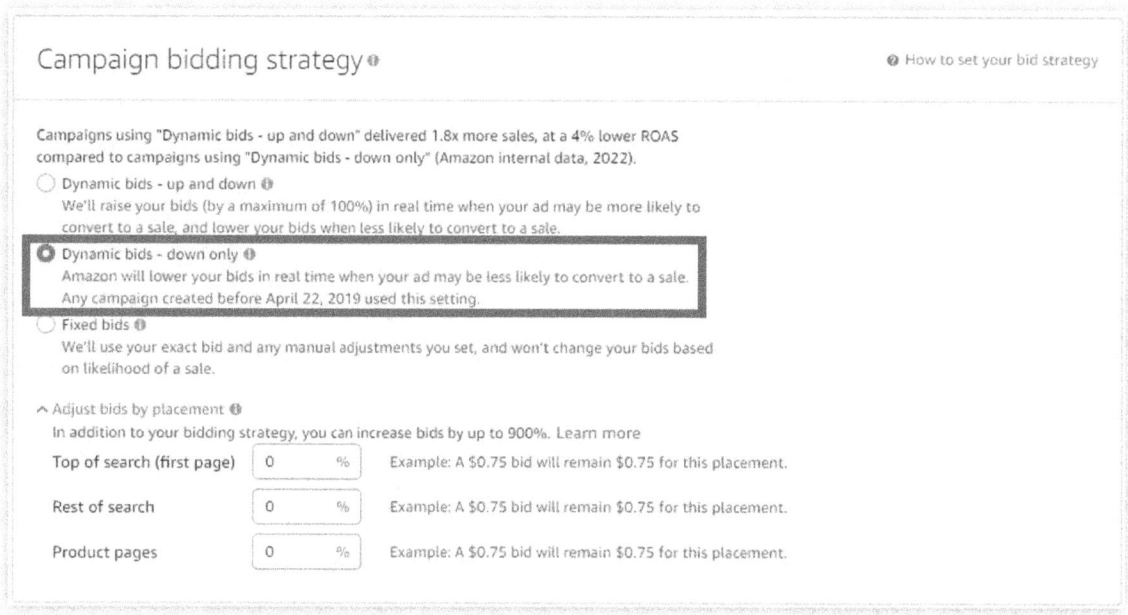

- Go to settings and fill in the campaign name field, "[Book Title] - Automatic Campaign."
- In the date fields, ensure no end date is indicated.
- In the daily budget field, write $10, which is a good starting amount. If you have a larger budget, go higher. Amazon does not always spend your daily budget. The amount you indicate is simply taken as a maximum. Some authors spend around $100+ per day, so the main idea is to spend as much as you reasonably can.

- Go to the bottom of the page and click **Launch Campaign**.

02 ›› Creating a Manual Keyword Campaign

- As you did in Step 1, go to choose your campaign type and click **Continue** in the sponsored products box.
- Click **Standard Ad**.
- Name your ad group "[Book Title] - Manual Keyword."

- Go to products and select the paperback for which you wish to run the ads.

- Under targeting, click **Manual Targeting**.

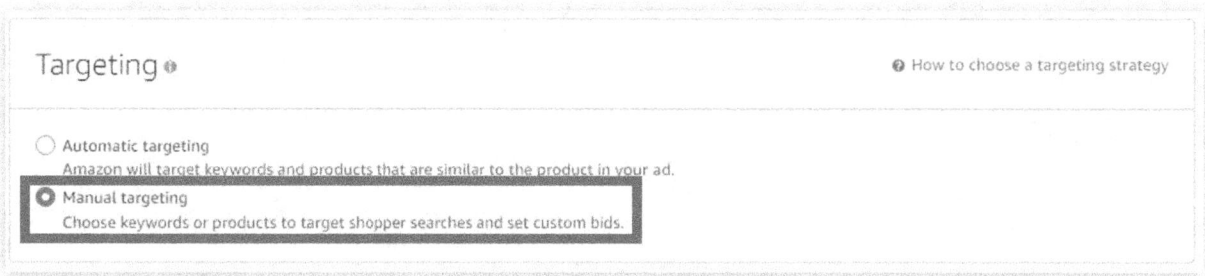

- Click **Keyword Targeting** since the aim of this campaign is to find winning keywords.

- In keyword targeting, under filter by, make sure that you click all three options, **Broad**, **Phrase**, and **Exact**, to enable you to reach as many readers who are doing pertinent searches as possible. Your goal is to find 50-100 winning keywords. From the list of those suggested by Amazon, select every relevant keyword.

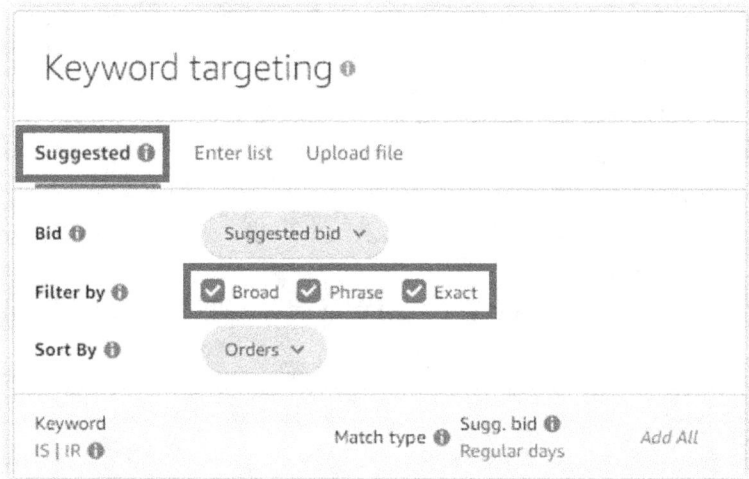

- Under the enter list option, select **Broad**, **Phrase**, and **Exact,** and enter all keywords that are relevant to your book. You can utilize Publisher Rocket, KDSpy, and BookBeam for this.

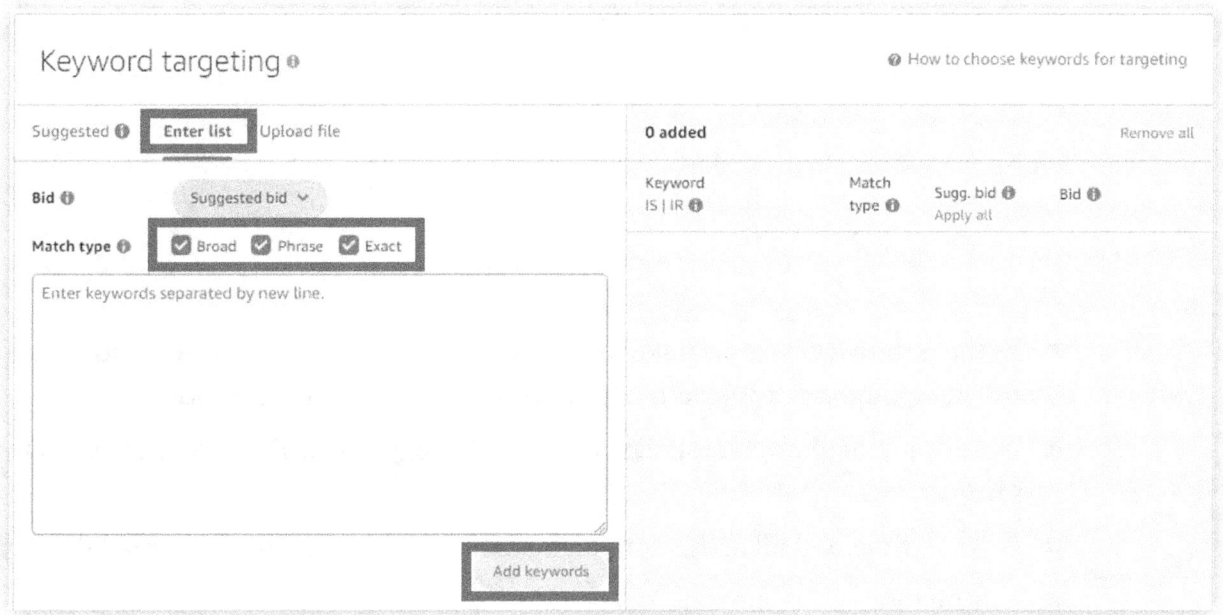

- A pop-up window will appear telling you how many keywords do not have a suggested bid. You can bid a bit lower for these keywords (say $0.40 instead of $0.80) because they do not have a suggested bid, which indicates they are less competitive.

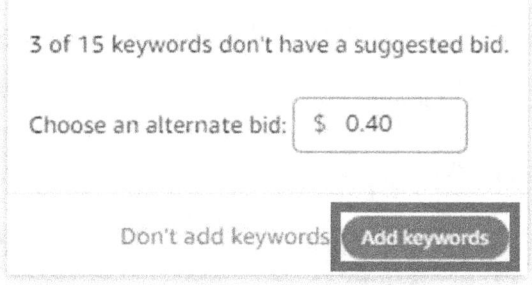

- You will also set your bid for the rest of the keywords. Amazon will suggest a range. Choose somewhere in the middle of the range. For instance, if Amazon suggests you bid between $0.30 and $0.52, bid somewhere in the middle, ensuring the amount is less than $1. If you bid too high, your profit will suffer. The highest you should go is around $0.80 when setting up the campaign.

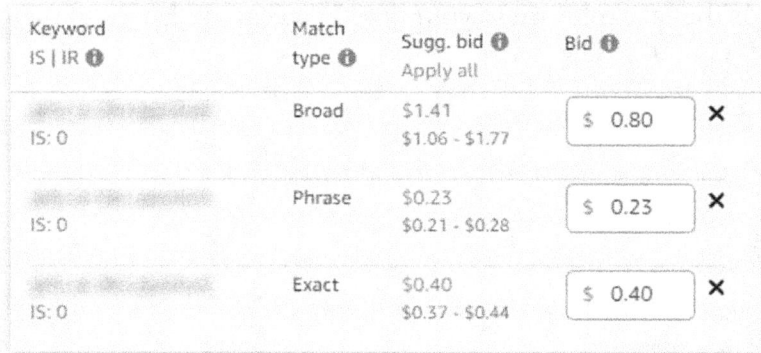

- In the negative keywords field, once again, only add keywords if you know Amazon might be targeting irrelevant keywords. Otherwise, leave it empty.
- Go to campaign and campaign bidding strategy. Click **Dynamic Bids—Down Only**.
- Go to settings and fill in the campaign name field, "[Book Title] - Manual Keyword."
- Ensure there is no end date.
- Fill the daily budget field with $10.
- Click **Launch Campaign**.

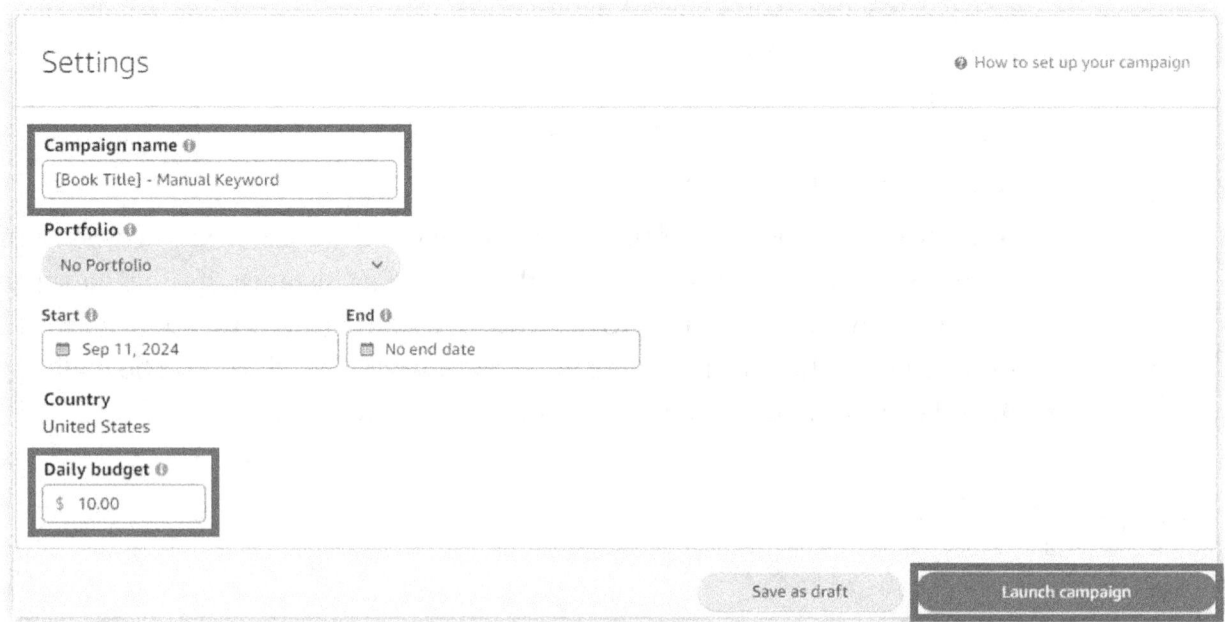

 **Creating a Manual Product Campaign**

- As you did in Steps 1 and 2, go to sponsored products and click **Standard Ad**.
- Name your ad group "[Book Title] - Manual Product."

- Go to products and select the book for which you wish to run the ads.
- Under targeting, click **Manual Targeting**.
- Instead of keyword targeting, select **Product Targeting**.

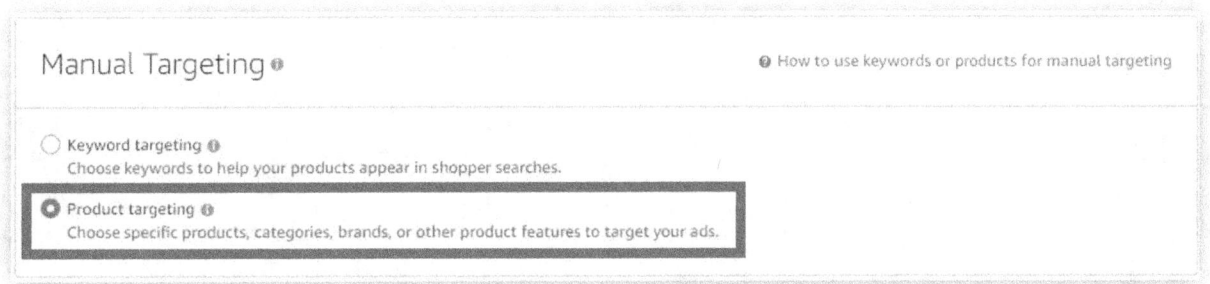

- You will see that Amazon suggests products and categories. Start by adding up to 4 relevant categories.

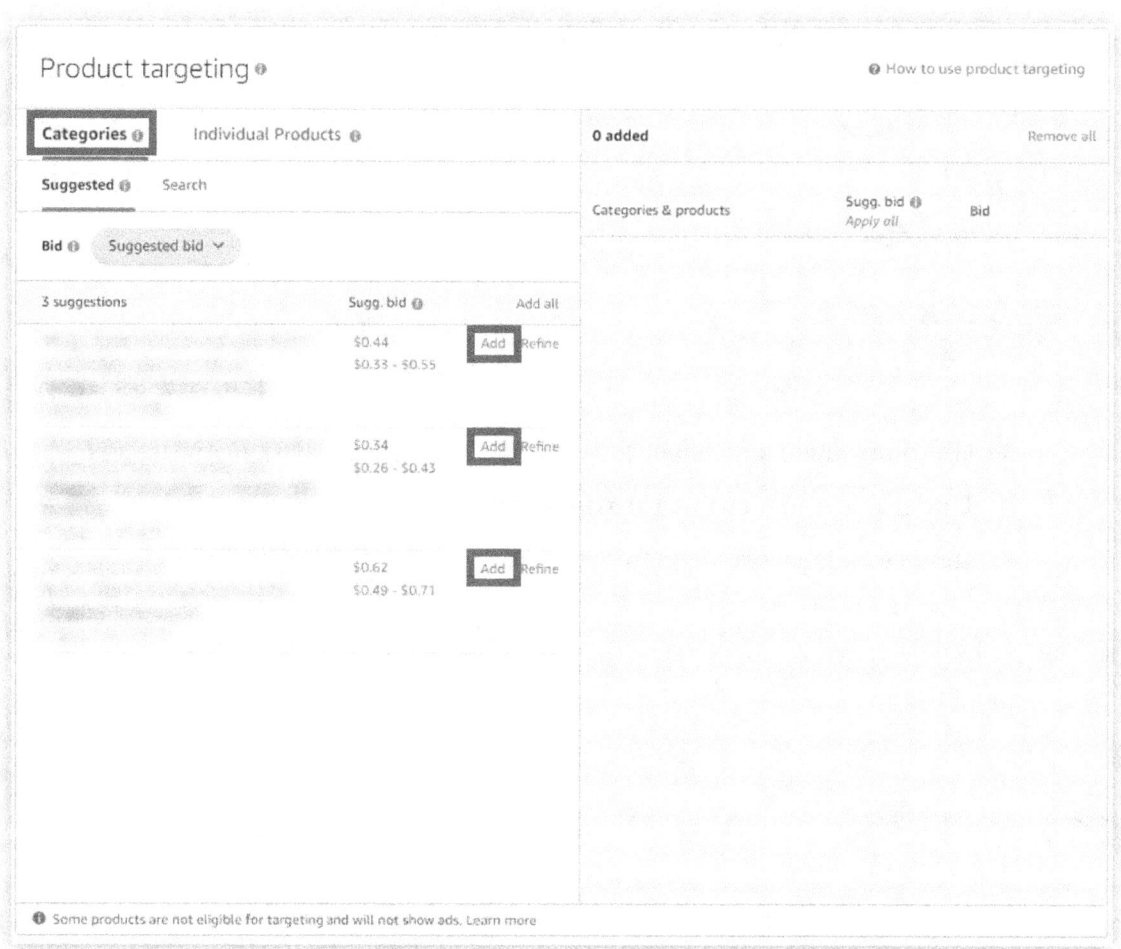

- Go to individual products and suggested, then select **Exact** and choose books that are in your niche.

    You have to look one by one because Amazon may suggest books with a large number of reviews; if your book is new, you don't want to compete with books with too many reviews. Instead, only choose relevant books that have less than 500 reviews.

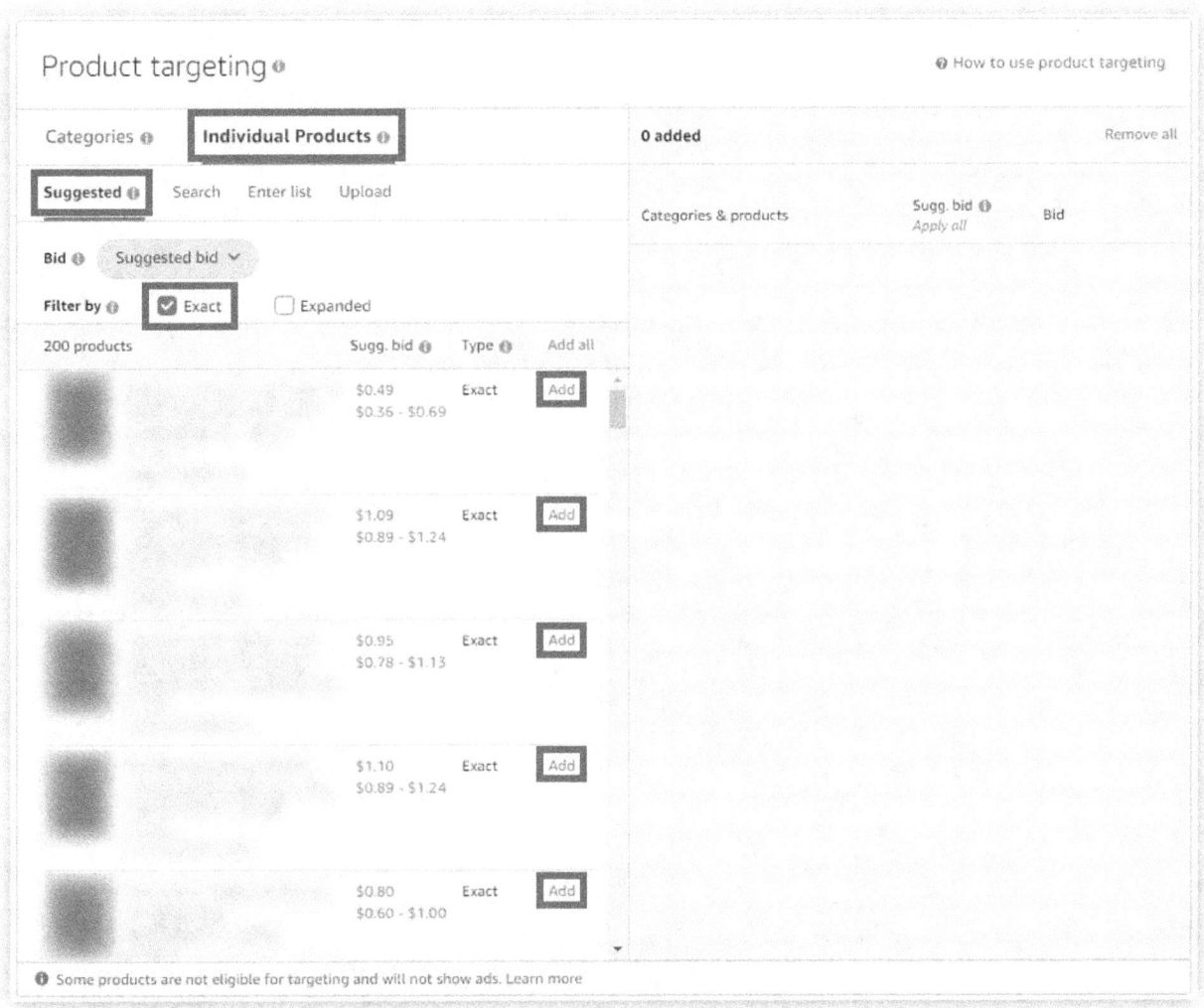

- Type in your competitor books' ASINs if they have fewer than 500 reviews and are not on the suggested list. Select between 25 and 50 books. Once your book has 200+ reviews, go back and add books with up to 1,000 reviews, as by this point, your book will be in a much better position to compete with books already selling well.

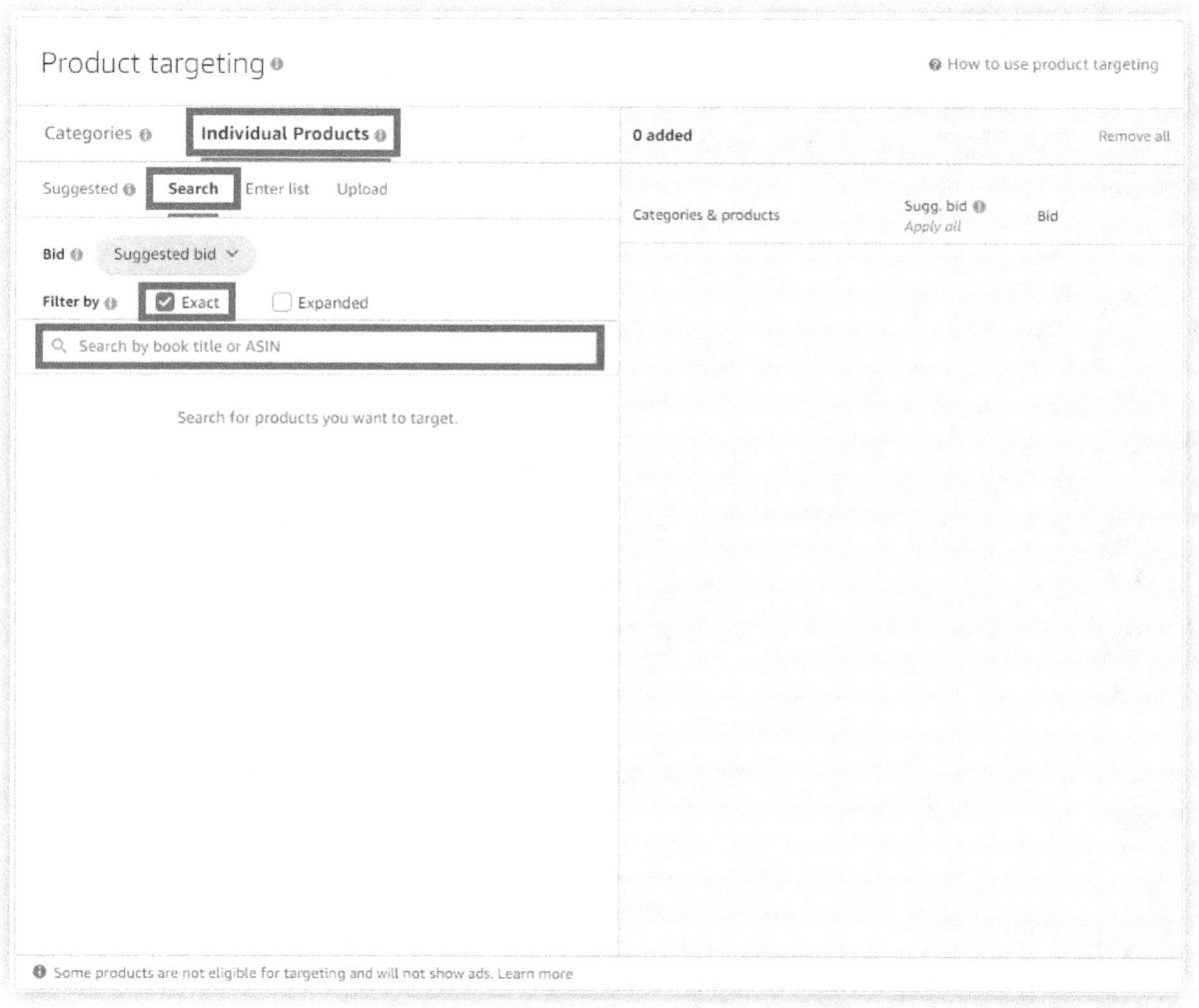

- Once again, when it comes to bidding, make bids in the middle range of the prices suggested by Amazon and keep your bids to under $1. When the range is above $1, set the bid to $0.80 when starting. Products without a suggested bid start at $0.40
- In the negative keywords field, only add keywords if you know Amazon might target keywords that have nothing to do with your book. Otherwise, leave it empty.
- Choose **Dynamic Bids—Down Only**.
- Name your campaign "[Book Title] - Product Targeting."
- Allocate a daily budget of around $10.
- Click **Launch Campaign**.

Phase 2: Determining Your List of Winning Keywords and Products

Now, it's time to use your results from Phase 1 to look for winning keywords. A winning keyword has garnered you at least two book sales, with an ACoS of 30% or under. Remember that the ACoS tells you how profitable the ad is. If you are making sales but your ACoS is high, lower your bid by about $0.10. The aim is to build up a list of profitable keywords and use your list of 50–100 winning keywords to optimize your ads. Simply run the three campaigns in Stage 1 (automatic, keyword, and manual campaigns) for 2 to 4 weeks without touching them so they have time to collect data that will help you make wise decisions.

To find your winning keywords, go into campaigns and then single country, where you will see each campaign on your dashboard.

365

Open the campaign you want to review. Click **Search Terms**.

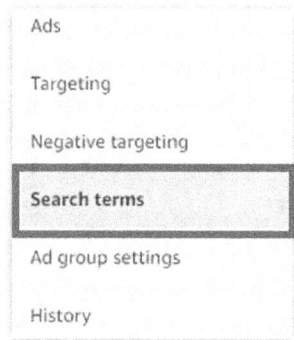

Then, set the date range to the last 30 days and click **Orders** twice, as doing so will place the keywords with the most orders at the top of your list (Ken Self-Publishing 2023c).

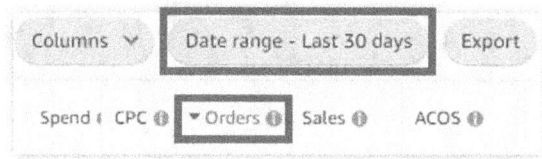

Now, go one by one and look for any customer search terms with over two sales and an ACoS of ≤30%. Keep a separate list of all these customer search terms. In your sheet, also jot down their CPC (cost per click).

These search terms are your winning keywords. Of course, in the case of your manual product campaign, you will be jotting down the ASIN of the books your ad appeared by instead of keywords.

Phase 3: Create a Winning Campaign

Now that you know which keywords work, you can use them to create a campaign with a very good chance of reaching your target market. The process is the same as that used in previous phases.

1. Choose the book you wish to advertise, go to **Manual Targeting**, and click **Keyword Targeting**.
2. Remove the check mark from Broad and Phrase, only leaving the check on Exact.
3. Add your keyword list to the available field/empty box (which will initially state, "Enter your list and separate each item with a new line."
4. To bid, use the CPC that your winning keywords had when you found them. In Campaign, select **Dynamic Bids—Down Only**.

5. Name the campaign "[Book Title] - Exact Keyword."
6. Allow the campaign to run, raising your daily budget slightly as it starts bringing in more sales.
7. For your product campaign, do the same, creating a separate campaign for your winning products. In other words, you should have two winning campaigns: one for keywords and the other for products.

Phase 4: Optimize Your Ads

In Phases 1 to 3, you completed all the hard work. Now, it's time to undertake a few tweaks to optimize your ads. Follow these strategies to improve your revenue and profit steadily:

1. Keep finding your winning keywords and add them to your existing Winning Keywords campaign.
2. Adjust the bids for your campaign in line with your ACoS. For instance, if your ACoS is too high, lower your bid by $0.10. When it is low (say 20%), consider raising your bid by $0.10.
3. Identify losing keywords and products (those with 15 clicks and no sales). Make them Negative Keywords or Products.
4. Keep working at optimizing your ads. Look at your CTR and optimize features that can make your target audience take notice—including your description, A+ Content, book cover, reviews, and more. If your ads are not converting into as many sales as you like, it may not be an issue with your Amazon ad strategy. Rather, the problem may be a description that doesn't address your audience's pain points, a boring book title, or a book cover that does not align with audience expectations for the genre. Additional issues include using keywords with too low a demand, using keywords that are too saturated, or failing to target pertinent keywords.

Outsourcing Your Ad Campaign

If you have a large enough budget to outsource your campaign, there are two companies that can run your ads for you.

BackedBy (www.publishingservicesbook.com/backed-by)

This company is staffed by a highly experienced team that can help you optimize your bids, reduce your ACoS, control your ad spend, and increase your campaign's profitability. We highly recommend them. Here's a sneak peek at what they offer:

- A dedicated account manager
- Daily bid adjustments

- Campaign creation & structuring
- Weekly KPI tracking
- Book launches at no extra cost
- Quick strategic responses
- 30 days money back guarantee

They are also affordable, so if you have the budget, consider investing in their service.

 **Exclusive Offer:** BackedBy is an affiliate partner of Publishing Services, and you can obtain **a 5% discount** on your first invoice by clicking this link: www.publishingservicesbook.com/backed-by.

Publishing Performance (www.publishingservicesbook.com/publishing-performance)

Unlike BackedBy, which runs human-created ad campaigns, this is an AI-based platform specifically designed to help authors sell more books on Amazon through strategies such as targeting high-performance keywords and running campaigns on autopilot. It's very easy to use.

You simply choose your marketplace (for instance, the US), add your book's URL, and then choose your budget (low, medium, or high). And that's all you have to do! You can add as many books as you like. Publishing Performance will run Amazon ads on all of them across any Amazon marketplace that offers the advertising options you select.

As we go to print, Publishing Performance is offering a $1 trial for 30 days. After that, you will be charged $39 monthly or $390 annually.

 **Exclusive Deal**: Go to www.publishingservicesbook.com/publishing-performance with the coupon code **PUBSERV15**, and you can obtain a recurring **15% discount** on this fee.

In addition to working on your ad campaign, continue working to improve the number of reviews your books obtain. Doing so will help you stand out from the competition and indicate that your work is a good time investment for your customers.

Your Amazon ad strategy will improve the more you work at it. Be patient and consistent, and take the time to do all the little things that can make a big difference to your results—including adjusting your bids, keeping your eye on your ACoS, and so forth. In the next chapter, we will cover a tool that can be very useful in gauging the profitability of your campaign: Publisher Champ.

Chapter 32

Publisher Champ—A Vital and Multifaceted Marketing Tool

Once you have started your ad campaigns, we highly recommend getting your hands on **Publisher Champ** (www.publishingservicesbook.com/publisher-champ). This marketing tool provides access to a wealth of information about your ad campaigns and your book's performance, enabling you to make smarter decisions. It links with Amazon Advertising, Kindle Direct Publishing, ACX, Meta, Kobo Writing Life, Draft2Digital, Barnes & Noble, and Facebook. Also, it's super cost-efficient at only $11.99 monthly or $136 yearly.

 **Exclusive Deal:** To obtain **10% off** the annual plan or 10% off the first 6 months of a monthly plan, use the coupon code **PUBLISHINGSERVICES**.

So, what exactly can Publisher Champ do for you?

Consider it the ultimate helper to streamline and supercharge your self-publishing journey. It automates data aggregation, centralizing, and spending across Amazon and Facebook so you can make smart decisions about where to put your money. Just a few of its many functions include:

- Analyzing your book performance across different formats and marketplaces
- Helping you manage your campaigns via its automated estimated profitable ACoS tool for your ads (With Publisher Champ, you can quickly test the profitability of your campaign and consolidate your ad spending across Amazon and Facebook for a unified view.)

- Monitoring gross versus net royalties and spending
- Automating performance analysis
- Providing comprehensive financial insights across all formats and marketplaces
- Informing you about what's working with your book series (Use your Sell-Through/Read-Through rates and revenue to make critical decisions about releasing your book series.)
- Notifying you every time you make a sale
- Auto-converting data to your preferred currency
- Auto-allocating royalties and spending to each book
- Providing you with a year-over-year analysis and monthly progress

Publisher Champ has customizable dashboards and widgets that enable you to track new releases and ad campaigns and personalize your KPIs. You can annotate key events on graphs and keep a detailed journal to identify patterns and improve sales.

How to Set Up Publisher Champ

Publisher Champ has simple instructions for synchronizing it with different platforms, whether you are using your smartphone (Apple or Android), Chrome, or Firefox. As an example, we will show you how to set up your account on Chrome, but you will find that the process is similar in other browsers and systems (Publisher Champ, n.d.).

1. Sign in to Amazon KDP at https://kdpreports.amazon.com/dashboard.
2. Install the Publisher Champ extension from the Chrome web store. (In the case of Firefox, you would install it from Firefox add-ons.)
3. Submit your cookies. Go to https://kdpreports.amazon.com/dashboard, open the Publisher Champ extension, and enter your Publisher Champ credentials. Click **Synchronize platforms with Publisher Champ**.
4. If successful, you should see the following message: "Congrats! The cookies were submitted successfully and account verified with KDP!"

You should be well on your way to marketing success with tools like Publisher Champ at hand. Next, we will look into how to maximize your publishing success and profits.

Chapter 33

Growing Your Publishing Business

In this chapter, we will cover three key ways to further develop a successful publishing business: writing your next book, publishing book collections, and translating your work.

Writing Your Next Book

If you want a successful publishing business, then you should definitely continue publishing after your first book. In fact, one of the best ways to market your work is to publish various books. That way, if your audience enjoys one of them, they are more likely to be interested in reading more of your work. Another reason is that when your book is new, it appears in Amazon's "Last 30 Days" and "Last 90 Days" new release lists. Someone may click on your new book and discover additional titles you've written.

Writing more than one book in your niche helps turn you into an authority and indicates that you are much more than a one-hit wonder. By the time you've finished writing one book, the good news is that all the other steps will be a lot easier—from finding the right keywords to honing your pre- and post-launch strategies.

There is a saying that self-publishing isn't really geared toward someone taking several years to write one book. If you look at online forums, many self-publishers claim that paid advertising begins to break even around your third book.

When writing your second book, best practices include:

- Remaining within the same niche as your first book
- Trying to solve another problem that your readers may have (Our example author, Cluck Norris, might write his second book on related topics such as chicken health, hatching and brooding chickens, small flock management, scaling to a larger chicken farm, specialized diets for egg-laying hens, building chicken coops or similar.)
- Creating a new bestselling title and subtitle
- Repeating the entire process of creating a great book (writing or hiring someone to write your outline, ghostwriting, editing, formatting, writing the description, review, cover design, and more)
- Utilizing your old ARC team (everyone who reviewed book #1) and finding new ARC readers

Following Up with Your ARC Team

In previous chapters, we discussed how to build your ARC team at the pre-launch stage. These same people can play a key role in boosting your rankings and getting others interested in your work when your second book is at the pre-launch stage. To ensure your ARC team is still relevant when you publish your second and subsequent books, make sure to:

- **Remain active on your Facebook page and the Facebook groups you are a member of.** Post snippets, polls, and news about your book, and send a newsletter to people on your mailing list.
- **Send personalized emails.** Use your Excel sheets to jot down any information that will help you remember who each reviewer is so you can personalize your emails as much as possible. If your ARC team feels connected to and invested in you, they will be far more likely to review new books and recommend your book to contacts. Build authentic relationships with the members of this team, and remember to ask them about important milestones and life events they mention to you.
- **Ask your ARC team for advice.** Their input is invaluable because they care about your success, and you know they can give honest advice for your next book.
- **Don't rest on your laurels when it comes to your ARC team.** By the time your second book comes around, your ARC team may have slightly dwindled. You may, therefore, have to invest a bit of time in building up your numbers.

How to Publish Book Collections for More Revenue

One marketing strategy we recommend is the creation of book collections. Self-publishers often refer to these as "book bundles," but you should refrain from using the word "bundles" on Amazon, as the publishing giant will reject your books if you do. There is a good reason for that. Using the word may imply that they are getting numerous separate books. A collection is different: it comprises multiple books published as one new book and offers an excellent ROI. Since collections contain books you've already written and released individually, you've already paid for the ghostwriting and editing, and collections take far less time to produce. Finally, they do not affect the sales of your original titles. They function as a great marketing tool because readers can access books at a cheaper price than if they purchased them individually.

Your book collection should effectively be treated as a new book and include the following features:

- A title (Remember to use the word "collection" instead of "bundle.")
- A new layout (You will have to ask your formatter to bundle the books.)
    - Title page
    - Copyright page
    - TOC (table of contents)
    - Book 1 title page
    - Book 1 introduction
    - Book 1 body chapters
    - Mid-book review page (optional)
    - Book 1 remaining body chapters
    - Review page (optional)
    - Book 1 conclusion
    - Book 1 references
    - Book 2 title page
    - Book 2 introduction
    - Book 2 body chapters
    - Mid-book review page (optional)
    - Book 2 remaining body chapters
    - Review page (optional)
    - Book 2 conclusion
    - Book 2 references

- ◊ Any additional information you wish to include (e.g., information about the author, other books by the author, and more)
  - Everything a book needs, including A+ content, a description, review pages (optional), and ARC readers
  - A new cover (Create a cover that features 3D images of the individual books.)

For audiobooks, you will simply use the individual files from both books, but you will need additional opening and closing credits. Your content should be laid out in the following way:

- Collection opening credits
- Book 1 opening credits
- Book 1 introduction
- Book 1 body chapters
- Book 1 mid-book review page (optional)
- Book 1 remaining body chapters
- Book 1 review page (optional)
- Book 1 conclusion
- Book 1 closing credits
- Book 2 opening credits
- Book 2 introduction
- Book 2 body chapters
- Book 2 mid-book review page (optional)
- Book 2 remaining body chapters
- Book 2 review page (optional)
- Book 2 conclusion
- Book 2 closing credits
- Collection closing credits

Translating Your Book for Global Reach

Another thing to keep in mind if you want your book to reach a wider audience is translation. If your market research indicates there is a demand for it, consider translating your book into the following languages:

- Spanish
- German
- French

In addition to translating your book's interior, you will also have to translate your cover, ensuring you don't exceed the permitted character counts for titles and subtitles. You will also need to translate your book description and A+ content and have your book narrated. You can hire a freelance translator from a platform like Upwork. Make it a point to hire a freelance proofreader to check that the translation is correct and that everything is correctly spelled.

Chapter 34

How to Transition and Sell Your Publishing Business

Once you publish a series of books that sell well, your publishing company will be a valuable brand you can profit from. If the timing is right, you can sell it for six or even seven figures and then start all over again by launching a new publishing business if you wish. In this chapter, we will take a look at all the steps you must take to make a profitable sale.

Why Would You Sell?

There are many reasons why you may want to sell your successful book publishing business. Perhaps you wish to pursue another career path. Maybe there is an investment opportunity you're keen to take advantage of, and you need a lump sum payment now. Or maybe you feel like publishing on a platform other than KDP. You may just want to take a break from publishing or reinvent your brand.

Some publishers build their brands and businesses with the intention of selling them once they reach a certain level of success. This is a legitimate business strategy. In that case, selling becomes part of your planned exit strategy to capitalize on the value you've built.

No matter what your motivation is, there are several options to consider when selling a publishing business.

Where Can You Sell Your Publishing Business?

We suggest selling your publishing business via Empire Flippers—a curated marketplace with global customers who've bought and sold over $520M worth of online businesses. If you visit their site, www.publishingservicesbook.com/empire-flippers, you will see that you can both buy and sell KDP book brands and other types of businesses. To sell your business on this platform, your account needs to be at least twelve months old and have made an average of $2000 within this time frame. Empire Flippers has its competitors, of course, but if you're looking for top-level support, dependability, and security, we think this company is the best option.

Its high sales volume means that the majority of serious buyers will probably consult its website first, so get ahead of your competitors by ensuring your business is listed where serious buyers can find you.

How Much Is Your Publishing Business Worth?

To work out how much you can sell your publishing business for, you will need to calculate your average net profits over the previous twelve-month period and use a specific multiplier.

This multiplier reflects the perceived value of your business based on its profitability, stability, and growth potential. For self-publishing, the multiplier depends on:

- The number of hours you work each week on the business
- The age of your business
- The average monthly gross revenue
- The average monthly net profit
- The total number of books published

Factors That May Decrease the Multiplier

- The overall business performance
- The niche you are publishing in
- Competition and the current demand for self-publishing businesses

Factors That May Increase the Multiplier

- Strong growth
- Brand recognition
- Competitive advantages (e.g., engaged email list or a strong social media presence)

We recommend that you take a look at Empire Flippers to check out the listing prices of a few KDP publishing businesses.

The site gives you information on these brands, including the price of sale, monthly net profit, monthly revenue, year of business creation, where the business is monetized, and monthly multiplier.

At the time of writing this book, we have found the example below.

The seller stated they work 1 hour per week on their business and will offer 30 days of email support to the buyer past the sale.

To get an idea of the value of your business, you can use Empire Flippers' free evaluation tool.

How Empire Flippers Can Help You Sell Your Business

To sell your publishing business via Empire Flippers, follow these steps:

 *Obtain a Free Valuation*

If you want to know what your business is worth, we recommend using the "Free Valuation" tool provided by Empire Flippers. It is totally commitment-free, meaning you can obtain a valuation and decide to sell your business on another marketplace (or not at all). The valuation is not the final price, but it gives you a good general idea of what your business is worth. Go to www.publishingservicesbook.com/empire-flippers and access the free online valuation tool.

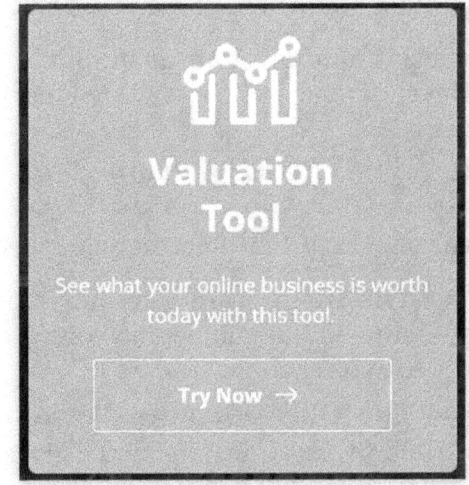

You will see that the questions asked are the same as mentioned above on how to calculate your multiplier.

 *Book a Consultation Call*

After having your business valued, the next step is to book a consultation call with Empire Flippers. Once again, this call is commitment-free and won't cost you a cent. It's simply an opportunity for you to pose any questions you have to the team.

 *Create a Profit-and-Loss Statement*

If you decide to go ahead, you will need to fill out a profit-and-loss statement for the past 12 months. This statement will contain all your income and expenses. For instance, your income may include the money you received from KDP, ACX, IngramSpark, Author's Republic, and others. Meanwhile, your expenses may include the cost of Facebook Ads, Amazon Marketing Services, your ghostwriter, your proofers and editors, and more.

You can access our free profit and loss template at www.publishingservicesbook.com/profit-and-loss.

04 ▶▶ *List Your Business on Empire Flippers*

Empire Flippers will study your profit-and-loss statement and all the other information you submit and will inform you of whether your business can be sold on their site. If the answer is "yes," they will provide you with an official valuation. If you are happy with the listing price, agree to it, and your business will be listed on the Empire Flippers marketplace.

05 ▶▶ *Speak to Potential Buyers*

At this stage, you will communicate with interested buyers, answering their questions and speaking to them via Zoom calls. A representative from Empire Flippers will also attend these calls. During the negotiation stage, potential buyers will most likely try to lower the listing price. However, we recommend that you only sell your business for what you feel is a good price. Bear in mind that all potential buyers must previously show Empire Flippers that they have the funds to buy your business. That means that they *can* actually buy your business at the full listing price if they wish to.

There are other ways that you can make the sale more valuable to the purchaser without lowering the price. For instance, you can offer to coach them after the sale, share your contacts with them, or recommend top professionals and tools to them. Your time and expertise will be worth a lot by this stage since you will have mastered all the steps required to produce and publish a winning book.

It is also important to bear in mind that Empire Flippers charges a 15% commission on the sale. However, if your business is listed for over $1 million, they take only 12%.

06 ▶▶ *The Migration Phase*

Once you accept the offer, the sale moves to the migration phase, which includes:

- **The Inspection Period:** In this phase the purchaser gains access to your account to make sure all the numbers in your profit-and-loss statement are accurate. This period lasts around two weeks.
- **The Due Diligence Period:** For sales of over $500,000, a third party will undertake additional due diligence. This period can last two to four weeks.

07 ▶▶ *Receive the Funds*

During the migration stage, the buyer will deposit the funds to Empire Flippers. Once the account transfer is complete, these funds will be released to you. You can choose to be paid through various methods, including a bank wire, Bitcoin, Payoneer, and more. Note that when you sell your business, you do not forfeit any money owed to you by KDP, bearing in mind that KDP has a sixty-day payment delay. That means that if you sell your business in May but haven't received your March and April payments yet, those amounts will be paid to you after the sale. You can back out of negotiations at any point *before* accepting the offer. Also, note that you can't sell just part of your KDP business on Empire Flippers; you have to sell 100% of it. Remember that your account will also need to be at least twelve months old.

Launching Another KDP Business

In time (or immediately after the sale), you can start a brand-new KDP business if you like. However, it's common to sign a non-compete agreement as part of the sale. This typically means you cannot publish in the same niche as the business you sold for a specific period. For example, if your previous books were about raising chickens, you might start publishing books on raising sheep but not ones directly related to chickens.

The specifics of the non-compete agreement can vary depending on the terms of the deal. In some cases, exceptions may be negotiated with the buyer, allowing for limited activities within the same niche under certain conditions. Always ensure these terms are clearly outlined in your agreement to avoid future conflicts.

And that's all there is to it! We wish you all the success as a self-publisher and entrepreneur!

Before You Start Searching for Those Keywords...

Congratulations, what a feat! You've made it through the ins and outs of self-publishing, from choosing your niche all the way to getting your book translated so you can reach readers the world over! You have seen how we kept our promise and left no stone unturned. We shared literally every bit of information you need to become a successful self-publisher.

As you have seen, it's a matter of ticking the items on a checklist: opening all necessary accounts, publishing your book in different formats, marketing and publicizing it, and building a community of followers and co-authors. Of course, there's another topic you've read about that is crucial to success, and that is ensuring your readers leave reviews. Can you do this for us, taking just 30 seconds to let others know what you thought of this book?

Thanks for your help. Writing this book has been quite a journey, and our team has dedicated significant time and effort to this project. Like you, we dream of achieving our self-publishing goals, and we hope we can count on your support to do so.

To leave your review on Amazon, go to

www.publishingservicesbook.com/leave-a-review or scan the QR code.

A Personal Note to Our Readers from Publishing Services' CEO

First, let me say congratulations—you made it to the end of this guide! By doing so, you've already taken a huge step forward in your self-publishing journey.

I hope you've found value in this book, not just in the tips and tutorials but in the encouragement of the whole Publishing Services team.

Traditionally, books end with a formulaic conclusion. But you don't always have to follow tradition. Creativity thrives when you take risks and make bold choices. That's why we're closing this book with something a little different: a personal note from me to you.

Self-publishing is an exciting and rewarding career, but let's be honest—it can feel overwhelming at times. Here's what I want you to remember: it's absolutely worth it.

Every moment of effort and every lesson learned is a step forward. You're here because you have something to share—something only you can offer—and there's power in that. Your words have the potential to inspire, inform, or move someone in ways you may never even know.

At Publishing Services, our mission is to help you succeed, whether it's guiding you through the publishing process, discussing your ideas, or simply being someone you can turn to when you need to vent your frustrations or feel stuck.

So, as you take the first step toward your creative and financial freedom, please remember you have everything it takes to succeed. Keep learning. Keep growing. Most importantly, keep believing in yourself. Whenever you need encouragement, guidance, or a partner in your success, we'll be here, ready to support you.

Thank you for letting us be a part of your journey. We're excited to see what you create.

With gratitude and excitement,

Sarah Eberstadt

CEO, Publishing Services

Tools & Software

Having the right tools and software can make the difference between a stressful, time-consuming process and a streamlined, professional production.

Below, you'll find a list of all the tools and software mentioned throughout the book, along with direct links to help you easily access and explore each one.

99 designs
- https://www.publishingservicesbook.com/99designs

ACX
- https://www.acx.com/

Ablurb Blurb Preview Tool
- https://www.publishingservicesbook.com/ablurb

Adobe InDesign
- https://www.adobe.com/products/indesign.html#modal-hash

Adobe Stock
- https://stock.adobe.com/

Amazon Author Central
- https://author.amazon.com/

Amazon Bestseller list
- https://www.publishingservicesbook.com/amazon-best-sellers

Amazon Review link
- https://www.amazon.com/review/create-review/?asin=ASIN

Amazon's Seller Central
- https://sellercentral.amazon.com/

APA (American Psychological Association)
- https://www.apa.org/

Apple Books
- https://www.apple.com/apple-books/

Atticus
- https://www.atticus.io/

Audible
- https://www.audible.com/

Author's Republic
- https://www.authorsrepublic.com/

BackedBy
- https://www.publishingservicesbook.com/backed-by
  - Get a **5% discount** on your first invoice by clicking the link.

Barnes & Noble
- https://www.barnesandnoble.com/

Bitly QR Codes
- https://www.publishingservicesbook.com/bitly

BlueInkReview
- https://www.publishingservicesbook.com/blue-ink-review

Book Bounty
- https://www.publishingservicesbook.com/book-bounty

Book Cover 3D Mockups tool
- https://www.publishingservicesbook.com/3d-mockups

Bookbeam
- https://www.publishingservicesbook.com/bookbeam
  - Use **PS10** to get **10% off** for the yearly plans or **PS50** to get **50% off** on the first month.

Booklaze
- https://www.publishingservicesbook.com/bookblaze

BookLife
- https://booklife.com/

Calibre
- https://calibre-ebook.com/

Canva
- https://www.canva.com/

ChatGPT
- https://chatgpt.com/

Chanticleer Book Reviews
- https://www.chantireviews.com/

City Book Review
- https://citybookreview.com/

CMOS (The Chicago Manual of Style)
- https://www.chicagomanualofstyle.org/home.html

Copyright Registration
- http://www.copyright.gov/registration/

Creative Market
- https://www.publishingservicesbook.com/creative-market

Critique Circle
- https://www.critiquecircle.com/landing

Dall-E
- https://openai.com/index/dall-e-2/

Depositphotos
- https://www.publishingservicesbook.com/depositphotos

Draft2Digital
- https://www.draft2digital.com/

draw.io
- https://app.diagrams.net/

DS Amazon Quick View on Google Chrome
- https://www.publishingservicesbook.com/ds-amazon-quick-view

Done for You KDP Reviews
- https://www.publishingservicesbook.com/dfy-kdp-reviews
  - Receive **$50 off** with the code **PS**

Duplichecker
- https://www.duplichecker.com/

Excalidraw
- https://excalidraw.com/

Facebook
- https://www.facebook.com

Feathered Quill
- https://featheredquill.com/

Findaway Voices by Shopify
- https://www.findawayvoices.com/

FigJam
- https://www.publishingservicesbook.com/figjam

Fiverr
- https://www.publishingservicesbook.com/fiverr

Foreword Reviews
- https://www.forewordreviews.com/

Getcovers
- https://www.publishingservicesbook.com/getcovers
  - Use coupon code **PS10** to get **10% off**.

GPTZero
- https://www.publishingservicesbook.com/gptzero

Grammarly
- https://www.publishingservicesbook.com/grammarly

GraphicRiver
- https://www.publishingservicesbook.com/graphic-river

IndieReader
- https://www.publishingservicesbook.com/indie-reader

IngramSpark
- https://www.ingramspark.com/

Instagram
- https://www.instagram.com/

ISBN
- **Australia ISBN agency Thorpe-Bowker**
  - www.myidentifiers.com.au
- **Bowkerlink**
  - www.bowkerlink.com
- **Canada ISBN agency email address**
  - isbn-canada@bac-lac.gc.ca
- **International ISBN agency**
  - www.isbn-international.org/agencies
- **New Zealand ISBN agency Thorpe-Bowker**
  - www.myidentifiers.com/nz
- **UK and Ireland's official IBSN agency**
  - www.isbn.nielsenbook.co.uk

ISBN converter
- https://www.publishingservicesbook.com/isbn-converter

ISBN Search
- https://isbnsearch.org/

ISBN from Bowker
- www.myidentifiers.com

iStock
- https://www.publishingservicesbook.com/istock

KDP
- https://kdp.amazon.com/

KDP A+ Content Guidelines
- https://www.publishingservicesbook.com/a-plus-guidelines

KDP Book Formatting Sizes
- https://www.publishingservicesbook.com/kdp-formatting-sizes

KDP Community Guidelines
- https://www.publishingservicesbook.com/community-guidelines

KDP's description formatting rules
- https://www.publishingservicesbook.com/kdp-formatting-rules

KDP Help Site
- https://kdp.amazon.com/en_US/help

KDP Payment Options
- https://www.publishingservicesbook.com/kdp-payment-options

KDP Royalty Calculator
- https://www.publishingservicesbook.com/kdp-royalty-calculator

KDSpy
- https://www.publishingservicesbook.com/kdspy

Kindlepreneur Book Review Blog
- https://www.publishingservicesbook.com/book-review-blogs

Kindlepreneur HTML Book Description Generator
- https://www.publishingservicesbook.com/html-generator

Kindlepreneur KENP Calculator
- https://www.publishingservicesbook.com/kenp-calculator

Kindlepreneur QR Code Generator
- https://www.publishingservicesbook.com/qr-code-generator

Kobo
- https://www.kobo.com/

KPC
- https://www.publishingservicesbook.com/kpc

Linkedin
- https://www.linkedin.com/feed/

Lulu
- https://www.lulu.com/

Meet Glimpse
- https://meetglimpse.com/

Midjourney
- https://www.midjourney.com/home

My QR Code
- www.myqrcode.com

Online Book Club
- https://onlinebookclub.org/

Originality.ai
- https://www.publishingservicesbook.com/originality-ai

pdfFiller
- https://www.publishingservicesbook.com/watermark

PeoplePerHour
- https://www.peopleperhour.com/

Perplexity
- https://www.perplexity.ai/

ProWritingAid
- https://www.publishingservicesbook.com/prowritingaid

- **Publishing Services**
  - https://www.publishingservices.com/
- **Publishing Services Copyright Page Template**
  - https://www.publishingservicesbook.com/copyright-page
- **Publishing Services Facebook Group**
  - https://www.facebook.com/groups/selfpublishingnetwork
- **Publishing Services Outline Template**
  - https://www.publishingservicesbook.com/outline-template
- **Publishing Services Outline Sample**
  - https://www.publishingservicesbook.com/outline-sample
- **Publishing Services Packages**
  - **A+ Content Package**
    - https://publishingservices.com/products/a-content-package
  - **AI Manuscript Developmental Editing & Humanization Package**
    - https://publishingservices.com/collections/pls-services/products/ai-manuscript-editing-humanization-package
  - **Author Bio Package**
    - https://publishingservices.com/products/amazon-author-bio-package
  - **Book Cover Design Package**
    - https://publishingservices.com/products/cover-design-package
  - **Book Description Package**
    - https://publishingservices.com/products/book-description-package
  - **Editing & Proofreading Package**
    - https://publishingservices.com/collections/pls-services/products/editing-proofreading-package
  - **Formatting Package**
    - https://publishingservices.com/products/ultimate-formatting-package
  - **Outline and Book Description Package**
    - https://publishingservices.com/products/book-outline-package
  - **Outline Quality Review Package**
    - https://publishingservices.com/products/outline-quality-review-package
  - **Premium Ghostwriting Package**
    - https://publishingservices.com/products/premium-ghostwriting-package-shortlist
  - **Pre-Existing Cover Resizing Package**
    - https://publishingservices.com/products/pre-existing-cover-resizing-package
  - **Review Page Package**
    - https://publishingservices.com/collections/pls-services/products/review-page-package
- **Publishing Services Reviewers Materials**
  - **Facebook Book Reviewers Spreadsheet**
    - https://www.publishingservicesbook.com/book-reviewers-spreadsheet
  - **Facebook Book Reviewers Spreadsheet Strategy 2**
    - https://www.publishingservicesbook.com/reviewers-spreadsheet-strategy-2
  - **Facebook Message Template**
    - https://www.publishingservicesbook.com/facebook-message-template
- **Publishing Services Support Email**
  - support@publishingservices.com
- **Publishing Services Trustpilot**
  - https://www.publishingservicesbook.com/trustpilot
- **Publisher Champ**
  - https://www.publishingservicesbook.com/publisher-champ
    - To obtain **10% off** the annual plan or **10% off** the first 6 months of a monthly plan, use the coupon code **PUBLISHINGSERVICES**
- **Publisher Rocket**
  - https://www.publishingservicesbook.com/publisher-rocket

Publishing Performance
- https://www.publishingservicesbook.com/publishing-performance
  ◊ Get **15% recurring discount** with code **PUBSERV15**

QR Code Generator
- www.qr-code-generator.com

QRCode Monkey
- www.qrcode-monkey.com

QuillBot
- https://www.publishingservicesbook.com/quillbot

Quora
- https://www.quora.com/

Readers' Favorite
- https://www.publishingservicesbook.com/readers-favorite

Reddit
- https://www.reddit.com/

Reedsy
- https://reedsy.com/

Reedsy Pen Name Generator
- https://www.publishingservicesbook.com/pen-name-generator

Scribophile
- https://www.scribophile.com/

Shutterstock
- https://www.publishingservicesbook.com/shutterstock

Tax Treat Calculator
- https://www.publishingservicesbook.com/tax-treaty-calculator

TikTok
- https://www.tiktok.com/

Trademark search
- https://www.uspto.gov/trademarks/search

Undetectable AI
- https://www.publishingservicesbook.com/undetectable-ai

Unsplash
- https://unsplash.com/

Upwork
- https://www.upwork.com/

Vellum
- https://vellum.pub/

Vellum FAQs
- https://www.publishingservicesbook.com/vellum-faq

Wikimedia Commons
- https://commons.wikimedia.org/

YouTube
- https://www.youtube.com/

Glossary

3D mockup – A visual representation of a book cover in three dimensions often used for marketing and promotional purposes.

A+ content – Enhanced product pages on Amazon that allow authors to include additional images, videos, and text to provide a more detailed description of their book.

ACoS (advertising cost of sale) – A metric used in Amazon Ads that shows how much an author is spending on advertising compared to the sales generated from that ad.

Amazon ads – Advertising campaigns run on Amazon to increase book visibility and sales.

Amazon marketplace – The platform where books are sold on Amazon, which includes global versions (US, UK, etc.).

ARC team (advanced review copy team) – A group of readers who get early access to a book before its release to provide reviews and feedback.

ASIN (Amazon standard identification number) – A unique identifier used by Amazon to catalog products, including books.

Author's bio – A short description of an author's background and credentials, often included on a book's Amazon page or website.

Audiobook – An audio version of a book, typically read by a narrator or produced using text-to-speech technology.

Audiobook opening and closing credits – The verbal acknowledgment of contributors to an audiobook, typically found at the beginning and end of the recording.

Back cover – The reverse side of a book's physical cover, often featuring a brief description of the book, an author bio, and other promotional elements.

Beta reader – A person who reads an early version of a book to offer feedback on plot, character, pacing, and other elements.

Bleed – The area of a book design that extends beyond the trim size, ensuring that content (e.g., images) reaches the edge of the page after trimming.

Book description – A written summary of a book that highlights its plot, themes, and key points to entice readers. It's often used on online book retailers' product pages.

Book distributors – Platforms that help authors distribute their books to multiple stores (e.g., Amazon, Barnes & Noble, Apple Books, etc.).

Book formatting – The process of preparing a manuscript for publication, ensuring it meets the technical requirements of the chosen publishing platform.

Book interior type – Refers to the choice between black-and-white or color printing and the use of cream or white paper, affecting the book's appearance, feel, and cost.

Book layout – The arrangement of text, images, and design elements inside a book, ensuring a visually pleasing and functional structure.

Book launch – The official release of a book to the public, often accompanied by marketing campaigns, reviews, and promotions.

Book rating – A numerical or star rating given by readers based on their review of a book.

Book spine – The edge of a book that is visible when it's on a shelf, typically displaying the book's title and author.

Book visibility – The degree to which a book is visible to readers on various platforms, like Amazon, through keywords, ads, and reviews.

Campaign ACoS – The advertising cost of sale for a specific campaign in Amazon Ads.

Citations – References to sources or external material used within the book to support claims or ideas.

Click-through rate (CTR) – The percentage of users who click on an ad compared to the number of people who viewed it.

Copyediting – The process of correcting errors in spelling, grammar, and punctuation and improving sentence structure in a manuscript.

Copywriting – The art and skill of writing compelling text for promotional materials, such as book descriptions, ad copy, or sales pages.

Cost per click (CPC) – The amount an author pays each time a user clicks on their ad.

Developmental editing – The process of editing a manuscript for structure, plot, pacing, and other big-picture elements.

Digital rights management (DRM) – Software that protects a digital book from unauthorized distribution, ensuring it can only be used by those who have purchased it.

Ebook – A digital version of a book, typically in EPUB format and readable on e-readers, tablets, or computers.

Editorial reviews – Professional reviews written by experts in the field or industry, often included on book covers or sales pages to boost credibility.

EPUB – A popular format for ebooks, compatible with most e-readers.

Full-page image – A single image that occupies an entire page of a book, often used in graphic novels or illustrated books.

Ghostwriter – A writer who is hired to write a book for someone else, typically credited as the author.

HTML code – The coding language used to create and format web pages, often used in ebook and book description formatting.

Hyphenation and justification – The process of adjusting word breaks and aligning text to ensure a clean, visually appealing layout in the manuscript.

ISBN (international standard book number) – A unique identifier for books that is used to track and catalog them in the publishing industry.

KPF file – Kindle format used by Amazon for books, often part of the ebook submission process.

Kindle countdown deals (KCD) – A promotional tool offered by Amazon that allows authors to offer their Kindle books at a discount for a limited time.

Kindle edition normalized pages (KENP) – A metric used by Amazon to track how much of an ebook is read by Kindle Unlimited subscribers, impacting royalty payments.

Line editing – The process of editing a manuscript for clarity, style, and sentence-level issues while maintaining the author's voice.

Line spacing – The vertical distance between lines of text in a book, which affects readability.

Margins – The blank space surrounding the text on a page, which is important for ensuring the text isn't cut off during printing.

Mechanical editing – The process of checking a manuscript for proper grammar, punctuation, spelling, and overall language mechanics.

Pen name – A pseudonym used by authors to publish books, often to maintain privacy or for branding purposes.

Page count – The total number of pages in a printed book, which can affect pricing, formatting, and printing options.

Plagiarism – The act of using someone else's work or ideas without permission or proper credit, considered unethical and illegal.

Preformatting – Preparing a manuscript by setting up fonts and layout before starting detailed formatting.

Printbook (Paperback/Hardback) – A physical version of a book that can be sold through online or brick-and-mortar retailers.

Printback/Printcover – The back and front cover of a print book, typically designed with printing specifications.

Proofreading – The final stage of editing, focusing on spotting and correcting errors in grammar, spelling, and punctuation.

Review page – A page placed in the book inviting readers to leave a review of a book.

Review link – A direct link to a platform where readers can leave a review for a book.

Royalty – The payment an author receives for each book sold, typically a percentage of the sale price.

RTF (rich text format) – A text file format that retains formatting across different platforms and word processors.

Signature framework – A unique method or structure that an author uses to outline, write, and organize their book, often a personalized or branded approach.

Stock images – Pre-licensed images that authors can purchase and use in their book's design or cover.

Subheadings – Titles or headings that fall under the main chapter or section heading used to break down content for easier reading.

TOC (table of contents) – A list of the chapters or sections of a book, often hyperlinked for ebooks, to allow readers to navigate through the content easily.

Trademark – A legally registered symbol, word, or phrase used to represent a product or brand, including books.

Vector graphics – Images created using mathematical equations, allowing for easy resizing without losing quality.

Watermark – A faint image or text added to a book or document to protect against unauthorized distribution or copying.

Widows and orphans – Design terms for lines of text that appear alone at the top or bottom of a page, which are avoided during formatting.

Zoning – Dividing content into sections or blocks to enhance structure and readability.

References

9designs. n.d. "How Cover Design Can Increase Book Visibility by 50% (or More). Accessed June 20, 2024. https://99designs.com/blog/tips/impact-book-cover-design-on-sales/.

ACX. n.d. "What's the Difference Between Exclusive Distribution and Non-exclusive Distribution?" Accessed September 1, 2024. https://help.acx.com/s/article/what-s-the-difference-between-exclusive-distribution-and-non-exclusive-distribution.

Allan, Scott. n.d. "How to Get an ISBN Number for a Self-Published Book." Selfpublishing.com. Accessed July 2, 2024. https://selfpublishing.com/isbn-number-self-published-book/.

Alliance of Independent Authors. 2024. "The Big Indie Author Data Drop 2024." Accessed September 27, 2024. https://www.allianceindependentauthors.org/wordpress/wp-content/uploads/2024/03/The-Big-Indie-Author-Data-Drop-2024.pdf.

Author Imprints. 2024. "The Myth of the eISBN: When ebooks Need an ISBN." January 13, 2024. https://www.authorimprints.com/myth-eisbn-every-ebook-edition-needs-unique-number/.

Author's Republic. 2022. "Your Audiobook Production Budget." May 26, 2022. https://www.authorsrepublic.com/learn/blog/64/your-audiobook-production-budget.

Baird, Chris A. 2023. "Lulu Self Publishing Review with Pros & Cons [2023]." Self Publishing Made Easy Now. June 20, 2023. https://selfpublishingmadeeasynow.com/lulu-self-publishing-review-with-pros-cons-2023/.

Barry KDP. 2024. "How PROFITABLE Keyword Research Actually Works on Amazon KDP | Amazon KDP Business Secrets." January 14, 2024. https://www.youtube.com/watch?v=N_Xi9hb4tDg.

Bidilică, Mihaela. 2023. "Self-Publishing Success Stories You Need to Hear About." Publish Drive. June 26, 2023. https://publishdrive.com/self-publishing-success-stories.html.

Bidilică, Mihaela. 2024. "Kobo & Kobo Plus: Key Players in Wide Publishing (+ Insights from Authors Who Use Kobo)." Publish Drive. April 11, 2024. https://publishdrive.com/kobo-distribution-and-benefits.html.

Booth, Doris. 2019. "Avoiding the Pitfalls of Publishing with Amazon Kindle Self-Publishing Platform." Authorlink. November 22, 2019. https://authorlink.com/news-and-views/rants/avoiding-the-pitfalls-of-publishing-with-amazon-kindle-self-publishing-platform/.

BrainyQuote. n.d. "Chickens Quotes." Accessed July 18, 2024. https://www.brainyquote.com/topics/chickens-quotes.

Brockbank, Michael. n.d. "15 Pros and Cons of Using the Free Reedsy Writing App." WriterSanctuary. Accessed June 27, 2024. https://writersanctuary.com/pros-cons-using-reedsy-writing-app/.

Cawley, Conor. 2024. "10 Key Visual Content Marketing Statistics in 2023." Tech.co. March 8, 2024. https://tech.co/digital-marketing/visual-content-marketing-statistics.

Chesson, Dave. 2021. "Smashwords Review." Kindlepreneur. July 20, 2021. https://kindlepreneur.com/review/smashwords-review/#:~:text=Smashwords%20makes%20it%20easy%20for,for%20easy%20off%2Dsite%20marketing.

Chesson, Dave. 2022a. "The Art and Science to Amazon Editorial Reviews." Kindlepreneur. December 13, 2022. https://kindlepreneur.com/amazon-editorial-reviews/.

Chesson, Dave. 2022b. "Author Networking: How to Partner with Other Authors." Kindlepreneur. July 31, 2022. https://kindlepreneur.com/amazon-editorial-reviews/.

Chesson, Dave. 2022c. "Amazon Popularity Effect: How Amazon Treats Book Discoverability." Kindlepreneur. November 4, 2022. https://kindlepreneur.com/amazon-popularity-effect-how-amazon-treats-book-discoverability/.

Chesson, Dave. 2023a. "Ultimate List of the Best Book Review Blogs." Kindlepreneur. January 20, 2023. https://kindlepreneur.com/book-review-blogs/.

Chesson, Dave. 2023b. "Draft2Digital Review: Read This Before You Sign Up." Kindlepreneur. June 27, 2023. https://kindlepreneur.com/draft2digital-review/.

Connolly, Brian. 2024. "How to Create Amazon A+ Content in 2024." JungleScout. April 5, 2024. https://www.junglescout.com/resources/articles/amazon-a-plus-content/.

Copyright.gov. n.d. "Fees." Accessed August 17, 2024. https://www.copyright.gov/about/fees.html.

Corson-Knowles, Tom. n.d. "Using Book Promotions Sites to Launch Your Book." Kindlepreneur. Accessed September 20, 2024. https://kindlepreneur.com/episode-7-book-promotions-sites-launch-book/.

Crossman, Cassandra. 2019. "The Ableist History of the Puzzle Piece for Autism." In the Loop About Neurodiversity. March 20, 2019. https://intheloopaboutneurodiversity.wordpress.com/2019/03/20/the-ableist-history-of-the-puzzle-piece-symbol-for-autism/#:~:text=Not%20only%20was%20the%20puzzle,used%20in%20this%20manner%20today.

Dollwet, Sean. 2023. "My Amazon KDP Account Was TERMINATED… How to NEVER Be Banned." YouTube Video, 1:09. September 18, 2023. https://www.youtube.com/watch?v=E8Q1tuYtBw4.

Empire Flippers. n.d. "Frequently Asked Questions (FAQ) from Sellers." January 24, 2025. https://empireflippers.com/how-to-sell-a-website-faq/.

Fox, Barry. n.d. "How to Find a Ghostwriter for Your Book – 10 Great Tips." Barry Fox. Accessed July 31, 2024. https://barryfox.us/looking-for-a-ghostwriter/.

Hamilton, Jason. "Amazon Closed My Account: What to Do About a Suspended KDP Account." Kindlepreneur (blog), June 27, 2023. https://kindlepreneur.com/amazon-account-suspension/.

Harrison, Mackenzie. n.d. "Color Psychology In Book Cover Design: How To Use Colors To Attract Readers." Book Brush. Accessed June 20, 2024. https://bookbrush.com/color-psychology-in-book-cover-design-how-to-use-colors-to-attract-readers/#:~:text=Blue%20is%20a%20great%20color,self%2Dhelp%20or%20spiritual%20books.

Haynes, Jesse. 2023a. "Barnes & Noble Press Review: Pros & Cons." J.J. Hebert. April 27, 2023. https://www.jjhebertonline.com/2023/04/27/barnes-noble-press-review-pros-cons/#:~:text=Higher%20Royalties%3A%20Barnes%20%26%20Noble%20Press,15%25%20offered%20by%20traditional%20publishers.

Haynes, Jesse. 2023b. "Lulu Publishing Review: Is It All It's Cracked Up to Be?" J.J. Hebert. February 23, 2023. https://www.jjhebertonline.com/2023/02/23/lulu-publishing-review-is-it-all-its-cracked-up-to-be/#:~:text=Lulu%2DPublishing%20is%20not%20worth,any%20website%20outside%20of%20Lulu.

Heimbigner, J. R. 2024. "17 Quotes To Help Get You Moving On Self-Publishing Your Next Book." The Freedom to Write (blog), August 27, 2024. Accessed November 12, 2024. https://medium.com/the-freedom-to-write/17-quotes-to-help-get-you-moving-on-self-publishing-your-next-book-6a71cc352be0.

Hill, Jessica. n.d. "Amazon KDP vs. IngramSpark: Who Should You Choose?" LaunchMyBook. Accessed July 30, 2024. https://www.launchmybook.com/amazon-kdp-vs-ingramspark/#:~:text=You'll%20have%20wider%20distribution,you%20just%20publish%20with%20KDP.

IBM. 2023. "Shedding Light on AI Bias with Real World Examples." Accessed October 26, 2023. https://www.ibm.com/think/topics/shedding-light-on-ai-bias-with-real-world-examples.

IngramSpark. 2019. "Understanding IngramSpark Title Processing and Availability." September 10, 2019. https://www.ingramspark.com/blog/ingramspark-title-availability.

Ken Self-Publishing Secrets. 2023a. "Complete A+ Content Guide for Amazon KDP | My Secret A+ Content Format Revealed." YouTube Video, 1:18. October 6, 2023. https://youtu.be/GU997iUK1YU?si=t1ua_anQiucQakNF.

Ken Self-Publishing Secrets. 2023b. "A Simple Book Launch Strategy to Maximize Sales and Rank on Page 1 | Amazon KDP." YouTube Video, 7:00. July 22, 2023. https://youtu.be/GU997iUK1YU?si=t1ua_anQiucQakNF.

Ken Self-Publishing Secrets. 2023c. "My SIMPLE & Profitable Ads Strategy for Amazon KDP | Beginner Amazon Ads Tutorial for KDP Authors." YouTube Video, 2:00. June 23, 2023. https://www.youtube.com/watch?v=1kxc0Z3FqvU.

Kindle Direct Publishing. n.d.-a "Metadata Guidelines for Books." Accessed June 10, 2024 (1). https://kdp.amazon.com/en_US/help/topic/G201097560.

Kindle Direct Publishing. n.d.-b. "International Standard Book Number (ISBN)." Accessed June 20, 2024. https://kdp.amazon.com/en_US/help/topic/G200672390#:~:text=We%20require%20you%20to%20inform,to%20disclose%20AI%2Dassisted%20content.

Kindle Direct Publishing. n.d.-c. "A+ Content Guidelines." Accessed July 20, 2024. https://kdp.amazon.com/en_US/help/topic/G4WB-7VPPEAREHAAD.

Kindle Direct Publishing. n.d.-d. "How to Enroll in KDP Select." Accessed July 25, 2024. https://kdp.amazon.com/en_US/help/topic/GD9PMU58BV24QFZ7#enroll.

Kindle Direct Publishing. n.d.-e. "Royalties in Kindle Unlimited." Accessed August 1, 2024. https://kdp.amazon.com/en_US/help/topic/G201541130#reporting.

Kindle Direct Publishing. n.d.-f. "Legal & Content Guidelines." Accessed June 16, 2024. https://kdp.amazon.com/en_US/help/topic/G200672390#:~:text=We%20require%20you%20to%20inform,to%20disclose%20AI%2Dassisted%20content.

Kindle Direct Publishing. n.d.-g. "Free Book Promotions." Accessed August 14, 2024. https://kdp.amazon.com/en_US/help/topic/G201298240.

Kindlepreneur. 2024. "How to Fill in Your 7 Kindle Keywords: 2024 UPDATE!." YouTube Video, 1:00. May 23, 2024(1). How to Fill in Your 7 Kindle Keywords: 2024 UPDATE!.

Kindlepreneur. n.d.-a. "Scheduling Book Promotion Sites To Increase Sales." YouTube Video, 1:00. Accessed September 23, 2024. https://youtu.be/wm0uGIpl5Lk?si=I2R3FP_YiwFbob0F.

Kindlepreneur. n.d.-b. "KENP Calculator: Know Exactly How Much Your KDP Select Books Make." Accessed August 1, 2024. https://kindlepreneur.com/kenp-calculator/.

Komnenic, Masha. 2023. "Copyright Examples." Termly. February 3, 2023. https://termly.io/resources/articles/copyright-examples/#:~:text=in%20this%20order%3A-,The%20copyright%20symbol%20%C2%A9%20or%20the%20word%20%E2%80%9Ccopyright%E2%80%9D,an%20organization%2C%20or%20a%20business.

Lerner, Harriet. 2014. *The Dance of Anger*. New York: Harper Collins.

LLC, Lightning Source. n.d. "Global Book Distribution | IngramSpark." https://www.ingramspark.com/how-it-works/distribute.

Maddieson, Ian. n.d. "Chapter Voicing in Plosives and Fricatives." The World Atlas of Language Structures Online. Accessed June 15, 2024. https://wals.info/chapter/4#:~:text=Plosives%20are%20the%20kinds%20of,being%20made%20in%20the%20mouth.

Metz, Ericka. 2024. "Key Amazon Advertising Stats You Need to Know in 2024." Vapa. August 27, 2024. https://www.vapa.ai/blogs/key-amazon-advertising-stats-need-know-2024.

Mongeau, Isabelle. "Audiobook Distribution: To Be Exclusive Or Not To Be?" Q'd Up. March 28, 2022. https://qd-up.com/blog/cover-2-cover/audiobook-distribution-acx-exclusive/#:~:text=So%2C%20if%20you%20choose%20ACX%20exclusive%2C%20you%20still%20have%20access,exclusive%20does%20have%20some%20limitations.

Nafees, Hammad. 2022. "Amazon KDP for Beginners: How Does Kindle Direct Publishing Work." Zonguru. June 20, 2022. https://www.zonguru.com/blog/how-does-kindle-direct-publishing-work.

Nielsen Book. 2021. "The Importance of Metadata for Discoverability and Sales." Accessed June 18, 2024. https://nielsenbook.co.uk/wp-content/uploads/2022/04/Nielsen-Metadata-Marketing-Report.pdf.

Nixon, Geoff. "How the Brain Reads and Understands Words." Gemm Learning, November 7, 2024. Accessed November 10, 2024. https://www.gemmlearning.com/blog/reading/how-brain-reads/.

Ortiz, Christopher. 2023. "Pubby Review – 2024 Guide for Authors." Self-Publishing School. August 14, 2023. https://self-publishing-school.com/pubby-review/.

Pangarkar, Tajammul. 2024. "Audiobooks Statistics 2024 By New Way of Storytelling." Scoop Market US. July 22, 2024. https://scoop.market.us/audiobooks-statistics/.

Publisher Champ. n.d. "How to Synchronize Your Chosen Platforms with Publisher Champ." Accessed August 30, 2024. https://www.publisherchamp.com/account-setup/.

Raiyn, Jamal. 2016. "The Role of Visual Learning in Improving Students' High-Order Thinking Skills." *Journal of Education and Practice* 7, no. 24 (2016): 115–21. http://files.eric.ed.gov/fulltext/EJ1112894.pdf.

Rapovets, Elena. 2024. "Creative Book Cover Design: Balancing Aesthetics and Genre Expectations." The Book Designer. February 29, 2024. https://www.thebookdesigner.com/creative-book-cover-design-aesthetics/.

Reedsy. 2022. "Revealed: The Real Marketing Value of a Professional Book Cover," Accessed November 11, 2024. https://blog.reedsy.com/marketing-value-professional-book-cover/.

Research and Markets. 2024. "Global Audiobooks Market by Genre (Fiction, Non-Fiction), Format (Abridged, Unabridged), Device, Distribution Channel, Users - Forecast 2024-2030." June 2024. Research and Markets. https://www.researchandmarkets.com/report/audio-book.

Roberts, Dale L. n.d. "What to Do if Your Amazon KDP Account is Suspended or Banned." Self Publishing With Dale. Accessed August 16, 2024. https://selfpublishingwithdale.com/index.php/2023/05/16/kdp-account-suspended/.

Robichaud, Meg. 2018. "You Can't Just Draw Purple People and Call It Diversity." Shopify UX. January 26, 2018. https://ux.shopify.com/you-cant-just-draw-purple-people-and-call-it-diversity-e2aa30f0c0e8.

Sarah. 2024. "Should I Do a KDP Preorder for My Book?" Spoonbridge Press. May 1, 2024. https://spoonbridgepress.com/kdp-preorder/#:~:text=you%20should%20know.-,KDP%20Preorders%20Aren't%20the%20Same%20as%20%E2%80%9CSchedule%20a%20Release,verification%20process%20ahead%20of%20time.

Sean Dollwet. 2024. "How to SELL Your Amazon KDP Business for 6 to 7 Figures (Full Tutorial)." YouTube Video, 0:04. October 14, 2024. https://www.youtube.com/watch?v=VKVbT-IgVtQ.

Smith, Laura. 2021. "How Book Covers Influence the Online Book Community." *Laura's Books and Blogs* (blog), July 14, 2021. Accessed on November 11, 2024. https://laurasbooksandblogs.com/how-book-covers-influence-community/.

Softonic. n.d. "DS Amazon Quick View." Accessed June 9, 2024. https://ds-amazon-quick-view.en.softonic.com/chrome/extension#:~:text=DS%20Amazon%20Quick%20View%3A%20A%20Productivity%20Extension%20for%20Amazon&text=DS%20Amazon%20Quick%20View%20is%20a%20handy%20tool%20for%20Amazon,to%20click%20on%20each%20product.

Sreepoorna. 2021. "Using Pen Name/Pseudonym for Amazon Self-Publishing." Pen2publishing. November 13, 2021. https://www.pen-2publishing.com/using-pen-name-for-amazon-publishing/#:~:text=Once%20your%20book%20is%20finished,'pen%20names'%20for%20decades.

Temple, Emily. 2021. "The 25 Most Iconic Book Covers in History." Lit Hub. October 7, 2021. https://lithub.com/the-25-most-iconic-book-covers-in-history/.

The Badger. 2024. "Amazon Advertising Stats (2024 Update)." June 21, 2024. https://www.adbadger.com/blog/amazon-advertising-stats/.

The Self-Publishing with Dale Podcast. 2024. "Publishing Audiobooks with Author's Republic | Review 2024." YouTube Video, 7:00. https://www.youtube.com/watch?v=6Ge7Aoyt_Sc.

Tortora, Daniel J. n.d.-a. "Why Publish on Apple Books? Pros and Cons for EBook Authors." Daniel J. Tortora. Accessed August 12, 2024. https://danieljtortora.com/blog/publish-apple-books-pros-and-cons.

Tortora, Daniel J. n.d.-b. "Amazon Editorial Reviews: How to Add in Author Central, with Tips and Guidelines." Daniel J. Tortora. Accessed July 2, 2024. https://danieljtortora.com/blog/amazon-editorial-reviews-author-central.

Tortora, Daniel J. n.d.-c. "Should You Self Publish on Kobo? Pros and Cons for Ebook Authors." Daniel J. Tortora. Accessed August 13, 2024. https://danieljtortora.com/blog/self-publish-kobo-writing-life-pros-and-cons.

VoiceOverAngela. 2021. "How to Choose a Narrator for your Audiobook." YouTube Video, 1:20. November 18, 2021. https://youtu.be/flgWoPPuuLY?si=Gj-Lc3-ehJjBGsJG.

www.ingramcontent.com/pod-product-compliance
Lightning Source LLC
Chambersburg PA
CBHW051207290426
44109CB00021B/2368